THE
CaΙvin AND HObbEs

PORTABLE COMPENDIUM

BOOK 4

BILL WATTERSON

Andrews McMeel
PUBLISHING®

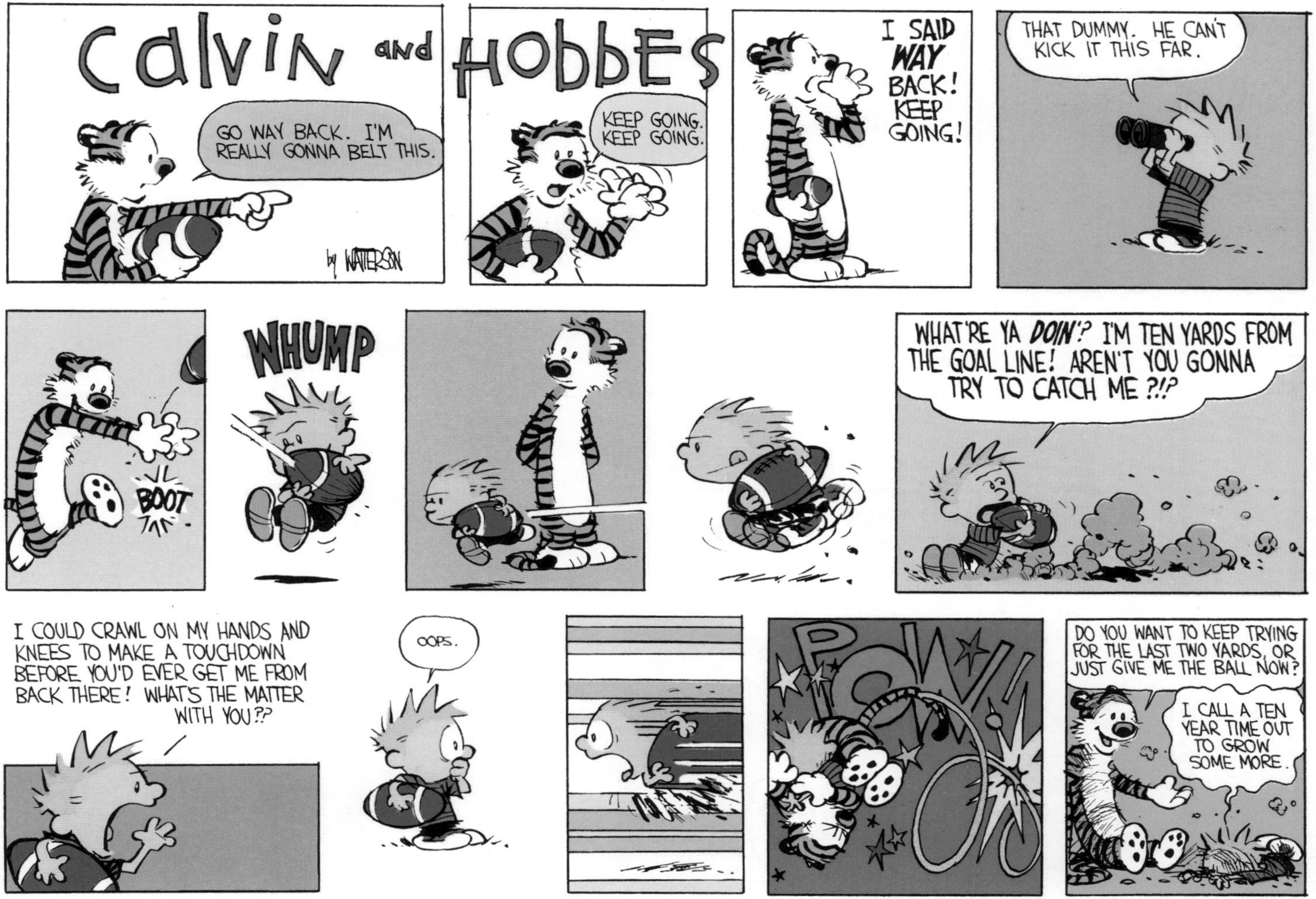
Calvin and HOBBES
GO WAY BACK. I'M REALLY GONNA BELT THIS.
by WATTERSON
KEEP GOING. KEEP GOING.
I SAID WAY BACK! KEEP GOING!
THAT DUMMY. HE CAN'T KICK IT THIS FAR.
BOOT
WHUMP
WHAT'RE YA DOIN'? I'M TEN YARDS FROM THE GOAL LINE! AREN'T YOU GONNA TRY TO CATCH ME ?!?
I COULD CRAWL ON MY HANDS AND KNEES TO MAKE A TOUCHDOWN BEFORE YOU'D EVER GET ME FROM BACK THERE! WHAT'S THE MATTER WITH YOU?!?
OOPS.
POW!!
DO YOU WANT TO KEEP TRYING FOR THE LAST TWO YARDS, OR JUST GIVE ME THE BALL NOW?
I CALL A TEN YEAR TIME OUT TO GROW SOME MORE.

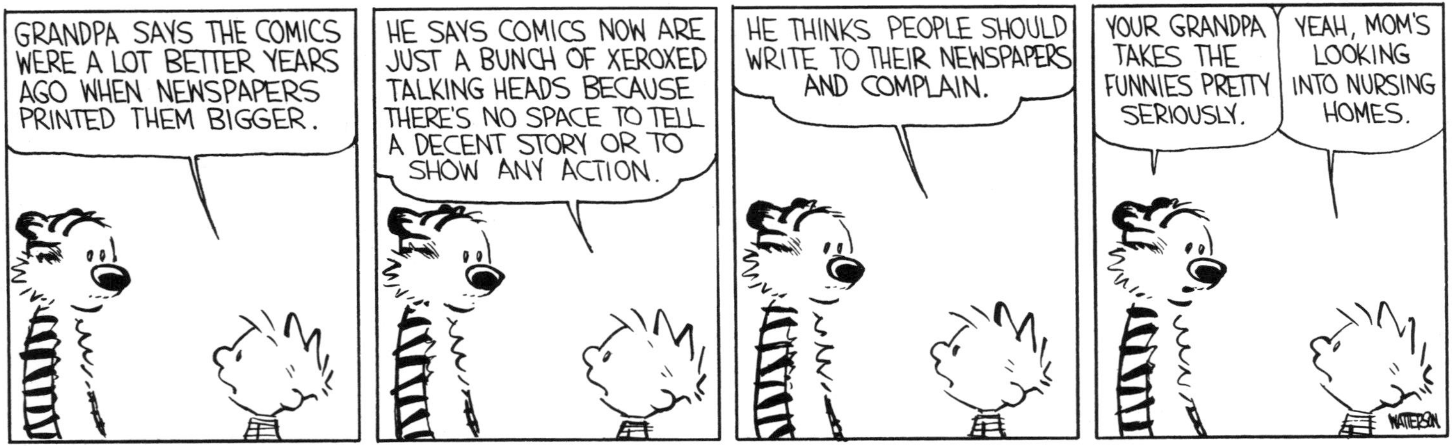
GRANDPA SAYS THE COMICS WERE A LOT BETTER YEARS AGO WHEN NEWSPAPERS PRINTED THEM BIGGER.
HE SAYS COMICS NOW ARE JUST A BUNCH OF XEROXED TALKING HEADS BECAUSE THERE'S NO SPACE TO TELL A DECENT STORY OR TO SHOW ANY ACTION.
HE THINKS PEOPLE SHOULD WRITE TO THEIR NEWSPAPERS AND COMPLAIN.
YOUR GRANDPA TAKES THE FUNNIES PRETTY SERIOUSLY.
YEAH, MOM'S LOOKING INTO NURSING HOMES.
WATTERSON

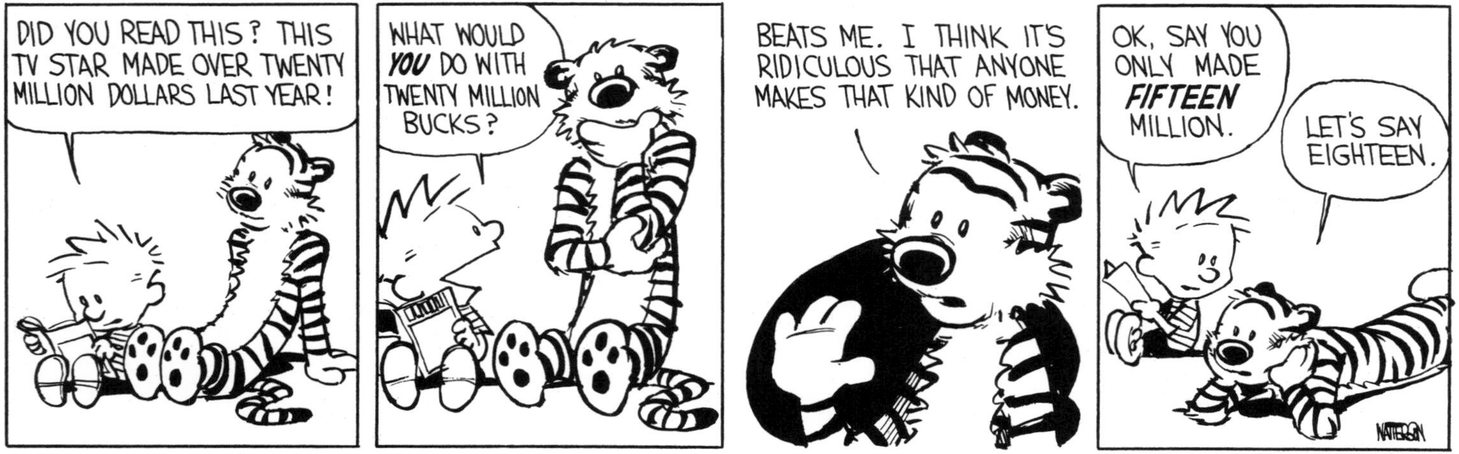
DID YOU READ THIS? THIS TV STAR MADE OVER TWENTY MILLION DOLLARS LAST YEAR!
WHAT WOULD *YOU* DO WITH TWENTY MILLION BUCKS?
BEATS ME. I THINK IT'S RIDICULOUS THAT ANYONE MAKES THAT KIND OF MONEY.
OK, SAY YOU ONLY MADE ***FIFTEEN*** MILLION.
LET'S SAY EIGHTEEN.
WATTERSON

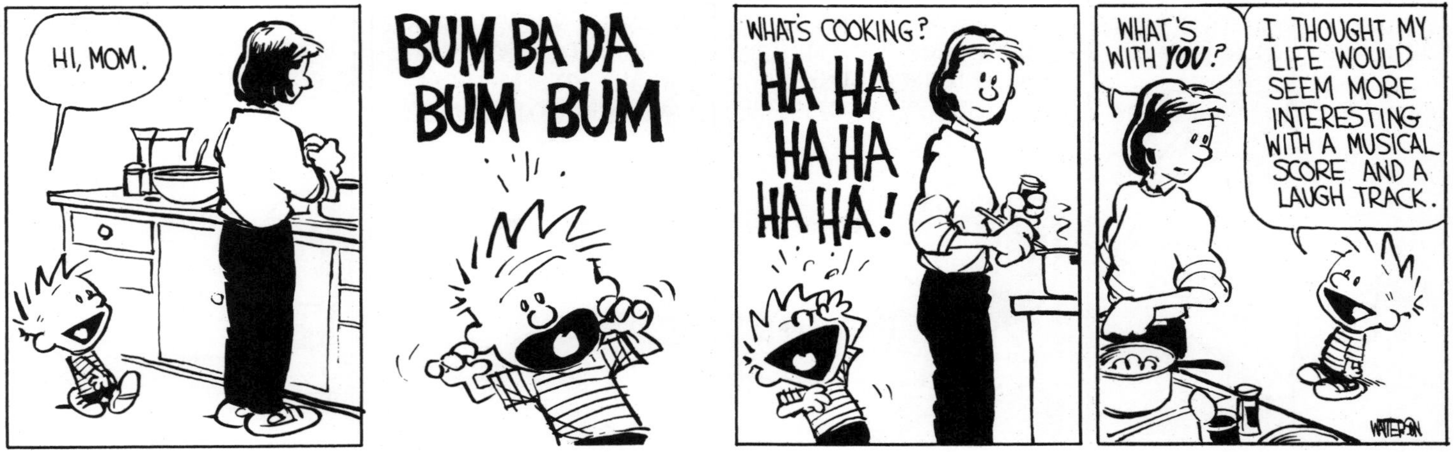
HI, MOM.
BUM BA DA BUM BUM
WHAT'S COOKING?
HA HA HA HA HA HA!
WHAT'S WITH **YOU**?
I THOUGHT MY LIFE WOULD SEEM MORE INTERESTING WITH A MUSICAL SCORE AND A LAUGH TRACK.
WATTERSON

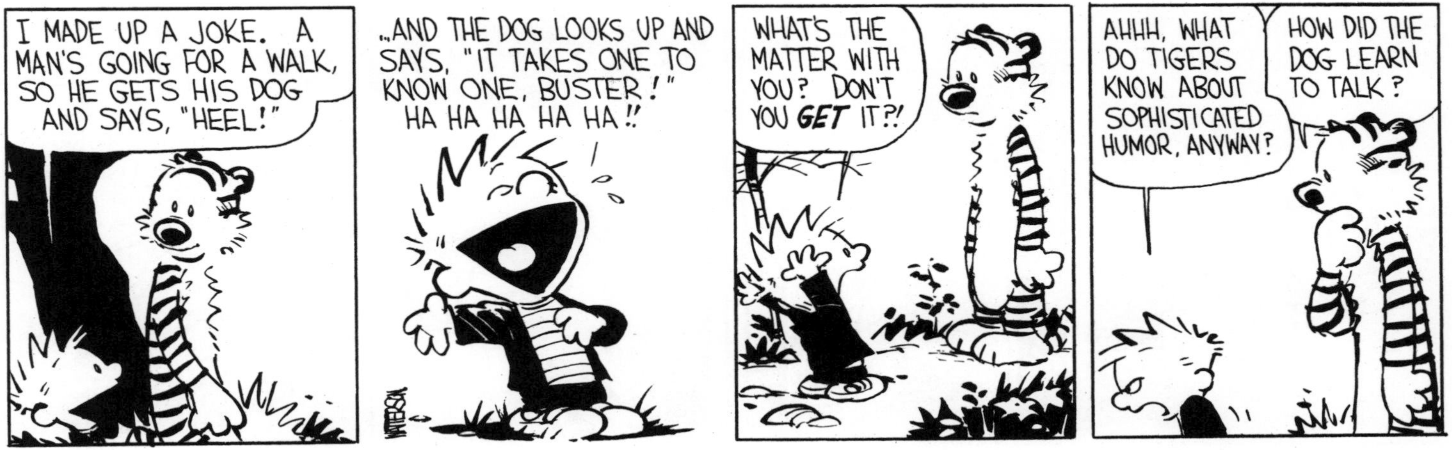
I MADE UP A JOKE. A MAN'S GOING FOR A WALK, SO HE GETS HIS DOG AND SAYS, "HEEL!"
...AND THE DOG LOOKS UP AND SAYS, "IT TAKES ONE TO KNOW ONE, BUSTER!" HA HA HA HA HA!!
WATTERSON
WHAT'S THE MATTER WITH YOU? DON'T YOU **GET** IT?!
AHHH, WHAT DO TIGERS KNOW ABOUT SOPHISTICATED HUMOR, ANYWAY?
HOW DID THE DOG LEARN TO TALK?

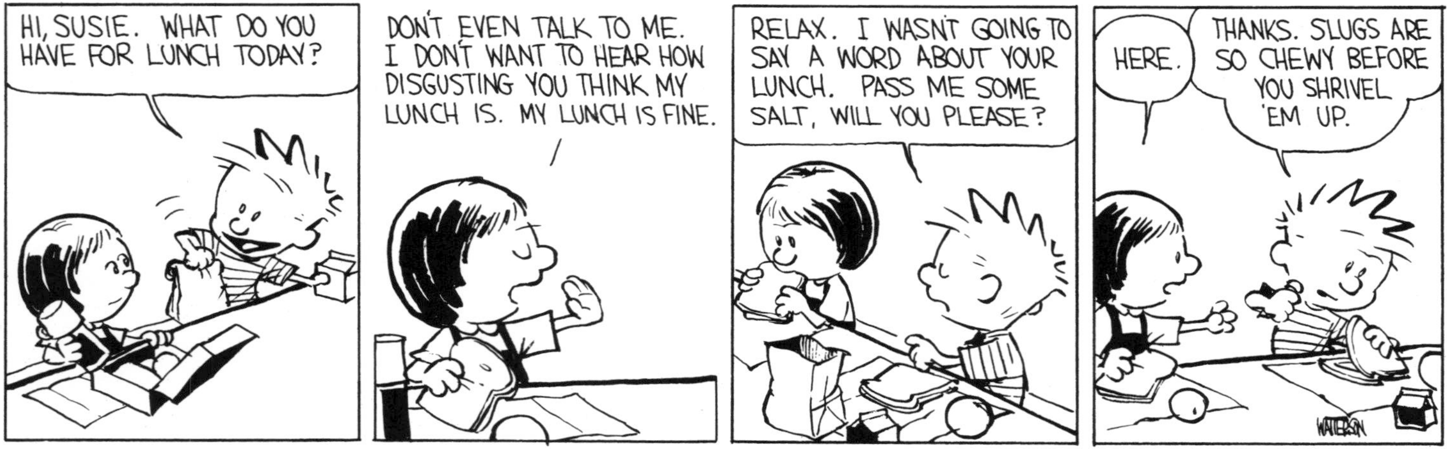
HI, SUSIE. WHAT DO YOU HAVE FOR LUNCH TODAY?
DON'T EVEN TALK TO ME. I DON'T WANT TO HEAR HOW DISGUSTING YOU THINK MY LUNCH IS. MY LUNCH IS FINE.
RELAX. I WASN'T GOING TO SAY A WORD ABOUT YOUR LUNCH. PASS ME SOME SALT, WILL YOU PLEASE?
HERE.
THANKS. SLUGS ARE SO CHEWY BEFORE YOU SHRIVEL 'EM UP.
WATTERSON

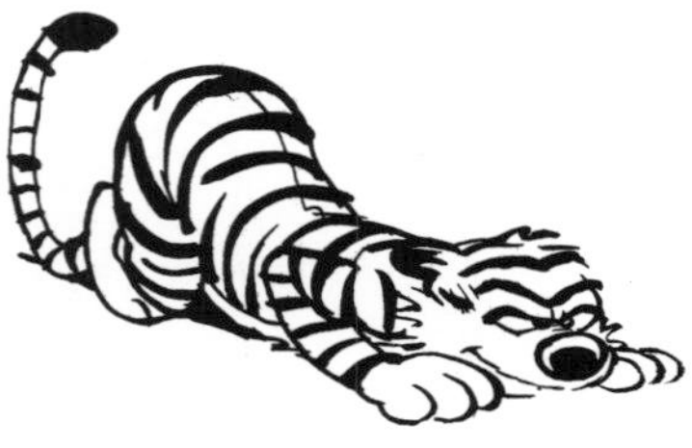

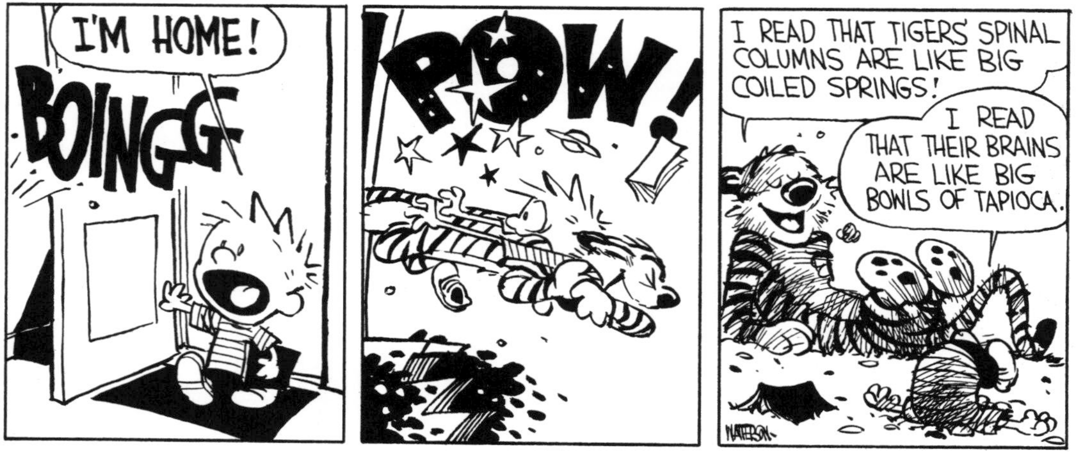
I'M HOME!
BOINGG
POW!
I READ THAT TIGERS' SPINAL COLUMNS ARE LIKE BIG COILED SPRINGS!
I READ THAT THEIR BRAINS ARE LIKE BIG BOWLS OF TAPIOCA.
WATTERSON

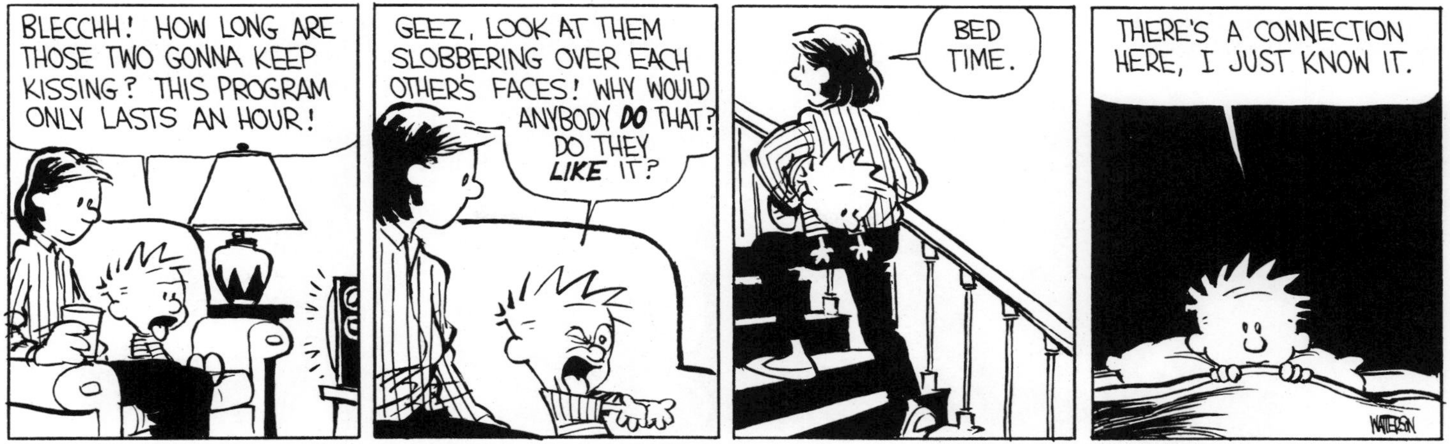
BLECCHH! HOW LONG ARE THOSE TWO GONNA KEEP KISSING? THIS PROGRAM ONLY LASTS AN HOUR!
GEEZ, LOOK AT THEM SLOBBERING OVER EACH OTHER'S FACES! WHY WOULD ANYBODY **DO** THAT? DO THEY **LIKE** IT?
BED TIME.
THERE'S A CONNECTION HERE, I JUST KNOW IT.

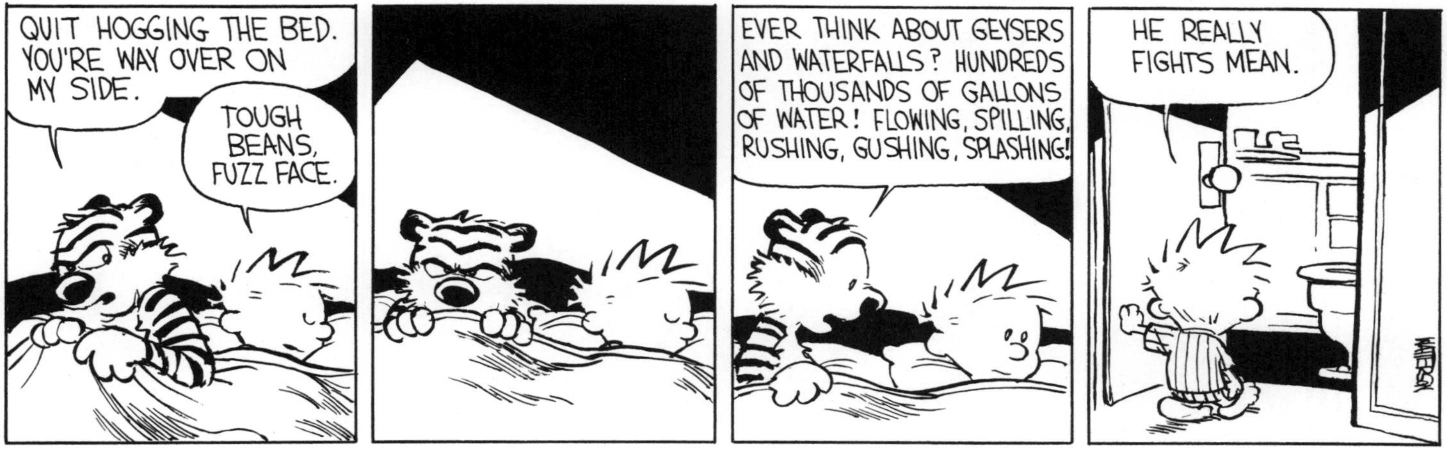
QUIT HOGGING THE BED. YOU'RE WAY OVER ON MY SIDE.
TOUGH BEANS, FUZZ FACE.
EVER THINK ABOUT GEYSERS AND WATERFALLS? HUNDREDS OF THOUSANDS OF GALLONS OF WATER! FLOWING, SPILLING, RUSHING, GUSHING, SPLASHING!
HE REALLY FIGHTS MEAN.

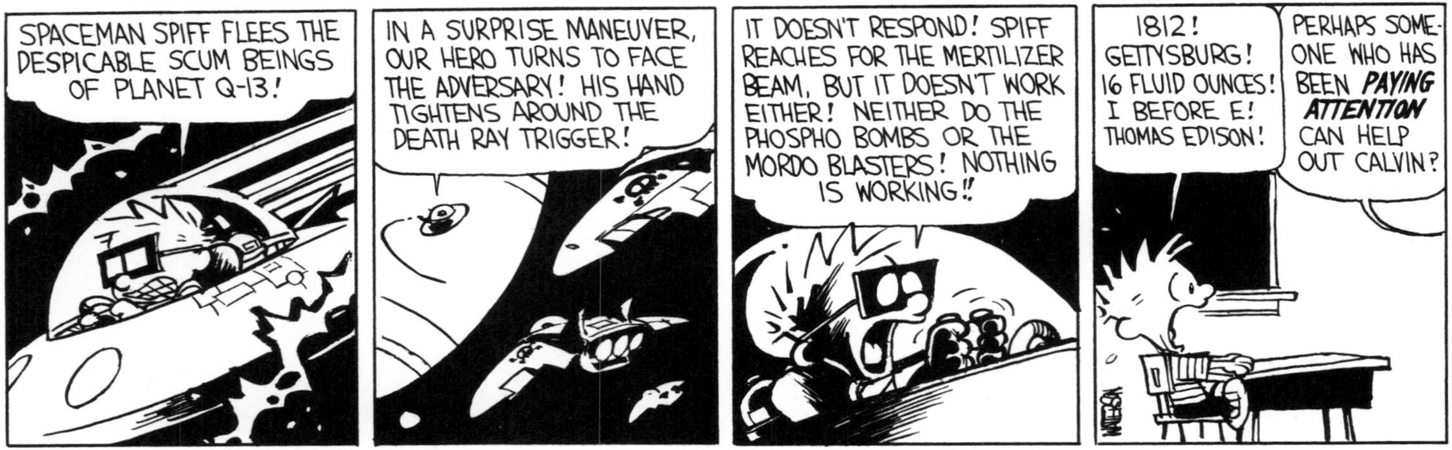
SPACEMAN SPIFF FLEES THE DESPICABLE SCUM BEINGS OF PLANET Q-13!
IN A SURPRISE MANEUVER, OUR HERO TURNS TO FACE THE ADVERSARY! HIS HAND TIGHTENS AROUND THE DEATH RAY TRIGGER!
IT DOESN'T RESPOND! SPIFF REACHES FOR THE MERTILIZER BEAM, BUT IT DOESN'T WORK EITHER! NEITHER DO THE PHOSPHO BOMBS OR THE MORDO BLASTERS! NOTHING IS WORKING!!
1812! GETTYSBURG! 16 FLUID OUNCES! I BEFORE E! THOMAS EDISON!
PERHAPS SOMEONE WHO HAS BEEN *PAYING ATTENTION* CAN HELP OUT CALVIN?
WATTERSON

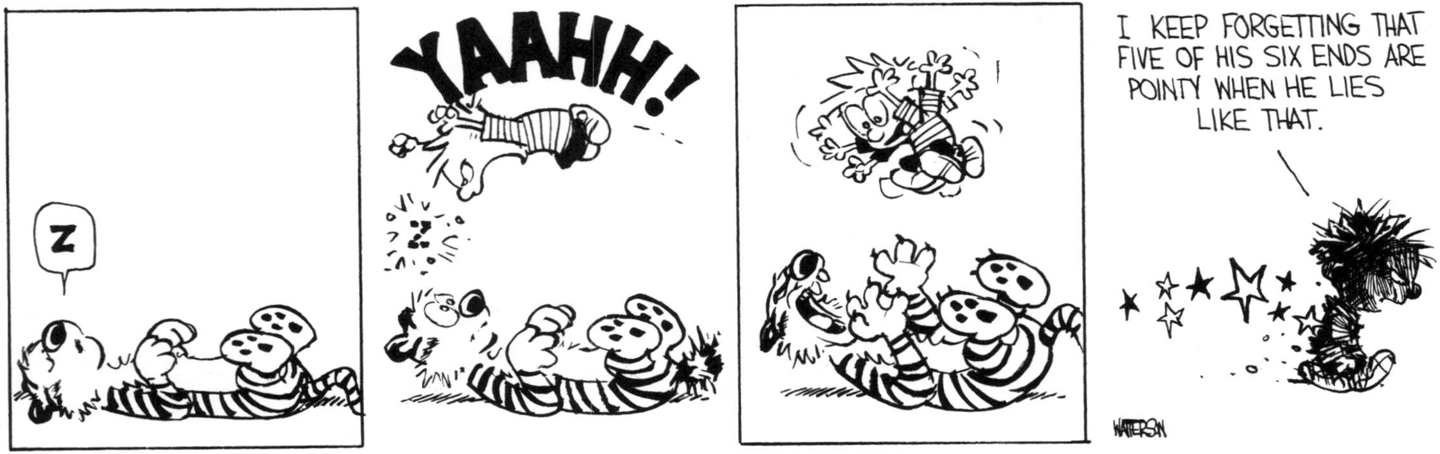
Z
YAAHH!
I KEEP FORGETTING THAT FIVE OF HIS SIX ENDS ARE POINTY WHEN HE LIES LIKE THAT.
WATTERSON

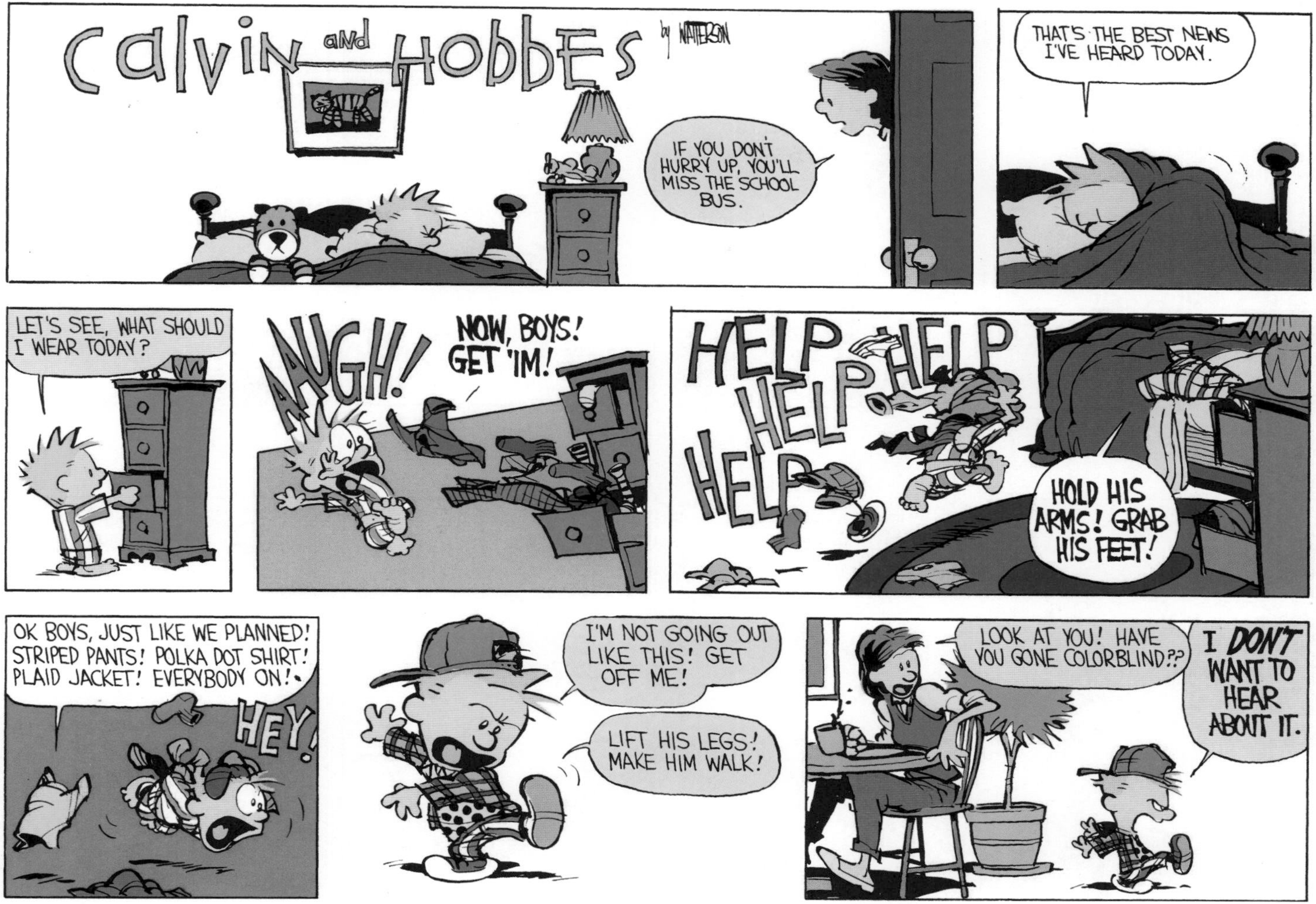
Calvin and HOBBES
by WATTERSON
IF YOU DON'T HURRY UP, YOU'LL MISS THE SCHOOL BUS.
THAT'S THE BEST NEWS I'VE HEARD TODAY.
LET'S SEE, WHAT SHOULD I WEAR TODAY?
AAUGH!
NOW, BOYS! GET 'IM!
HELP HELP HELP HELP HELP
HOLD HIS ARMS! GRAB HIS FEET!
OK BOYS, JUST LIKE WE PLANNED! STRIPED PANTS! POLKA DOT SHIRT! PLAID JACKET! EVERYBODY ON!
HEY!
I'M NOT GOING OUT LIKE THIS! GET OFF ME!
LIFT HIS LEGS! MAKE HIM WALK!
LOOK AT YOU! HAVE YOU GONE COLORBLIND?
I DON'T WANT TO HEAR ABOUT IT.

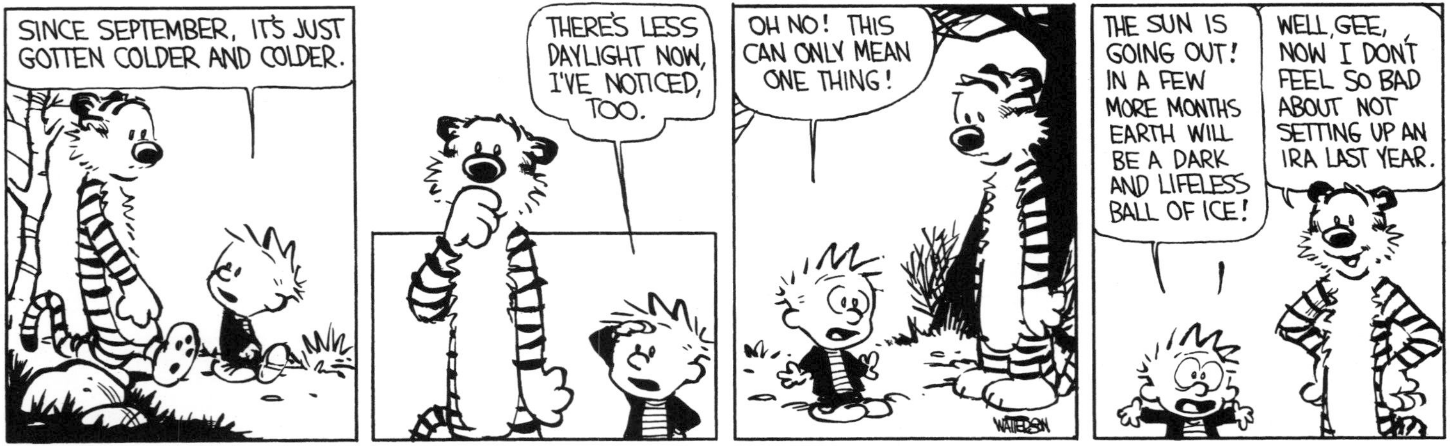
SINCE SEPTEMBER, IT'S JUST GOTTEN COLDER AND COLDER.
THERE'S LESS DAYLIGHT NOW, I'VE NOTICED, TOO.
OH NO! THIS CAN ONLY MEAN ONE THING!
THE SUN IS GOING OUT! IN A FEW MORE MONTHS EARTH WILL BE A DARK AND LIFELESS BALL OF ICE!
WELL, GEE, NOW I DON'T FEEL SO BAD ABOUT NOT SETTING UP AN IRA LAST YEAR.
WATTERSON

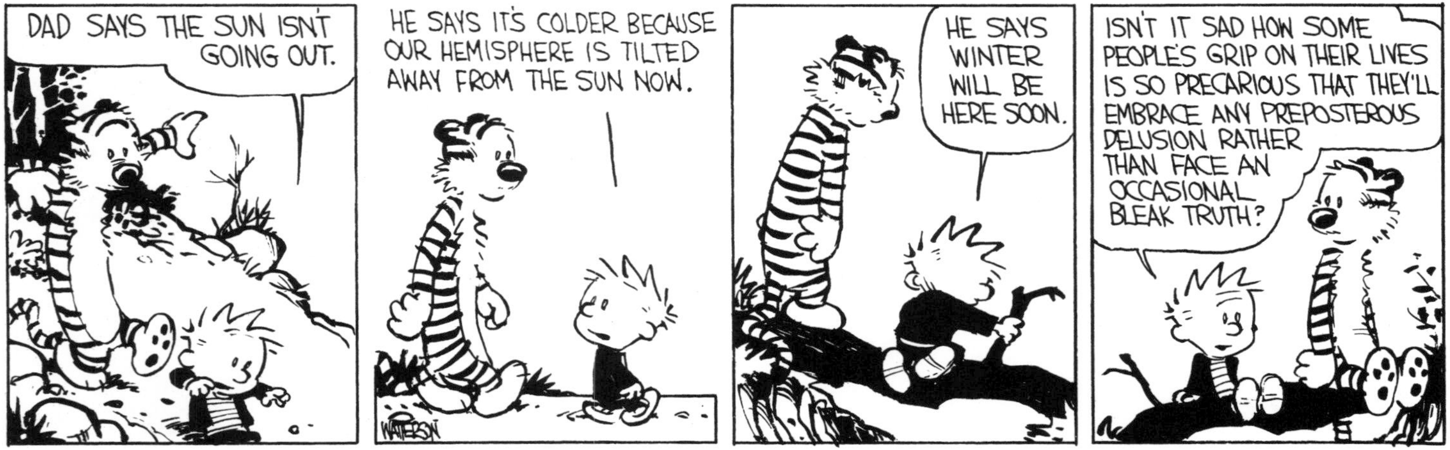
DAD SAYS THE SUN ISN'T GOING OUT.
HE SAYS IT'S COLDER BECAUSE OUR HEMISPHERE IS TILTED AWAY FROM THE SUN NOW.
WATTERSON
HE SAYS WINTER WILL BE HERE SOON.
ISN'T IT SAD HOW SOME PEOPLE'S GRIP ON THEIR LIVES IS SO PRECARIOUS THAT THEY'LL EMBRACE ANY PREPOSTEROUS DELUSION RATHER THAN FACE AN OCCASIONAL BLEAK TRUTH?

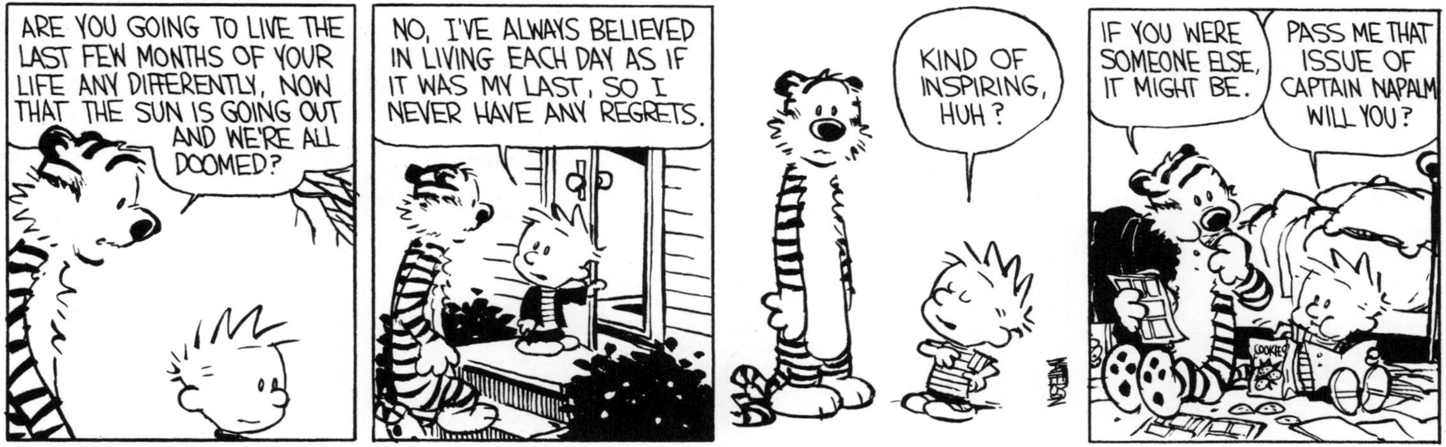
ARE YOU GOING TO LIVE THE LAST FEW MONTHS OF YOUR LIFE ANY DIFFERENTLY, NOW THAT THE SUN IS GOING OUT AND WE'RE ALL DOOMED?
NO, I'VE ALWAYS BELIEVED IN LIVING EACH DAY AS IF IT WAS MY LAST, SO I NEVER HAVE ANY REGRETS.
KIND OF INSPIRING, HUH?
WATTERSON
IF YOU WERE SOMEONE ELSE, IT MIGHT BE.
PASS ME THAT ISSUE OF CAPTAIN NAPALM WILL YOU?
COOKIES

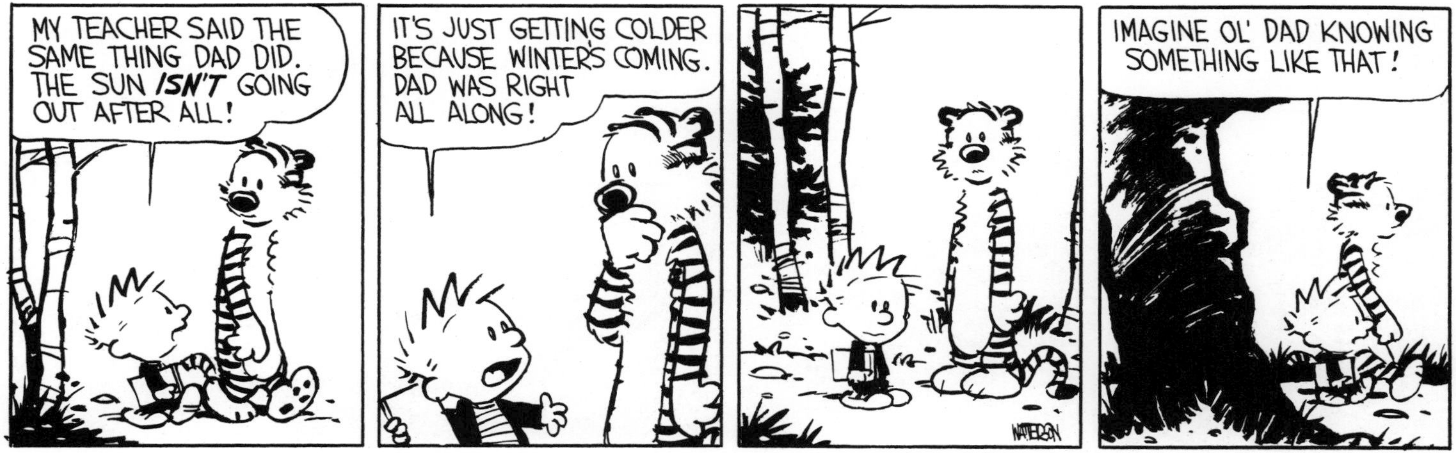
MY TEACHER SAID THE SAME THING DAD DID. THE SUN *ISN'T* GOING OUT AFTER ALL!
IT'S JUST GETTING COLDER BECAUSE WINTER'S COMING. DAD WAS RIGHT ALL ALONG!
WATTERSON
IMAGINE OL' DAD KNOWING SOMETHING LIKE THAT!

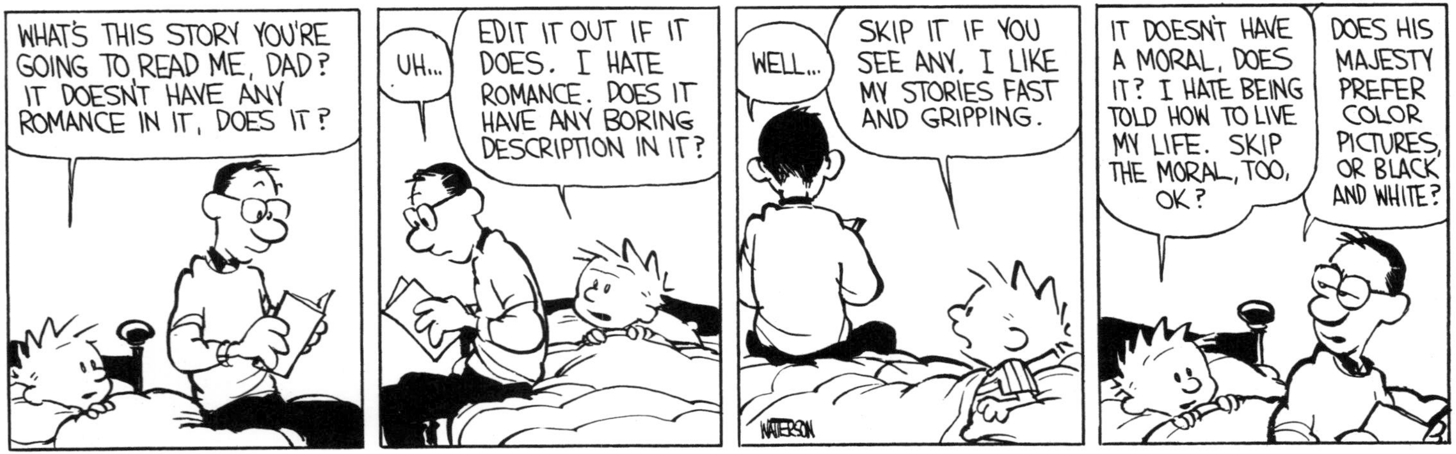
WHAT'S THIS STORY YOU'RE GOING TO READ ME, DAD? IT DOESN'T HAVE ANY ROMANCE IN IT, DOES IT?
UH...
EDIT IT OUT IF IT DOES. I HATE ROMANCE. DOES IT HAVE ANY BORING DESCRIPTION IN IT?
WELL...
SKIP IT IF YOU SEE ANY. I LIKE MY STORIES FAST AND GRIPPING.
IT DOESN'T HAVE A MORAL, DOES IT? I HATE BEING TOLD HOW TO LIVE MY LIFE. SKIP THE MORAL, TOO, OK?
DOES HIS MAJESTY PREFER COLOR PICTURES, OR BLACK AND WHITE?

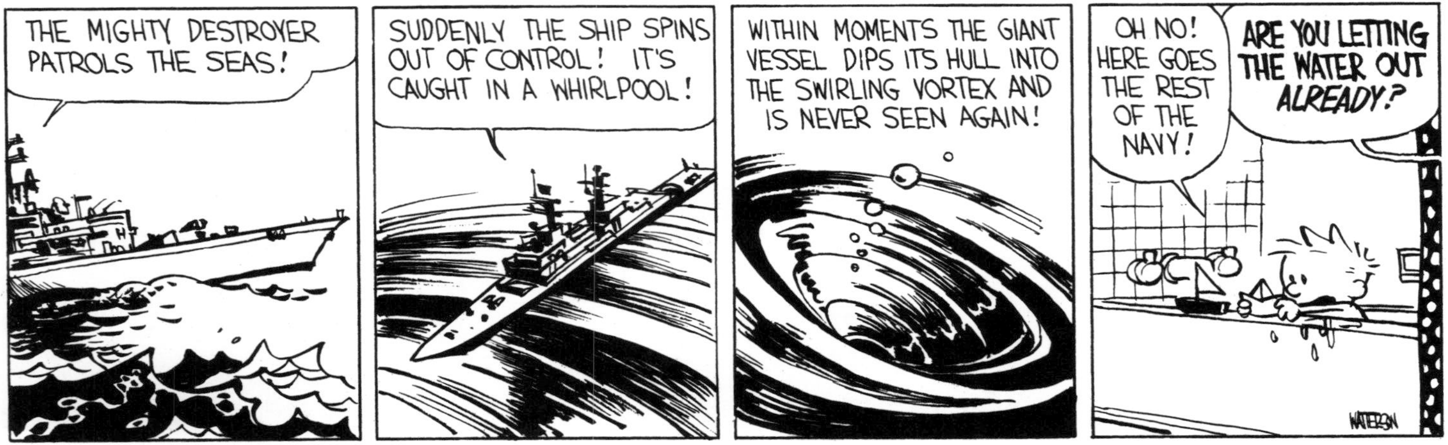
THE MIGHTY DESTROYER PATROLS THE SEAS!
SUDDENLY THE SHIP SPINS OUT OF CONTROL! IT'S CAUGHT IN A WHIRLPOOL!
WITHIN MOMENTS THE GIANT VESSEL DIPS ITS HULL INTO THE SWIRLING VORTEX AND IS NEVER SEEN AGAIN!
OH NO! HERE GOES THE REST OF THE NAVY!
ARE YOU LETTING THE WATER OUT *ALREADY*?

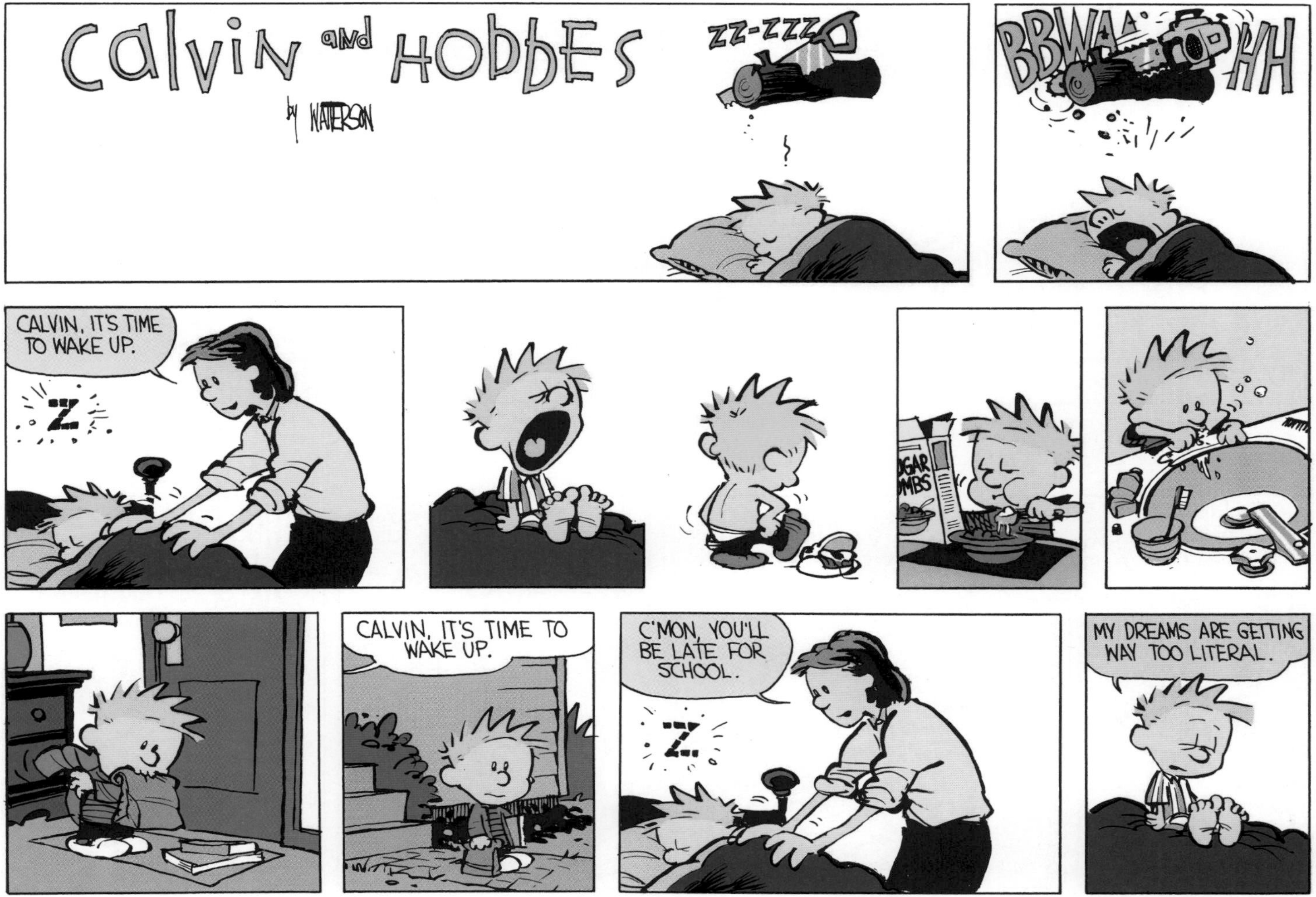
Calvin and HOBBES
by WATTERSON
ZZ-ZZZ
BBWAAAHH
CALVIN, IT'S TIME TO WAKE UP.
Z
CALVIN, IT'S TIME TO WAKE UP.
C'MON, YOU'LL BE LATE FOR SCHOOL.
Z
MY DREAMS ARE GETTING WAY TOO LITERAL.

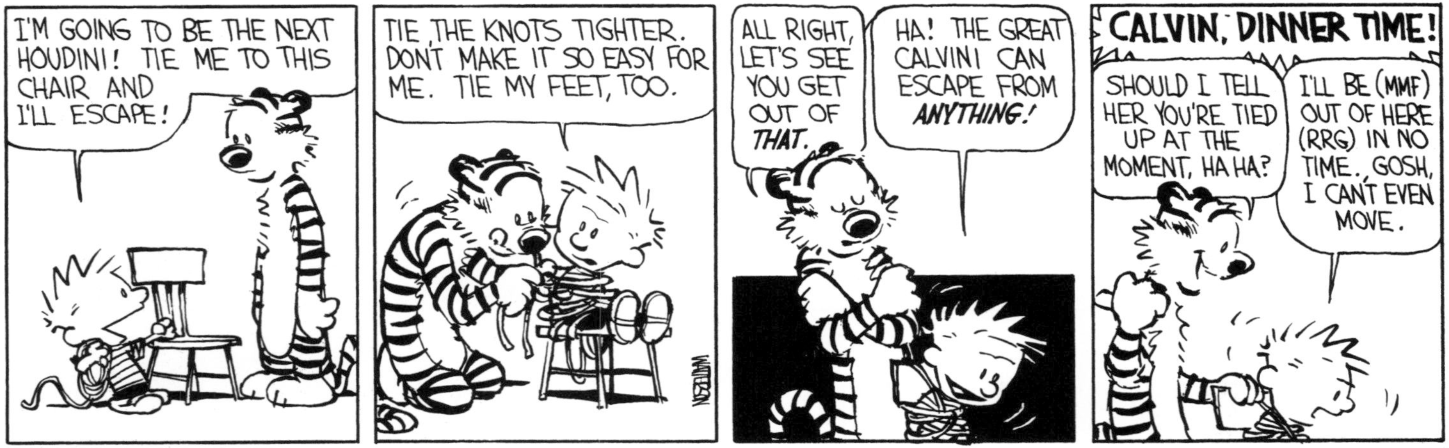
I'M GOING TO BE THE NEXT HOUDINI! TIE ME TO THIS CHAIR AND I'LL ESCAPE!
TIE THE KNOTS TIGHTER. DON'T MAKE IT SO EASY FOR ME. TIE MY FEET, TOO.
ALL RIGHT, LET'S SEE YOU GET OUT OF *THAT*.
HA! THE GREAT CALVINI CAN ESCAPE FROM *ANYTHING!*
CALVIN, DINNER TIME!
SHOULD I TELL HER YOU'RE TIED UP AT THE MOMENT, HA HA?
I'LL BE (MMF) OUT OF HERE (RRG) IN NO TIME. GOSH, I CAN'T EVEN MOVE.

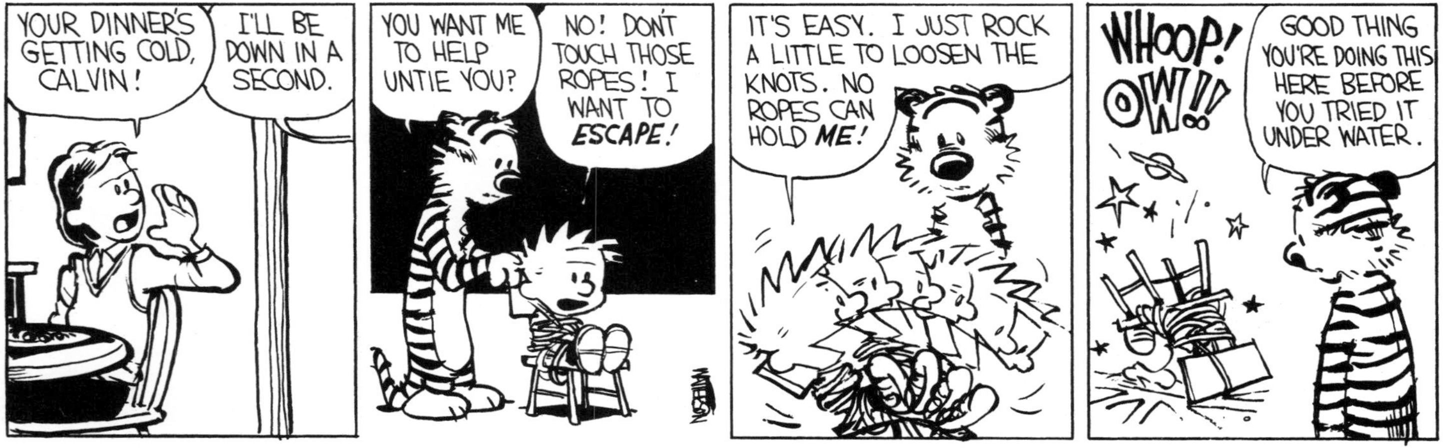
YOUR DINNER'S GETTING COLD, CALVIN!
I'LL BE DOWN IN A SECOND.
YOU WANT ME TO HELP UNTIE YOU?
NO! DON'T TOUCH THOSE ROPES! I WANT TO *ESCAPE!*
IT'S EASY. I JUST ROCK A LITTLE TO LOOSEN THE KNOTS. NO ROPES CAN HOLD *ME!*
WHOOP! OW!!!
GOOD THING YOU'RE DOING THIS HERE BEFORE YOU TRIED IT UNDER WATER.

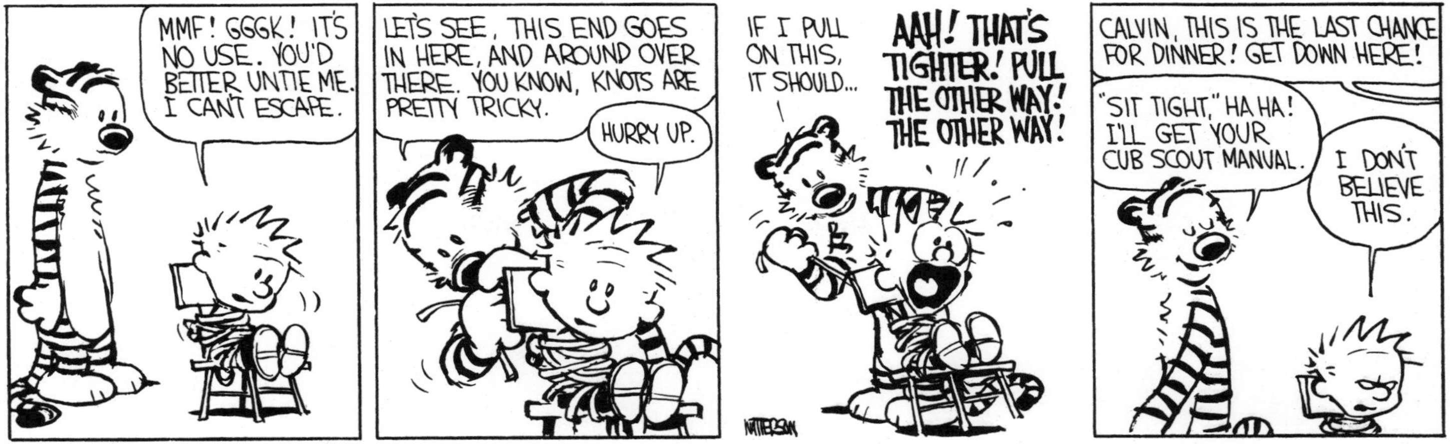
MMF! GGGK! IT'S NO USE. YOU'D BETTER UNTIE ME. I CAN'T ESCAPE.
LET'S SEE, THIS END GOES IN HERE, AND AROUND OVER THERE. YOU KNOW, KNOTS ARE PRETTY TRICKY.
HURRY UP.
IF I PULL ON THIS, IT SHOULD...
AAH! THAT'S TIGHTER! PULL THE OTHER WAY! THE OTHER WAY!
WATTERSON
CALVIN, THIS IS THE LAST CHANCE FOR DINNER! GET DOWN HERE!
"SIT TIGHT," HA HA! I'LL GET YOUR CUB SCOUT MANUAL.
I DON'T BELIEVE THIS.

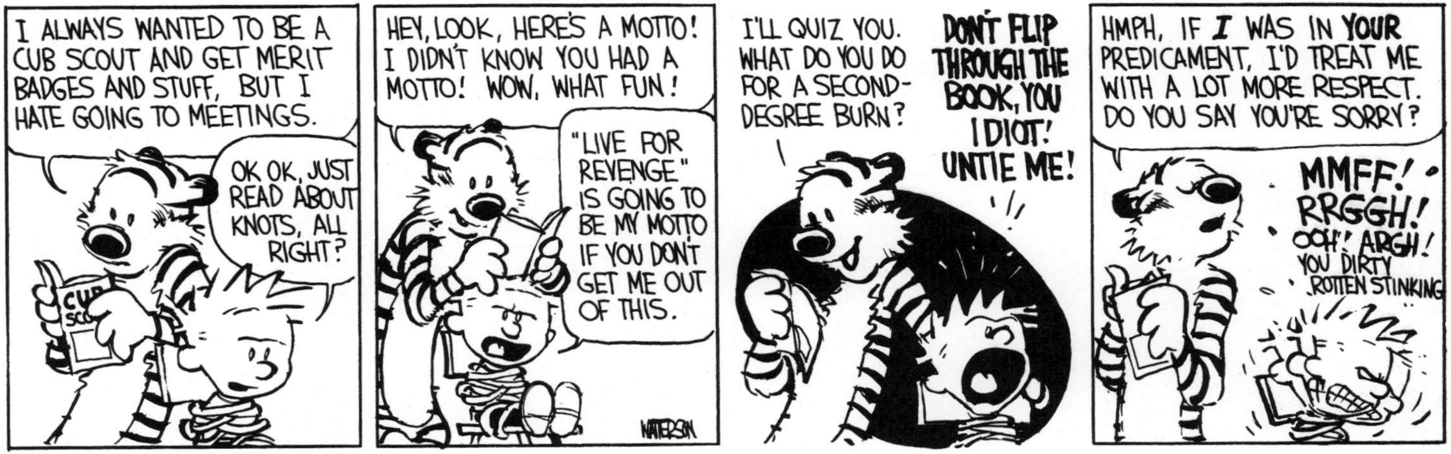
I ALWAYS WANTED TO BE A CUB SCOUT AND GET MERIT BADGES AND STUFF, BUT I HATE GOING TO MEETINGS.
OK OK, JUST READ ABOUT KNOTS, ALL RIGHT?
HEY, LOOK, HERE'S A MOTTO! I DIDN'T KNOW YOU HAD A MOTTO! WOW, WHAT FUN!
"LIVE FOR REVENGE" IS GOING TO BE MY MOTTO IF YOU DON'T GET ME OUT OF THIS.
WATTERSON
I'LL QUIZ YOU. WHAT DO YOU DO FOR A SECOND-DEGREE BURN?
DON'T FLIP THROUGH THE BOOK, YOU IDIOT! UNTIE ME!
HMPH, IF I WAS IN YOUR PREDICAMENT, I'D TREAT ME WITH A LOT MORE RESPECT. DO YOU SAY YOU'RE SORRY?
MMFF! RRGGH! OOH! ARGH! YOU DIRTY ROTTEN STINKING

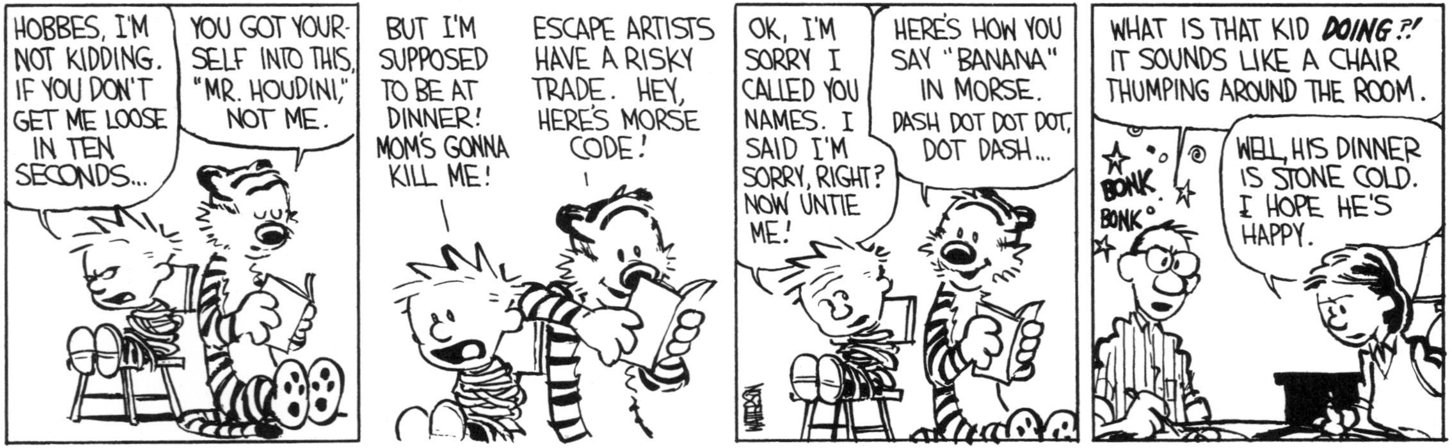
HOBBES, I'M NOT KIDDING. IF YOU DON'T GET ME LOOSE IN TEN SECONDS...
YOU GOT YOURSELF INTO THIS, "MR. HOUDINI," NOT ME.
BUT I'M SUPPOSED TO BE AT DINNER! MOM'S GONNA KILL ME!
ESCAPE ARTISTS HAVE A RISKY TRADE. HEY, HERE'S MORSE CODE!
OK, I'M SORRY I CALLED YOU NAMES. I SAID I'M SORRY, RIGHT? NOW UNTIE ME!
HERE'S HOW YOU SAY "BANANA" IN MORSE. DASH DOT DOT DOT, DOT DASH...
WHAT IS THAT KID **DOING** ?! IT SOUNDS LIKE A CHAIR THUMPING AROUND THE ROOM.
BONK
BONK
WELL, HIS DINNER IS STONE COLD. I HOPE HE'S HAPPY.

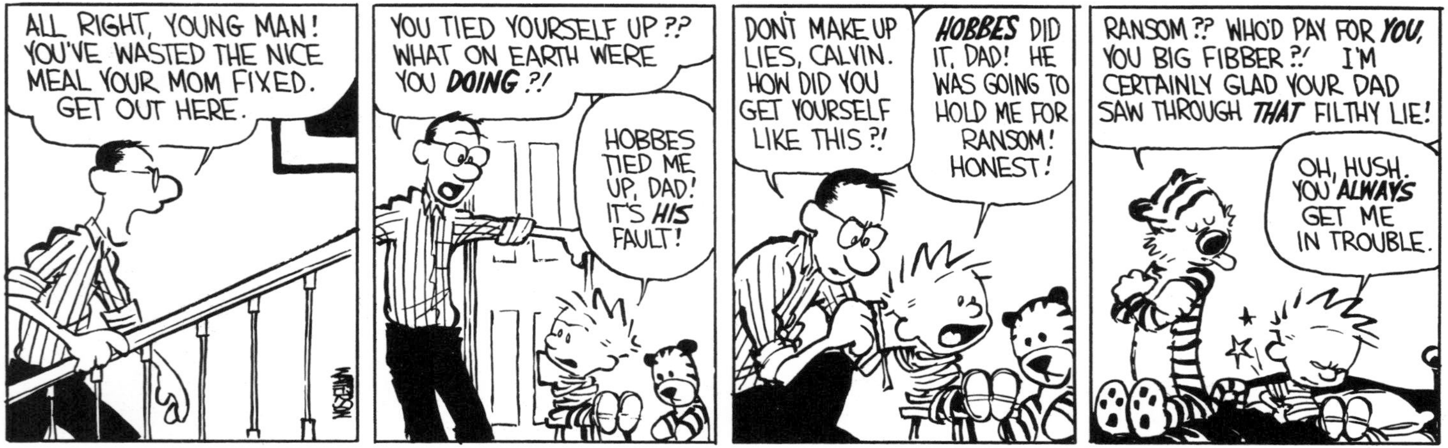
ALL RIGHT, YOUNG MAN! YOU'VE WASTED THE NICE MEAL YOUR MOM FIXED. GET OUT HERE.
YOU TIED YOURSELF UP ?? WHAT ON EARTH WERE YOU **DOING** ?!
HOBBES TIED ME UP, DAD! IT'S **HIS** FAULT!
DON'T MAKE UP LIES, CALVIN. HOW DID YOU GET YOURSELF LIKE THIS ?!
HOBBES DID IT, DAD! HE WAS GOING TO HOLD ME FOR RANSOM! HONEST!
RANSOM ?? WHO'D PAY FOR **YOU**, YOU BIG FIBBER ?! I'M CERTAINLY GLAD YOUR DAD SAW THROUGH **THAT** FILTHY LIE!
OH, HUSH. YOU **ALWAYS** GET ME IN TROUBLE.

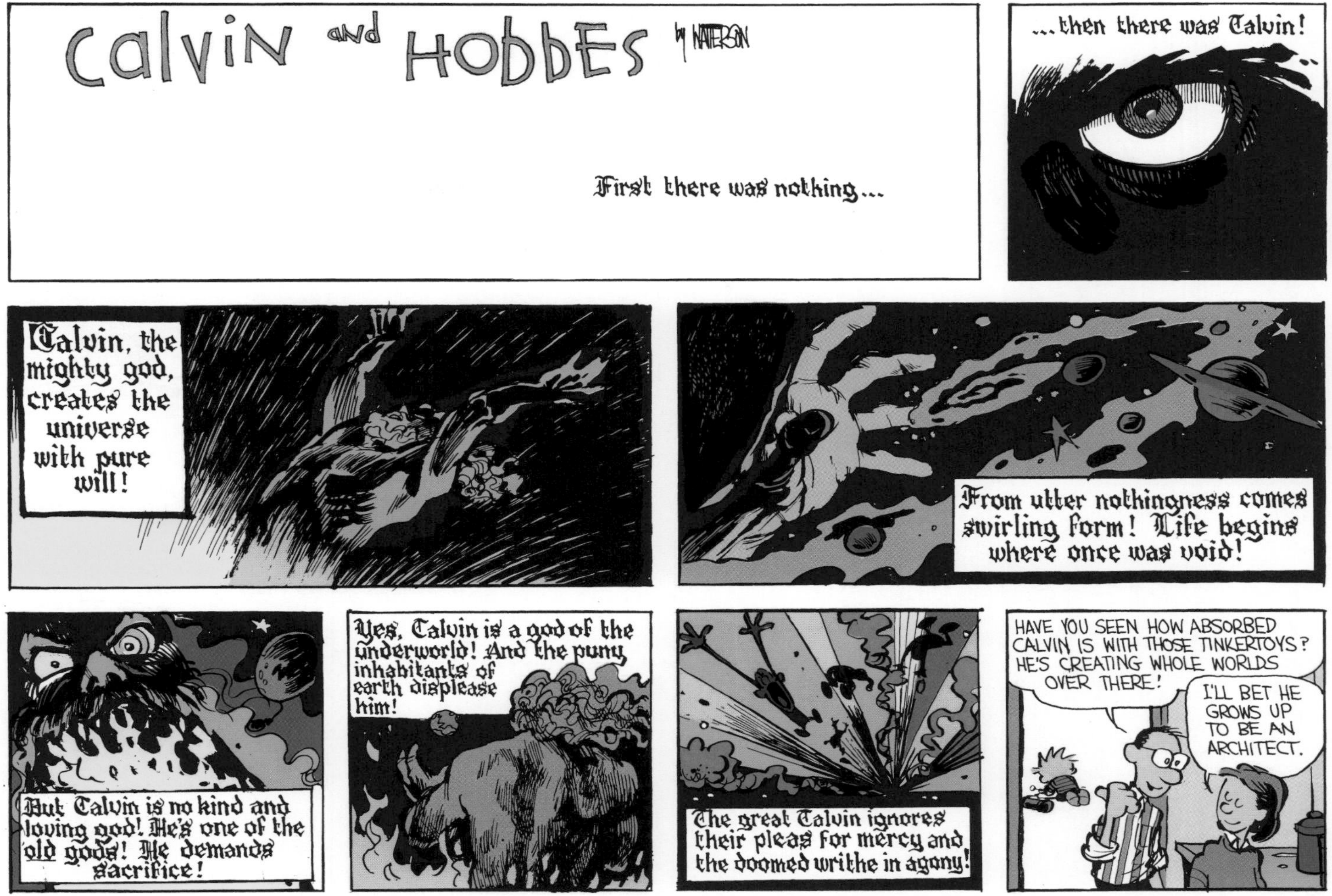
Calvin and Hobbes
by WATTERSON
First there was nothing...
...then there was Calvin!
Calvin, the mighty god, creates the universe with pure will!
From utter nothingness comes swirling form! Life begins where once was void!
But Calvin is no kind and loving god! He's one of the old gods! He demands sacrifice!
Yes, Calvin is a god of the underworld! And the puny inhabitants of earth displease him!
The great Calvin ignores their pleas for mercy and the doomed writhe in agony!
HAVE YOU SEEN HOW ABSORBED CALVIN IS WITH THOSE TINKERTOYS? HE'S CREATING WHOLE WORLDS OVER THERE!
I'LL BET HE GROWS UP TO BE AN ARCHITECT.

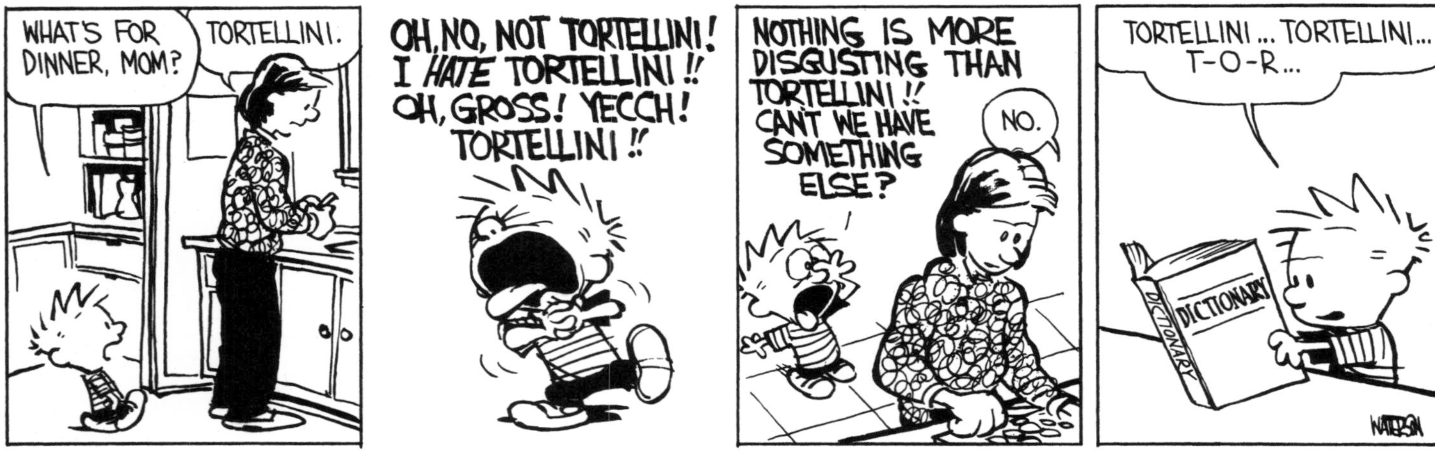
WHAT'S FOR DINNER, MOM?
TORTELLINI.
OH, NO, NOT TORTELLINI! I HATE TORTELLINI!! OH, GROSS! YECCH! TORTELLINI!!
NOTHING IS MORE DISGUSTING THAN TORTELLINI!! CAN'T WE HAVE SOMETHING ELSE?
NO.
TORTELLINI... TORTELLINI... T-O-R...
DICTIONARY
DICTIONARY
WATTERSON

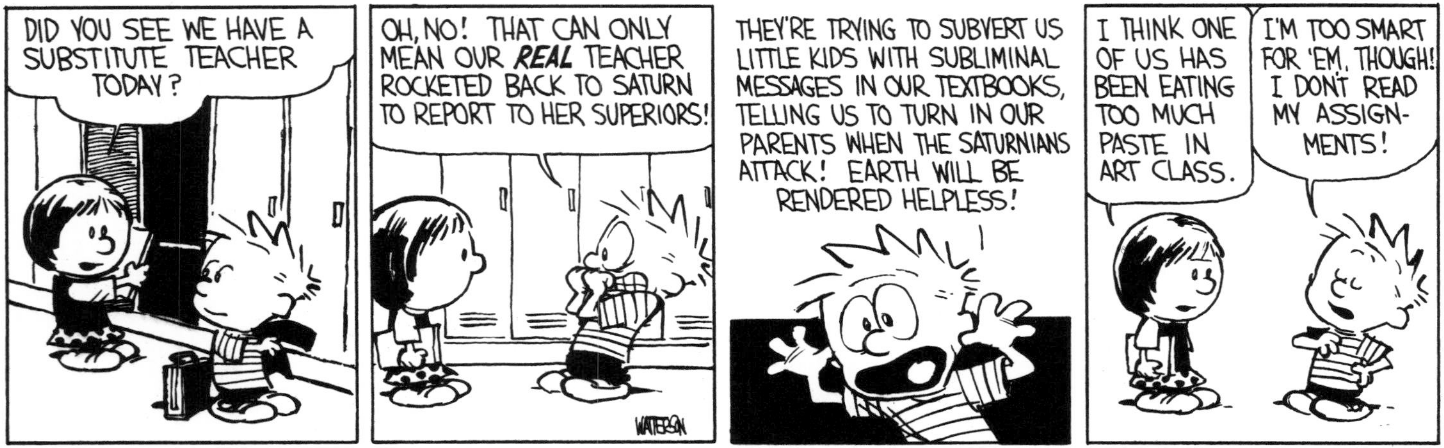
DID YOU SEE WE HAVE A SUBSTITUTE TEACHER TODAY?
OH, NO! THAT CAN ONLY MEAN OUR REAL TEACHER ROCKETED BACK TO SATURN TO REPORT TO HER SUPERIORS!
WATTERSON
THEY'RE TRYING TO SUBVERT US LITTLE KIDS WITH SUBLIMINAL MESSAGES IN OUR TEXTBOOKS, TELLING US TO TURN IN OUR PARENTS WHEN THE SATURNIANS ATTACK! EARTH WILL BE RENDERED HELPLESS!
I THINK ONE OF US HAS BEEN EATING TOO MUCH PASTE IN ART CLASS.
I'M TOO SMART FOR 'EM, THOUGH! I DON'T READ MY ASSIGNMENTS!

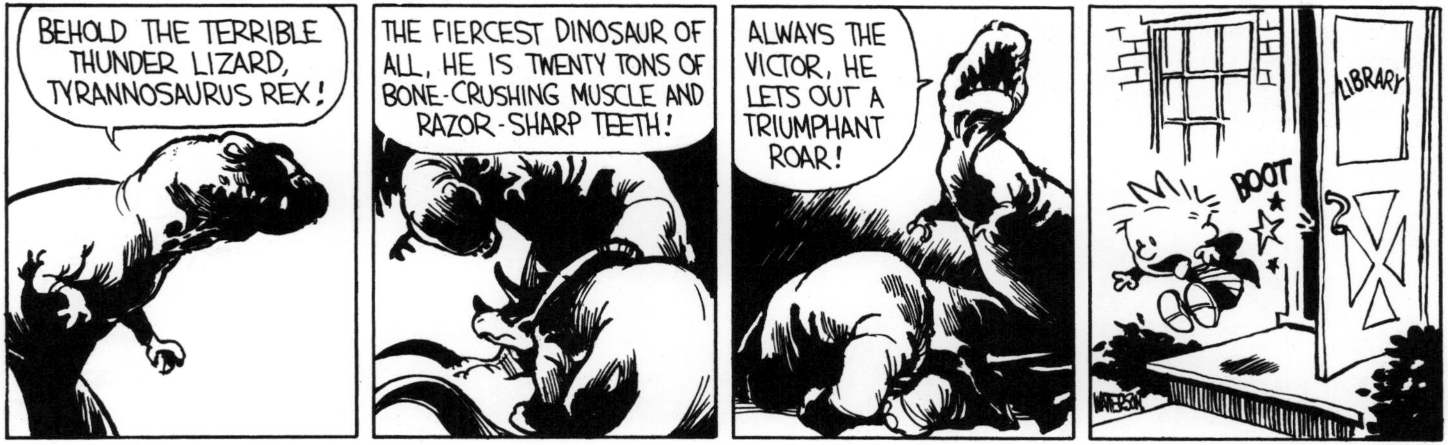
BEHOLD THE TERRIBLE THUNDER LIZARD, TYRANNOSAURUS REX!
THE FIERCEST DINOSAUR OF ALL, HE IS TWENTY TONS OF BONE-CRUSHING MUSCLE AND RAZOR-SHARP TEETH!
ALWAYS THE VICTOR, HE LETS OUT A TRIUMPHANT ROAR!
LIBRARY
BOOT
WATTERSON

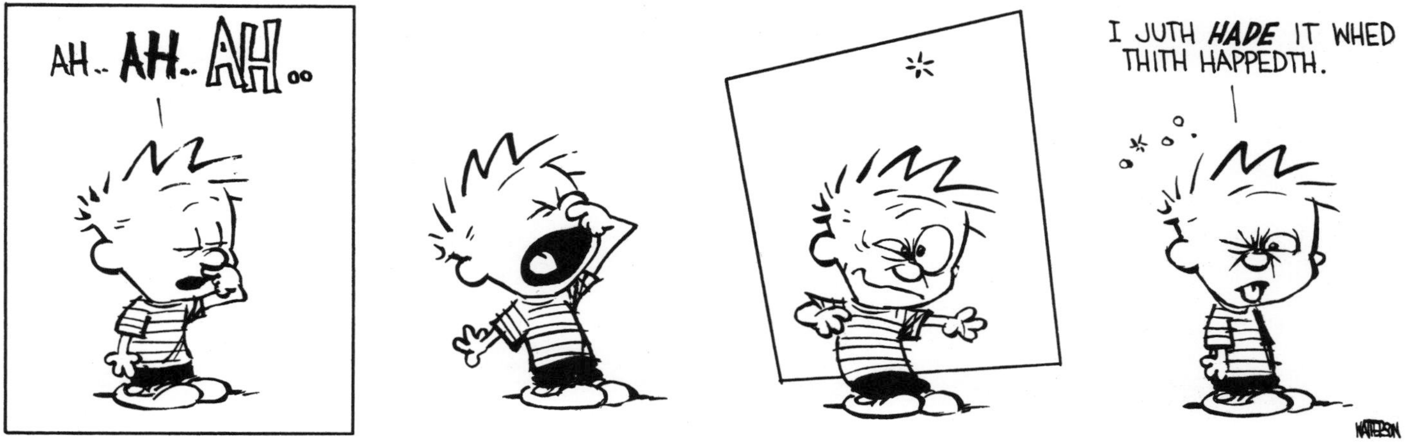
AH.. AH.. AH..
I JUTH HADE IT WHED THITH HAPPEDTH.
WATTERSON

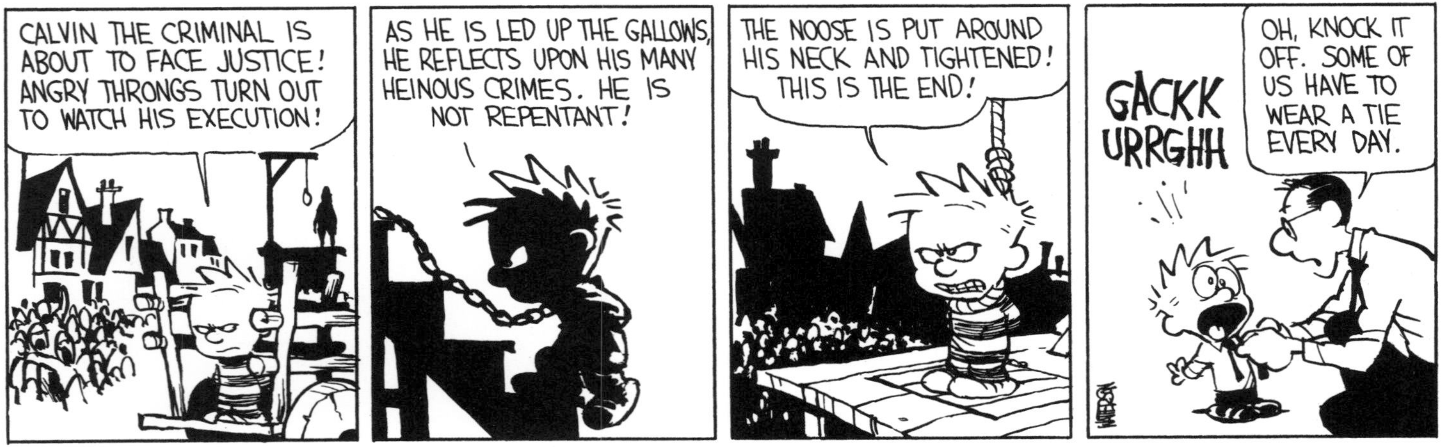
CALVIN THE CRIMINAL IS ABOUT TO FACE JUSTICE! ANGRY THRONGS TURN OUT TO WATCH HIS EXECUTION!
AS HE IS LED UP THE GALLOWS, HE REFLECTS UPON HIS MANY HEINOUS CRIMES. HE IS NOT REPENTANT!
THE NOOSE IS PUT AROUND HIS NECK AND TIGHTENED! THIS IS THE END!
GACKK URRGHH
OH, KNOCK IT OFF. SOME OF US HAVE TO WEAR A TIE EVERY DAY.
WATTERSON

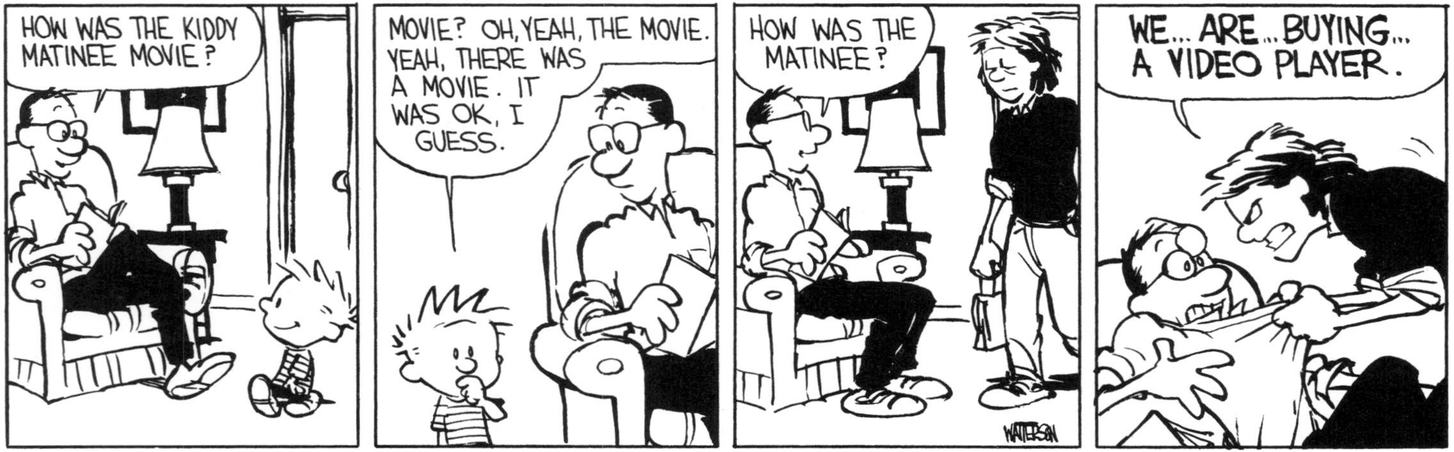
HOW WAS THE KIDDY MATINEE MOVIE?
MOVIE? OH, YEAH, THE MOVIE. YEAH, THERE WAS A MOVIE. IT WAS OK, I GUESS.
HOW WAS THE MATINEE?
WATTERSON
WE... ARE... BUYING... A VIDEO PLAYER.

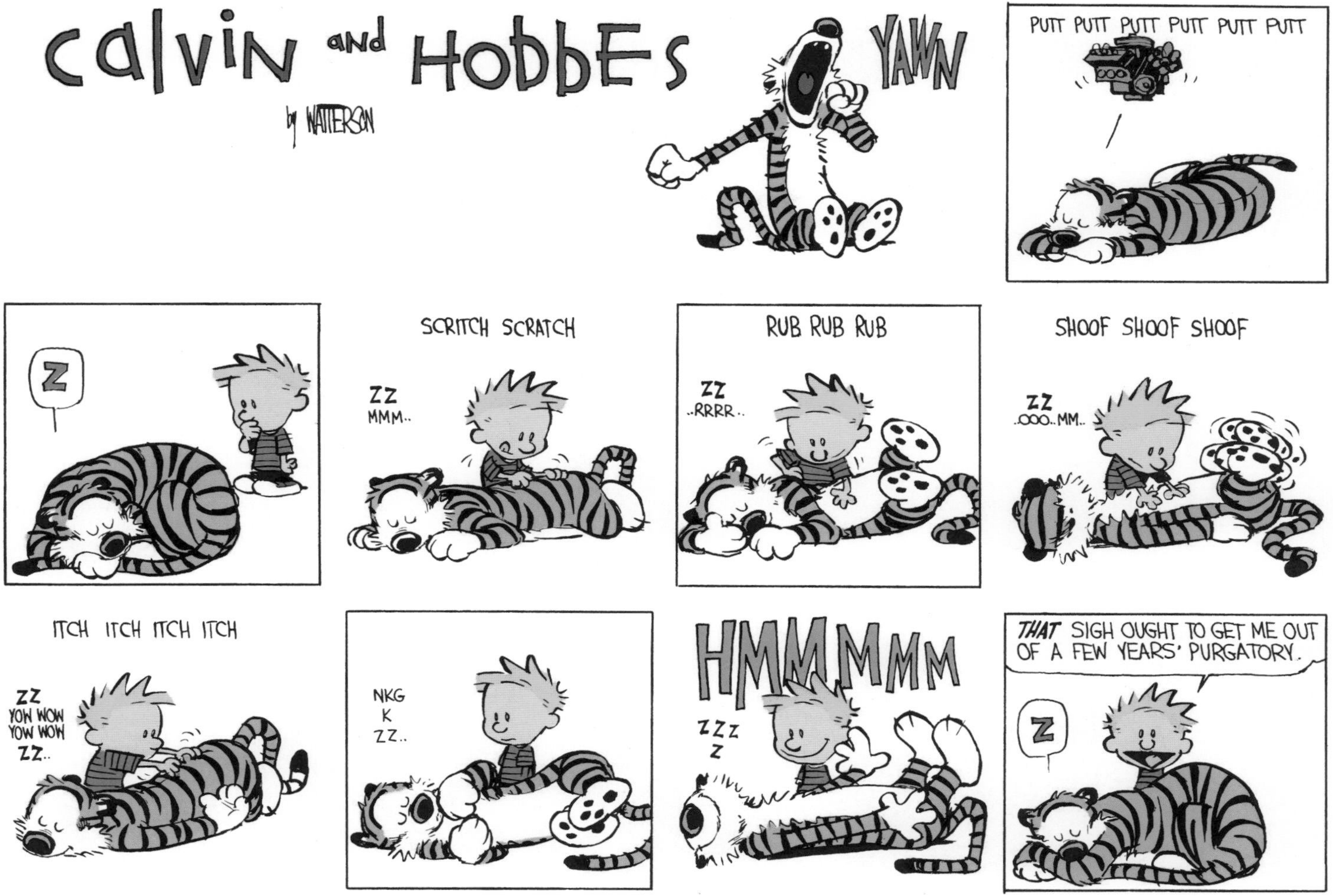
Calvin and HOBBES
by WATTERSON
YAWN
PUTT PUTT PUTT PUTT PUTT PUTT
Z
SCRITCH SCRATCH
ZZ
MMM..
RUB RUB RUB
ZZ
..RRRR..
SHOOF SHOOF SHOOF
ZZ
..OOO..MM..
ITCH ITCH ITCH ITCH
ZZ
YOW WOW
YOW WOW
ZZ..
NKG
K
ZZ..
HMMMMMM
ZZZ
Z
THAT SIGH OUGHT TO GET ME OUT OF A FEW YEARS' PURGATORY.
Z

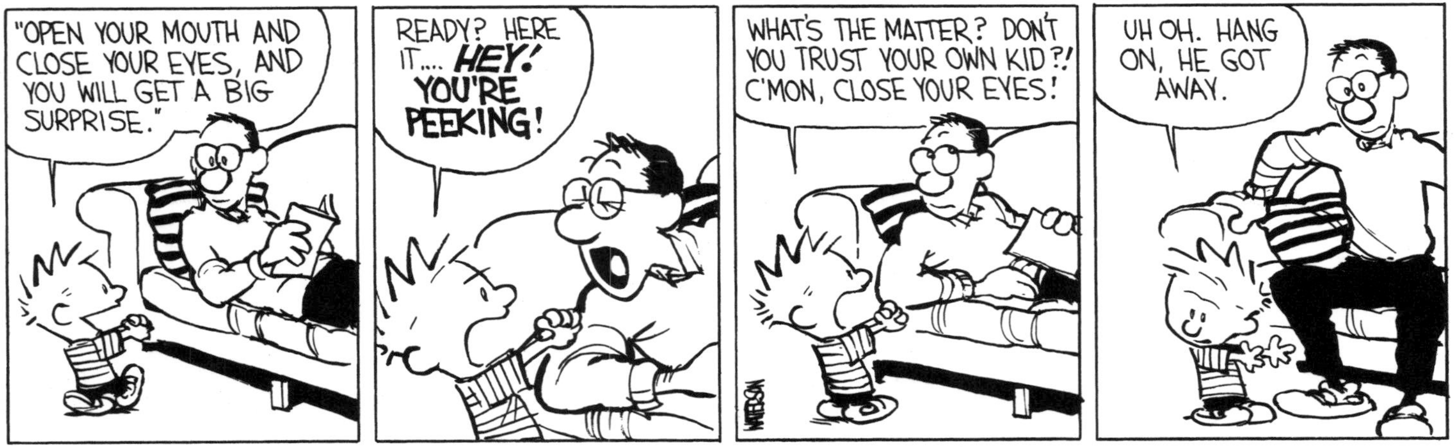
"OPEN YOUR MOUTH AND CLOSE YOUR EYES, AND YOU WILL GET A BIG SURPRISE."
READY? HERE IT.... HEY! YOU'RE PEEKING!
WHAT'S THE MATTER? DON'T YOU TRUST YOUR OWN KID?! C'MON, CLOSE YOUR EYES!
UH OH. HANG ON, HE GOT AWAY.

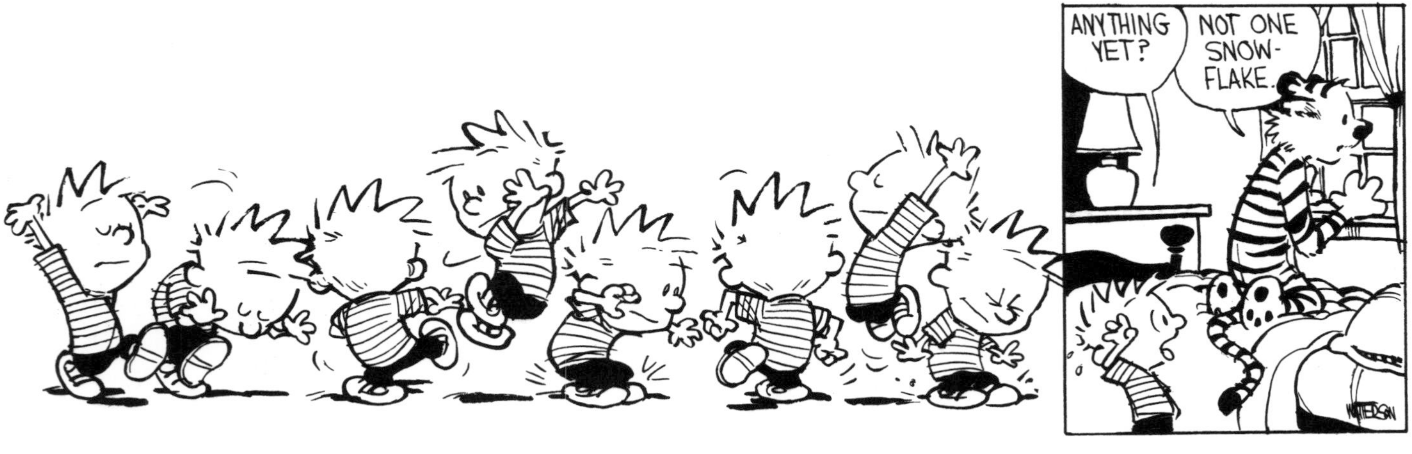
ANYTHING YET?
NOT ONE SNOW-FLAKE.

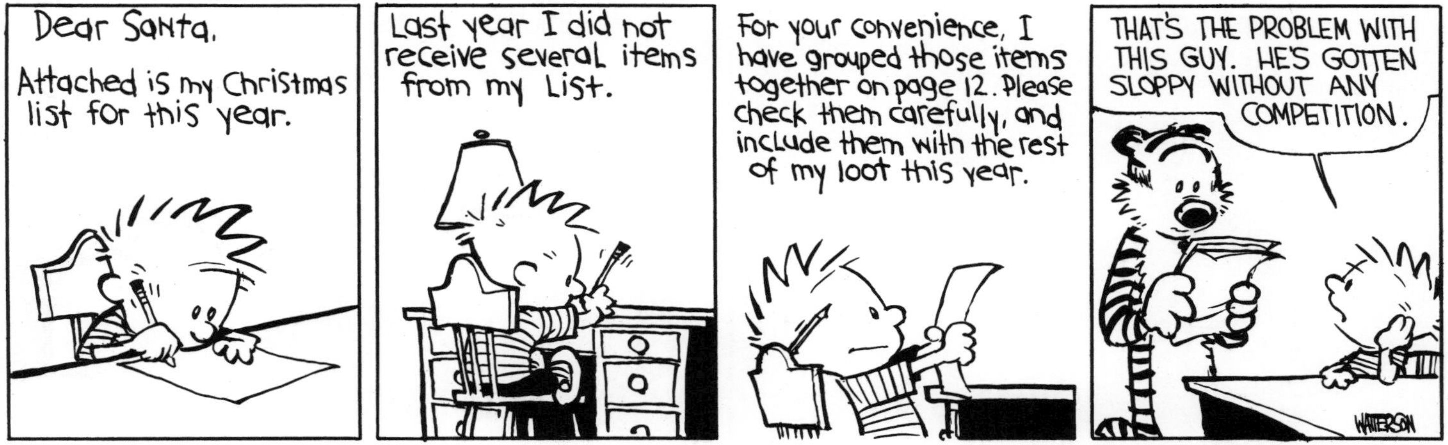
Dear Santa.
Attached is my Christmas list for this year.
Last year I did not receive several items from my List.
For your convenience, I have grouped those items together on page 12. Please check them carefully, and include them with the rest of my loot this year.
THAT'S THE PROBLEM WITH THIS GUY. HE'S GOTTEN SLOPPY WITHOUT ANY COMPETITION.
WATTERSON

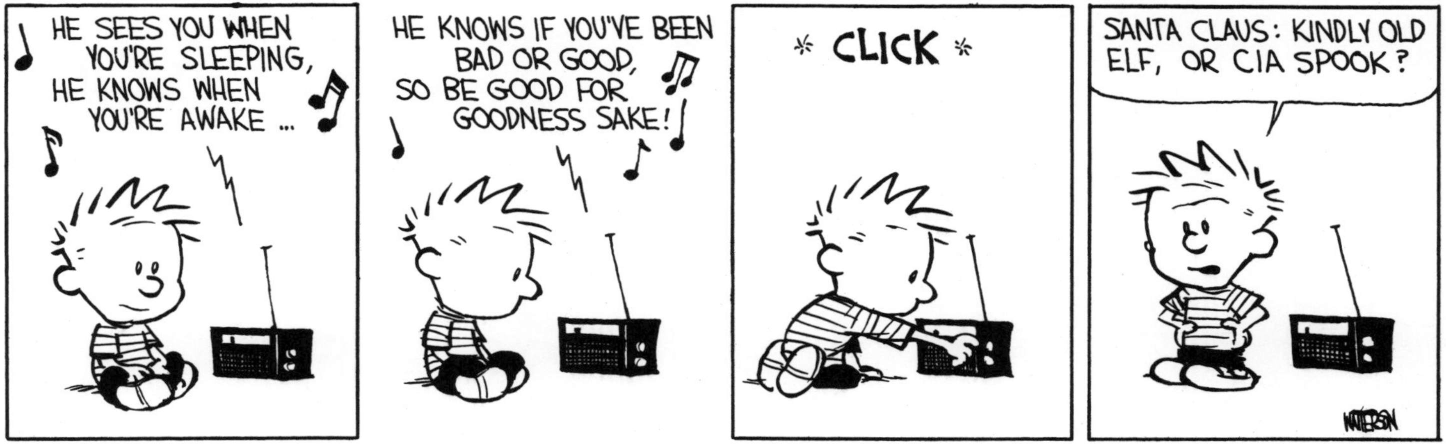
HE SEES YOU WHEN YOU'RE SLEEPING, HE KNOWS WHEN YOU'RE AWAKE ...
HE KNOWS IF YOU'VE BEEN BAD OR GOOD, SO BE GOOD FOR GOODNESS SAKE!
CLICK
SANTA CLAUS: KINDLY OLD ELF, OR CIA SPOOK?
WATTERSON

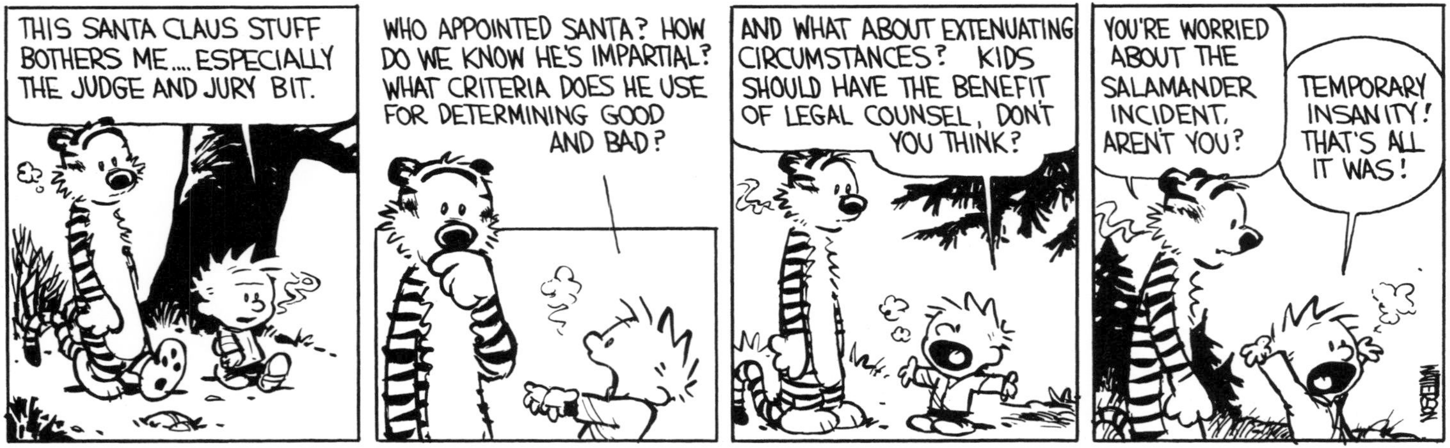
THIS SANTA CLAUS STUFF BOTHERS ME.... ESPECIALLY THE JUDGE AND JURY BIT.
WHO APPOINTED SANTA? HOW DO WE KNOW HE'S IMPARTIAL? WHAT CRITERIA DOES HE USE FOR DETERMINING GOOD AND BAD?
AND WHAT ABOUT EXTENUATING CIRCUMSTANCES? KIDS SHOULD HAVE THE BENEFIT OF LEGAL COUNSEL, DON'T YOU THINK?
YOU'RE WORRIED ABOUT THE SALAMANDER INCIDENT, AREN'T YOU?
TEMPORARY INSANITY! THAT'S ALL IT WAS!
WATTERSON

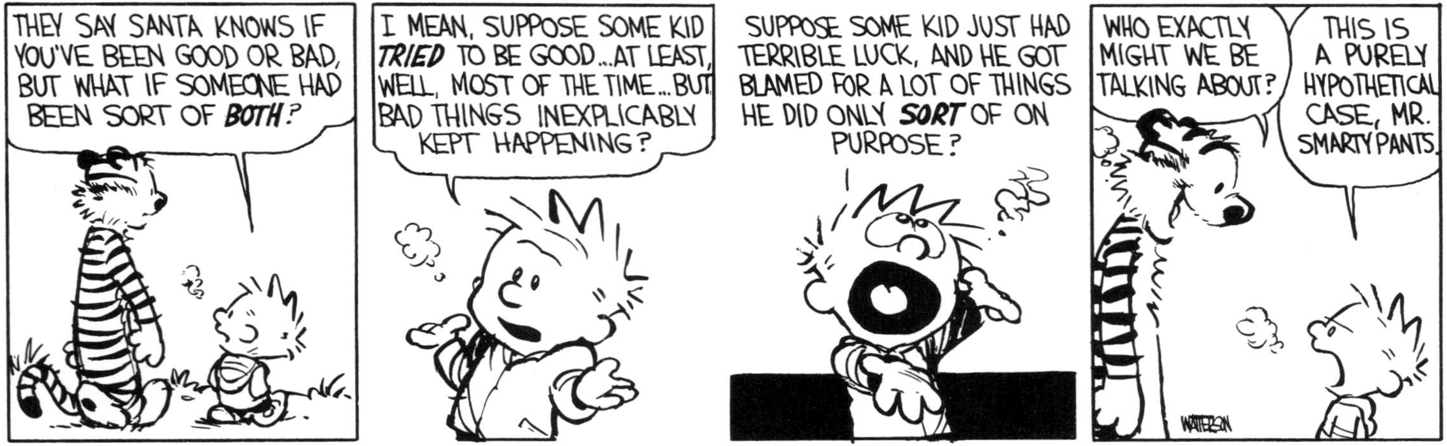
THEY SAY SANTA KNOWS IF YOU'VE BEEN GOOD OR BAD, BUT WHAT IF SOMEONE HAD BEEN SORT OF **BOTH**?
I MEAN, SUPPOSE SOME KID **TRIED** TO BE GOOD...AT LEAST, WELL, MOST OF THE TIME...BUT BAD THINGS INEXPLICABLY KEPT HAPPENING?
SUPPOSE SOME KID JUST HAD TERRIBLE LUCK, AND HE GOT BLAMED FOR A LOT OF THINGS HE DID ONLY **SORT** OF ON PURPOSE?
WHO EXACTLY MIGHT WE BE TALKING ABOUT?
THIS IS A PURELY HYPOTHETICAL CASE, MR. SMARTY PANTS.
WATTERSON

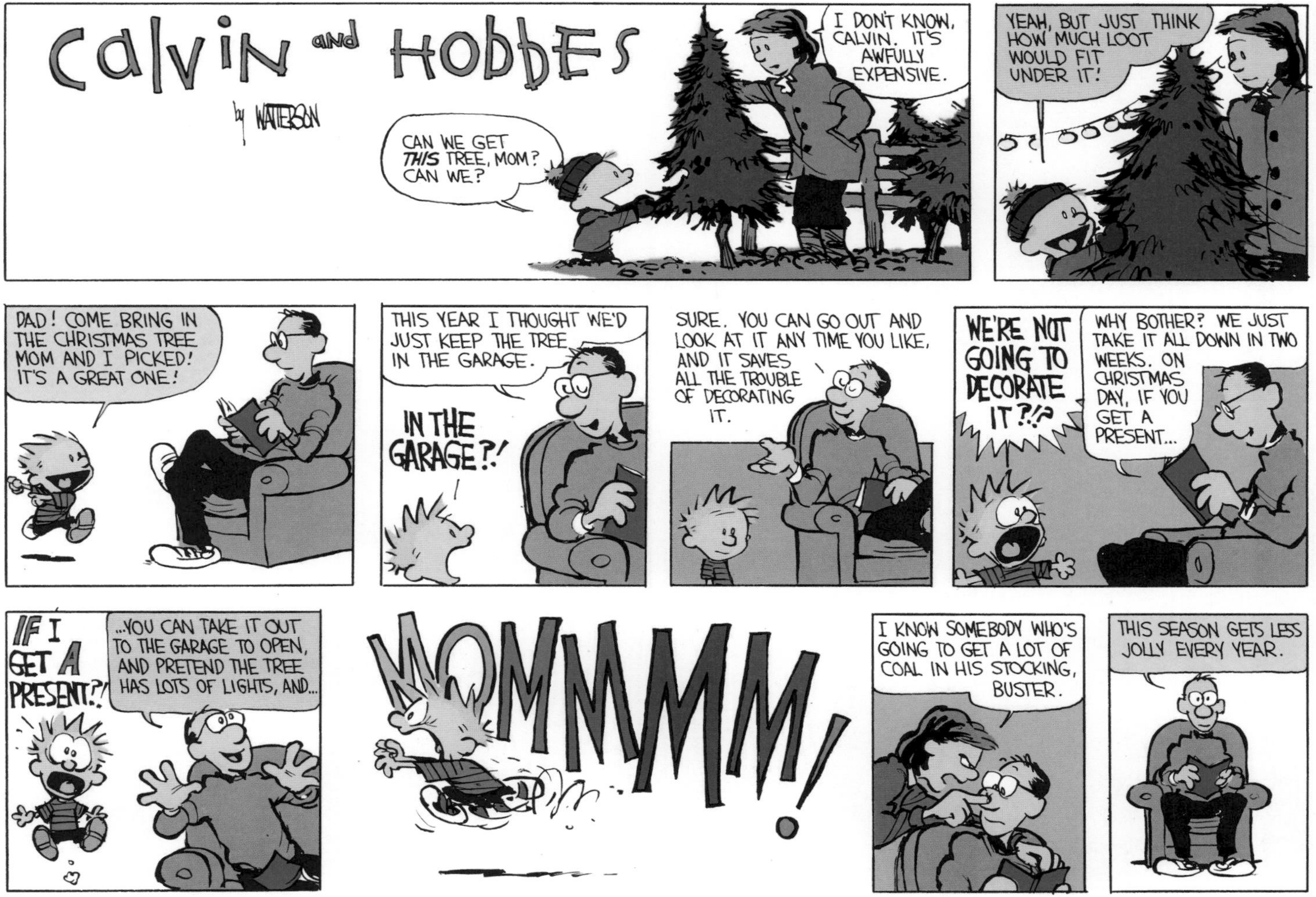
Calvin and Hobbes
by WATTERSON
CAN WE GET THIS TREE, MOM? CAN WE?
I DON'T KNOW, CALVIN. IT'S AWFULLY EXPENSIVE.
YEAH, BUT JUST THINK HOW MUCH LOOT WOULD FIT UNDER IT!
DAD! COME BRING IN THE CHRISTMAS TREE MOM AND I PICKED! IT'S A GREAT ONE!
THIS YEAR I THOUGHT WE'D JUST KEEP THE TREE IN THE GARAGE.
IN THE GARAGE?!
SURE. YOU CAN GO OUT AND LOOK AT IT ANY TIME YOU LIKE,
AND IT SAVES ALL THE TROUBLE OF DECORATING IT.
WE'RE NOT GOING TO DECORATE IT?!?
WHY BOTHER? WE JUST TAKE IT ALL DOWN IN TWO WEEKS. ON CHRISTMAS DAY, IF YOU GET A PRESENT...
IF I GET A PRESENT?!
...YOU CAN TAKE IT OUT TO THE GARAGE TO OPEN, AND PRETEND THE TREE HAS LOTS OF LIGHTS, AND...
MOMMMM!
I KNOW SOMEBODY WHO'S GOING TO GET A LOT OF COAL IN HIS STOCKING, BUSTER.
THIS SEASON GETS LESS JOLLY EVERY YEAR.

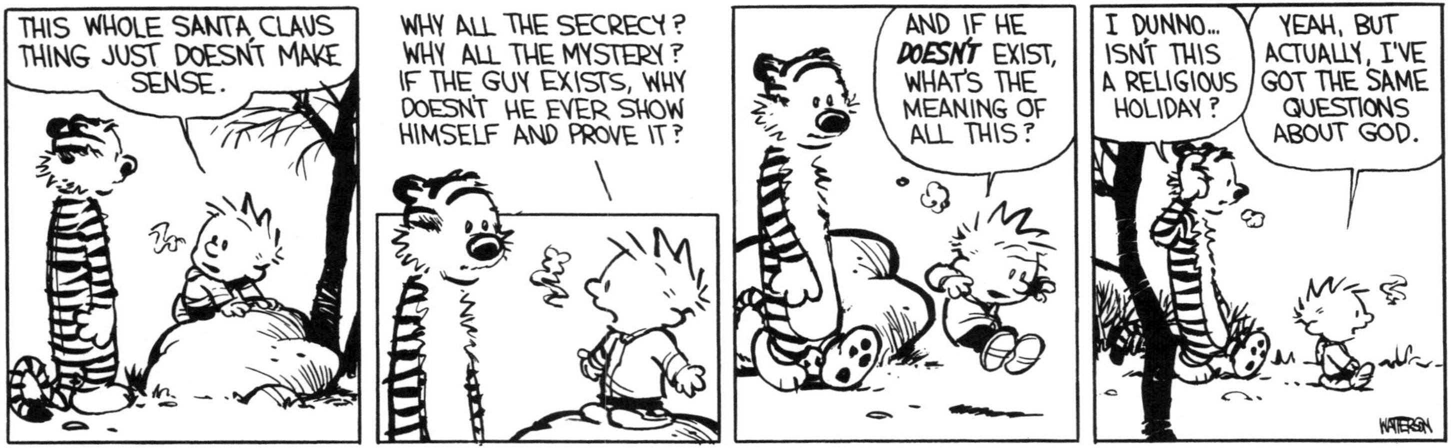
THIS WHOLE SANTA CLAUS THING JUST DOESN'T MAKE SENSE.
WHY ALL THE SECRECY? WHY ALL THE MYSTERY? IF THE GUY EXISTS, WHY DOESN'T HE EVER SHOW HIMSELF AND PROVE IT?
AND IF HE ***DOESN'T*** EXIST, WHAT'S THE MEANING OF ALL THIS?
I DUNNO... ISN'T THIS A RELIGIOUS HOLIDAY?
YEAH, BUT ACTUALLY, I'VE GOT THE SAME QUESTIONS ABOUT GOD.
WATTERSON

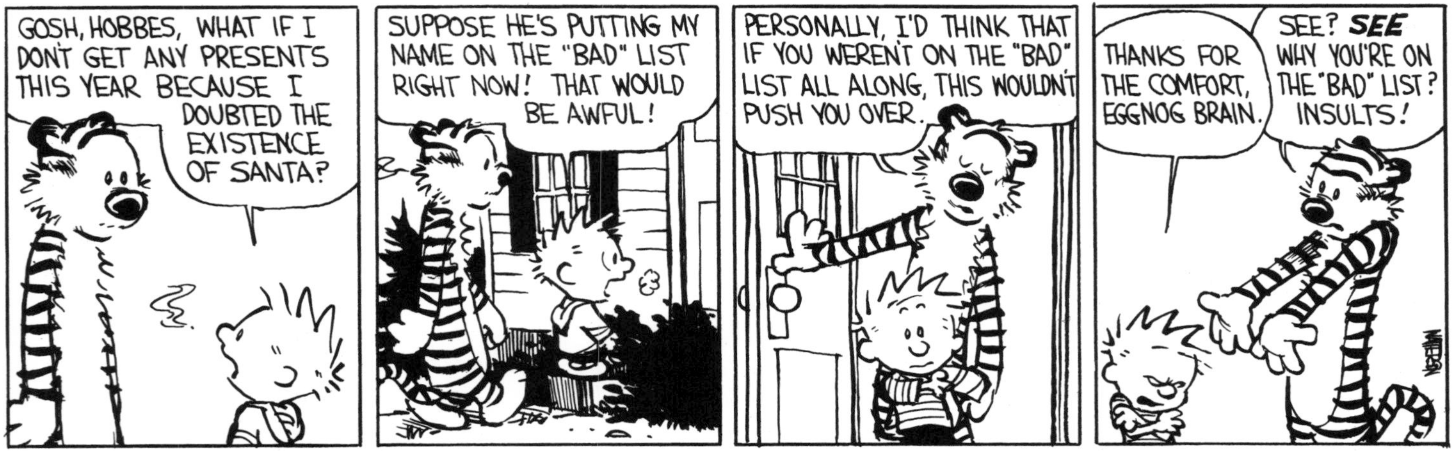
GOSH, HOBBES, WHAT IF I DON'T GET ANY PRESENTS THIS YEAR BECAUSE I DOUBTED THE EXISTENCE OF SANTA?
SUPPOSE HE'S PUTTING MY NAME ON THE "BAD" LIST RIGHT NOW! THAT WOULD BE AWFUL!
PERSONALLY, I'D THINK THAT IF YOU WEREN'T ON THE "BAD" LIST ALL ALONG, THIS WOULDN'T PUSH YOU OVER.
THANKS FOR THE COMFORT, EGGNOG BRAIN.
SEE? ***SEE*** WHY YOU'RE ON THE "BAD" LIST? INSULTS!
WATTERSON

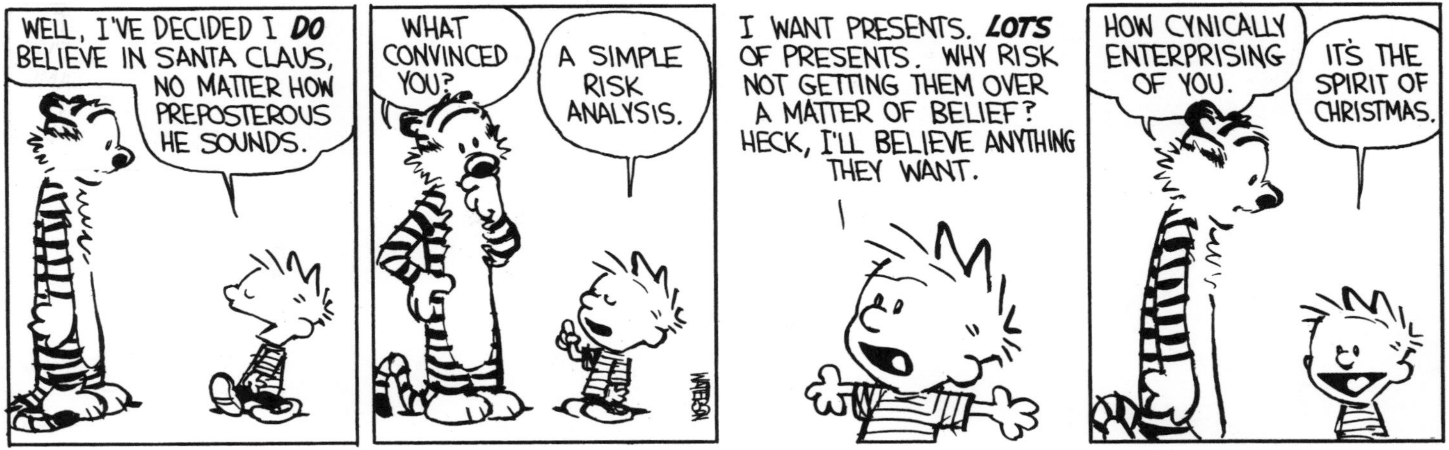
WELL, I'VE DECIDED I **DO** BELIEVE IN SANTA CLAUS, NO MATTER HOW PREPOSTEROUS HE SOUNDS.
WHAT CONVINCED YOU?
A SIMPLE RISK ANALYSIS.
I WANT PRESENTS. ***LOTS*** OF PRESENTS. WHY RISK NOT GETTING THEM OVER A MATTER OF BELIEF? HECK, I'LL BELIEVE ANYTHING THEY WANT.
HOW CYNICALLY ENTERPRISING OF YOU.
IT'S THE SPIRIT OF CHRISTMAS.

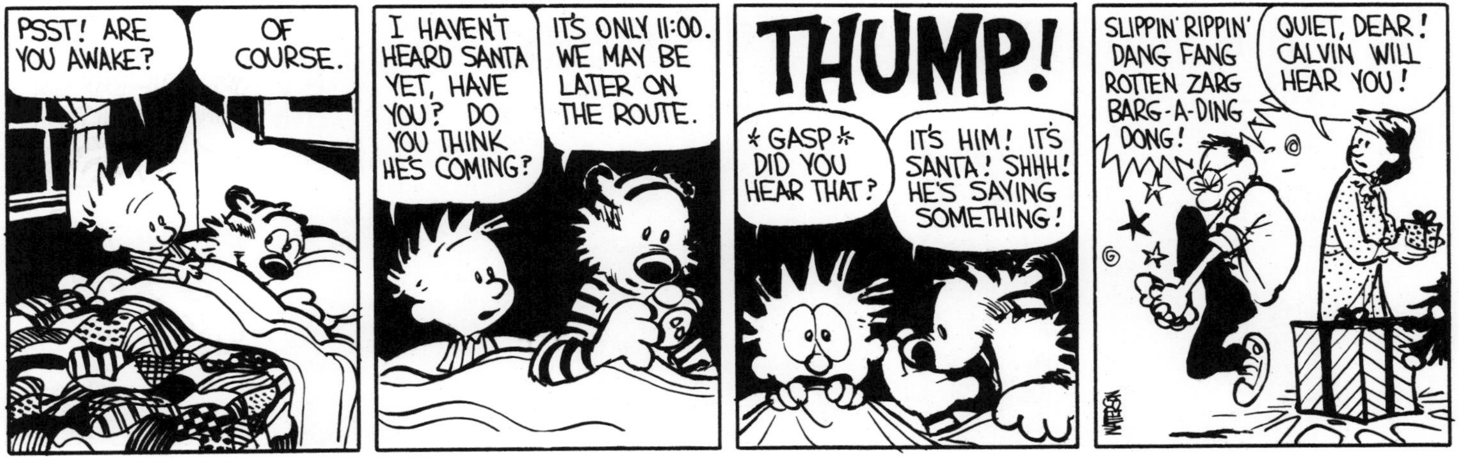
PSST! ARE YOU AWAKE?
OF COURSE.
I HAVEN'T HEARD SANTA YET, HAVE YOU? DO YOU THINK HE'S COMING?
IT'S ONLY 11:00. WE MAY BE LATER ON THE ROUTE.
THUMP!
GASP DID YOU HEAR THAT?
IT'S HIM! IT'S SANTA! SHHH! HE'S SAYING SOMETHING!
SLIPPIN' RIPPIN' DANG FANG ROTTEN ZARG BARG-A-DING DONG!
QUIET, DEAR! CALVIN WILL HEAR YOU!

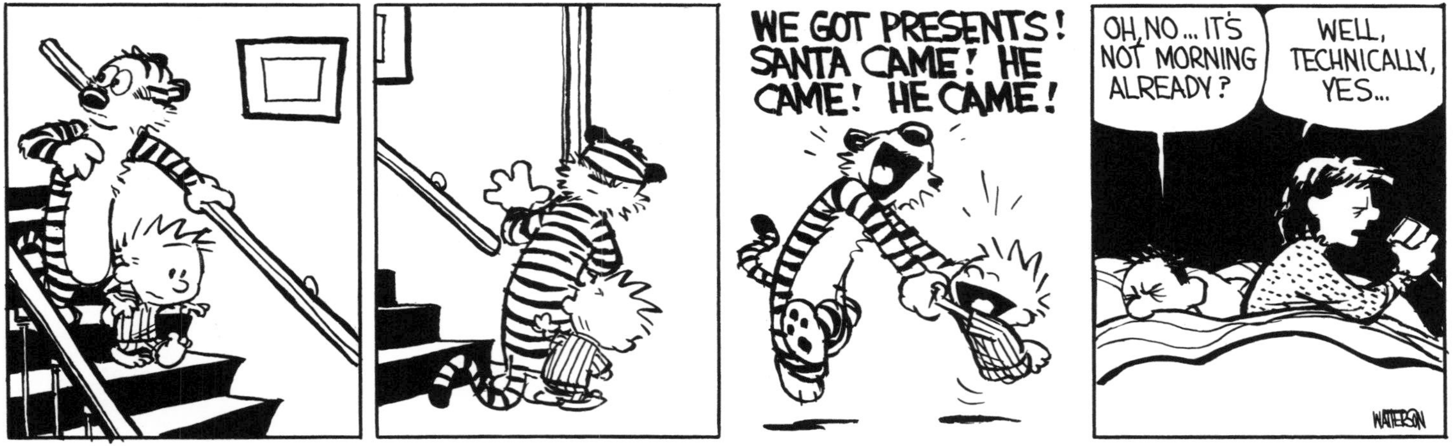
WE GOT PRESENTS! SANTA CAME! HE CAME! HE CAME!
OH, NO... IT'S NOT MORNING ALREADY?
WELL, TECHNICALLY, YES...
WATTERSON

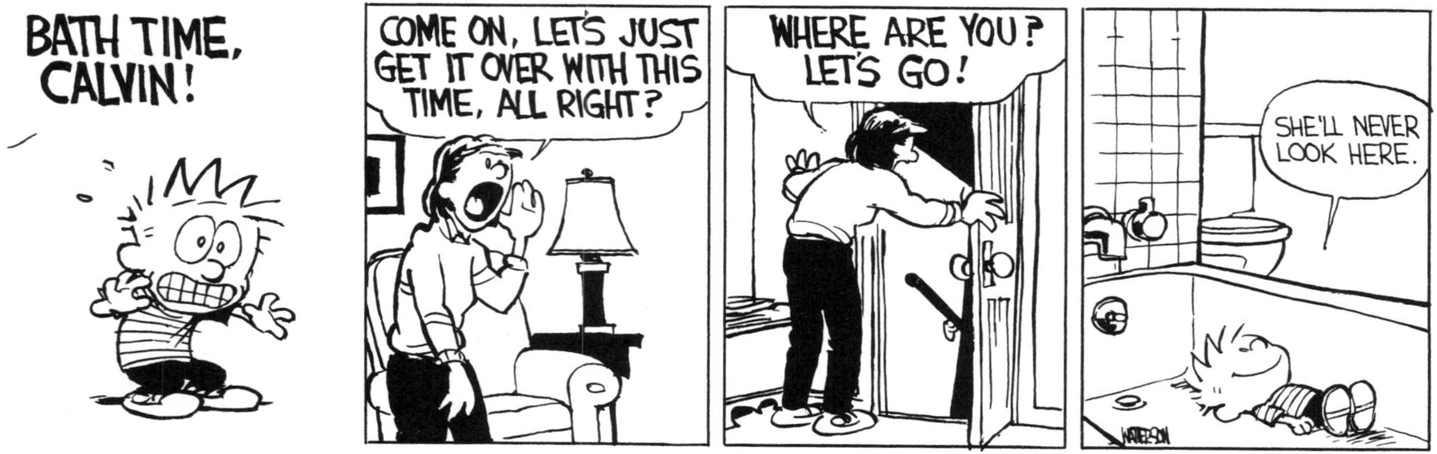
BATH TIME, CALVIN!
COME ON, LET'S JUST GET IT OVER WITH THIS TIME, ALL RIGHT?
WHERE ARE YOU? LET'S GO!
SHE'LL NEVER LOOK HERE.
WATTERSON

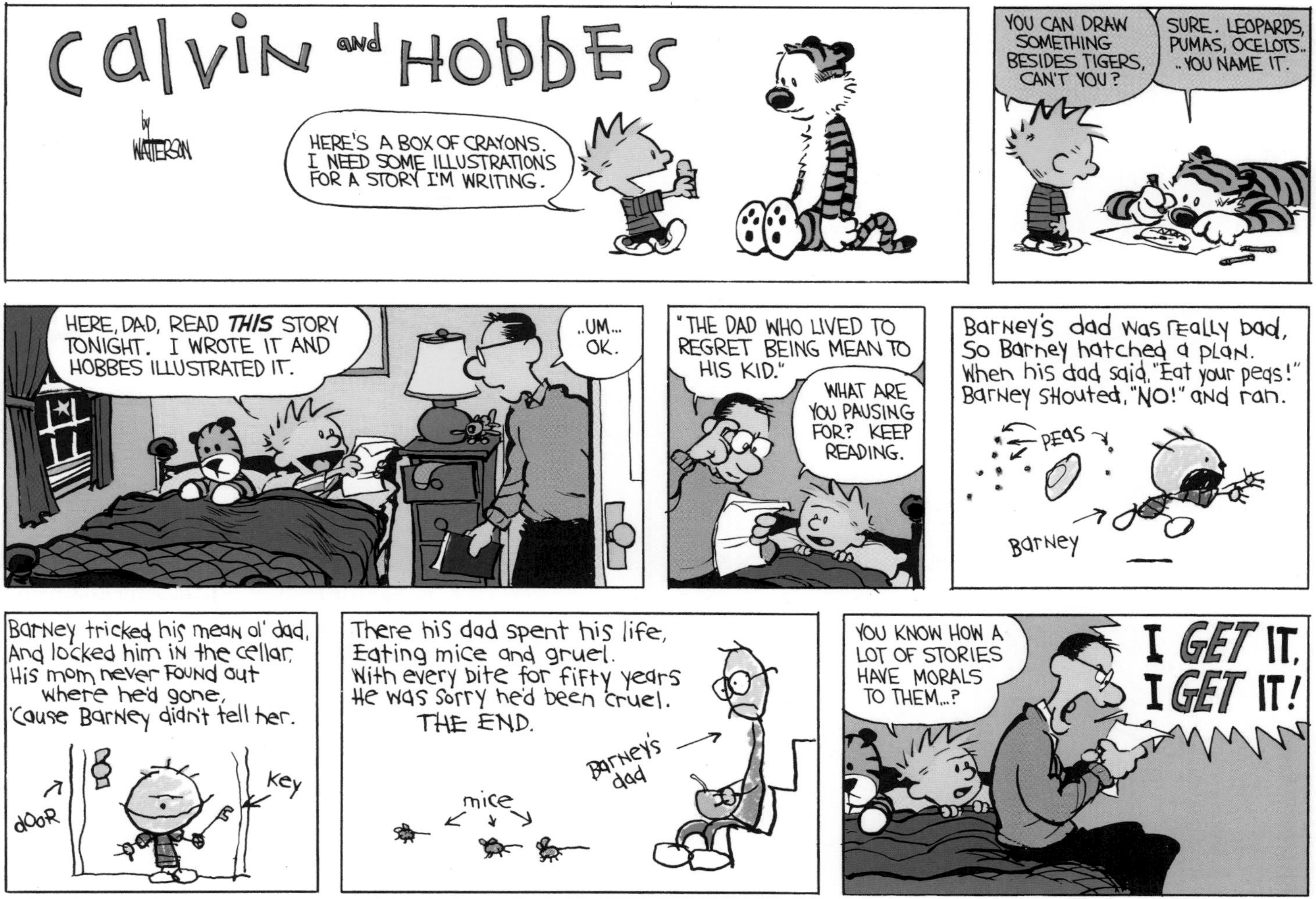
Calvin and HOBBES
by WATTERSON
HERE'S A BOX OF CRAYONS. I NEED SOME ILLUSTRATIONS FOR A STORY I'M WRITING.
YOU CAN DRAW SOMETHING BESIDES TIGERS, CAN'T YOU?
SURE. LEOPARDS, PUMAS, OCELOTS.. ..YOU NAME IT.
HERE, DAD, READ THIS STORY TONIGHT. I WROTE IT AND HOBBES ILLUSTRATED IT.
..UM... OK.
"THE DAD WHO LIVED TO REGRET BEING MEAN TO HIS KID."
WHAT ARE YOU PAUSING FOR? KEEP READING.
Barney's dad was really bad, So Barney hatched a plan. When his dad said, "Eat your peas!" Barney shouted, "NO!" and ran.
PEAS
Barney
Barney tricked his mean ol' dad, And locked him in the cellar, His mom never found out where he'd gone, 'Cause Barney didn't tell her.
door
Key
There his dad spent his life, Eating mice and gruel. With every bite for fifty years He was sorry he'd been cruel.
THE END.
Barney's dad
mice
YOU KNOW HOW A LOT OF STORIES HAVE MORALS TO THEM...?
I GET IT, I GET IT!

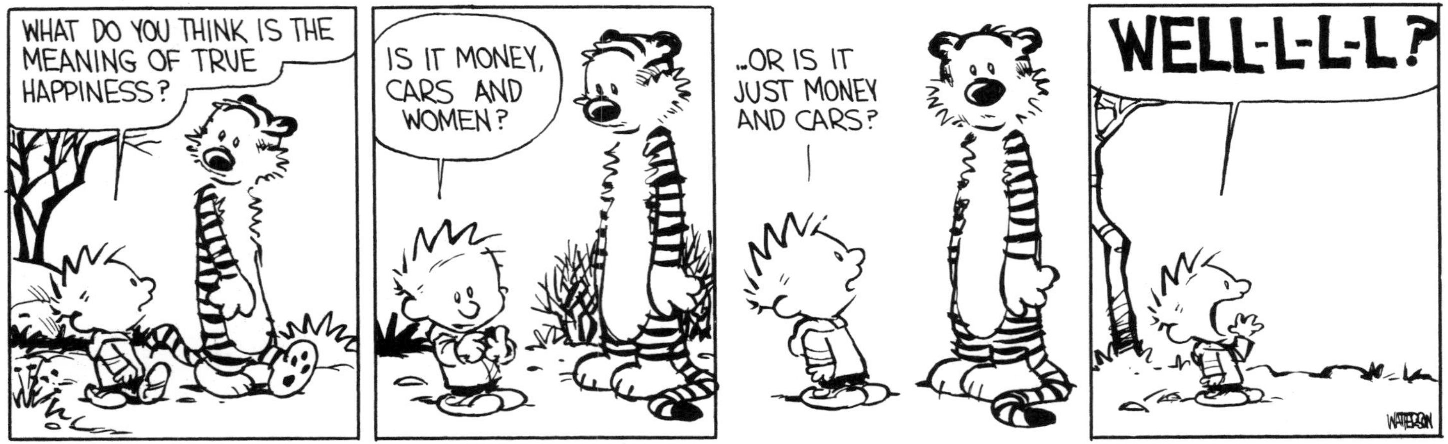
WHAT DO YOU THINK IS THE MEANING OF TRUE HAPPINESS?
IS IT MONEY, CARS AND WOMEN?
..OR IS IT JUST MONEY AND CARS?
WELL-L-L-L?
WATTERSON

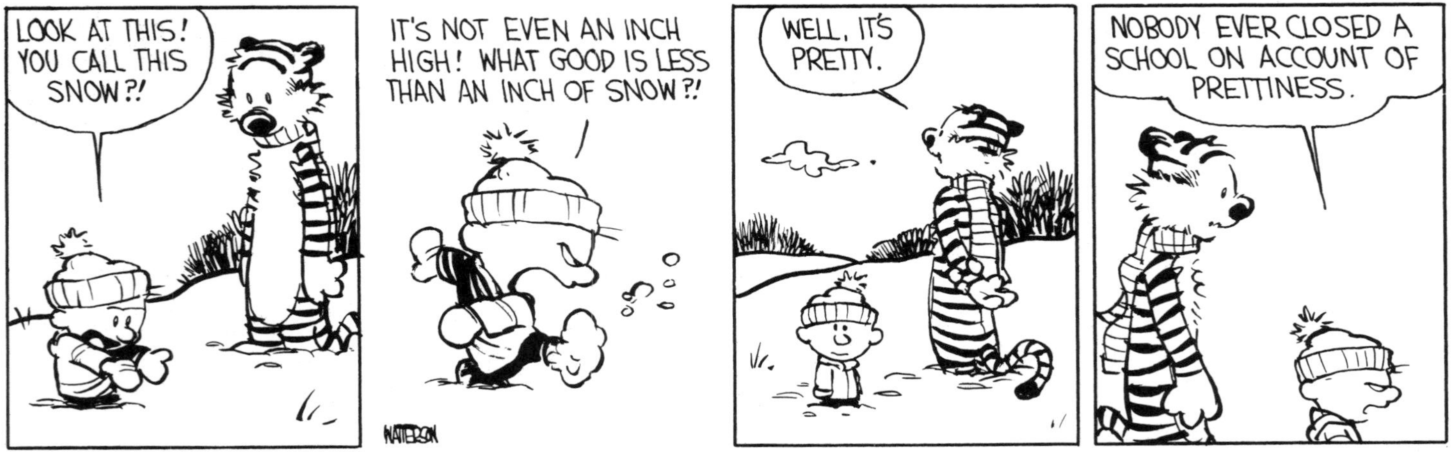
LOOK AT THIS! YOU CALL THIS SNOW?!
IT'S NOT EVEN AN INCH HIGH! WHAT GOOD IS LESS THAN AN INCH OF SNOW?!
WATTERSON
WELL, IT'S PRETTY.
NOBODY EVER CLOSED A SCHOOL ON ACCOUNT OF PRETTINESS.

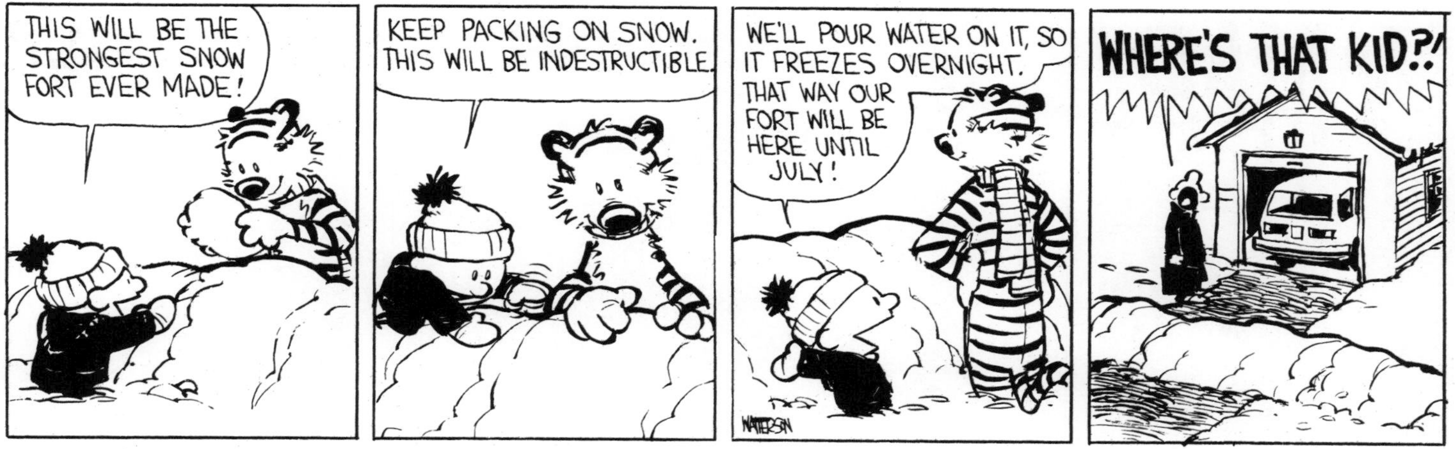
THIS WILL BE THE STRONGEST SNOW FORT EVER MADE!
KEEP PACKING ON SNOW. THIS WILL BE INDESTRUCTIBLE.
WE'LL POUR WATER ON IT, SO IT FREEZES OVERNIGHT.
THAT WAY OUR FORT WILL BE HERE UNTIL JULY!
WATTERSON
WHERE'S THAT KID?!

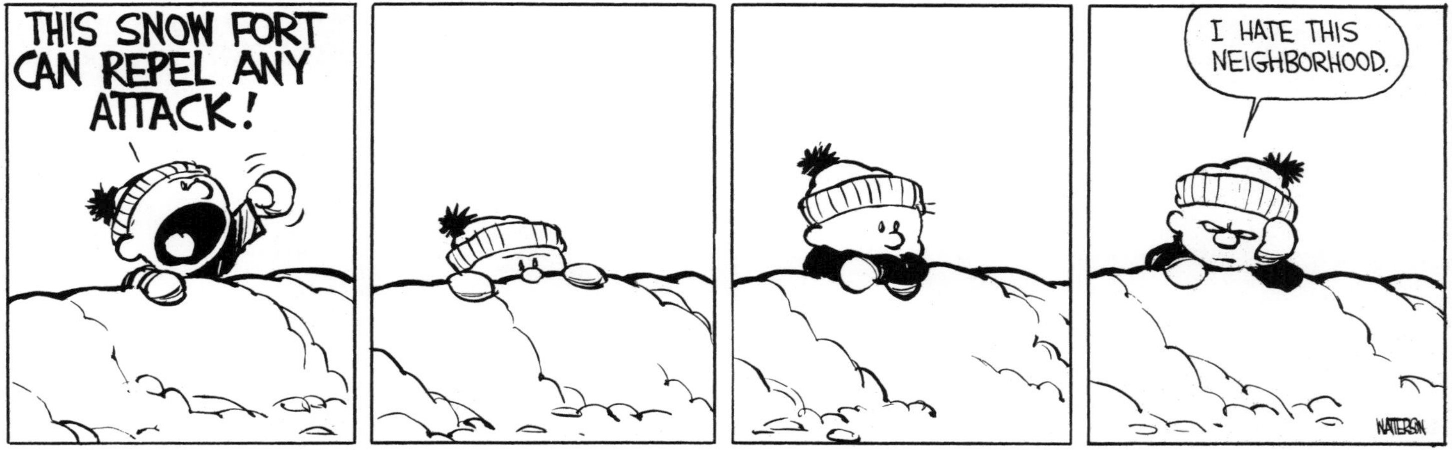
THIS SNOW FORT CAN REPEL ANY ATTACK!
I HATE THIS NEIGHBORHOOD.
WATTERSON

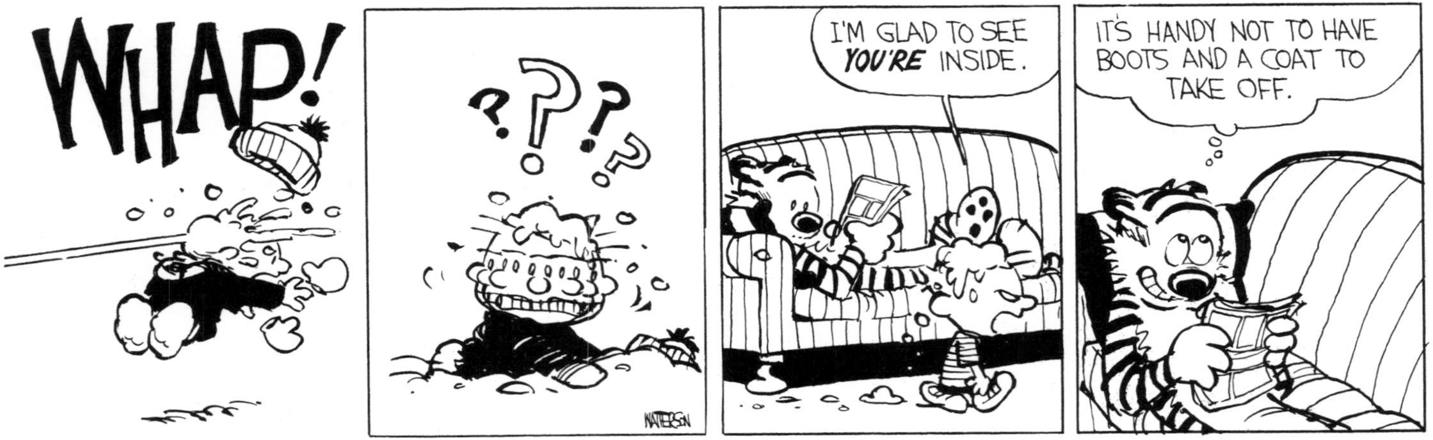
WHAP!
I'M GLAD TO SEE *YOU'RE* INSIDE.
IT'S HANDY NOT TO HAVE BOOTS AND A COAT TO TAKE OFF.

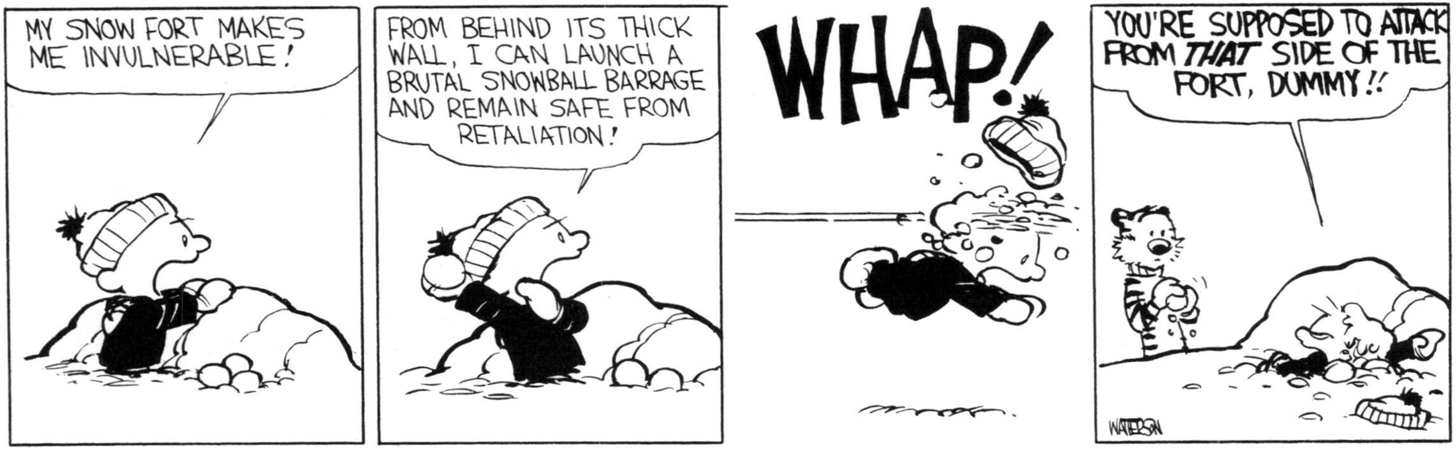
MY SNOW FORT MAKES ME INVULNERABLE!
FROM BEHIND ITS THICK WALL, I CAN LAUNCH A BRUTAL SNOWBALL BARRAGE AND REMAIN SAFE FROM RETALIATION!
WHAP!
YOU'RE SUPPOSED TO ATTACK FROM *THAT* SIDE OF THE FORT, DUMMY!!

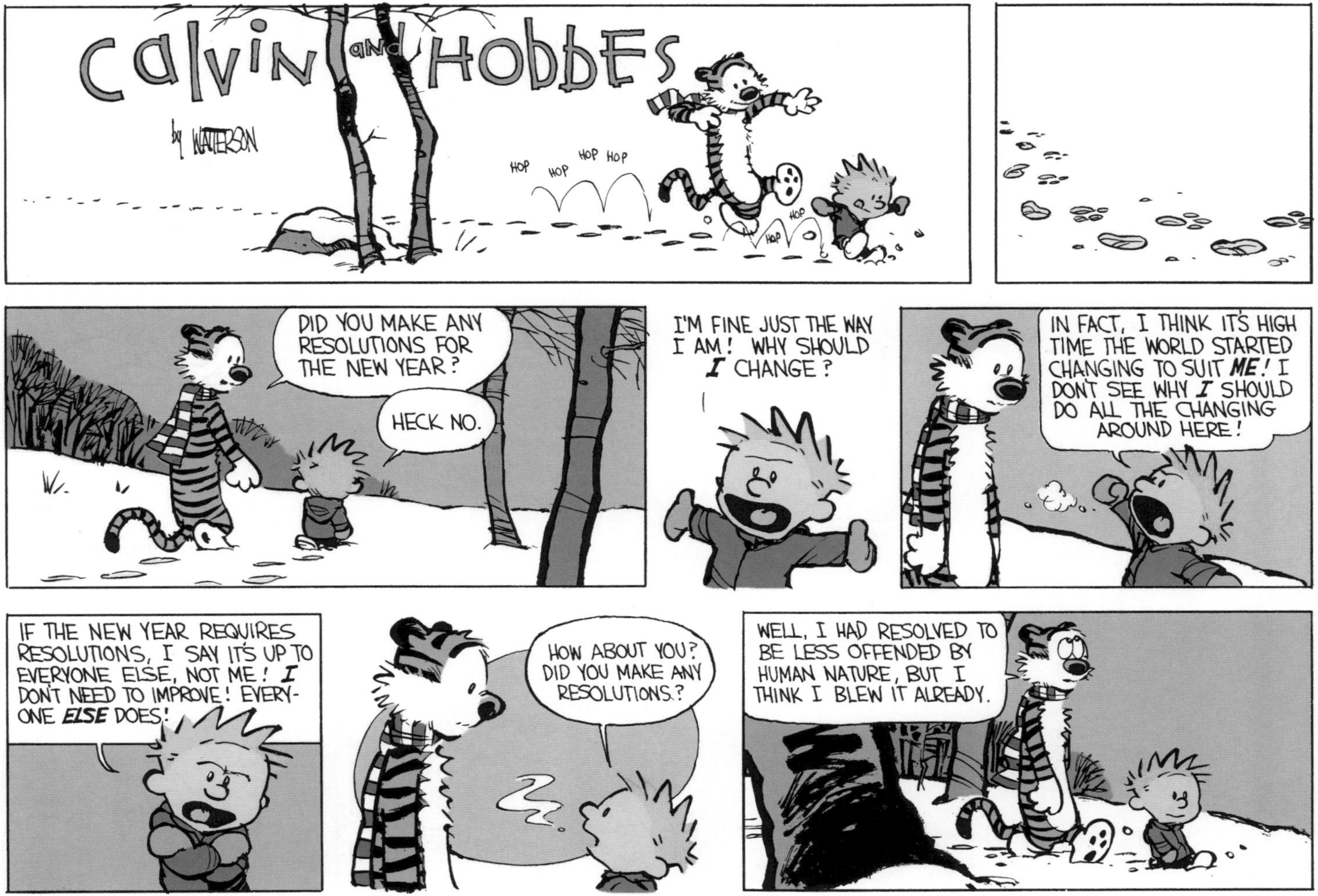
Calvin and HOBBES
by WATTERSON
HOP HOP HOP HOP
HOP HOP
DID YOU MAKE ANY RESOLUTIONS FOR THE NEW YEAR?
HECK NO.
I'M FINE JUST THE WAY I AM! WHY SHOULD I CHANGE?
IN FACT, I THINK IT'S HIGH TIME THE WORLD STARTED CHANGING TO SUIT ME! I DON'T SEE WHY I SHOULD DO ALL THE CHANGING AROUND HERE!
IF THE NEW YEAR REQUIRES RESOLUTIONS, I SAY IT'S UP TO EVERYONE ELSE, NOT ME! I DON'T NEED TO IMPROVE! EVERYONE ELSE DOES!
HOW ABOUT YOU? DID YOU MAKE ANY RESOLUTIONS?
WELL, I HAD RESOLVED TO BE LESS OFFENDED BY HUMAN NATURE, BUT I THINK I BLEW IT ALREADY.

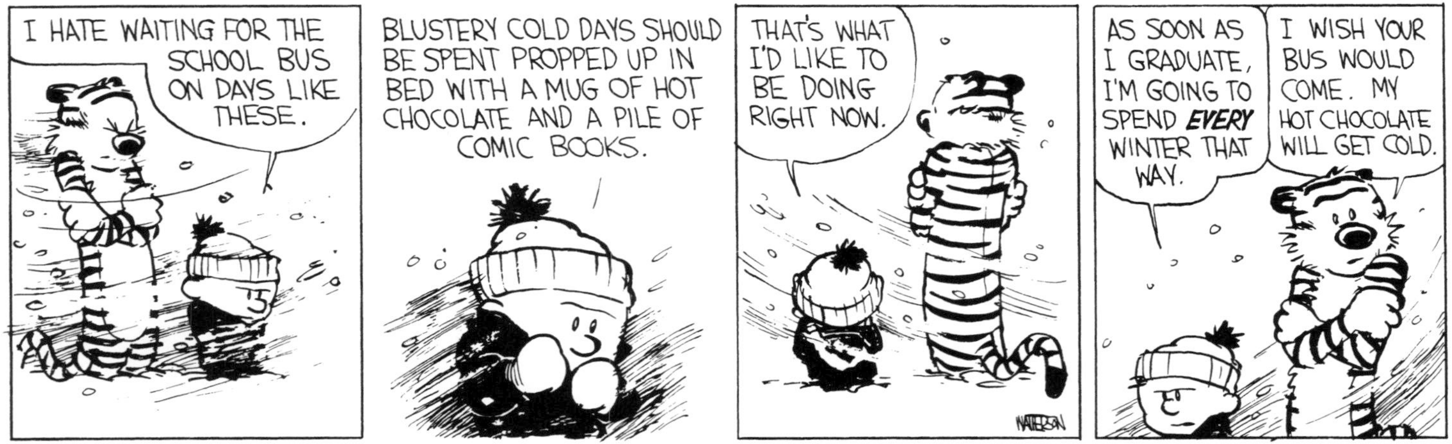
I HATE WAITING FOR THE SCHOOL BUS ON DAYS LIKE THESE.
BLUSTERY COLD DAYS SHOULD BE SPENT PROPPED UP IN BED WITH A MUG OF HOT CHOCOLATE AND A PILE OF COMIC BOOKS.
THAT'S WHAT I'D LIKE TO BE DOING RIGHT NOW.
AS SOON AS I GRADUATE, I'M GOING TO SPEND **EVERY** WINTER THAT WAY.
I WISH YOUR BUS WOULD COME. MY HOT CHOCOLATE WILL GET COLD.
WATTERSON

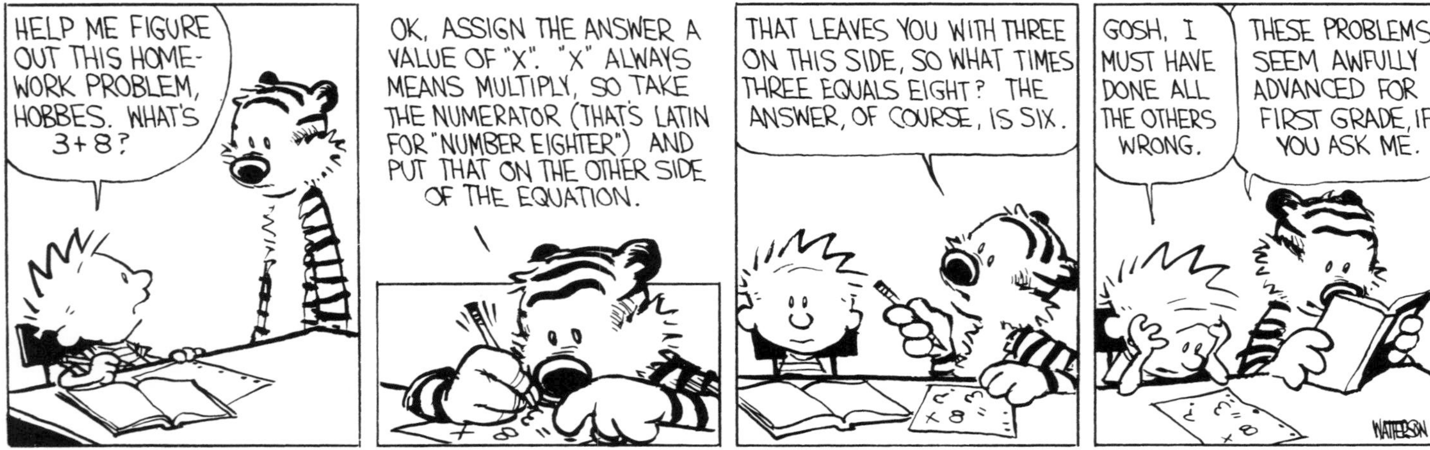
HELP ME FIGURE OUT THIS HOME-WORK PROBLEM, HOBBES. WHAT'S 3+8?
OK, ASSIGN THE ANSWER A VALUE OF "X". "X" ALWAYS MEANS MULTIPLY, SO TAKE THE NUMERATOR (THAT'S LATIN FOR "NUMBER EIGHTER") AND PUT THAT ON THE OTHER SIDE OF THE EQUATION.
THAT LEAVES YOU WITH THREE ON THIS SIDE, SO WHAT TIMES THREE EQUALS EIGHT? THE ANSWER, OF COURSE, IS SIX.
GOSH, I MUST HAVE DONE ALL THE OTHERS WRONG.
THESE PROBLEMS SEEM AWFULLY ADVANCED FOR FIRST GRADE, IF YOU ASK ME.
WATTERSON

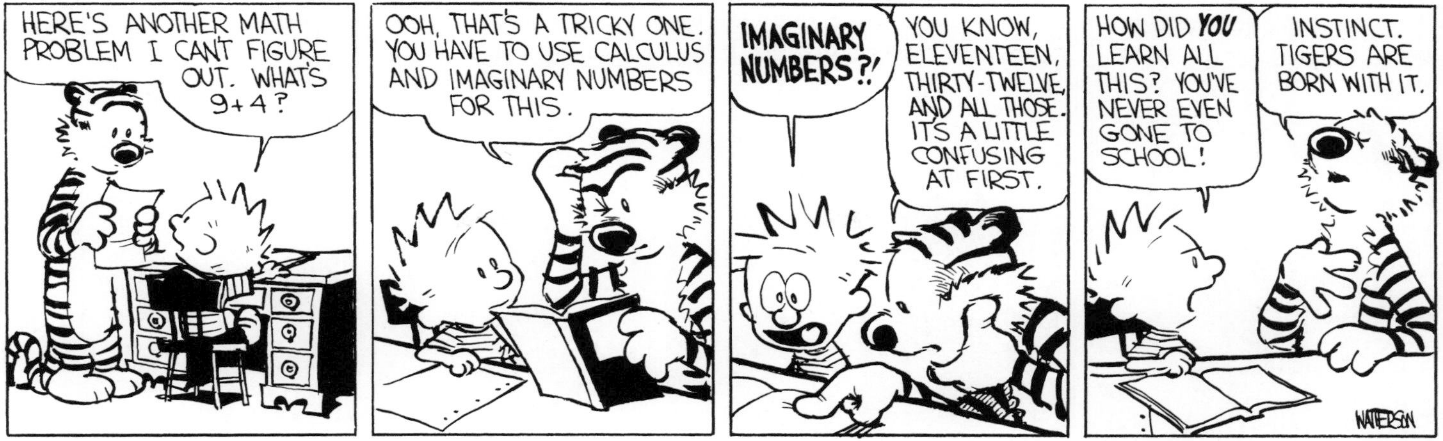
HERE'S ANOTHER MATH PROBLEM I CAN'T FIGURE OUT. WHAT'S 9+4?
OOH, THAT'S A TRICKY ONE. YOU HAVE TO USE CALCULUS AND IMAGINARY NUMBERS FOR THIS.
IMAGINARY NUMBERS?!
YOU KNOW, ELEVENTEEN, THIRTY-TWELVE, AND ALL THOSE. IT'S A LITTLE CONFUSING AT FIRST.
HOW DID YOU LEARN ALL THIS? YOU'VE NEVER EVEN GONE TO SCHOOL!
INSTINCT. TIGERS ARE BORN WITH IT.
WATTERSON

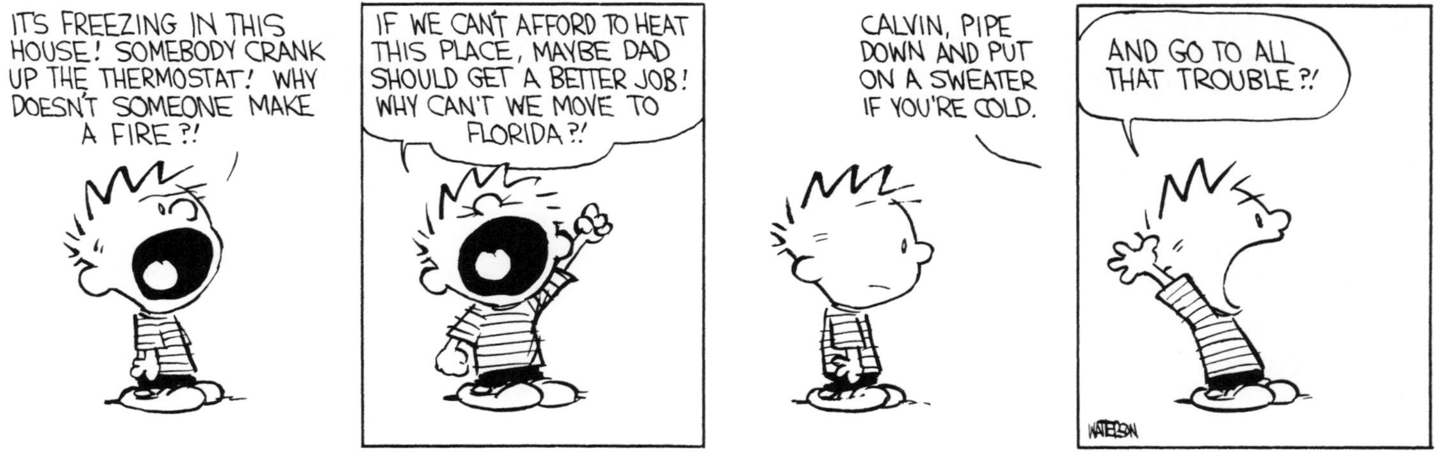
IT'S FREEZING IN THIS HOUSE! SOMEBODY CRANK UP THE THERMOSTAT! WHY DOESN'T SOMEONE MAKE A FIRE?!
IF WE CAN'T AFFORD TO HEAT THIS PLACE, MAYBE DAD SHOULD GET A BETTER JOB! WHY CAN'T WE MOVE TO FLORIDA?!
CALVIN, PIPE DOWN AND PUT ON A SWEATER IF YOU'RE COLD.
AND GO TO ALL THAT TROUBLE?!
WATTERSON

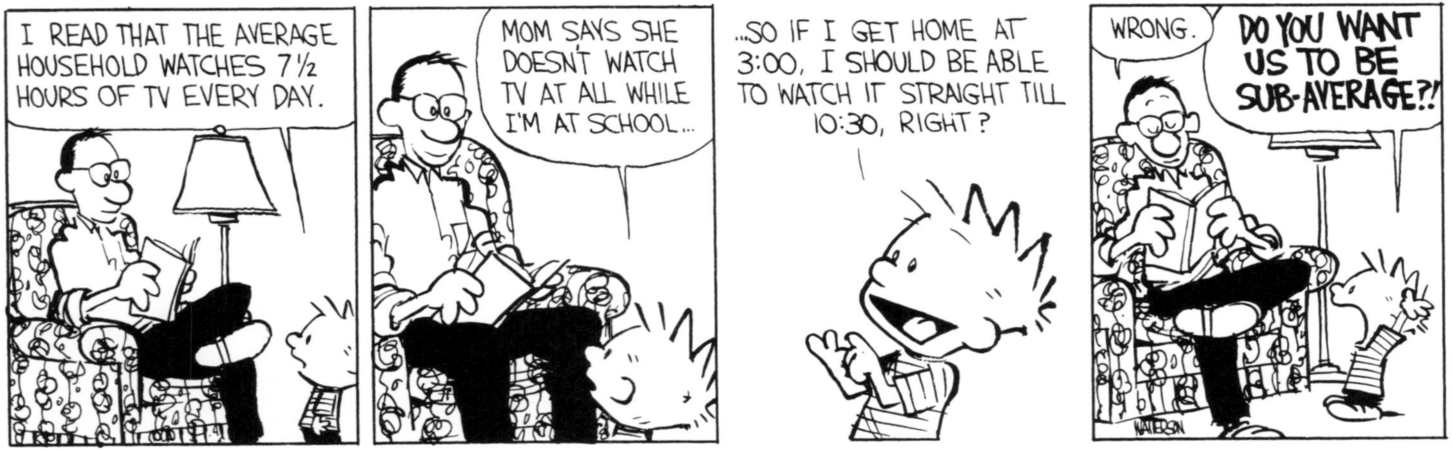
I READ THAT THE AVERAGE HOUSEHOLD WATCHES 7½ HOURS OF TV EVERY DAY.
MOM SAYS SHE DOESN'T WATCH TV AT ALL WHILE I'M AT SCHOOL...
...SO IF I GET HOME AT 3:00, I SHOULD BE ABLE TO WATCH IT STRAIGHT TILL 10:30, RIGHT?
WRONG.
DO YOU WANT US TO BE SUB-AVERAGE?!
WATTERSON

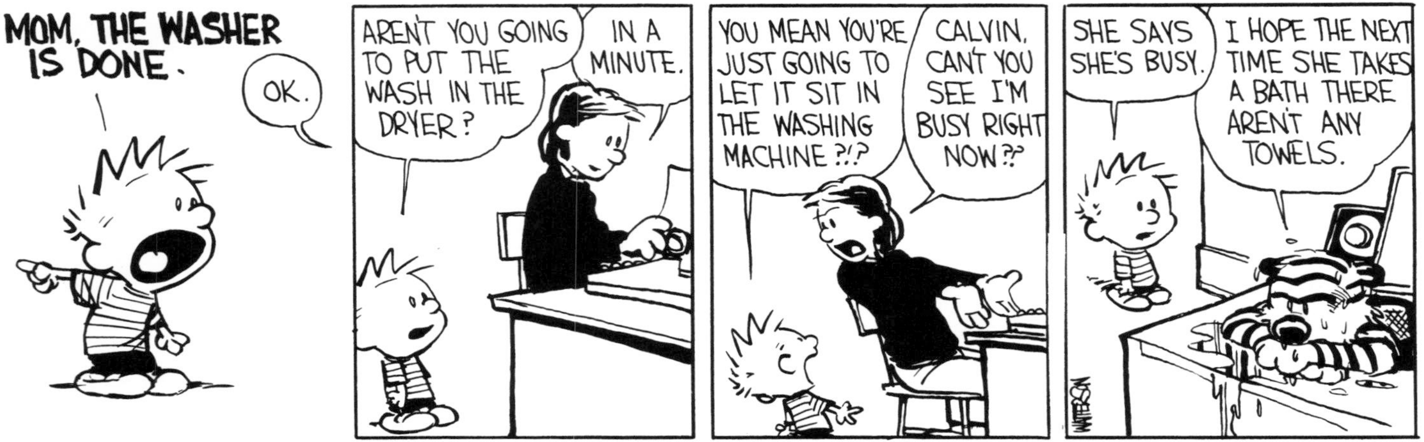
MOM, THE WASHER IS DONE.
OK.
AREN'T YOU GOING TO PUT THE WASH IN THE DRYER?
IN A MINUTE.
YOU MEAN YOU'RE JUST GOING TO LET IT SIT IN THE WASHING MACHINE?!?
CALVIN, CAN'T YOU SEE I'M BUSY RIGHT NOW?!?
SHE SAYS SHE'S BUSY.
I HOPE THE NEXT TIME SHE TAKES A BATH THERE AREN'T ANY TOWELS.
WATTERSON

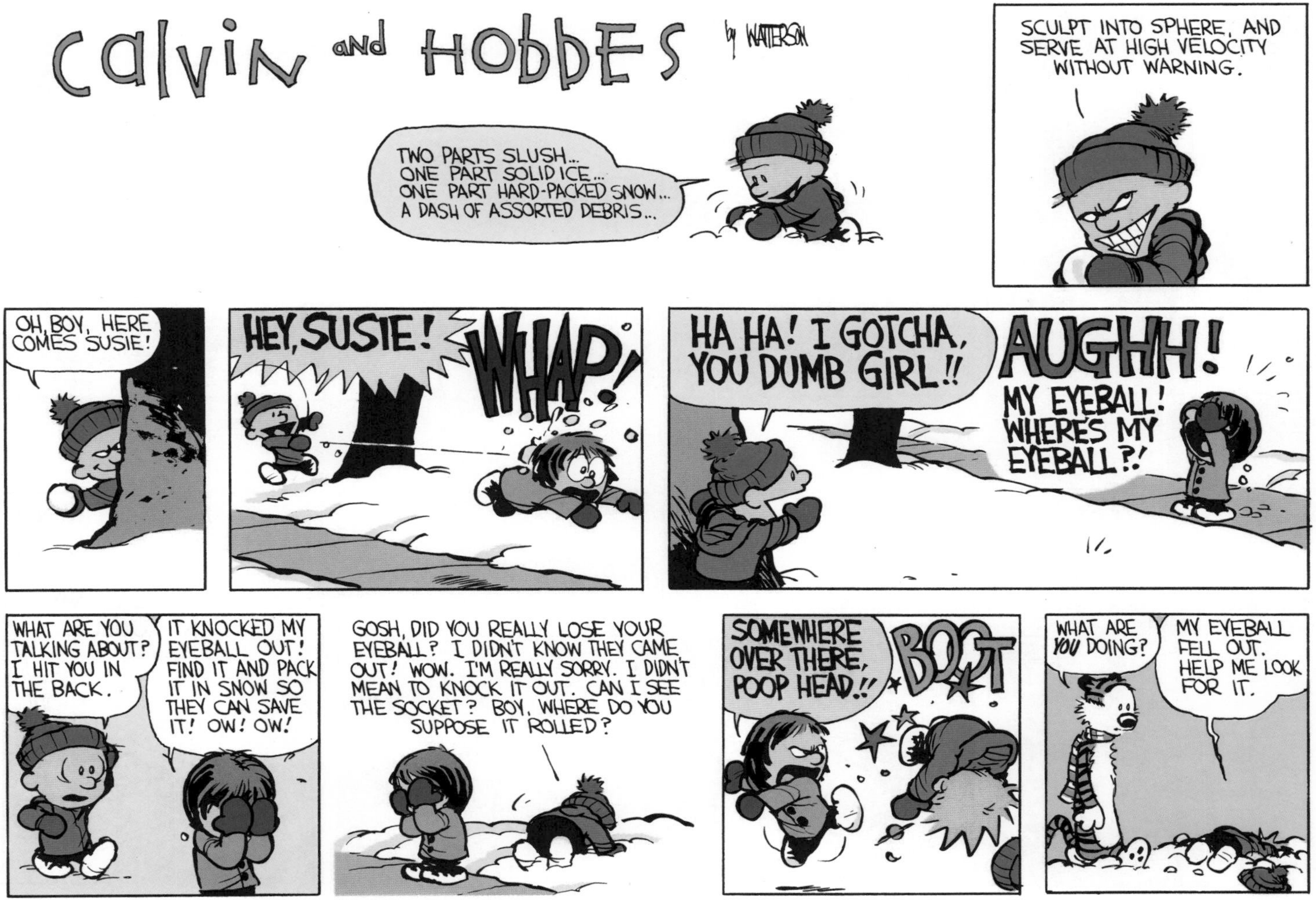
Calvin and HOBBES
by WATTERSON
TWO PARTS SLUSH... ONE PART SOLID ICE... ONE PART HARD-PACKED SNOW... A DASH OF ASSORTED DEBRIS...
SCULPT INTO SPHERE, AND SERVE AT HIGH VELOCITY WITHOUT WARNING.
OH, BOY, HERE COMES SUSIE!
HEY, SUSIE!
WHAP!
HA HA! I GOTCHA, YOU DUMB GIRL!!
AUGHH!
MY EYEBALL! WHERE'S MY EYEBALL?!
WHAT ARE YOU TALKING ABOUT? I HIT YOU IN THE BACK.
IT KNOCKED MY EYEBALL OUT! FIND IT AND PACK IT IN SNOW SO THEY CAN SAVE IT! OW! OW!
GOSH, DID YOU REALLY LOSE YOUR EYEBALL? I DIDN'T KNOW THEY CAME OUT! WOW. I'M REALLY SORRY. I DIDN'T MEAN TO KNOCK IT OUT. CAN I SEE THE SOCKET? BOY, WHERE DO YOU SUPPOSE IT ROLLED?
SOMEWHERE OVER THERE, POOP HEAD!!
BOOT
WHAT ARE *YOU* DOING?
MY EYEBALL FELL OUT. HELP ME LOOK FOR IT.

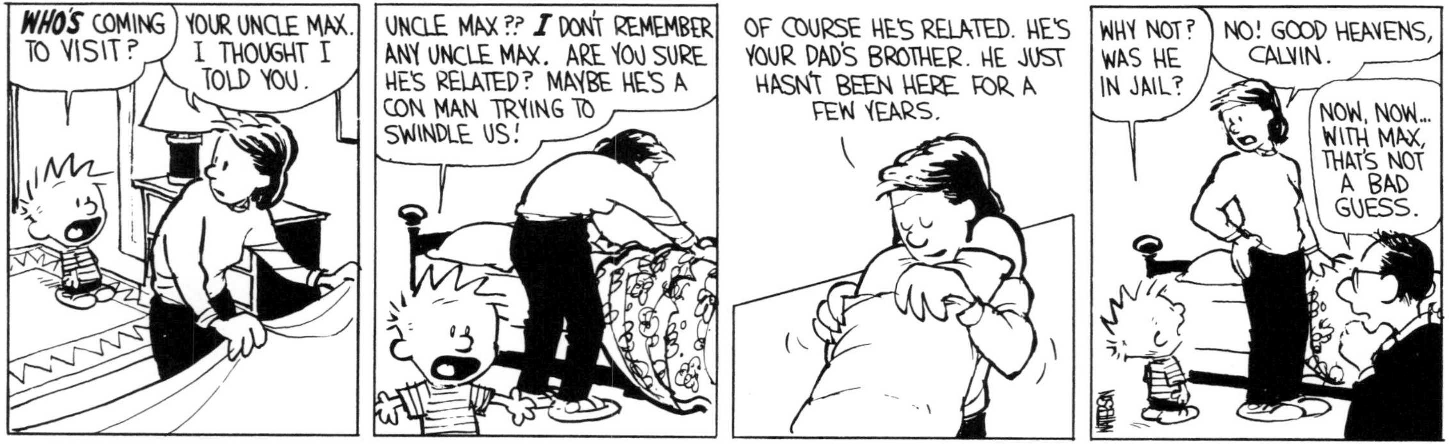
WHO'S COMING TO VISIT?
YOUR UNCLE MAX. I THOUGHT I TOLD YOU.
UNCLE MAX?? I DON'T REMEMBER ANY UNCLE MAX. ARE YOU SURE HE'S RELATED? MAYBE HE'S A CON MAN TRYING TO SWINDLE US!
OF COURSE HE'S RELATED. HE'S YOUR DAD'S BROTHER. HE JUST HASN'T BEEN HERE FOR A FEW YEARS.
WHY NOT? WAS HE IN JAIL?
NO! GOOD HEAVENS, CALVIN.
NOW, NOW... WITH MAX, THAT'S NOT A BAD GUESS.
WATTERSON

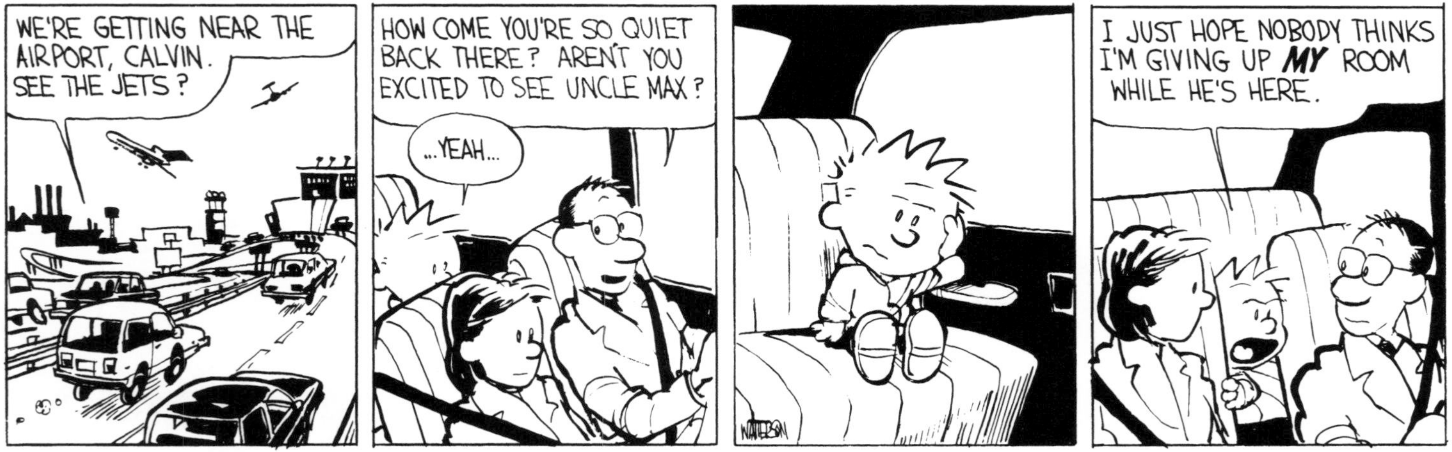
WE'RE GETTING NEAR THE AIRPORT, CALVIN. SEE THE JETS?
HOW COME YOU'RE SO QUIET BACK THERE? AREN'T YOU EXCITED TO SEE UNCLE MAX?
...YEAH...
WATTERSON
I JUST HOPE NOBODY THINKS I'M GIVING UP MY ROOM WHILE HE'S HERE.

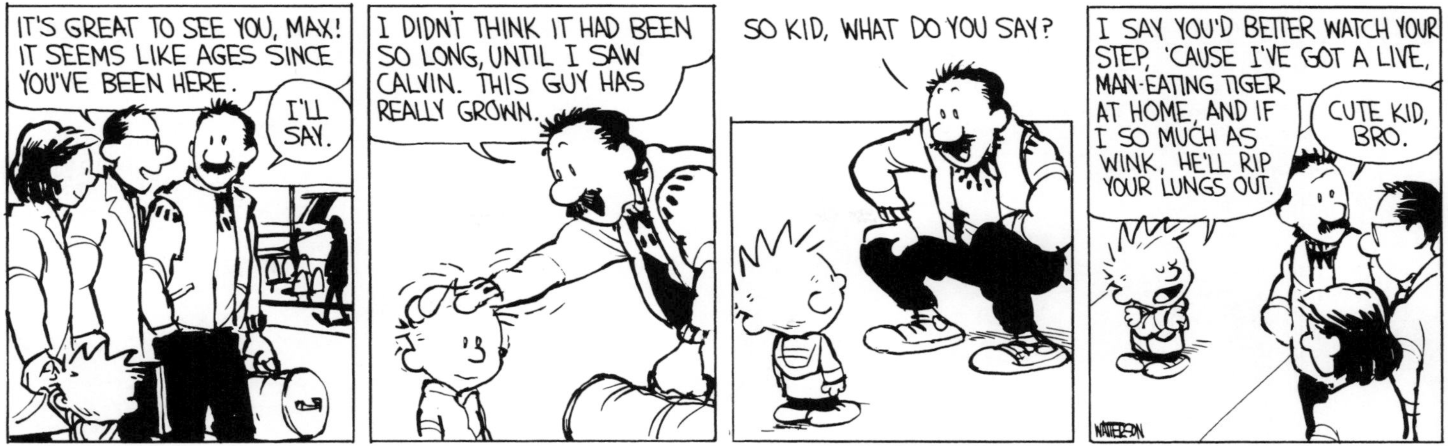
IT'S GREAT TO SEE YOU, MAX! IT SEEMS LIKE AGES SINCE YOU'VE BEEN HERE.
I'LL SAY.
I DIDN'T THINK IT HAD BEEN SO LONG, UNTIL I SAW CALVIN. THIS GUY HAS REALLY GROWN.
SO KID, WHAT DO YOU SAY?
I SAY YOU'D BETTER WATCH YOUR STEP, 'CAUSE I'VE GOT A LIVE, MAN-EATING TIGER AT HOME, AND IF I SO MUCH AS WINK, HE'LL RIP YOUR LUNGS OUT.
CUTE KID, BRO.
WATTERSON

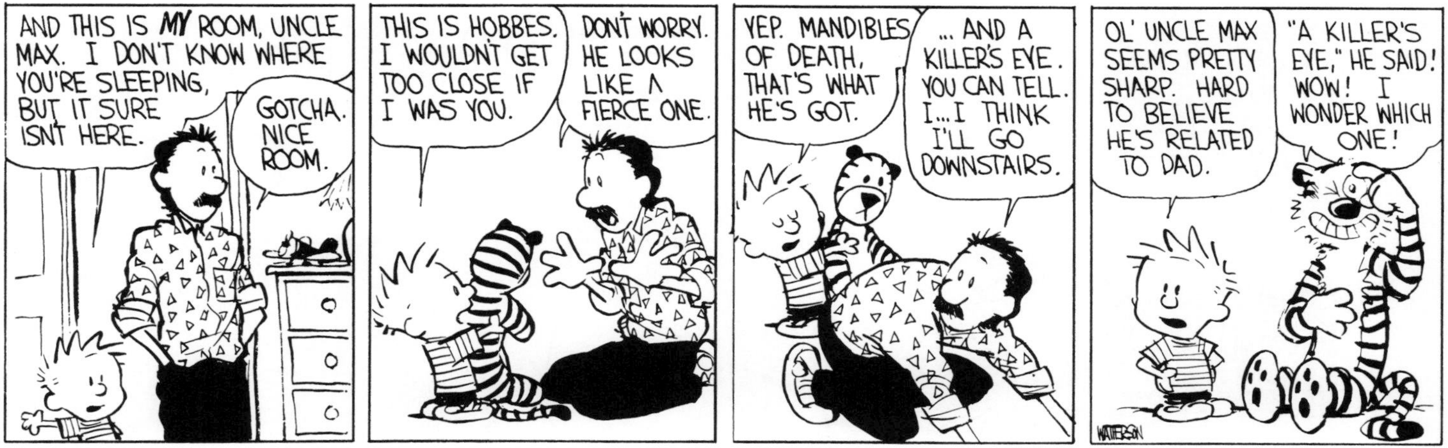
AND THIS IS *MY* ROOM, UNCLE MAX. I DON'T KNOW WHERE YOU'RE SLEEPING, BUT IT SURE ISN'T HERE.
GOTCHA. NICE ROOM.
THIS IS HOBBES. I WOULDN'T GET TOO CLOSE IF I WAS YOU.
DON'T WORRY. HE LOOKS LIKE A FIERCE ONE.
YEP. MANDIBLES OF DEATH, THAT'S WHAT HE'S GOT.
... AND A KILLER'S EYE. YOU CAN TELL. I...I THINK I'LL GO DOWNSTAIRS.
OL' UNCLE MAX SEEMS PRETTY SHARP. HARD TO BELIEVE HE'S RELATED TO DAD.
"A KILLER'S EYE," HE SAID! WOW! I WONDER WHICH ONE!
WATTERSON

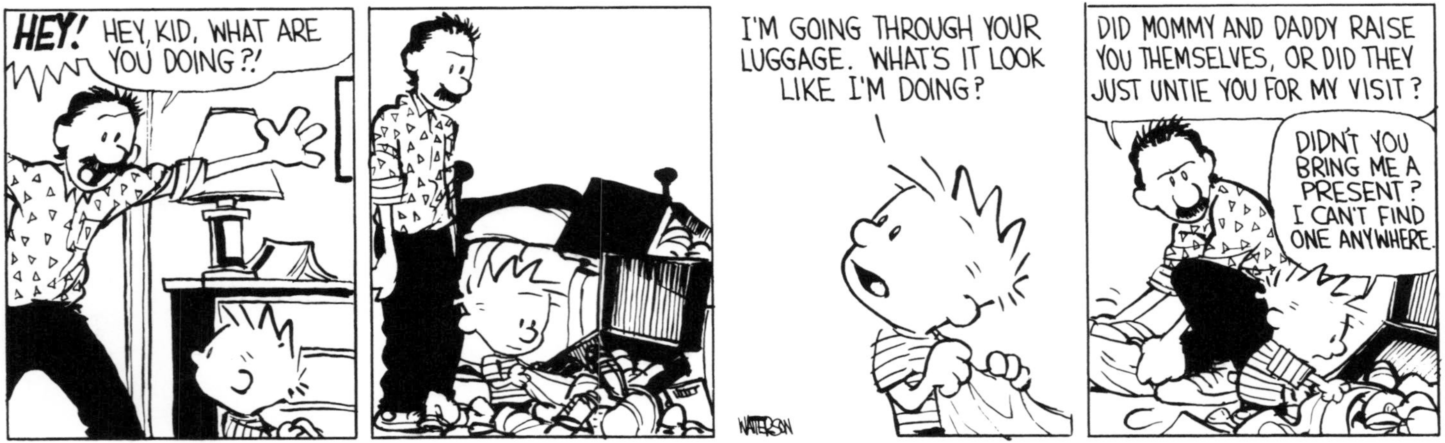
HEY!
HEY, KID, WHAT ARE YOU DOING?!
I'M GOING THROUGH YOUR LUGGAGE. WHAT'S IT LOOK LIKE I'M DOING?
DID MOMMY AND DADDY RAISE YOU THEMSELVES, OR DID THEY JUST UNTIE YOU FOR MY VISIT?
DIDN'T YOU BRING ME A PRESENT? I CAN'T FIND ONE ANYWHERE.

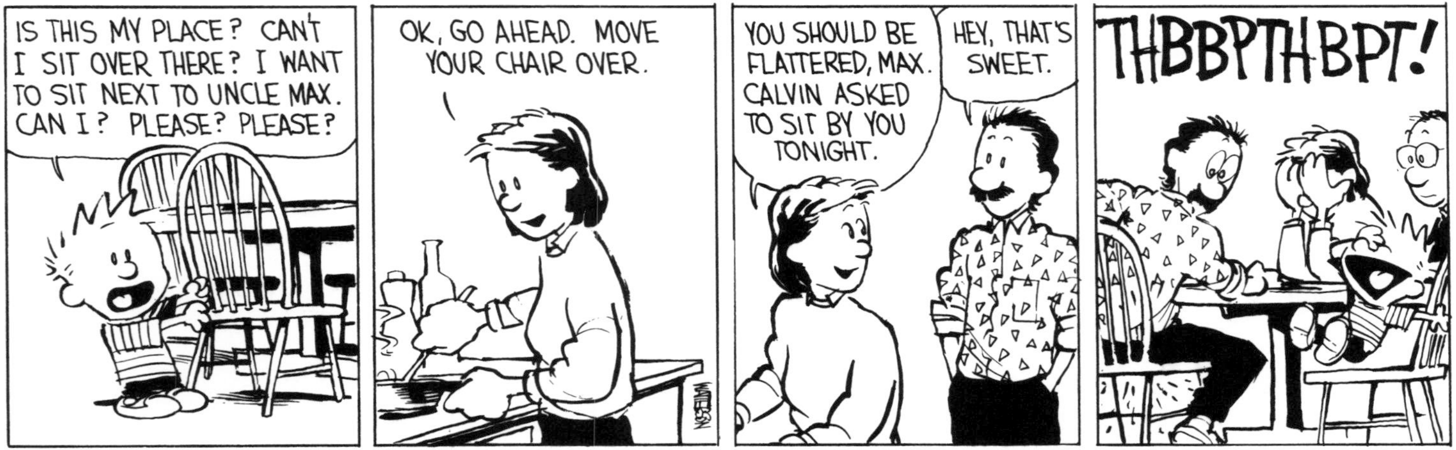
IS THIS MY PLACE? CAN'T I SIT OVER THERE? I WANT TO SIT NEXT TO UNCLE MAX. CAN I? PLEASE? PLEASE?
OK, GO AHEAD. MOVE YOUR CHAIR OVER.
YOU SHOULD BE FLATTERED, MAX. CALVIN ASKED TO SIT BY YOU TONIGHT.
HEY, THAT'S SWEET.
THBBPTHBPT!

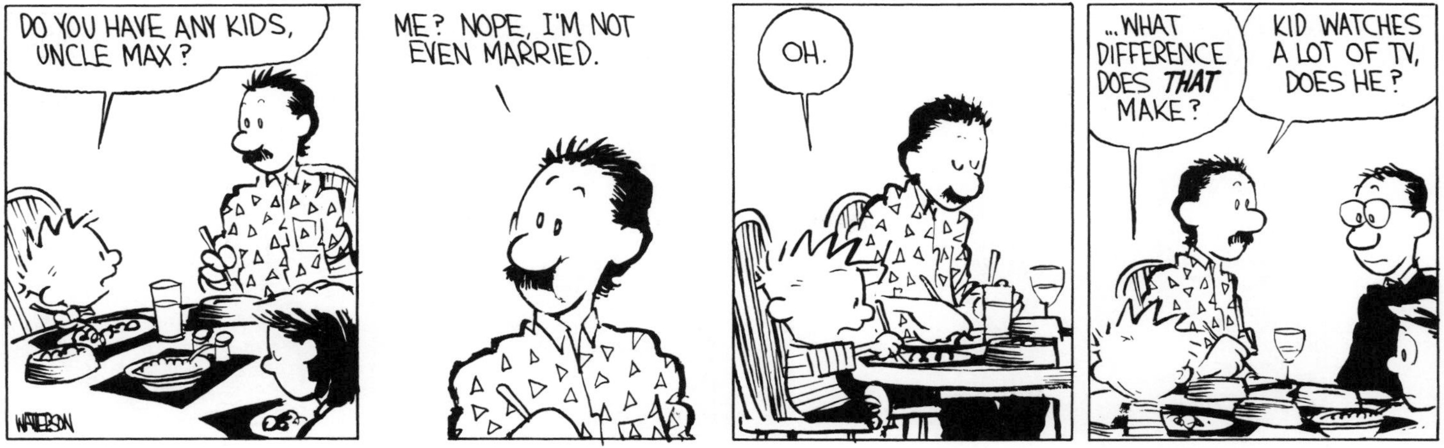
DO YOU HAVE ANY KIDS, UNCLE MAX?
ME? NOPE, I'M NOT EVEN MARRIED.
OH.
...WHAT DIFFERENCE DOES **THAT** MAKE?
KID WATCHES A LOT OF TV, DOES HE?
WATTERSON

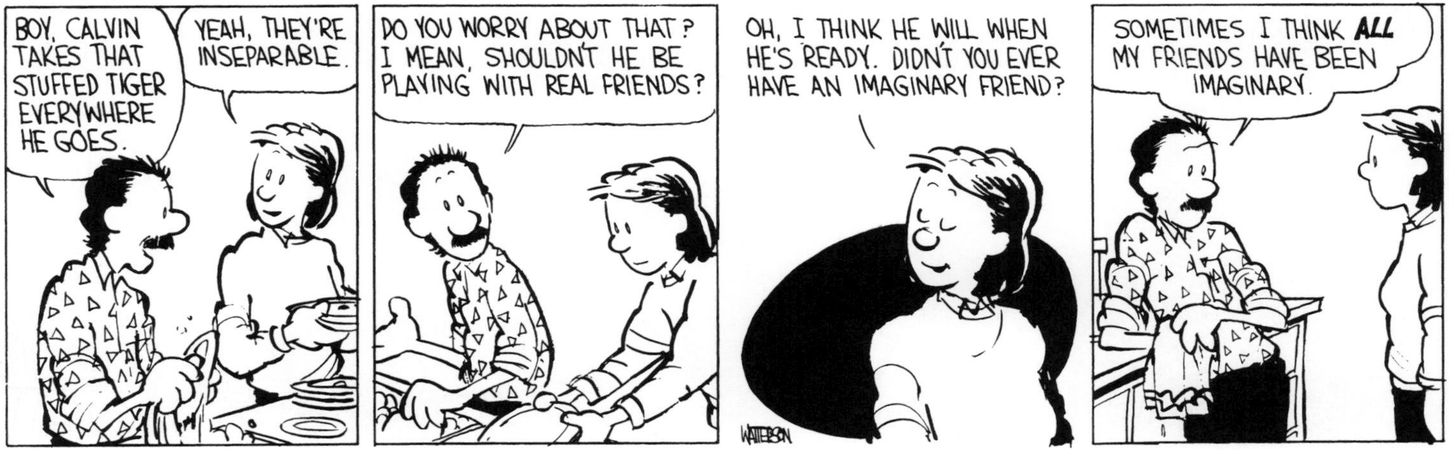
BOY, CALVIN TAKES THAT STUFFED TIGER EVERYWHERE HE GOES.
YEAH, THEY'RE INSEPARABLE.
DO YOU WORRY ABOUT THAT? I MEAN, SHOULDN'T HE BE PLAYING WITH REAL FRIENDS?
OH, I THINK HE WILL WHEN HE'S READY. DIDN'T YOU EVER HAVE AN IMAGINARY FRIEND?
WATTERSON
SOMETIMES I THINK **ALL** MY FRIENDS HAVE BEEN IMAGINARY.

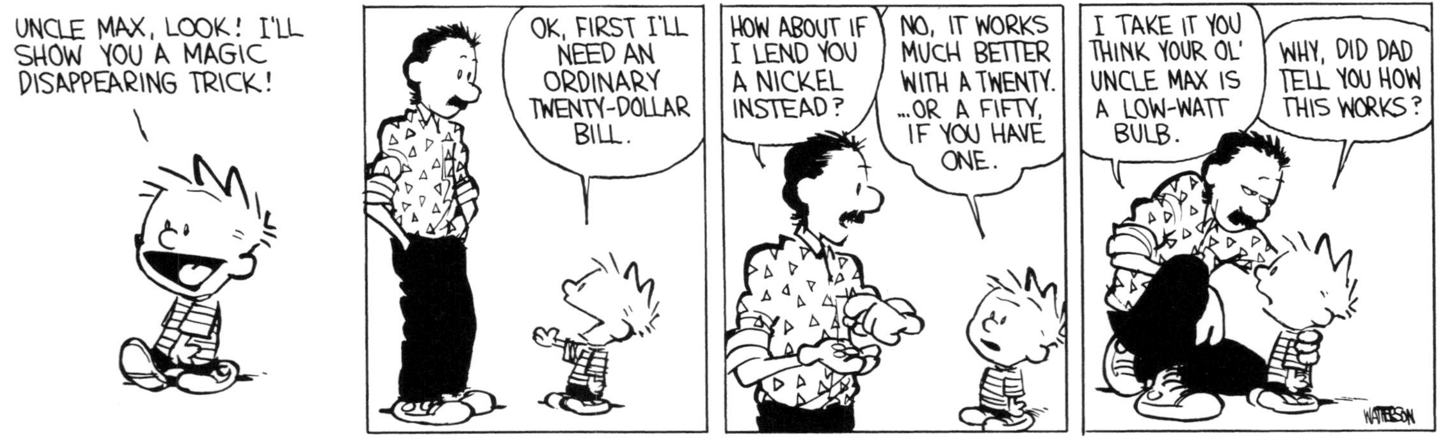
UNCLE MAX, LOOK! I'LL SHOW YOU A MAGIC DISAPPEARING TRICK!
OK, FIRST I'LL NEED AN ORDINARY TWENTY-DOLLAR BILL.
HOW ABOUT IF I LEND YOU A NICKEL INSTEAD?
NO, IT WORKS MUCH BETTER WITH A TWENTY. ...OR A FIFTY, IF YOU HAVE ONE.
I TAKE IT YOU THINK YOUR OL' UNCLE MAX IS A LOW-WATT BULB.
WHY, DID DAD TELL YOU HOW THIS WORKS?
WATTERSON

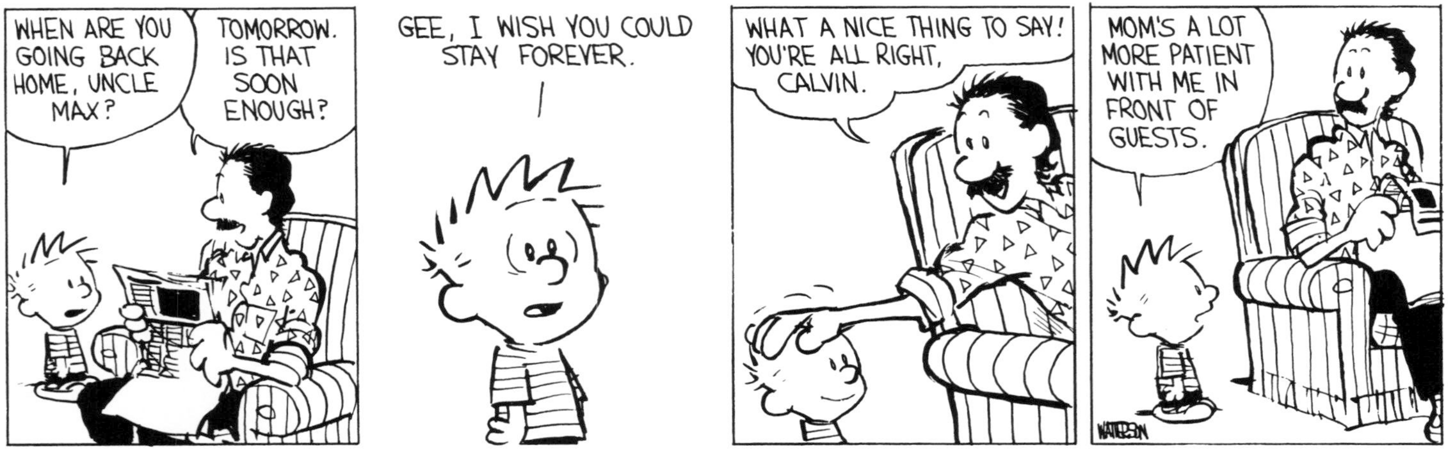
WHEN ARE YOU GOING BACK HOME, UNCLE MAX?
TOMORROW. IS THAT SOON ENOUGH?
GEE, I WISH YOU COULD STAY FOREVER.
WHAT A NICE THING TO SAY! YOU'RE ALL RIGHT, CALVIN.
MOM'S A LOT MORE PATIENT WITH ME IN FRONT OF GUESTS.
WATTERSON

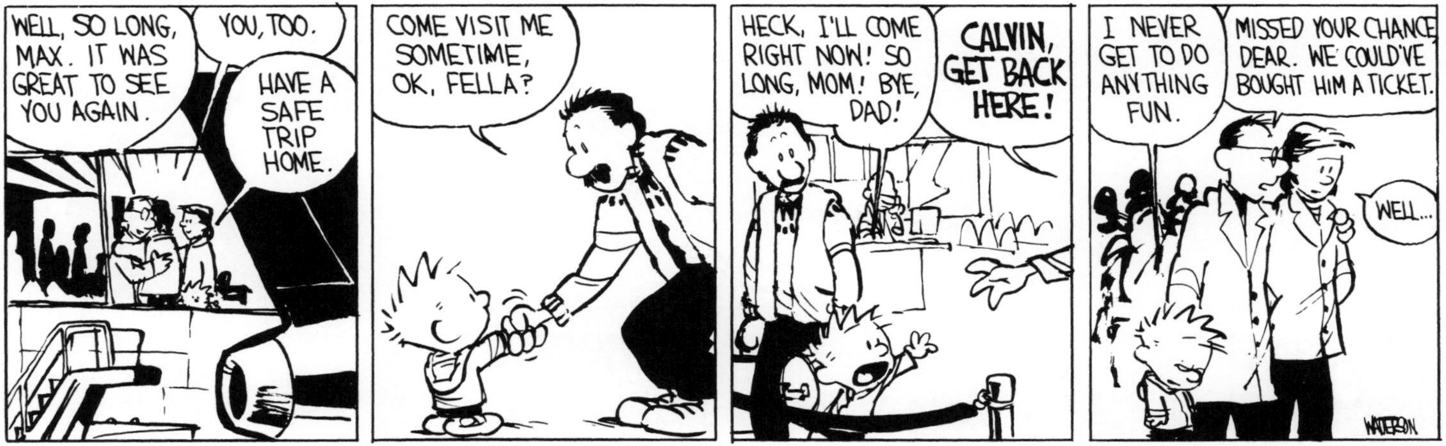
WELL, SO LONG, MAX. IT WAS GREAT TO SEE YOU AGAIN.
YOU, TOO.
HAVE A SAFE TRIP HOME.
COME VISIT ME SOMETIME, OK, FELLA?
HECK, I'LL COME RIGHT NOW! SO LONG, MOM! BYE, DAD!
CALVIN, GET BACK HERE!
I NEVER GET TO DO ANYTHING FUN.
MISSED YOUR CHANCE, DEAR. WE COULD'VE BOUGHT HIM A TICKET.
WELL...
WATTERSON

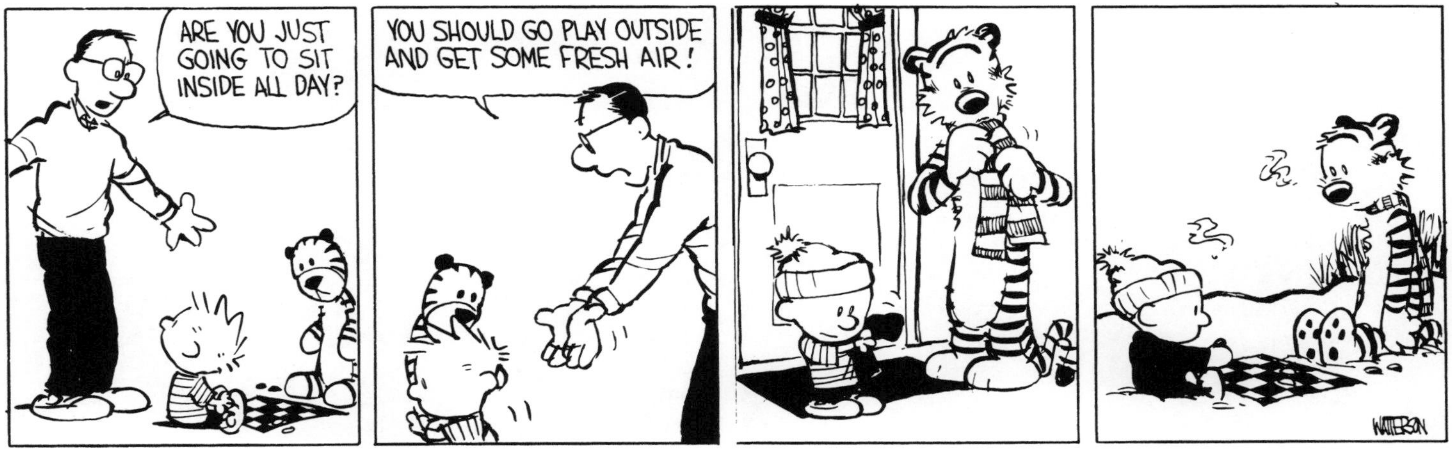
ARE YOU JUST GOING TO SIT INSIDE ALL DAY?
YOU SHOULD GO PLAY OUTSIDE AND GET SOME FRESH AIR!
WATTERSON

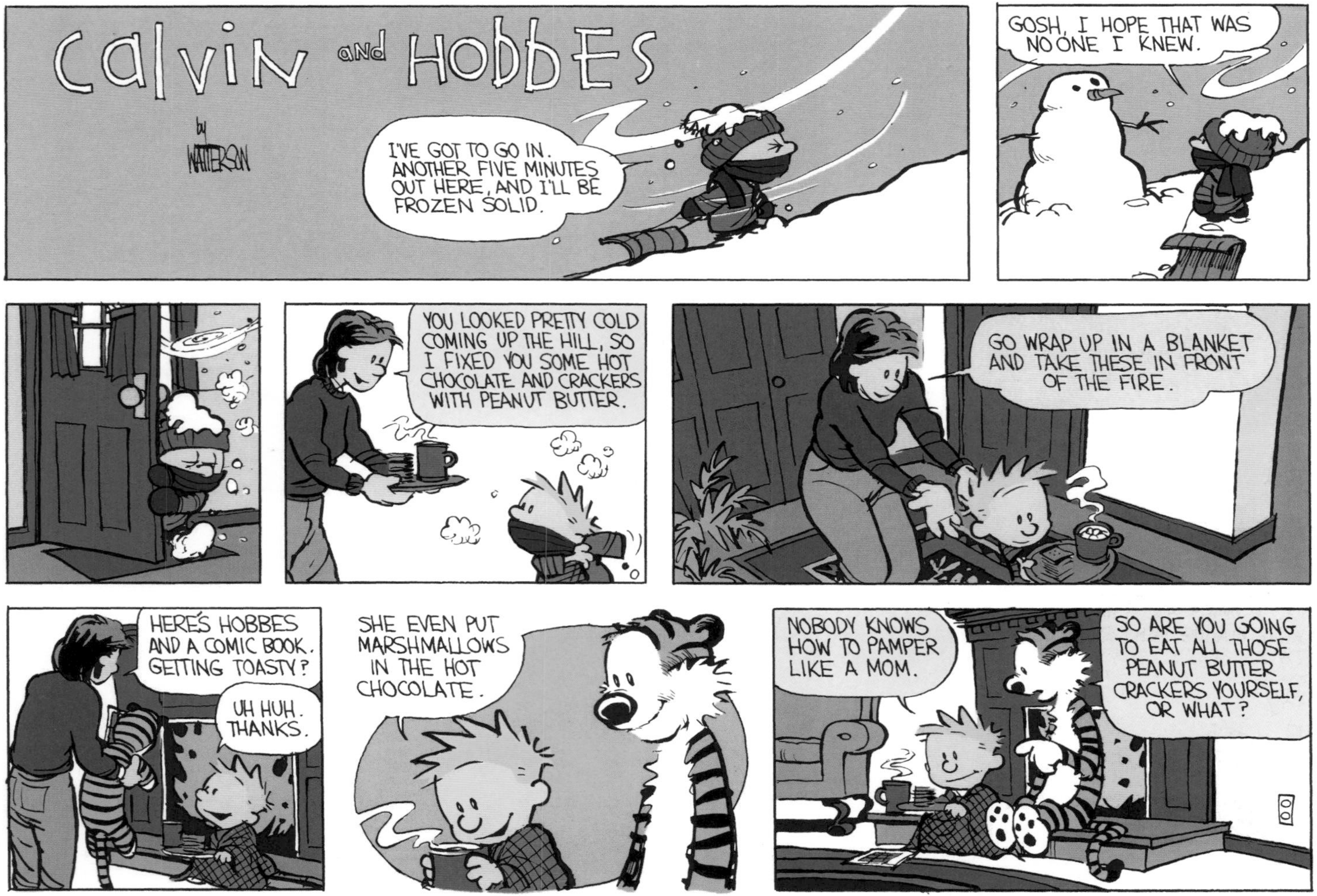
Calvin and HOBBES
by WATTERSON
I'VE GOT TO GO IN. ANOTHER FIVE MINUTES OUT HERE, AND I'LL BE FROZEN SOLID.
GOSH, I HOPE THAT WAS NO ONE I KNEW.
YOU LOOKED PRETTY COLD COMING UP THE HILL, SO I FIXED YOU SOME HOT CHOCOLATE AND CRACKERS WITH PEANUT BUTTER.
GO WRAP UP IN A BLANKET AND TAKE THESE IN FRONT OF THE FIRE.
HERE'S HOBBES AND A COMIC BOOK. GETTING TOASTY?
UH HUH. THANKS.
SHE EVEN PUT MARSHMALLOWS IN THE HOT CHOCOLATE.
NOBODY KNOWS HOW TO PAMPER LIKE A MOM.
SO ARE YOU GOING TO EAT ALL THOSE PEANUT BUTTER CRACKERS YOURSELF, OR WHAT?

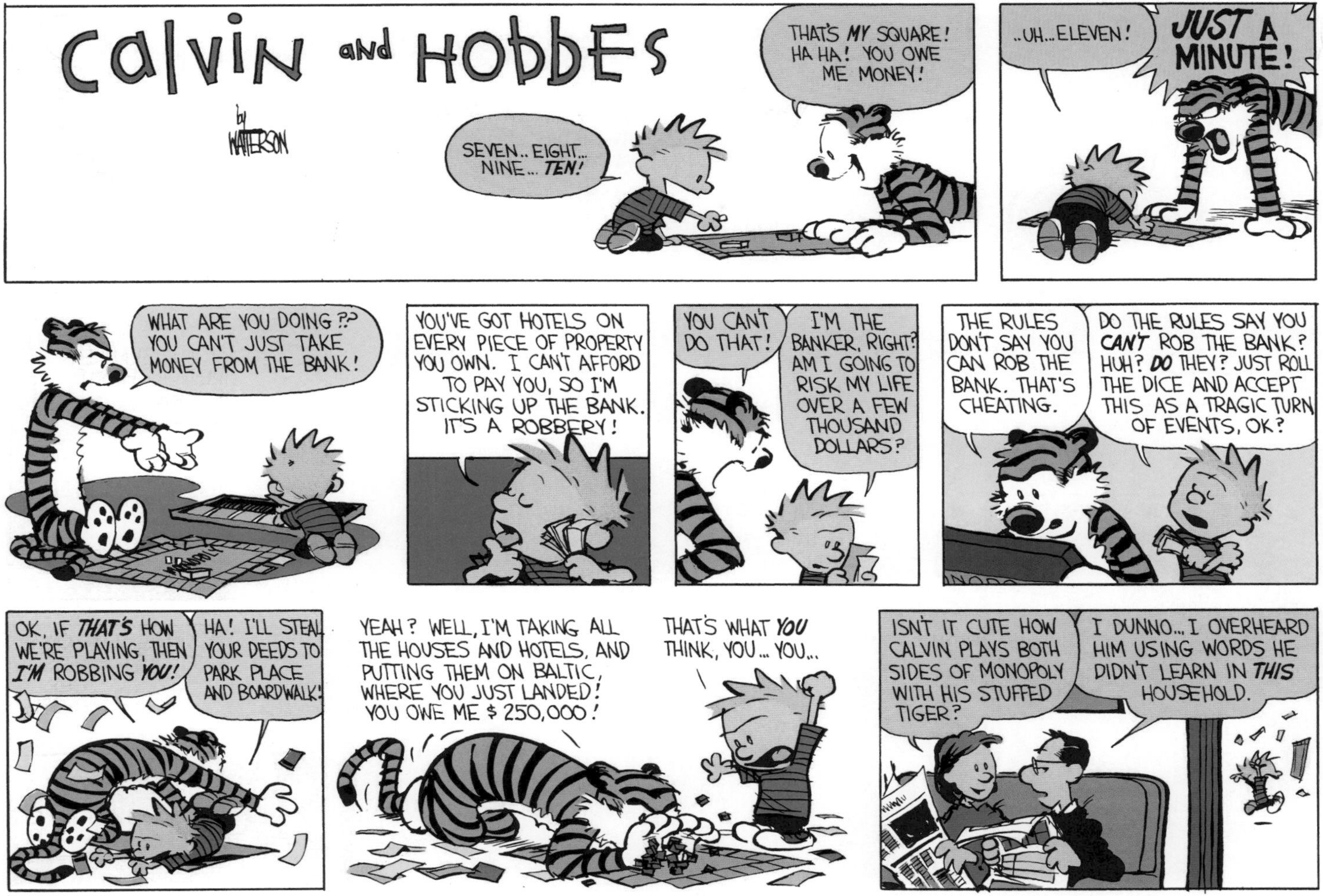
Calvin and HOBBES
by WATTERSON
SEVEN.. EIGHT... NINE... TEN!
THAT'S MY SQUARE! HA HA! YOU OWE ME MONEY!
..UH... ELEVEN!
JUST A MINUTE!
WHAT ARE YOU DOING ?!? YOU CAN'T JUST TAKE MONEY FROM THE BANK!
YOU'VE GOT HOTELS ON EVERY PIECE OF PROPERTY YOU OWN. I CAN'T AFFORD TO PAY YOU, SO I'M STICKING UP THE BANK. IT'S A ROBBERY!
YOU CAN'T DO THAT!
I'M THE BANKER, RIGHT? AM I GOING TO RISK MY LIFE OVER A FEW THOUSAND DOLLARS?
THE RULES DON'T SAY YOU CAN ROB THE BANK. THAT'S CHEATING.
DO THE RULES SAY YOU CAN'T ROB THE BANK? HUH? DO THEY? JUST ROLL THE DICE AND ACCEPT THIS AS A TRAGIC TURN OF EVENTS, OK?
OK, IF THAT'S HOW WE'RE PLAYING, THEN I'M ROBBING YOU!
HA! I'LL STEAL YOUR DEEDS TO PARK PLACE AND BOARDWALK!
YEAH? WELL, I'M TAKING ALL THE HOUSES AND HOTELS, AND PUTTING THEM ON BALTIC, WHERE YOU JUST LANDED! YOU OWE ME $ 250,000!
THAT'S WHAT YOU THINK, YOU... YOU...
ISN'T IT CUTE HOW CALVIN PLAYS BOTH SIDES OF MONOPOLY WITH HIS STUFFED TIGER?
I DUNNO... I OVERHEARD HIM USING WORDS HE DIDN'T LEARN IN THIS HOUSEHOLD.

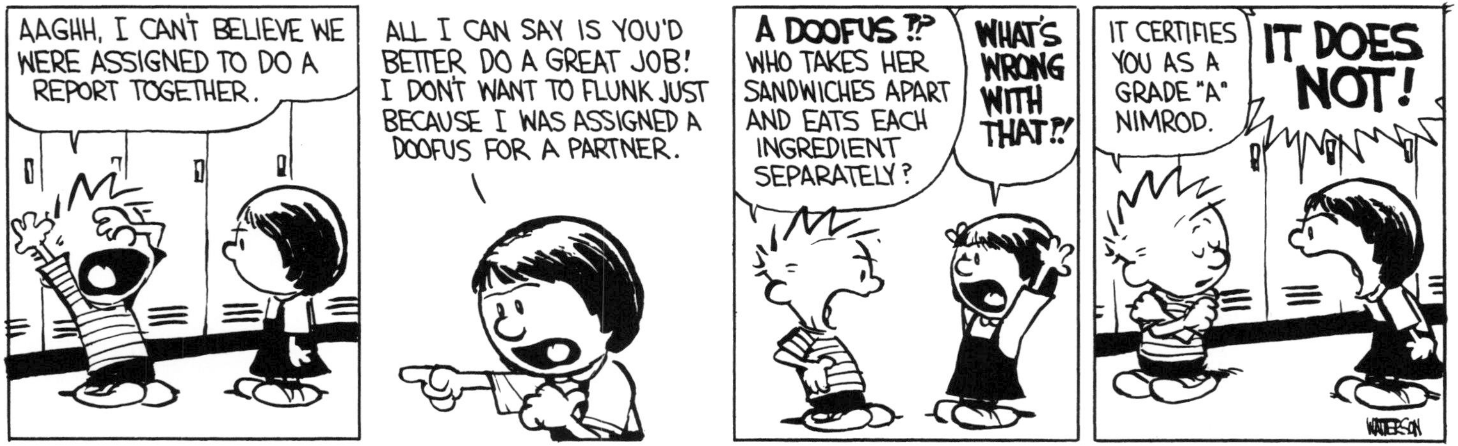
AAGHH, I CAN'T BELIEVE WE WERE ASSIGNED TO DO A REPORT TOGETHER.
ALL I CAN SAY IS YOU'D BETTER DO A GREAT JOB! I DON'T WANT TO FLUNK JUST BECAUSE I WAS ASSIGNED A DOOFUS FOR A PARTNER.
A DOOFUS ?!? WHO TAKES HER SANDWICHES APART AND EATS EACH INGREDIENT SEPARATELY?
WHAT'S WRONG WITH THAT?!
IT CERTIFIES YOU AS A GRADE "A" NIMROD.
IT DOES NOT!

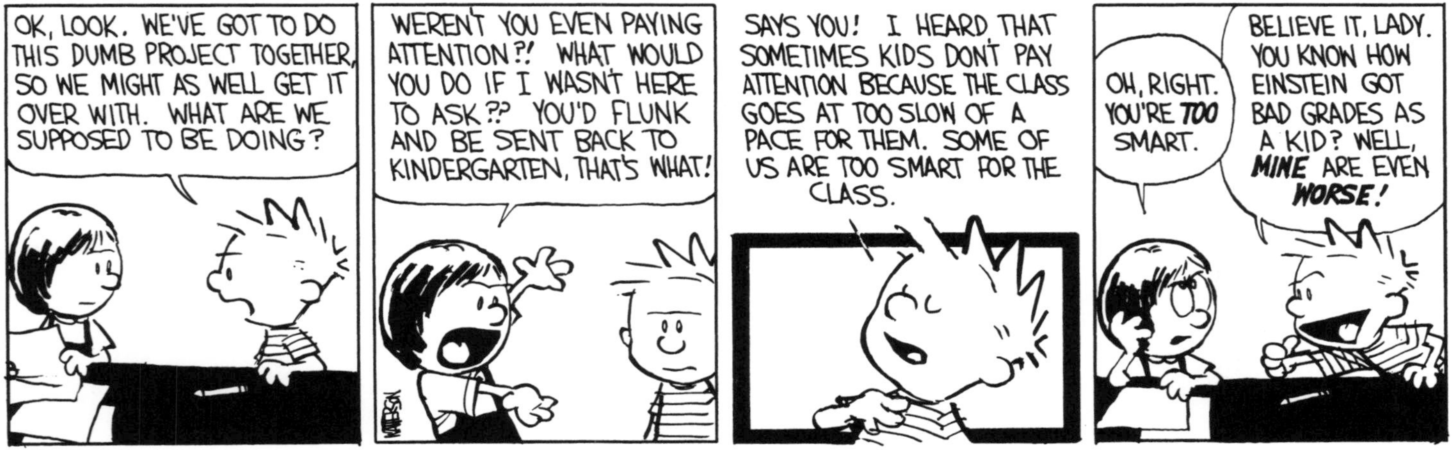
OK, LOOK. WE'VE GOT TO DO THIS DUMB PROJECT TOGETHER, SO WE MIGHT AS WELL GET IT OVER WITH. WHAT ARE WE SUPPOSED TO BE DOING?
WEREN'T YOU EVEN PAYING ATTENTION?! WHAT WOULD YOU DO IF I WASN'T HERE TO ASK?!? YOU'D FLUNK AND BE SENT BACK TO KINDERGARTEN, THAT'S WHAT!
SAYS YOU! I HEARD THAT SOMETIMES KIDS DON'T PAY ATTENTION BECAUSE THE CLASS GOES AT TOO SLOW OF A PACE FOR THEM. SOME OF US ARE TOO SMART FOR THE CLASS.
OH, RIGHT. YOU'RE *TOO* SMART.
BELIEVE IT, LADY. YOU KNOW HOW EINSTEIN GOT BAD GRADES AS A KID? WELL, ***MINE*** ARE EVEN ***WORSE***!

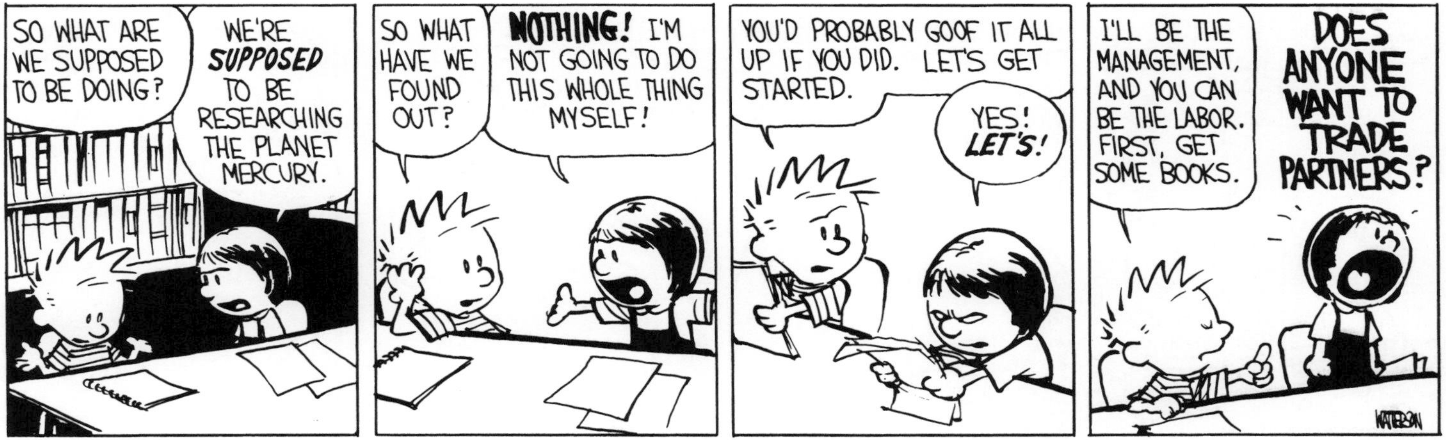
SO WHAT ARE WE SUPPOSED TO BE DOING?
WE'RE **SUPPOSED** TO BE RESEARCHING THE PLANET MERCURY.
SO WHAT HAVE WE FOUND OUT?
NOTHING! I'M NOT GOING TO DO THIS WHOLE THING MYSELF!
YOU'D PROBABLY GOOF IT ALL UP IF YOU DID. LET'S GET STARTED.
YES! ***LET'S!***
I'LL BE THE MANAGEMENT, AND YOU CAN BE THE LABOR. FIRST, GET SOME BOOKS.
DOES ANYONE WANT TO TRADE PARTNERS?
WATTERSON

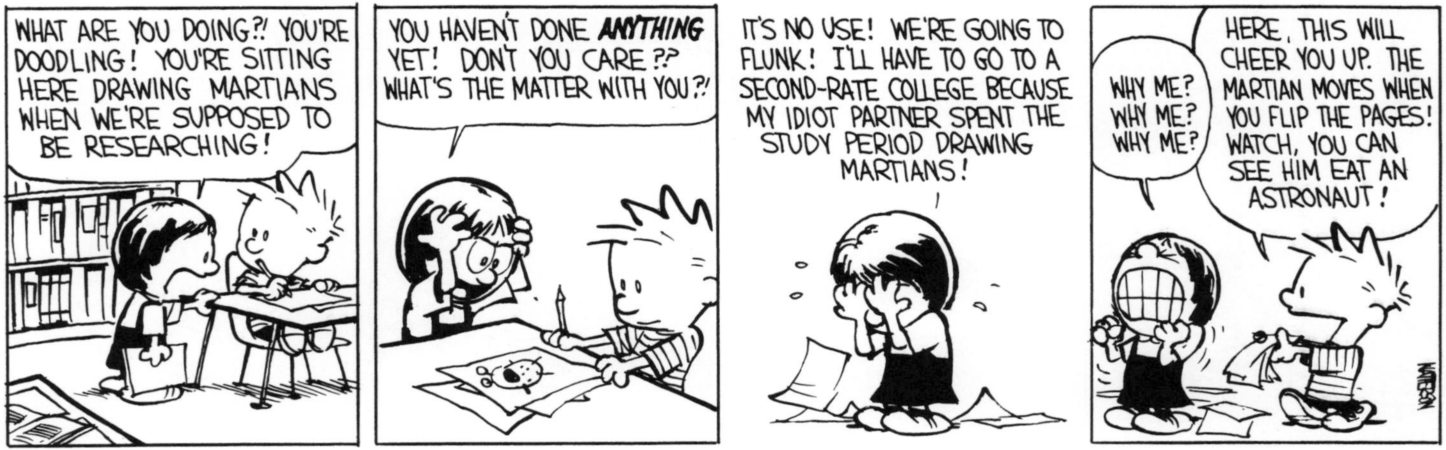
WHAT ARE YOU DOING?! YOU'RE DOODLING! YOU'RE SITTING HERE DRAWING MARTIANS WHEN WE'RE SUPPOSED TO BE RESEARCHING!
YOU HAVEN'T DONE **ANYTHING** YET! DON'T YOU CARE?? WHAT'S THE MATTER WITH YOU?!
IT'S NO USE! WE'RE GOING TO FLUNK! I'LL HAVE TO GO TO A SECOND-RATE COLLEGE BECAUSE MY IDIOT PARTNER SPENT THE STUDY PERIOD DRAWING MARTIANS!
WHY ME? WHY ME? WHY ME?
HERE, THIS WILL CHEER YOU UP. THE MARTIAN MOVES WHEN YOU FLIP THE PAGES! WATCH, YOU CAN SEE HIM EAT AN ASTRONAUT!
WATTERSON

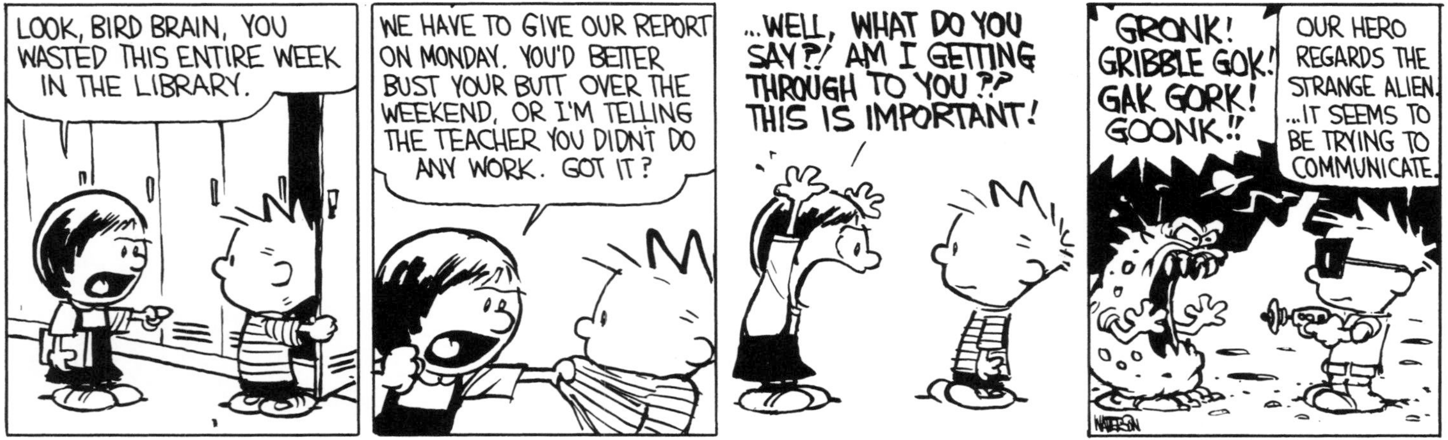
LOOK, BIRD BRAIN, YOU WASTED THIS ENTIRE WEEK IN THE LIBRARY.
WE HAVE TO GIVE OUR REPORT ON MONDAY. YOU'D BETTER BUST YOUR BUTT OVER THE WEEKEND, OR I'M TELLING THE TEACHER YOU DIDN'T DO ANY WORK. GOT IT?
...WELL, WHAT DO YOU SAY?! AM I GETTING THROUGH TO YOU?? THIS IS IMPORTANT!
GRONK! GRIBBLE GOK! GAK GORK! GOONK!!
OUR HERO REGARDS THE STRANGE ALIEN. ...IT SEEMS TO BE TRYING TO COMMUNICATE.
WATTERSON

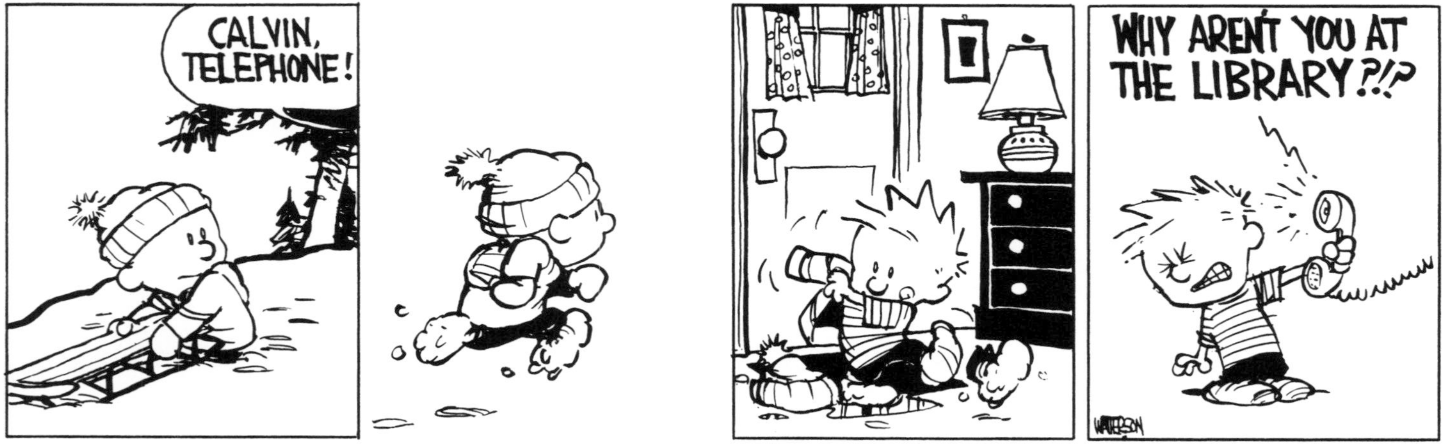
CALVIN, TELEPHONE!
WHY AREN'T YOU AT THE LIBRARY?!?
WATTERSON

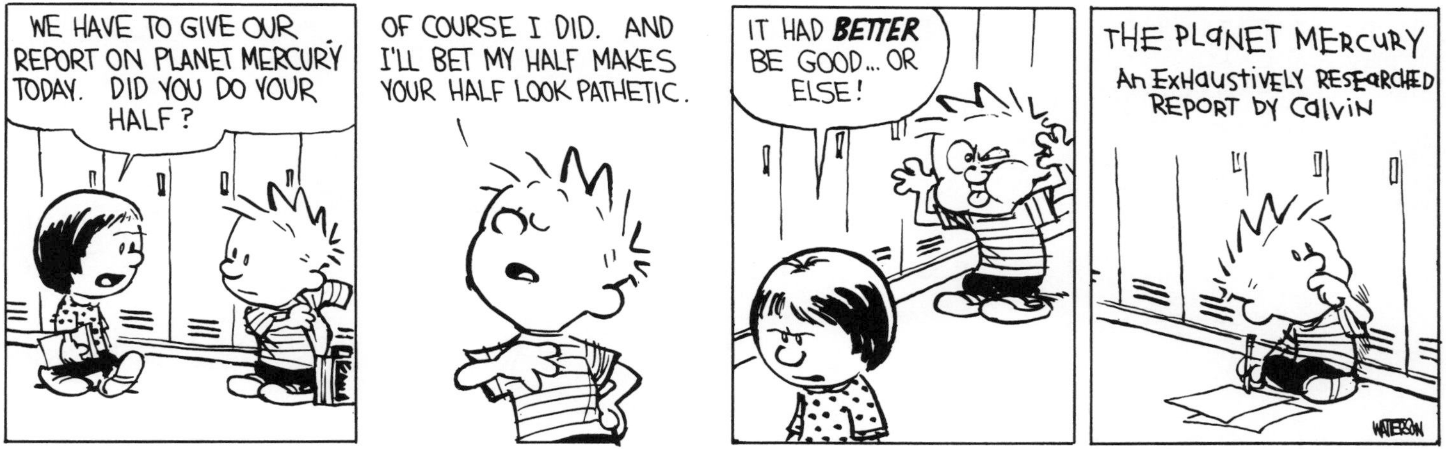
WE HAVE TO GIVE OUR REPORT ON PLANET MERCURY TODAY. DID YOU DO YOUR HALF?
OF COURSE I DID. AND I'LL BET MY HALF MAKES YOUR HALF LOOK PATHETIC.
IT HAD BETTER BE GOOD... OR ELSE!
THE PLANET MERCURY
An Exhaustively Researched Report by Calvin

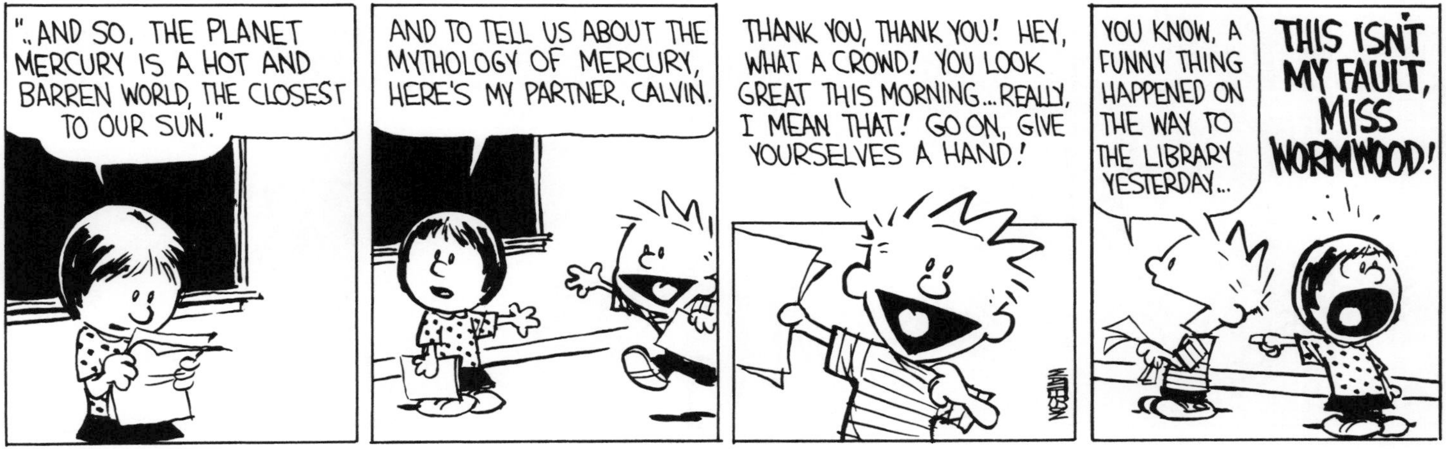
"..AND SO, THE PLANET MERCURY IS A HOT AND BARREN WORLD, THE CLOSEST TO OUR SUN."
AND TO TELL US ABOUT THE MYTHOLOGY OF MERCURY, HERE'S MY PARTNER, CALVIN.
THANK YOU, THANK YOU! HEY, WHAT A CROWD! YOU LOOK GREAT THIS MORNING...REALLY, I MEAN THAT! GO ON, GIVE YOURSELVES A HAND!
YOU KNOW, A FUNNY THING HAPPENED ON THE WAY TO THE LIBRARY YESTERDAY...
THIS ISN'T MY FAULT, MISS WORMWOOD!

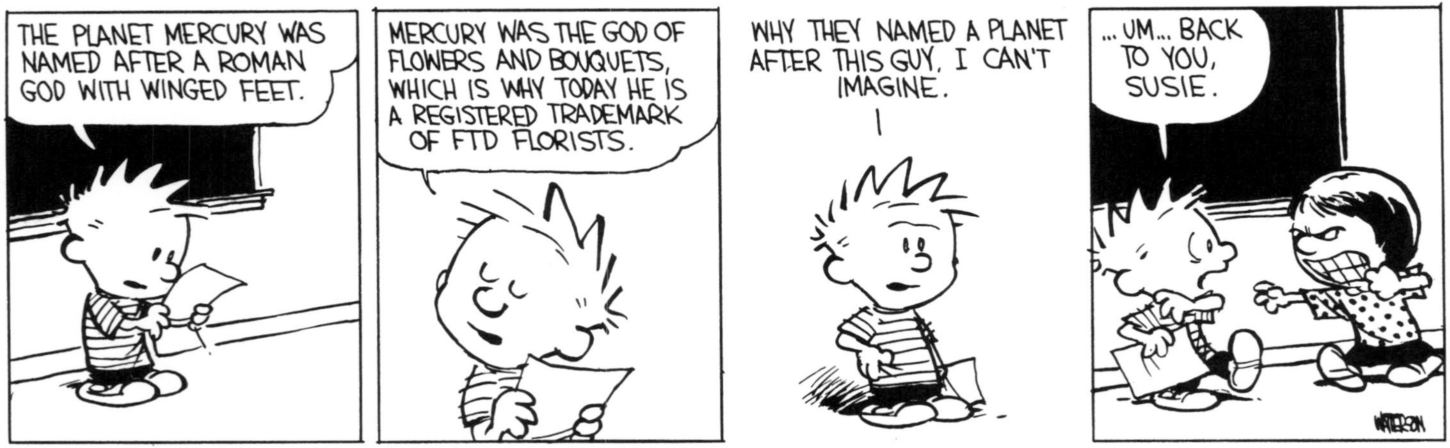
THE PLANET MERCURY WAS NAMED AFTER A ROMAN GOD WITH WINGED FEET.
MERCURY WAS THE GOD OF FLOWERS AND BOUQUETS, WHICH IS WHY TODAY HE IS A REGISTERED TRADEMARK OF FTD FLORISTS.
WHY THEY NAMED A PLANET AFTER THIS GUY, I CAN'T IMAGINE.
...UM... BACK TO YOU, SUSIE.

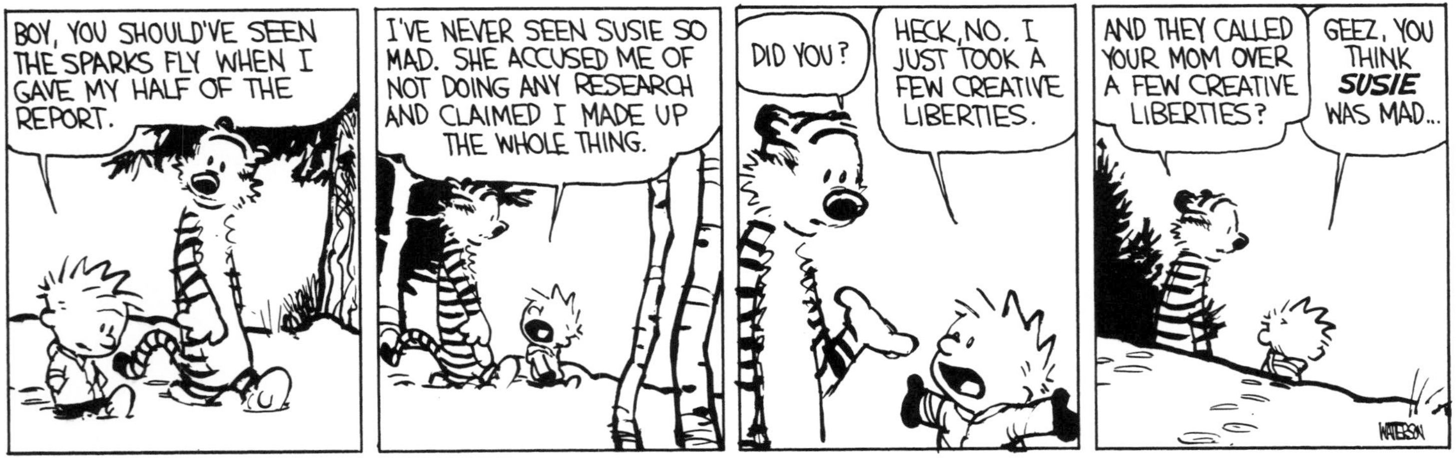
BOY, YOU SHOULD'VE SEEN THE SPARKS FLY WHEN I GAVE MY HALF OF THE REPORT.
I'VE NEVER SEEN SUSIE SO MAD. SHE ACCUSED ME OF NOT DOING ANY RESEARCH AND CLAIMED I MADE UP THE WHOLE THING.
DID YOU?
HECK, NO. I JUST TOOK A FEW CREATIVE LIBERTIES.
AND THEY CALLED YOUR MOM OVER A FEW CREATIVE LIBERTIES?
GEEZ, YOU THINK ***SUSIE*** WAS MAD...

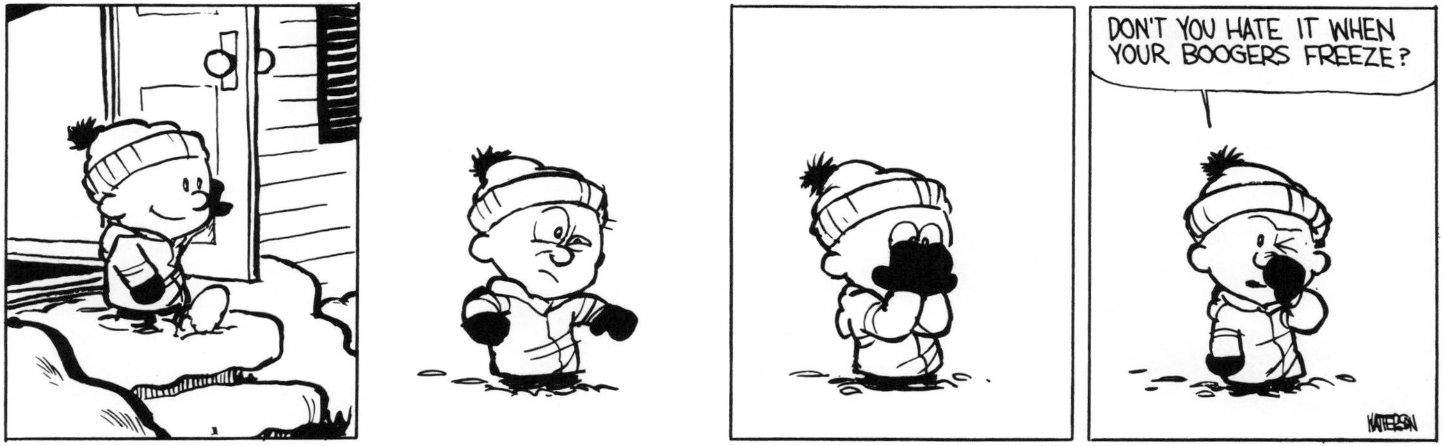
DON'T YOU HATE IT WHEN YOUR BOOGERS FREEZE?

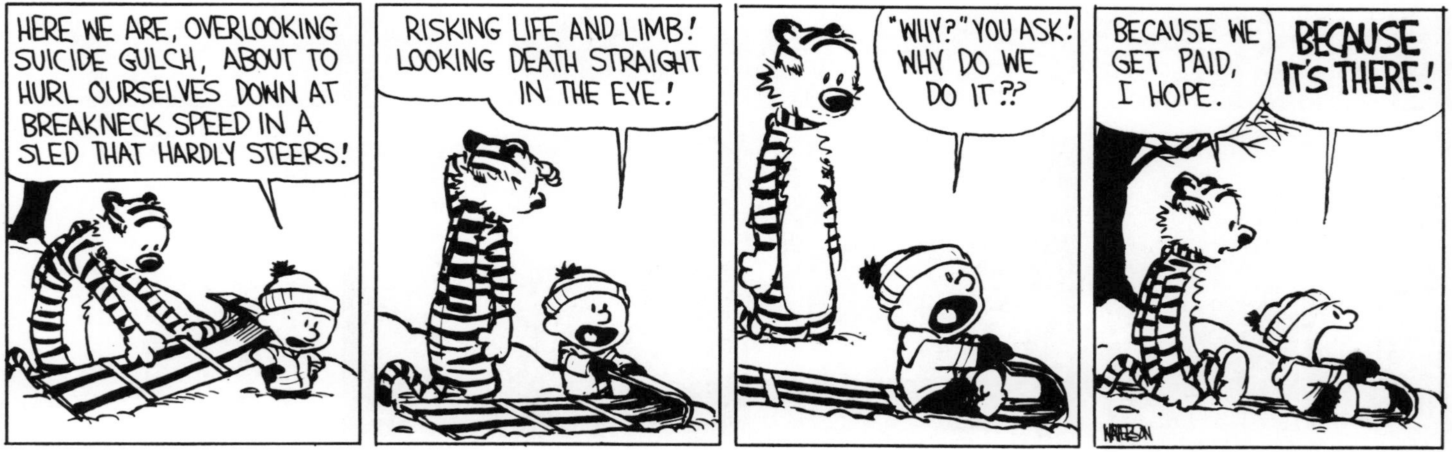
HERE WE ARE, OVERLOOKING SUICIDE GULCH, ABOUT TO HURL OURSELVES DOWN AT BREAKNECK SPEED IN A SLED THAT HARDLY STEERS!
RISKING LIFE AND LIMB! LOOKING DEATH STRAIGHT IN THE EYE!
"WHY?" YOU ASK! WHY DO WE DO IT??
BECAUSE WE GET PAID, I HOPE.
BECAUSE IT'S THERE!

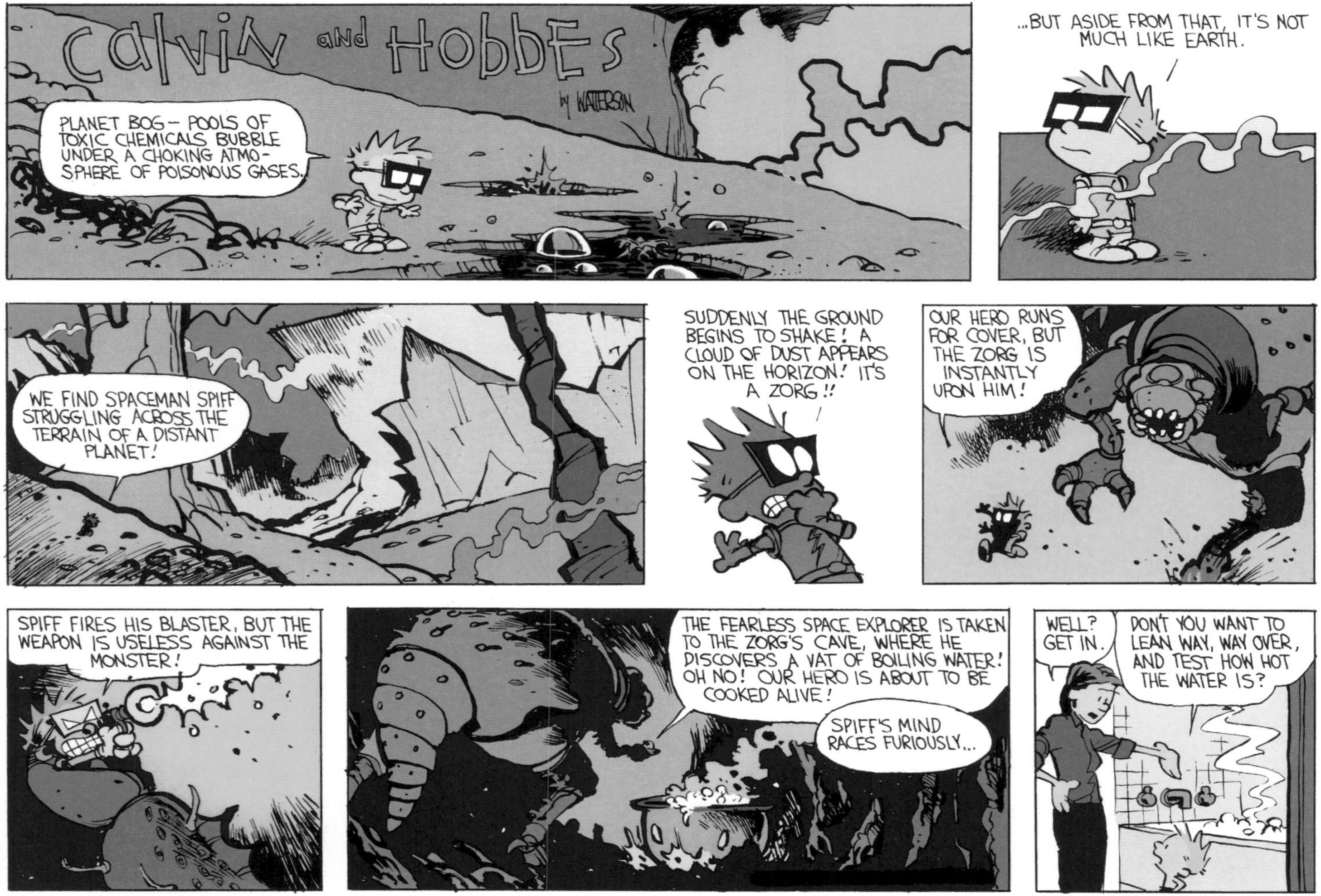
Calvin and Hobbes
by WATTERSON
PLANET BOG — POOLS OF TOXIC CHEMICALS BUBBLE UNDER A CHOKING ATMO-SPHERE OF POISONOUS GASES.
...BUT ASIDE FROM THAT, IT'S NOT MUCH LIKE EARTH.
WE FIND SPACEMAN SPIFF STRUGGLING ACROSS THE TERRAIN OF A DISTANT PLANET!
SUDDENLY THE GROUND BEGINS TO SHAKE! A CLOUD OF DUST APPEARS ON THE HORIZON! IT'S A ZORG!!
OUR HERO RUNS FOR COVER, BUT THE ZORG IS INSTANTLY UPON HIM!
SPIFF FIRES HIS BLASTER, BUT THE WEAPON IS USELESS AGAINST THE MONSTER!
THE FEARLESS SPACE EXPLORER IS TAKEN TO THE ZORG'S CAVE, WHERE HE DISCOVERS A VAT OF BOILING WATER! OH NO! OUR HERO IS ABOUT TO BE COOKED ALIVE!
SPIFF'S MIND RACES FURIOUSLY...
WELL? GET IN.
DON'T YOU WANT TO LEAN WAY, WAY OVER, AND TEST HOW HOT THE WATER IS?

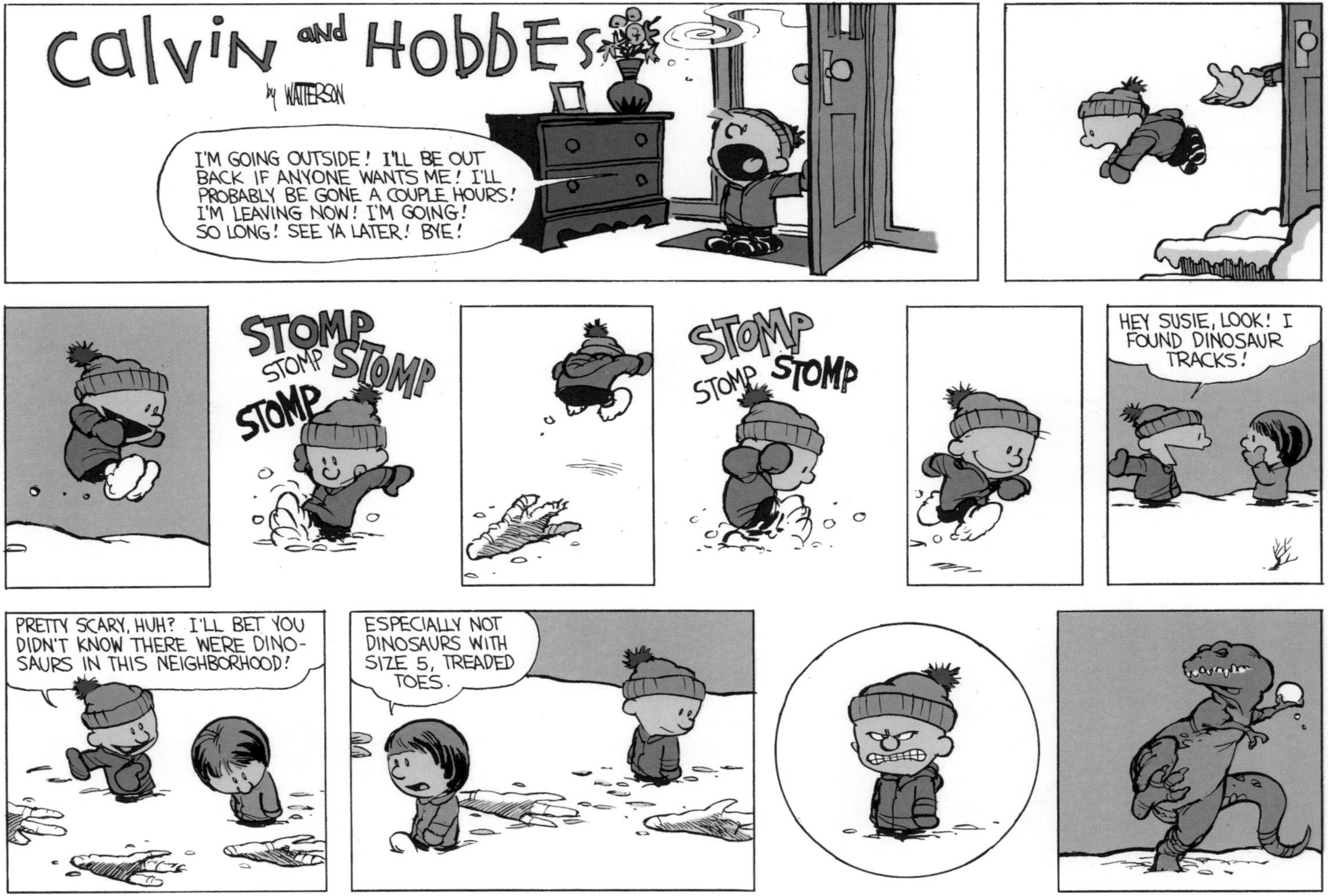
Calvin and Hobbes
by WATTERSON
I'M GOING OUTSIDE! I'LL BE OUT BACK IF ANYONE WANTS ME! I'LL PROBABLY BE GONE A COUPLE HOURS! I'M LEAVING NOW! I'M GOING! SO LONG! SEE YA LATER! BYE!
STOMP STOMP STOMP STOMP
STOMP STOMP STOMP
HEY SUSIE, LOOK! I FOUND DINOSAUR TRACKS!
PRETTY SCARY, HUH? I'LL BET YOU DIDN'T KNOW THERE WERE DINO-SAURS IN THIS NEIGHBORHOOD!
ESPECIALLY NOT DINOSAURS WITH SIZE 5, TREADED TOES.

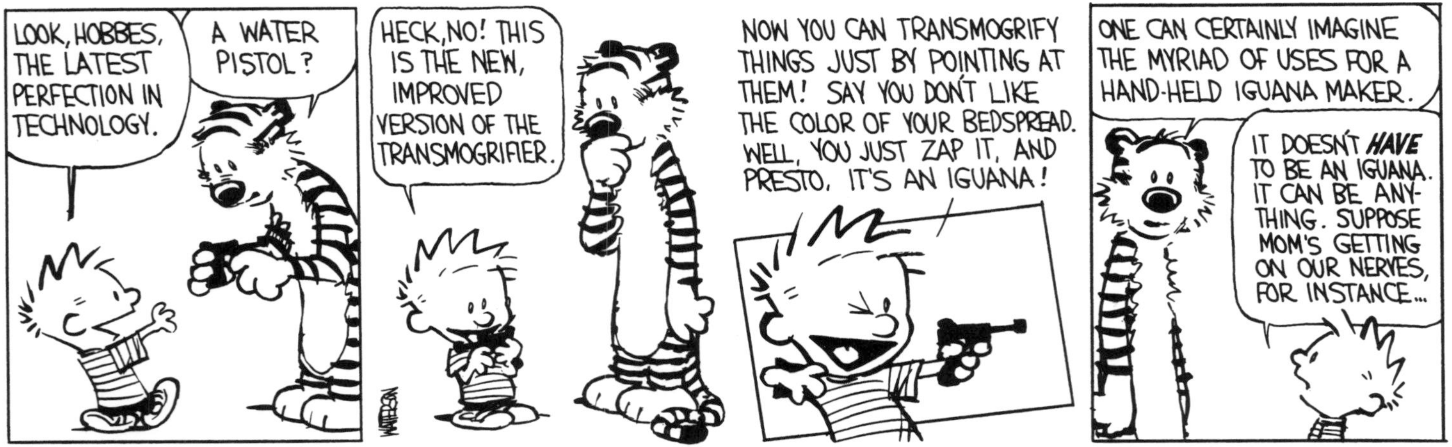
LOOK, HOBBES, THE LATEST PERFECTION IN TECHNOLOGY.
A WATER PISTOL?
HECK, NO! THIS IS THE NEW, IMPROVED VERSION OF THE TRANSMOGRIFIER.
NOW YOU CAN TRANSMOGRIFY THINGS JUST BY POINTING AT THEM! SAY YOU DON'T LIKE THE COLOR OF YOUR BEDSPREAD. WELL, YOU JUST ZAP IT, AND PRESTO, IT'S AN IGUANA!
ONE CAN CERTAINLY IMAGINE THE MYRIAD OF USES FOR A HAND-HELD IGUANA MAKER.
IT DOESN'T **HAVE** TO BE AN IGUANA. IT CAN BE ANYTHING. SUPPOSE MOM'S GETTING ON OUR NERVES, FOR INSTANCE...

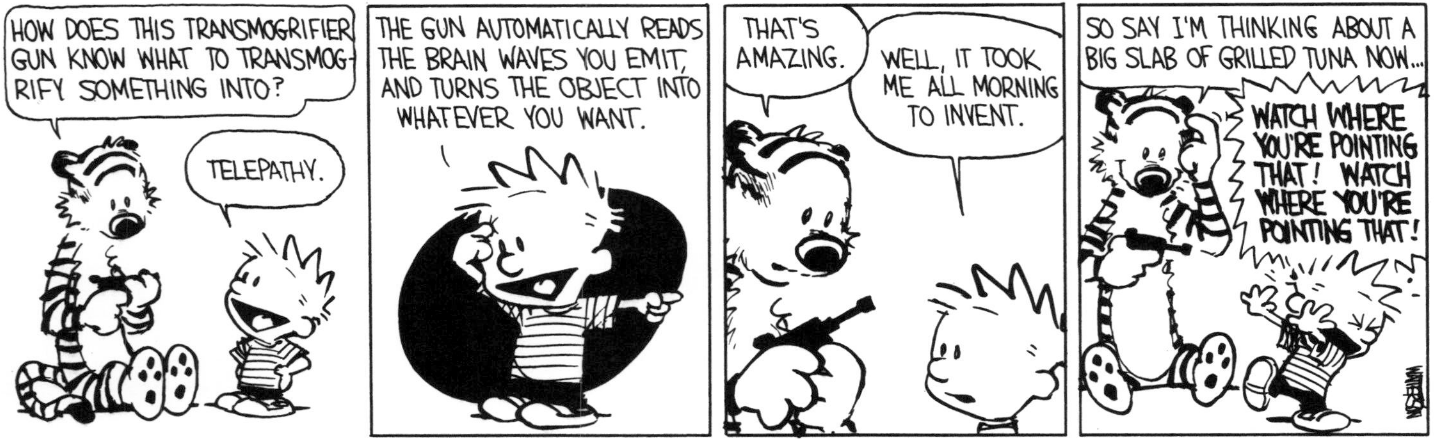
HOW DOES THIS TRANSMOGRIFIER GUN KNOW WHAT TO TRANSMOGRIFY SOMETHING INTO?
TELEPATHY.
THE GUN AUTOMATICALLY READS THE BRAIN WAVES YOU EMIT, AND TURNS THE OBJECT INTO WHATEVER YOU WANT.
THAT'S AMAZING.
WELL, IT TOOK ME ALL MORNING TO INVENT.
SO SAY I'M THINKING ABOUT A BIG SLAB OF GRILLED TUNA NOW...
WATCH WHERE YOU'RE POINTING THAT! WATCH WHERE YOU'RE POINTING THAT!

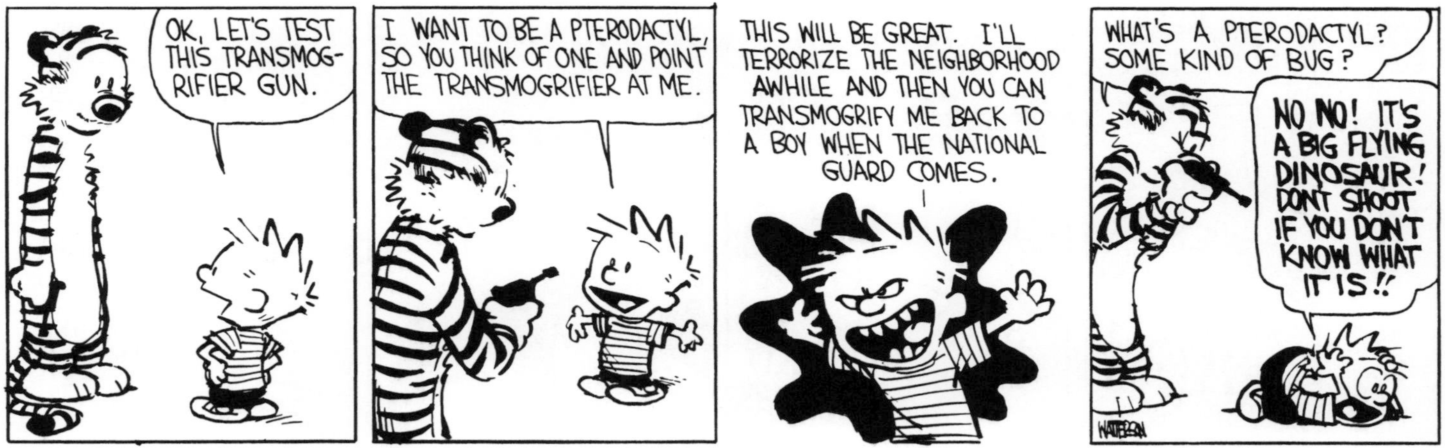
OK, LET'S TEST THIS TRANSMOG-RIFIER GUN.
I WANT TO BE A PTERODACTYL, SO YOU THINK OF ONE AND POINT THE TRANSMOGRIFIER AT ME.
THIS WILL BE GREAT. I'LL TERRORIZE THE NEIGHBORHOOD AWHILE AND THEN YOU CAN TRANSMOGRIFY ME BACK TO A BOY WHEN THE NATIONAL GUARD COMES.
WHAT'S A PTERODACTYL? SOME KIND OF BUG?
NO NO! IT'S A BIG FLYING DINOSAUR! DON'T SHOOT IF YOU DON'T KNOW WHAT IT IS!!

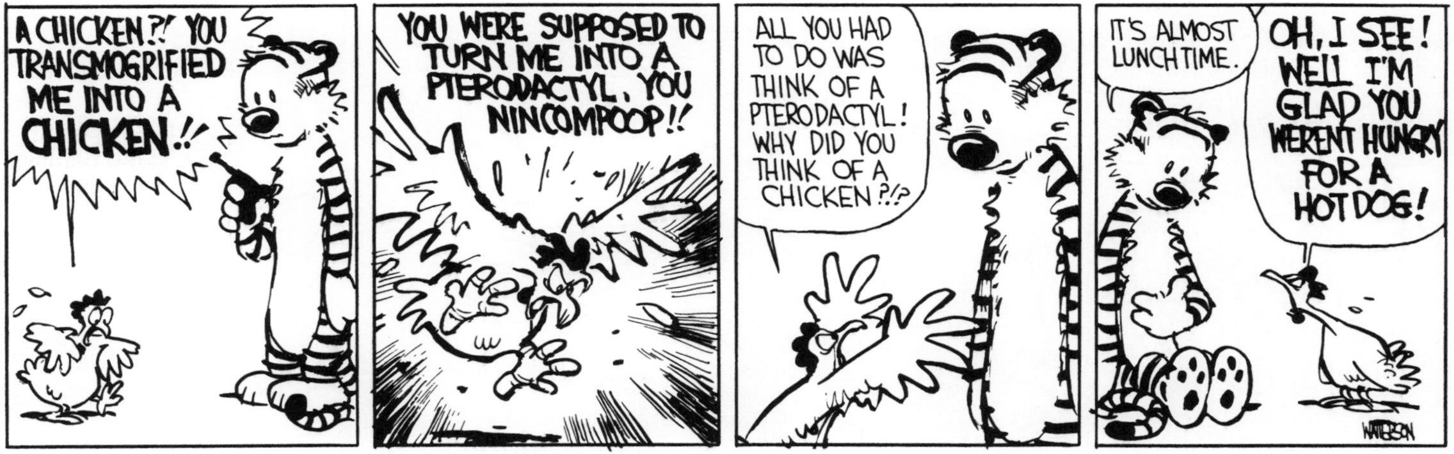
A CHICKEN?! YOU TRANSMOGRIFIED ME INTO A CHICKEN!!
YOU WERE SUPPOSED TO TURN ME INTO A PTERODACTYL, YOU NINCOMPOOP!!
ALL YOU HAD TO DO WAS THINK OF A PTERODACTYL! WHY DID YOU THINK OF A CHICKEN?!?
IT'S ALMOST LUNCHTIME.
OH, I SEE! WELL I'M GLAD YOU WEREN'T HUNGRY FOR A HOT DOG!

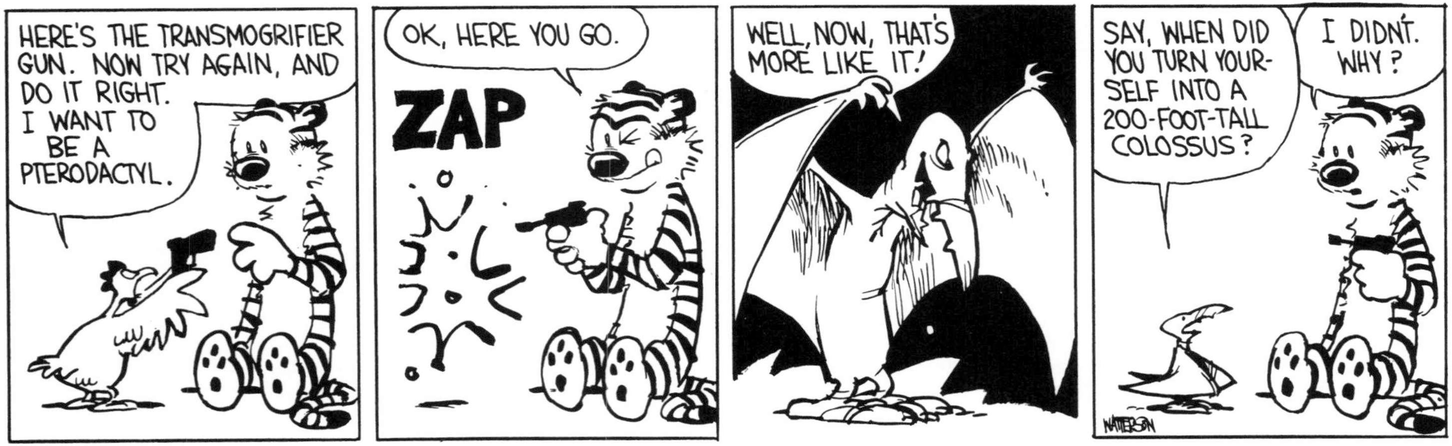
HERE'S THE TRANSMOGRIFIER GUN. NOW TRY AGAIN, AND DO IT RIGHT. I WANT TO BE A PTERODACTYL.
OK, HERE YOU GO.
ZAP
WELL, NOW, THAT'S MORE LIKE IT!
SAY, WHEN DID YOU TURN YOURSELF INTO A 200-FOOT-TALL COLOSSUS?
I DIDN'T. WHY?

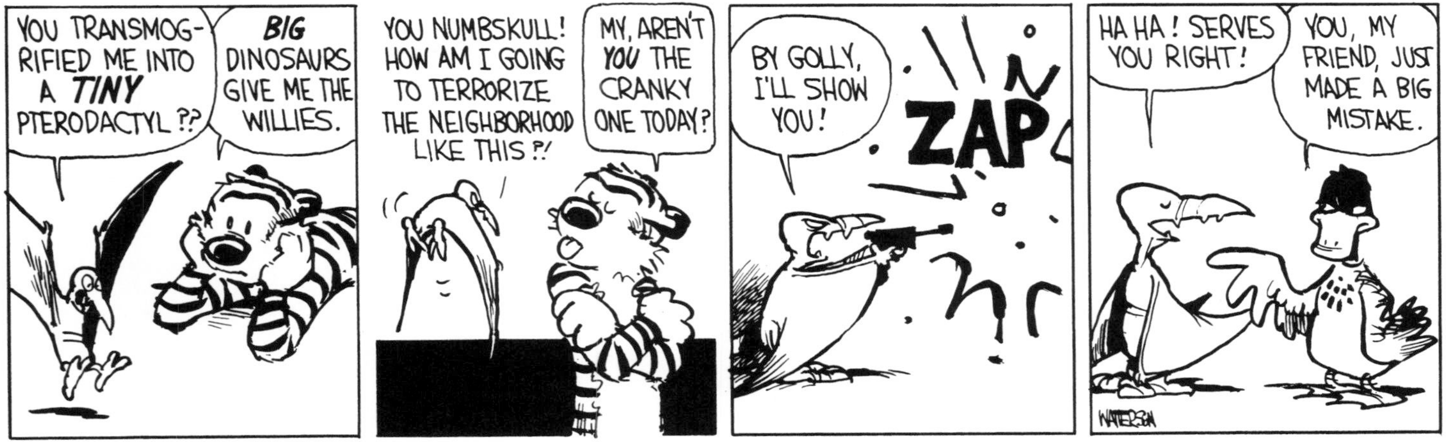
YOU TRANSMOGRIFIED ME INTO A *TINY* PTERODACTYL ?!?
BIG DINOSAURS GIVE ME THE WILLIES.
YOU NUMBSKULL! HOW AM I GOING TO TERRORIZE THE NEIGHBORHOOD LIKE THIS ?!
MY, AREN'T *YOU* THE CRANKY ONE TODAY?
BY GOLLY, I'LL SHOW YOU!
ZAP
HA HA! SERVES YOU RIGHT!
YOU, MY FRIEND, JUST MADE A BIG MISTAKE.

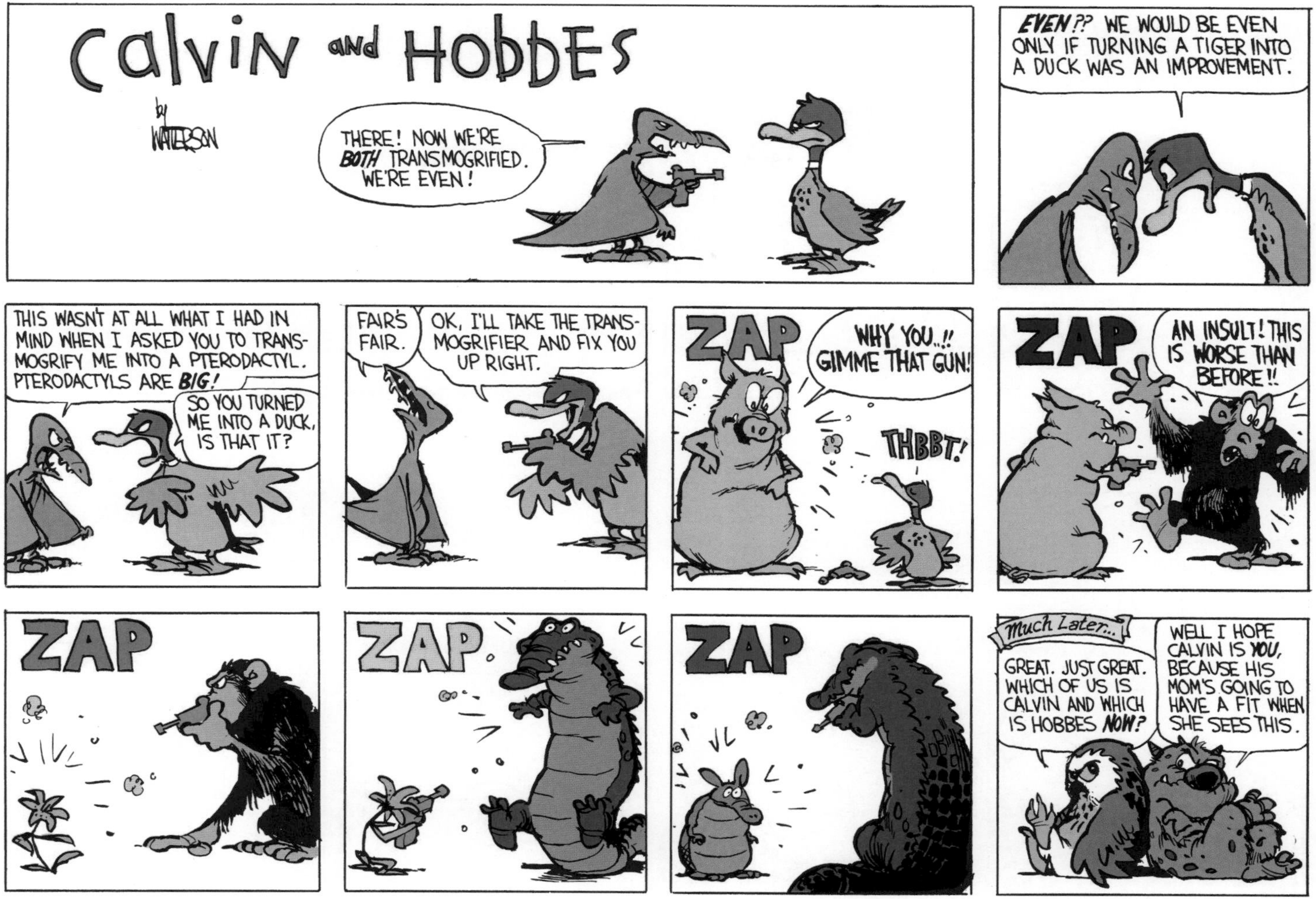
Calvin and HOBBES
by WATTERSON
THERE! NOW WE'RE BOTH TRANSMOGRIFIED. WE'RE EVEN!
EVEN?? WE WOULD BE EVEN ONLY IF TURNING A TIGER INTO A DUCK WAS AN IMPROVEMENT.
THIS WASN'T AT ALL WHAT I HAD IN MIND WHEN I ASKED YOU TO TRANSMOGRIFY ME INTO A PTERODACTYL. PTERODACTYLS ARE BIG!
SO YOU TURNED ME INTO A DUCK, IS THAT IT?
FAIR'S FAIR.
OK, I'LL TAKE THE TRANSMOGRIFIER AND FIX YOU UP RIGHT.
ZAP
WHY YOU..!! GIMME THAT GUN!
THBBT!
ZAP
AN INSULT! THIS IS WORSE THAN BEFORE!!
ZAP
ZAP
ZAP
Much Later...
GREAT. JUST GREAT. WHICH OF US IS CALVIN AND WHICH IS HOBBES NOW?
WELL I HOPE CALVIN IS YOU, BECAUSE HIS MOM'S GOING TO HAVE A FIT WHEN SHE SEES THIS.

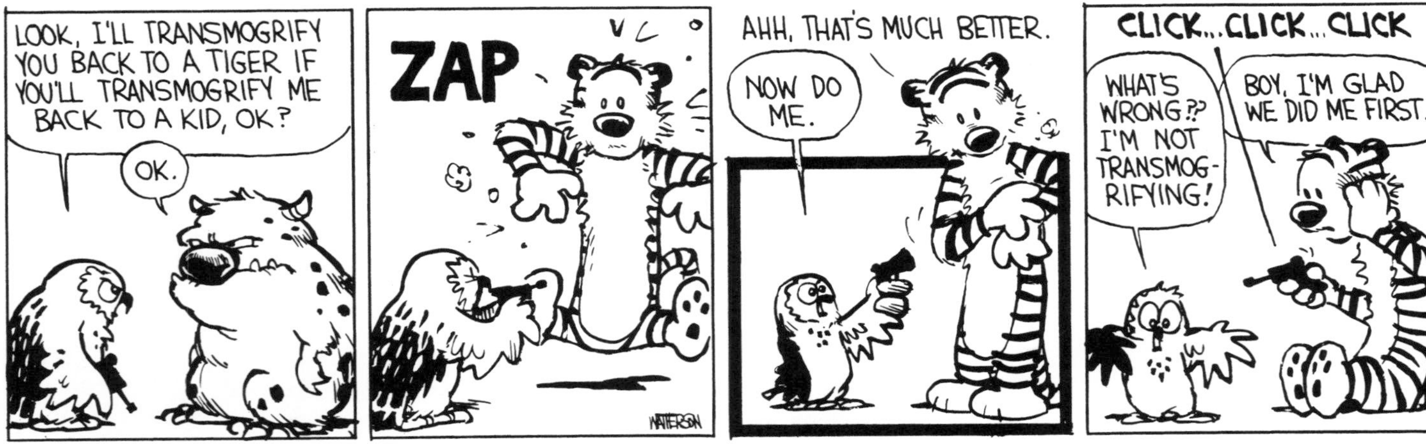
LOOK, I'LL TRANSMOGRIFY YOU BACK TO A TIGER IF YOU'LL TRANSMOGRIFY ME BACK TO A KID, OK?
OK.
ZAP
AHH, THAT'S MUCH BETTER.
NOW DO ME.
WATTERSON
CLICK...CLICK...CLICK
WHAT'S WRONG?? I'M NOT TRANSMOG-RIFYING!
BOY, I'M GLAD WE DID ME FIRST.

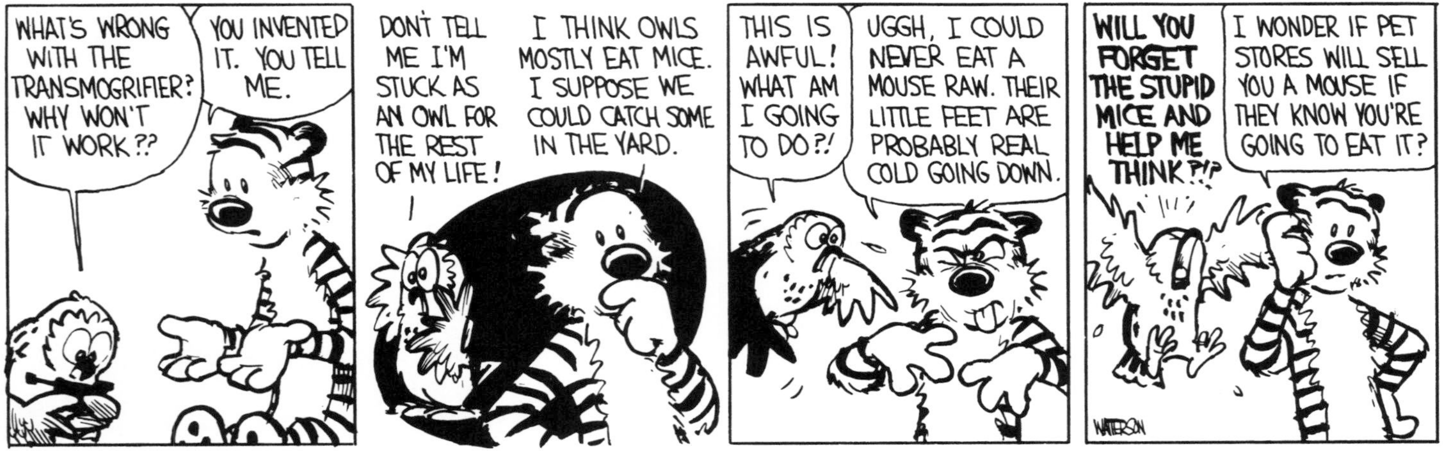
WHAT'S WRONG WITH THE TRANSMOGRIFIER? WHY WON'T IT WORK??
YOU INVENTED IT. YOU TELL ME.
DON'T TELL ME I'M STUCK AS AN OWL FOR THE REST OF MY LIFE!
I THINK OWLS MOSTLY EAT MICE. I SUPPOSE WE COULD CATCH SOME IN THE YARD.
THIS IS AWFUL! WHAT AM I GOING TO DO?!
UGGH, I COULD NEVER EAT A MOUSE RAW. THEIR LITTLE FEET ARE PROBABLY REAL COLD GOING DOWN.
WILL YOU FORGET THE STUPID MICE AND HELP ME THINK?!?
I WONDER IF PET STORES WILL SELL YOU A MOUSE IF THEY KNOW YOU'RE GOING TO EAT IT?
WATTERSON

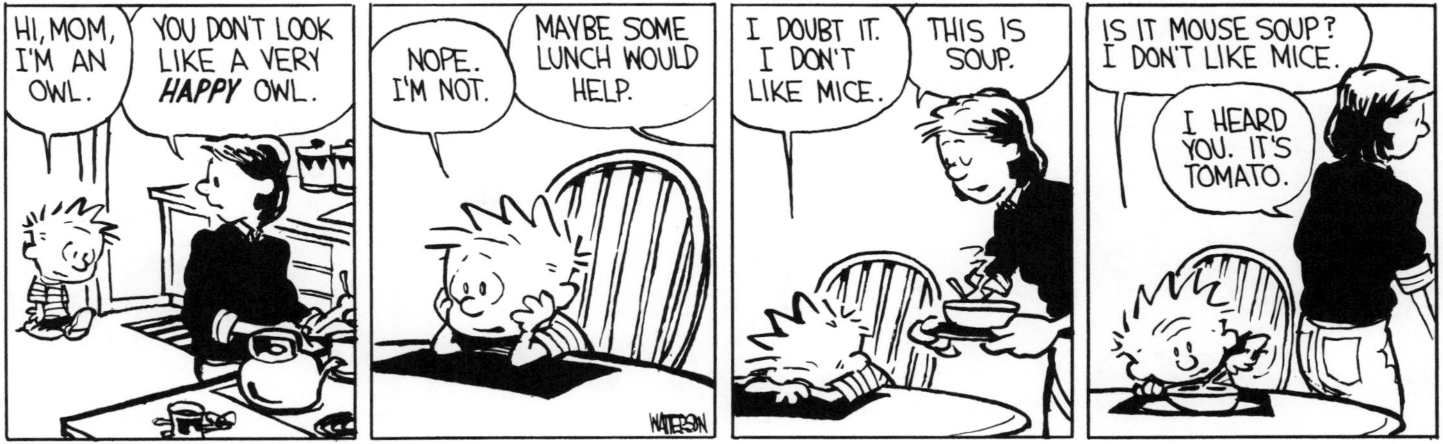
HI, MOM, I'M AN OWL.
YOU DON'T LOOK LIKE A VERY ***HAPPY*** OWL.
NOPE. I'M NOT.
MAYBE SOME LUNCH WOULD HELP.
WATTERSON
I DOUBT IT. I DON'T LIKE MICE.
THIS IS SOUP.
IS IT MOUSE SOUP? I DON'T LIKE MICE.
I HEARD YOU. IT'S TOMATO.

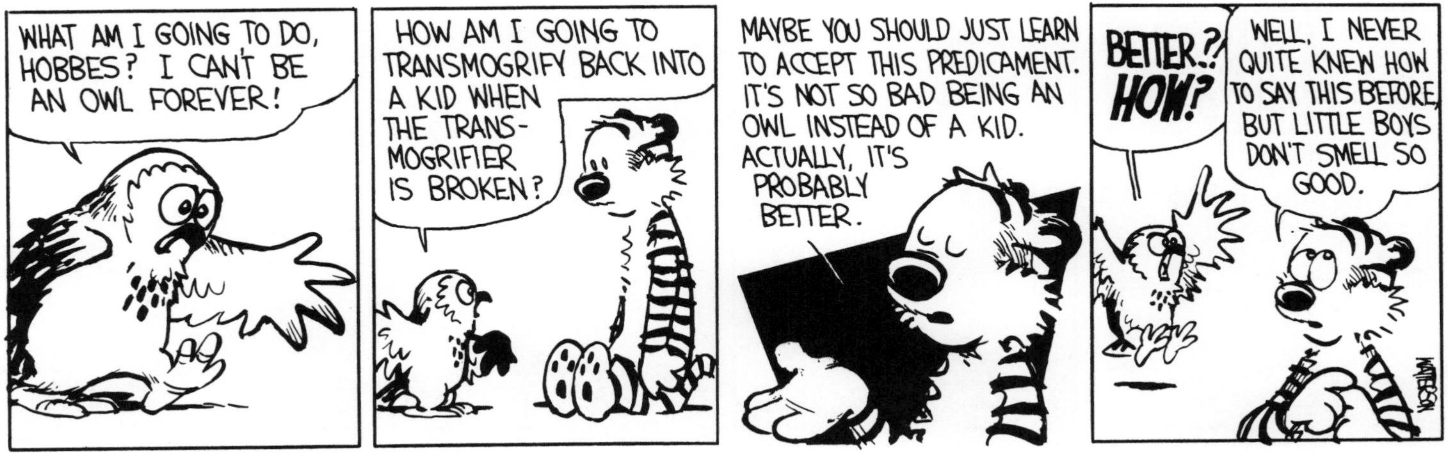
WHAT AM I GOING TO DO, HOBBES? I CAN'T BE AN OWL FOREVER!
HOW AM I GOING TO TRANSMOGRIFY BACK INTO A KID WHEN THE TRANS-MOGRIFIER IS BROKEN?
MAYBE YOU SHOULD JUST LEARN TO ACCEPT THIS PREDICAMENT. IT'S NOT SO BAD BEING AN OWL INSTEAD OF A KID. ACTUALLY, IT'S PROBABLY BETTER.
BETTER?! HOW?
WELL, I NEVER QUITE KNEW HOW TO SAY THIS BEFORE, BUT LITTLE BOYS DON'T SMELL SO GOOD.
WATTERSON

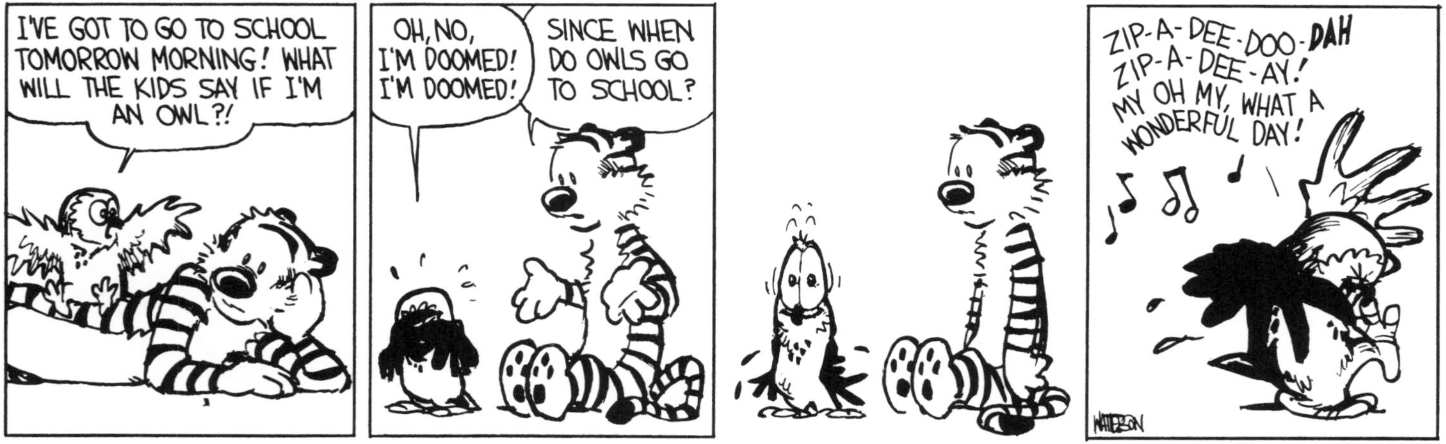
I'VE GOT TO GO TO SCHOOL TOMORROW MORNING! WHAT WILL THE KIDS SAY IF I'M AN OWL?!
OH, NO, I'M DOOMED! I'M DOOMED!
SINCE WHEN DO OWLS GO TO SCHOOL?
ZIP-A-DEE-DOO-DAH ZIP-A-DEE-AY! MY OH MY, WHAT A WONDERFUL DAY!
WATTERSON

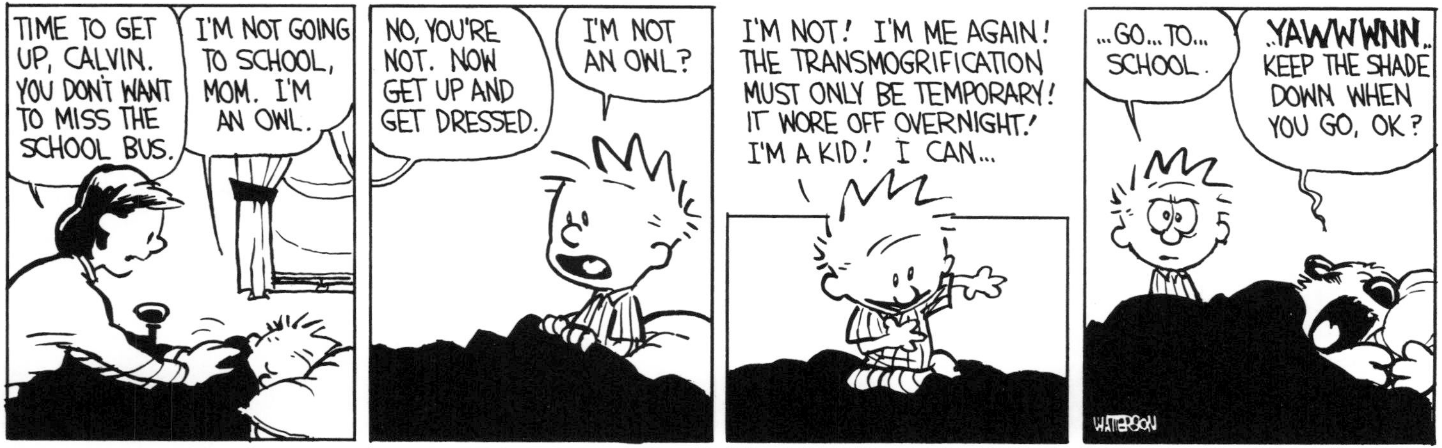
TIME TO GET UP, CALVIN. YOU DON'T WANT TO MISS THE SCHOOL BUS.
I'M NOT GOING TO SCHOOL, MOM. I'M AN OWL.
NO, YOU'RE NOT. NOW GET UP AND GET DRESSED.
I'M NOT AN OWL?
I'M NOT! I'M ME AGAIN! THE TRANSMOGRIFICATION MUST ONLY BE TEMPORARY! IT WORE OFF OVERNIGHT! I'M A KID! I CAN...
...GO...TO... SCHOOL.
..YAWWWNN.. KEEP THE SHADE DOWN WHEN YOU GO, OK?
WATTERSON

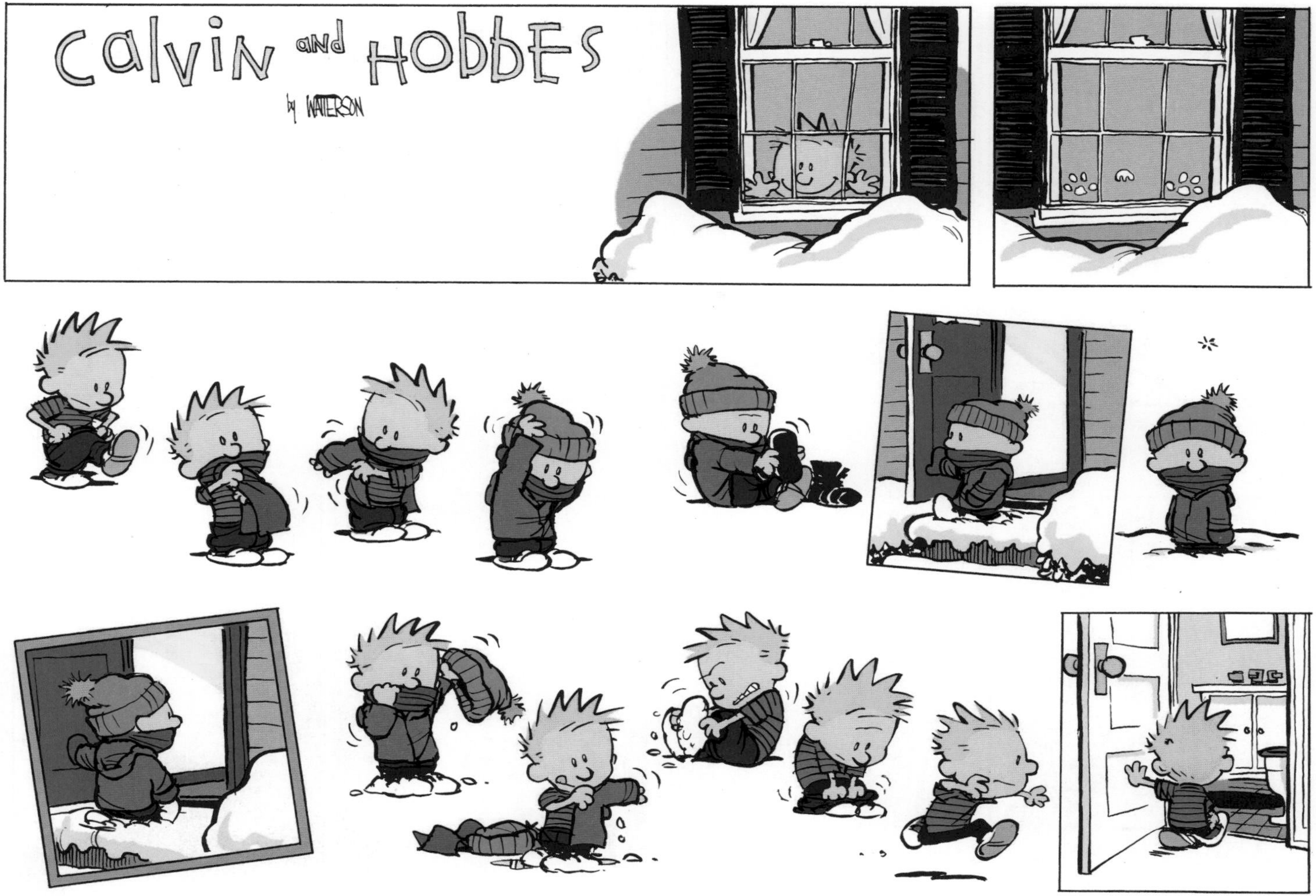
Calvin and HOBBES
by WATTERSON

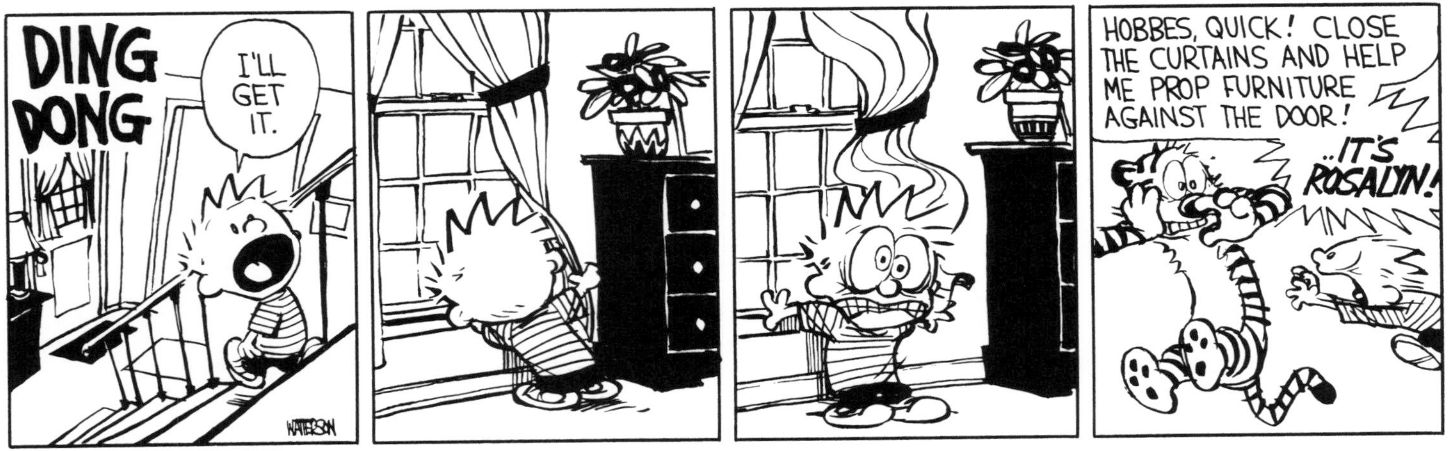
DING DONG
I'LL GET IT.
WATTERSON
HOBBES, QUICK! CLOSE THE CURTAINS AND HELP ME PROP FURNITURE AGAINST THE DOOR!
..IT'S ROSALYN!

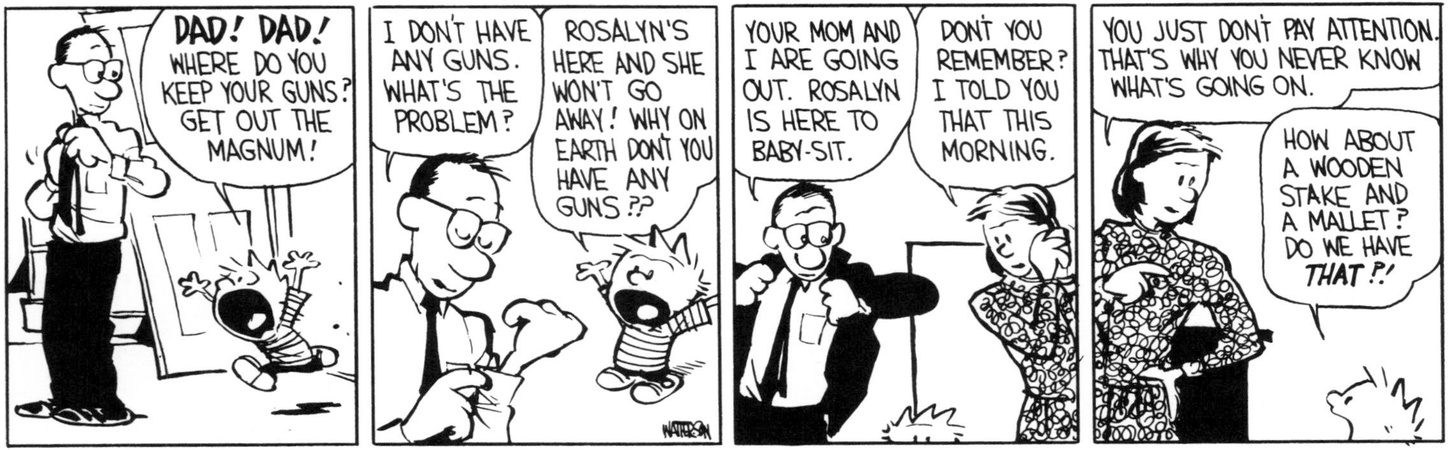
DAD! DAD! WHERE DO YOU KEEP YOUR GUNS? GET OUT THE MAGNUM!
I DON'T HAVE ANY GUNS. WHAT'S THE PROBLEM?
ROSALYN'S HERE AND SHE WON'T GO AWAY! WHY ON EARTH DON'T YOU HAVE ANY GUNS ??
WATTERSON
YOUR MOM AND I ARE GOING OUT. ROSALYN IS HERE TO BABY-SIT.
DON'T YOU REMEMBER? I TOLD YOU THAT THIS MORNING.
YOU JUST DON'T PAY ATTENTION. THAT'S WHY YOU NEVER KNOW WHAT'S GOING ON.
HOW ABOUT A WOODEN STAKE AND A MALLET? DO WE HAVE *THAT*?!

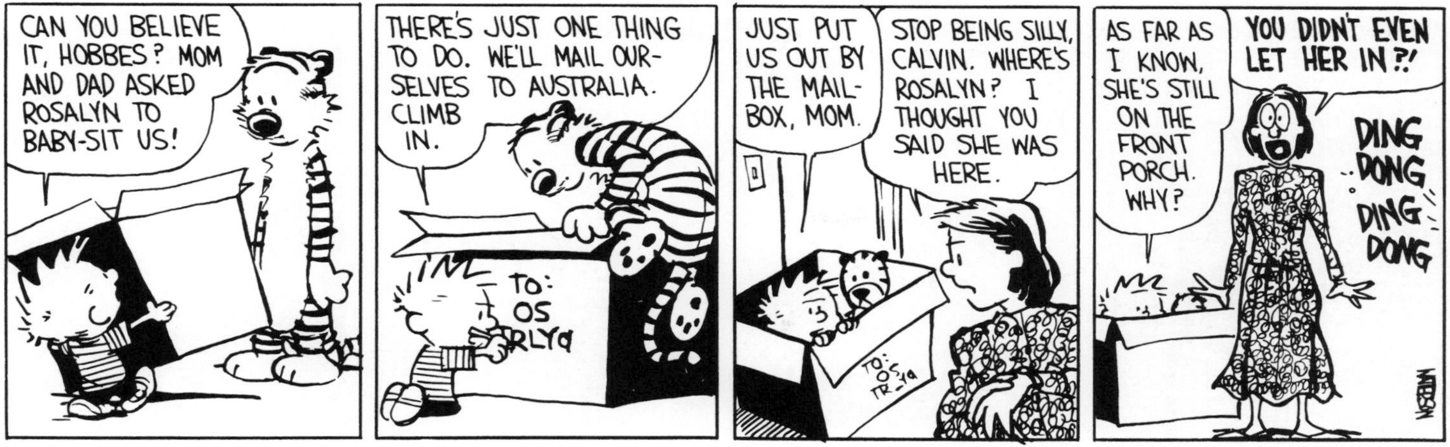
CAN YOU BELIEVE IT, HOBBES? MOM AND DAD ASKED ROSALYN TO BABY-SIT US!
THERE'S JUST ONE THING TO DO. WE'LL MAIL OURSELVES TO AUSTRALIA. CLIMB IN.
JUST PUT US OUT BY THE MAILBOX, MOM.
STOP BEING SILLY, CALVIN. WHERE'S ROSALYN? I THOUGHT YOU SAID SHE WAS HERE.
AS FAR AS I KNOW, SHE'S STILL ON THE FRONT PORCH. WHY?
YOU DIDN'T EVEN LET HER IN?!
DING DONG DING DONG
WATTERSON

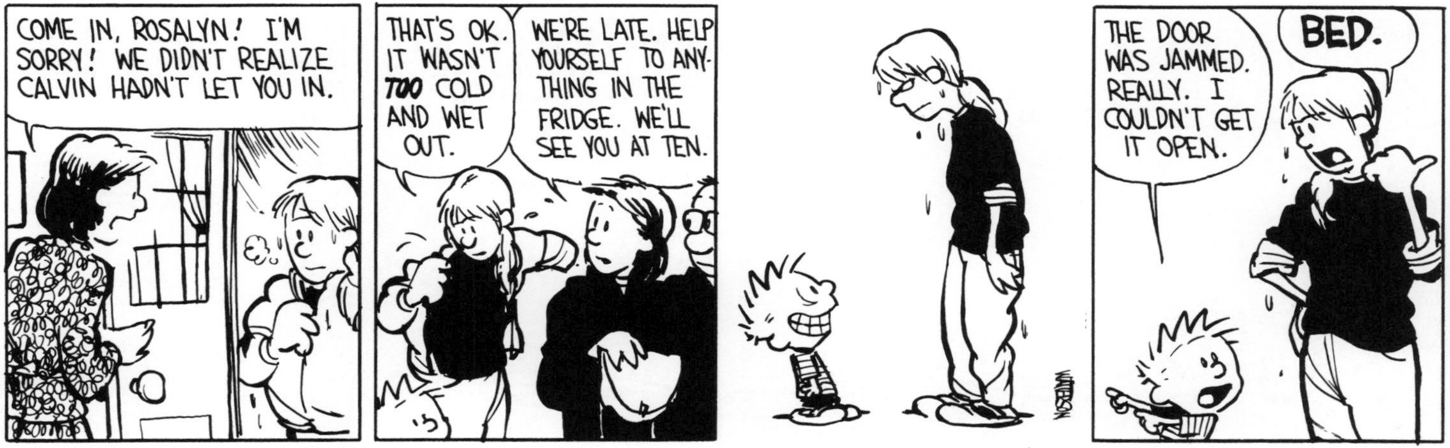
COME IN, ROSALYN! I'M SORRY! WE DIDN'T REALIZE CALVIN HADN'T LET YOU IN.
THAT'S OK. IT WASN'T *TOO* COLD AND WET OUT.
WE'RE LATE. HELP YOURSELF TO ANYTHING IN THE FRIDGE. WE'LL SEE YOU AT TEN.
WATTERSON
THE DOOR WAS JAMMED. REALLY. I COULDN'T GET IT OPEN.
BED.

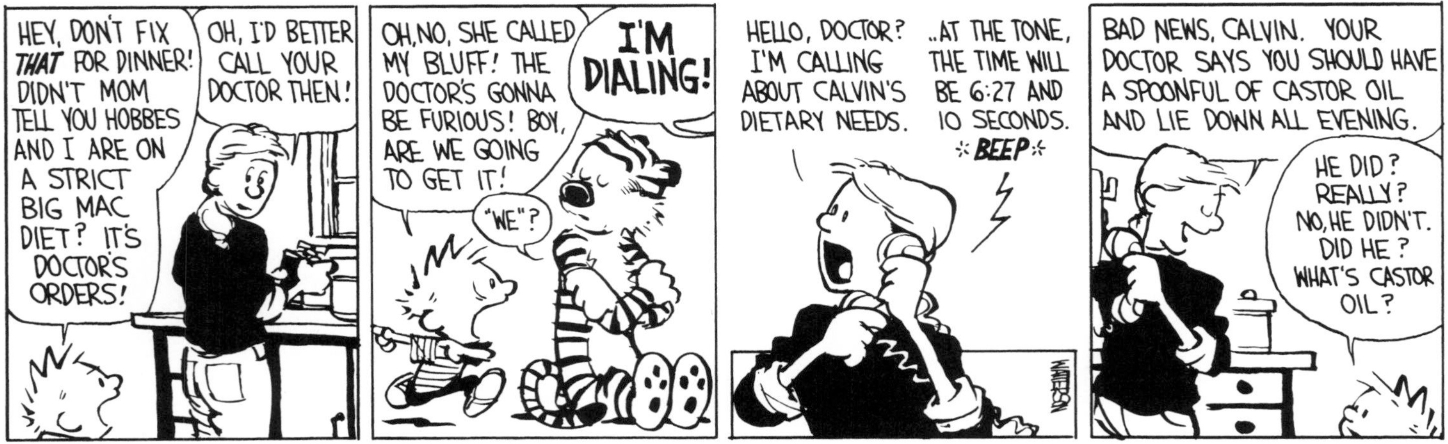
HEY, DON'T FIX *THAT* FOR DINNER! DIDN'T MOM TELL YOU HOBBES AND I ARE ON A STRICT BIG MAC DIET? IT'S DOCTOR'S ORDERS!
OH, I'D BETTER CALL YOUR DOCTOR THEN!
OH, NO, SHE CALLED MY BLUFF! THE DOCTOR'S GONNA BE FURIOUS! BOY, ARE WE GOING TO GET IT!
"WE"?
I'M DIALING!
HELLO, DOCTOR? I'M CALLING ABOUT CALVIN'S DIETARY NEEDS.
..AT THE TONE, THE TIME WILL BE 6:27 AND 10 SECONDS.
BEEP
BAD NEWS, CALVIN. YOUR DOCTOR SAYS YOU SHOULD HAVE A SPOONFUL OF CASTOR OIL AND LIE DOWN ALL EVENING.
HE DID? REALLY? NO, HE DIDN'T. DID HE? WHAT'S CASTOR OIL?

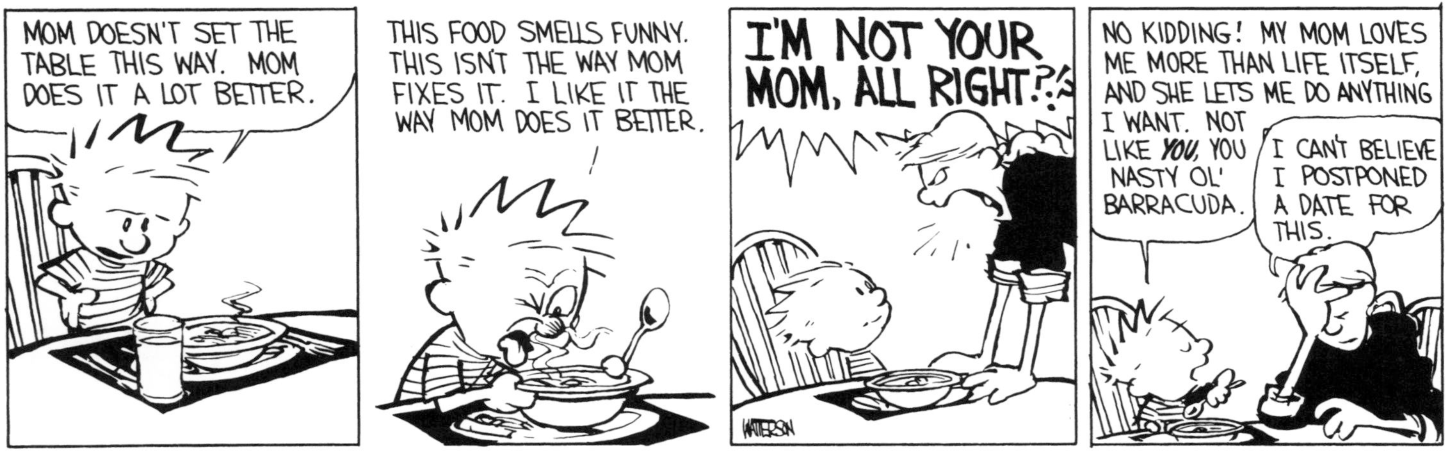
MOM DOESN'T SET THE TABLE THIS WAY. MOM DOES IT A LOT BETTER.
THIS FOOD SMELLS FUNNY. THIS ISN'T THE WAY MOM FIXES IT. I LIKE IT THE WAY MOM DOES IT BETTER.
I'M NOT YOUR MOM, ALL RIGHT?!
NO KIDDING! MY MOM LOVES ME MORE THAN LIFE ITSELF, AND SHE LETS ME DO ANYTHING I WANT. NOT LIKE *YOU*, YOU NASTY OL' BARRACUDA.
I CAN'T BELIEVE I POSTPONED A DATE FOR THIS.

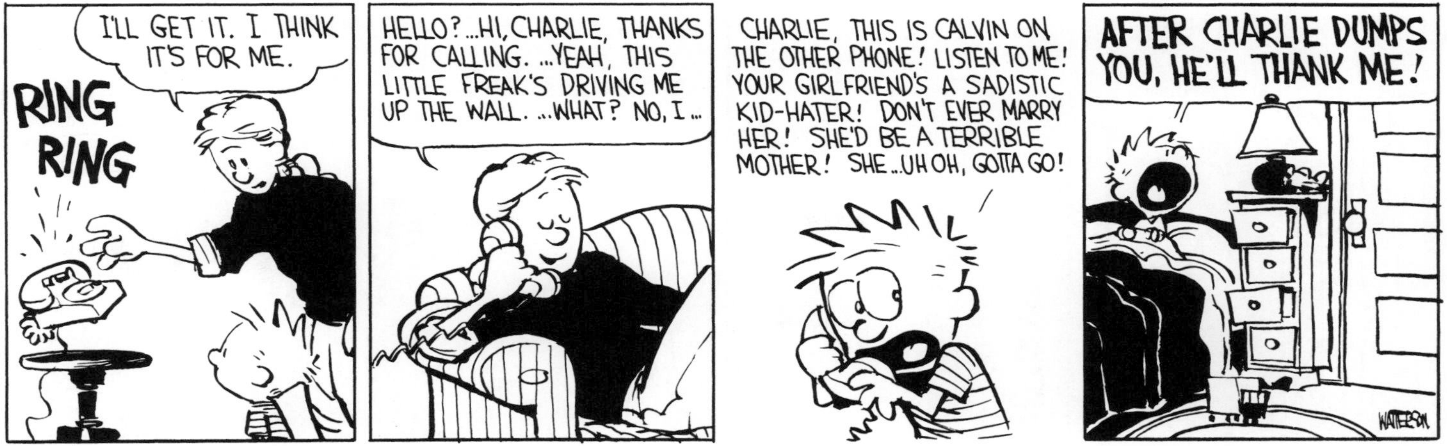
I'LL GET IT. I THINK IT'S FOR ME.
RING RING
HELLO? ...HI, CHARLIE, THANKS FOR CALLING. ...YEAH, THIS LITTLE FREAK'S DRIVING ME UP THE WALL. ...WHAT? NO, I ...
CHARLIE, THIS IS CALVIN ON THE OTHER PHONE! LISTEN TO ME! YOUR GIRLFRIEND'S A SADISTIC KID-HATER! DON'T EVER MARRY HER! SHE'D BE A TERRIBLE MOTHER! SHE...UH OH, GOTTA GO!
AFTER CHARLIE DUMPS YOU, HE'LL THANK ME!
WATTERSON

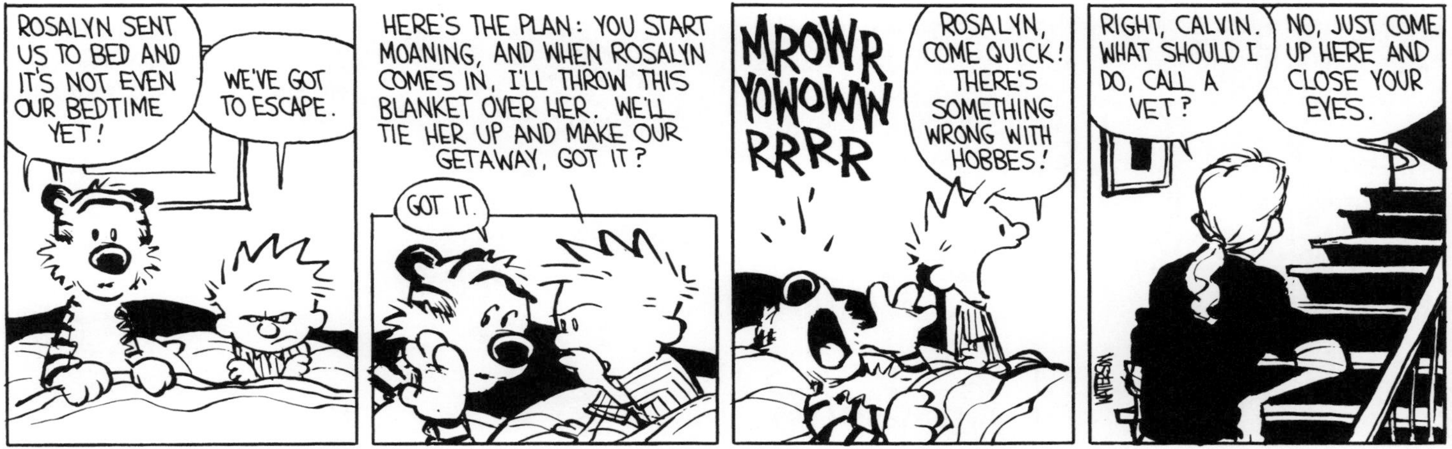
ROSALYN SENT US TO BED AND IT'S NOT EVEN OUR BEDTIME YET!
WE'VE GOT TO ESCAPE.
HERE'S THE PLAN: YOU START MOANING, AND WHEN ROSALYN COMES IN, I'LL THROW THIS BLANKET OVER HER. WE'LL TIE HER UP AND MAKE OUR GETAWAY, GOT IT?
GOT IT.
MROWR YOWOWW RRRR
ROSALYN, COME QUICK! THERE'S SOMETHING WRONG WITH HOBBES!
WATTERSON
RIGHT, CALVIN. WHAT SHOULD I DO, CALL A VET?
NO, JUST COME UP HERE AND CLOSE YOUR EYES.

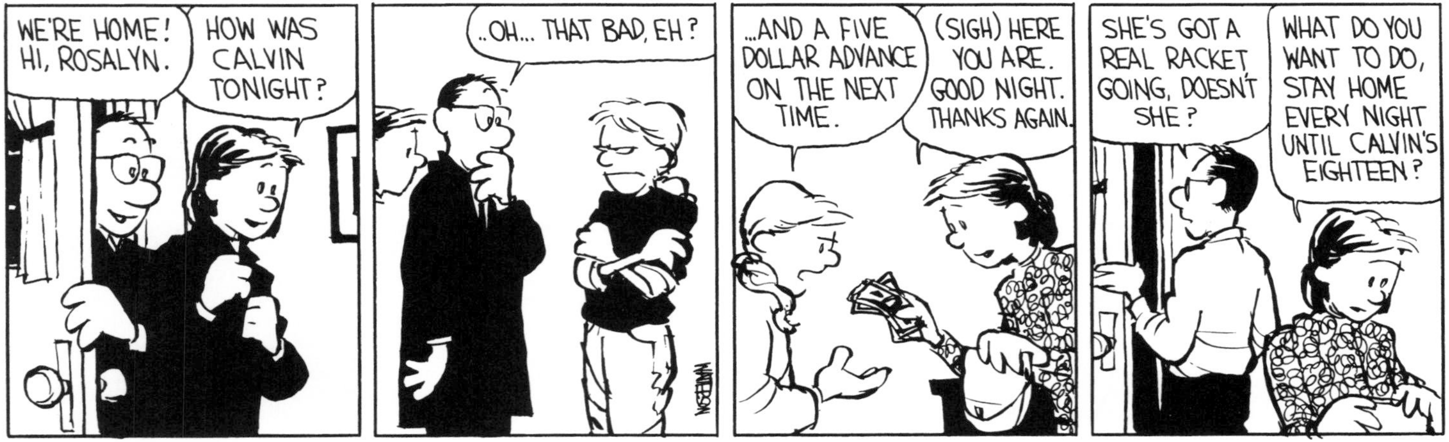
WE'RE HOME! HI, ROSALYN.
HOW WAS CALVIN TONIGHT?
..OH... THAT BAD, EH?
...AND A FIVE DOLLAR ADVANCE ON THE NEXT TIME.
(SIGH) HERE YOU ARE. GOOD NIGHT. THANKS AGAIN.
SHE'S GOT A REAL RACKET GOING, DOESN'T SHE?
WHAT DO YOU WANT TO DO, STAY HOME EVERY NIGHT UNTIL CALVIN'S EIGHTEEN?

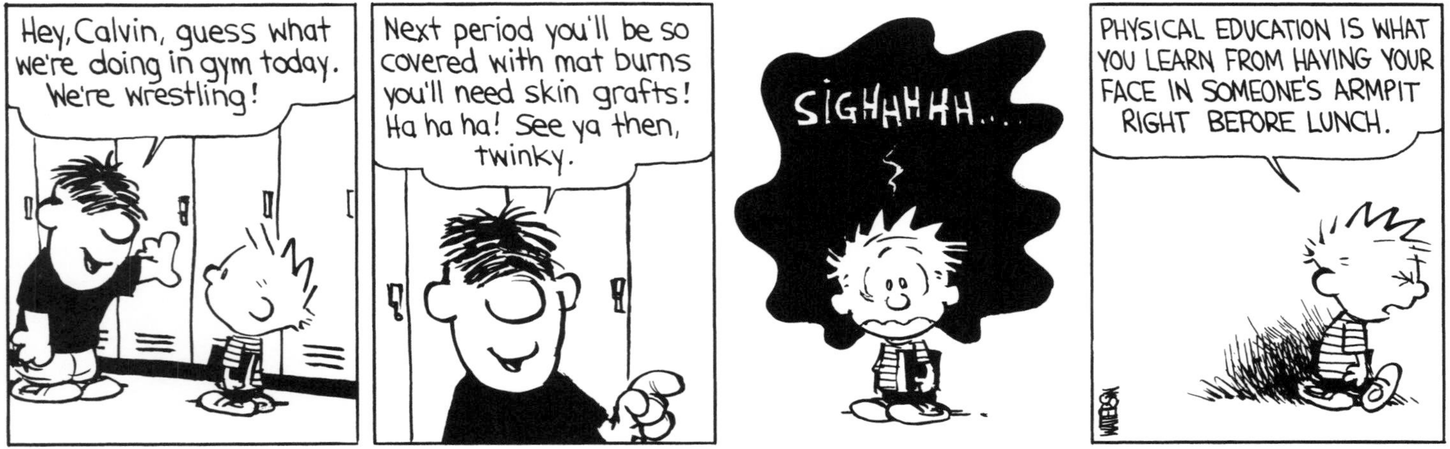
Hey, Calvin, guess what we're doing in gym today. We're wrestling!
Next period you'll be so covered with mat burns you'll need skin grafts! Ha ha ha! See ya then, twinky.
SIGHHHHH...
PHYSICAL EDUCATION IS WHAT YOU LEARN FROM HAVING YOUR FACE IN SOMEONE'S ARMPIT RIGHT BEFORE LUNCH.

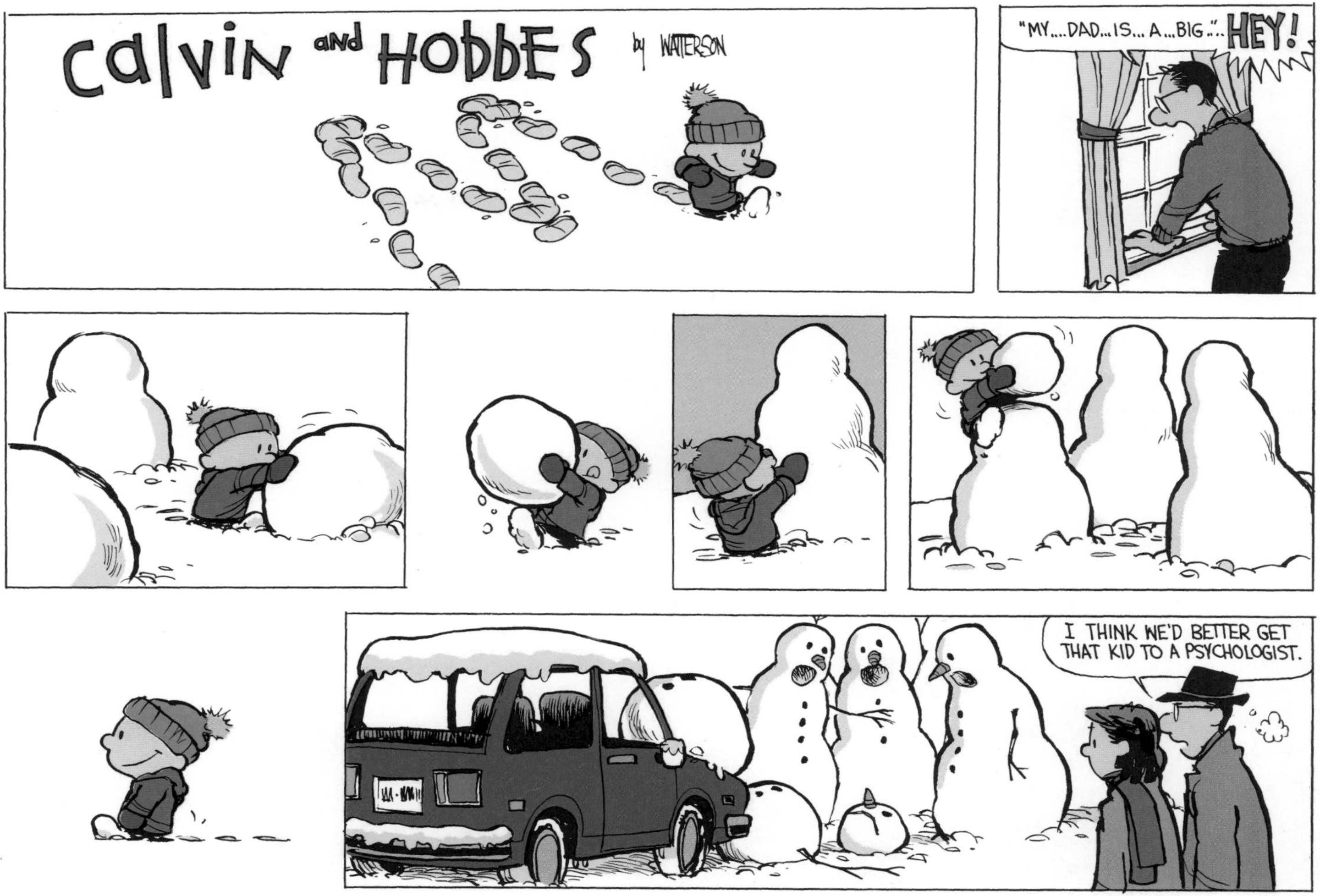
Calvin and HOBBES by WATTERSON
"MY.... DAD... IS... A... BIG..."... HEY!
I THINK WE'D BETTER GET THAT KID TO A PSYCHOLOGIST.

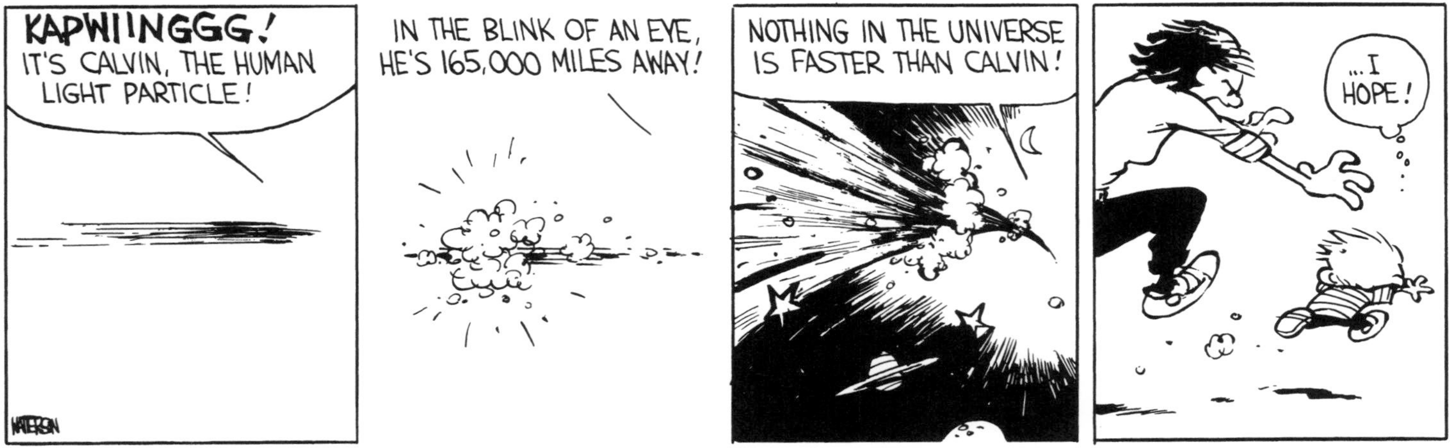
KAPWIINGGG!
IT'S CALVIN, THE HUMAN LIGHT PARTICLE!
IN THE BLINK OF AN EYE, HE'S 165,000 MILES AWAY!
NOTHING IN THE UNIVERSE IS FASTER THAN CALVIN!
...I HOPE!

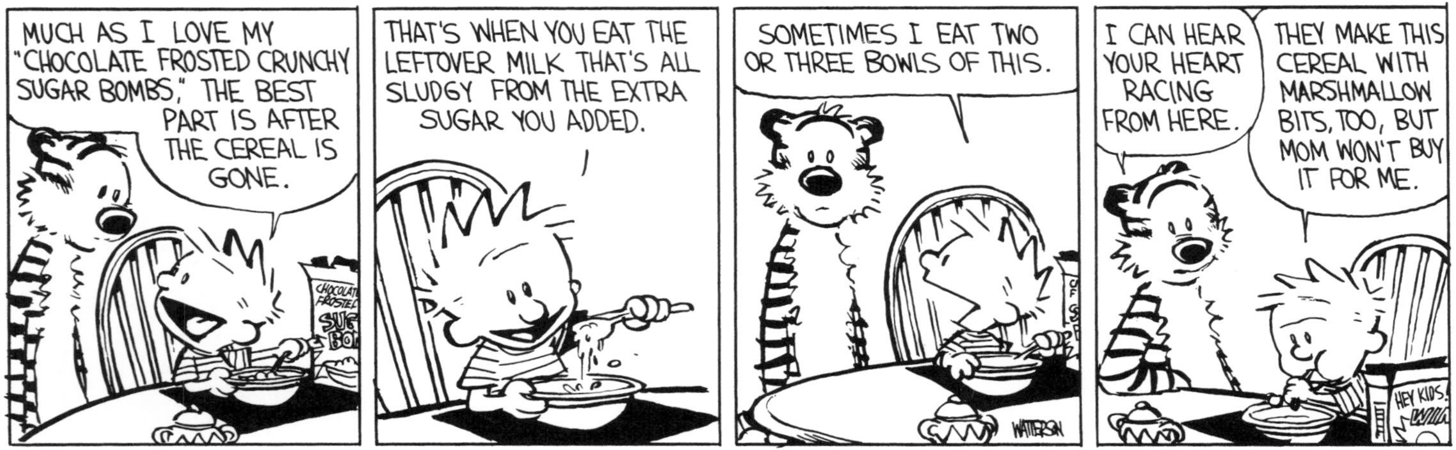
MUCH AS I LOVE MY "CHOCOLATE FROSTED CRUNCHY SUGAR BOMBS," THE BEST PART IS AFTER THE CEREAL IS GONE.
CHOCOLATE FROSTED SUG BOI
THAT'S WHEN YOU EAT THE LEFTOVER MILK THAT'S ALL SLUDGY FROM THE EXTRA SUGAR YOU ADDED.
SOMETIMES I EAT TWO OR THREE BOWLS OF THIS.
I CAN HEAR YOUR HEART RACING FROM HERE.
THEY MAKE THIS CEREAL WITH MARSHMALLOW BITS, TOO, BUT MOM WON'T BUY IT FOR ME.
HEY KIDS!

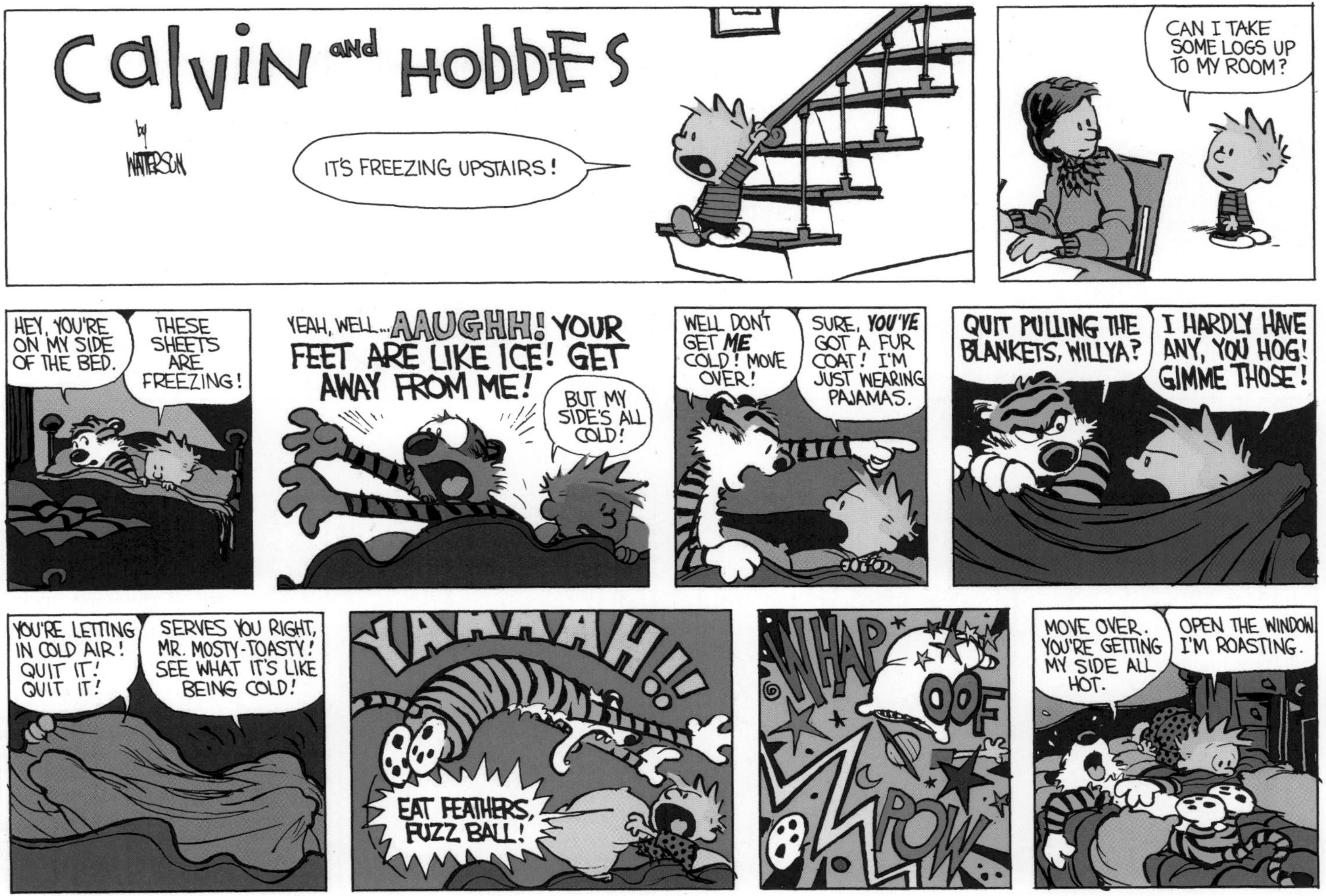
Calvin and HOBBES
by WATTERSON
IT'S FREEZING UPSTAIRS!
CAN I TAKE SOME LOGS UP TO MY ROOM?
HEY, YOU'RE ON MY SIDE OF THE BED.
THESE SHEETS ARE FREEZING!
YEAH, WELL... AAUGHH! YOUR FEET ARE LIKE ICE! GET AWAY FROM ME!
BUT MY SIDE'S ALL COLD!
WELL DON'T GET ME COLD! MOVE OVER!
SURE, YOU'VE GOT A FUR COAT! I'M JUST WEARING PAJAMAS.
QUIT PULLING THE BLANKETS, WILLYA?
I HARDLY HAVE ANY, YOU HOG! GIMME THOSE!
YOU'RE LETTING IN COLD AIR! QUIT IT! QUIT IT!
SERVES YOU RIGHT, MR. MOSTY-TOASTY! SEE WHAT IT'S LIKE BEING COLD!
YAAAAAH!!!
EAT FEATHERS, FUZZ BALL!
WHAP
OOF
POW
MOVE OVER. YOU'RE GETTING MY SIDE ALL HOT.
OPEN THE WINDOW. I'M ROASTING.

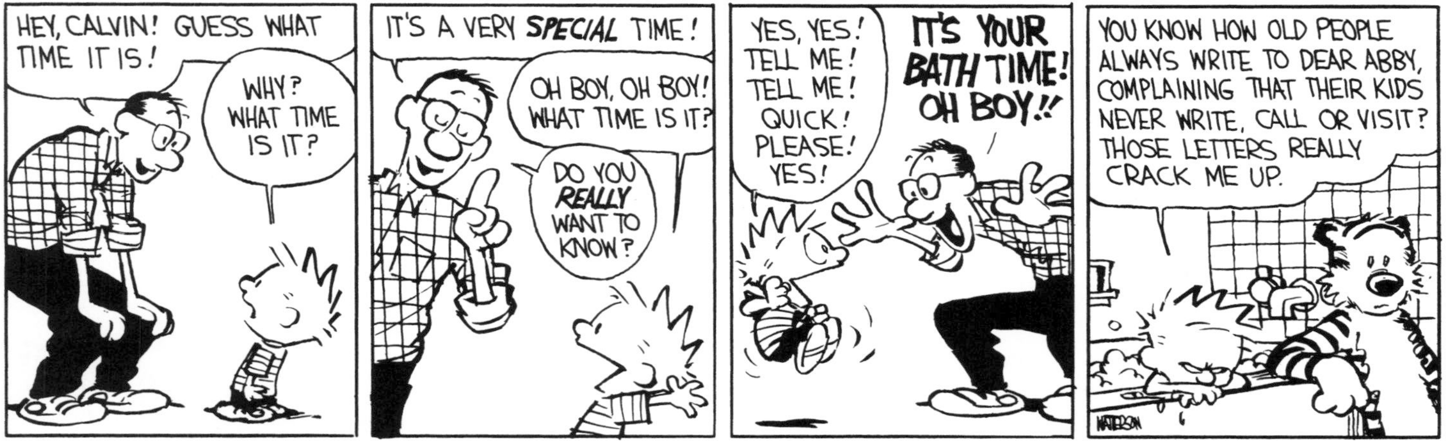
HEY, CALVIN! GUESS WHAT TIME IT IS!
WHY? WHAT TIME IS IT?
IT'S A VERY SPECIAL TIME!
OH BOY, OH BOY! WHAT TIME IS IT?
DO YOU REALLY WANT TO KNOW?
YES, YES! TELL ME! TELL ME! QUICK! PLEASE! YES!
IT'S YOUR BATH TIME! OH BOY!!
YOU KNOW HOW OLD PEOPLE ALWAYS WRITE TO DEAR ABBY, COMPLAINING THAT THEIR KIDS NEVER WRITE, CALL OR VISIT? THOSE LETTERS REALLY CRACK ME UP.
WATTERSON

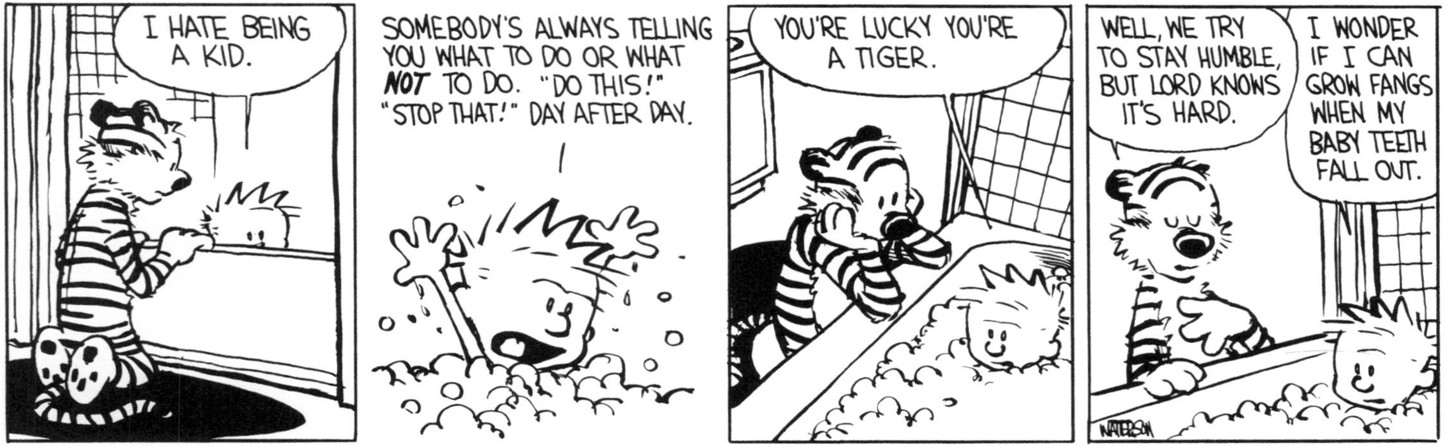
I HATE BEING A KID.
SOMEBODY'S ALWAYS TELLING YOU WHAT TO DO OR WHAT NOT TO DO. "DO THIS!" "STOP THAT!" DAY AFTER DAY.
YOU'RE LUCKY YOU'RE A TIGER.
WELL, WE TRY TO STAY HUMBLE, BUT LORD KNOWS IT'S HARD.
I WONDER IF I CAN GROW FANGS WHEN MY BABY TEETH FALL OUT.
WATTERSON

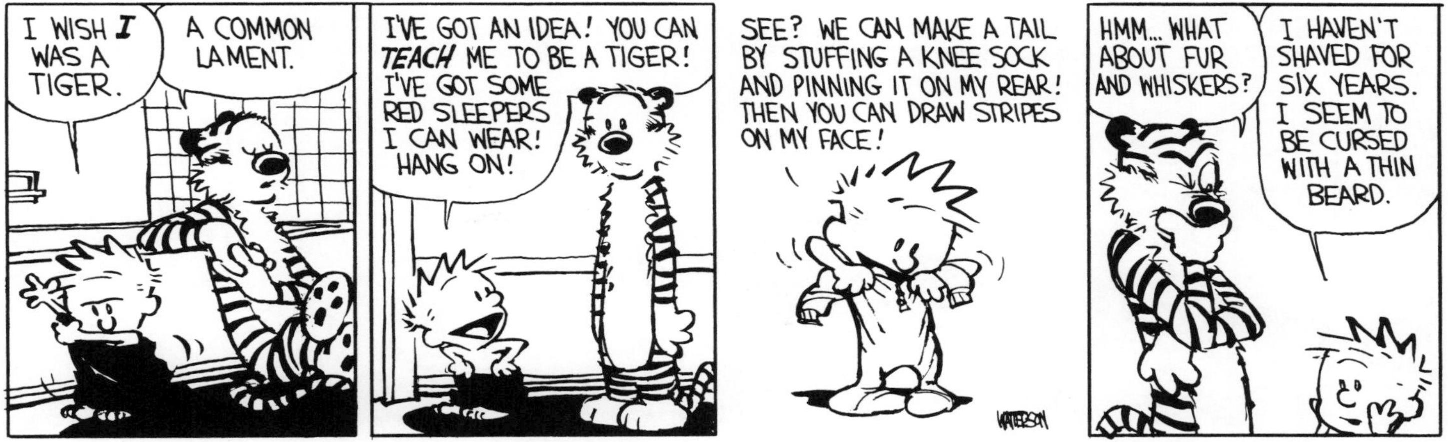
I WISH I WAS A TIGER.
A COMMON LAMENT.
I'VE GOT AN IDEA! YOU CAN TEACH ME TO BE A TIGER! I'VE GOT SOME RED SLEEPERS I CAN WEAR! HANG ON!
SEE? WE CAN MAKE A TAIL BY STUFFING A KNEE SOCK AND PINNING IT ON MY REAR! THEN YOU CAN DRAW STRIPES ON MY FACE!
HMM... WHAT ABOUT FUR AND WHISKERS?
I HAVEN'T SHAVED FOR SIX YEARS. I SEEM TO BE CURSED WITH A THIN BEARD.

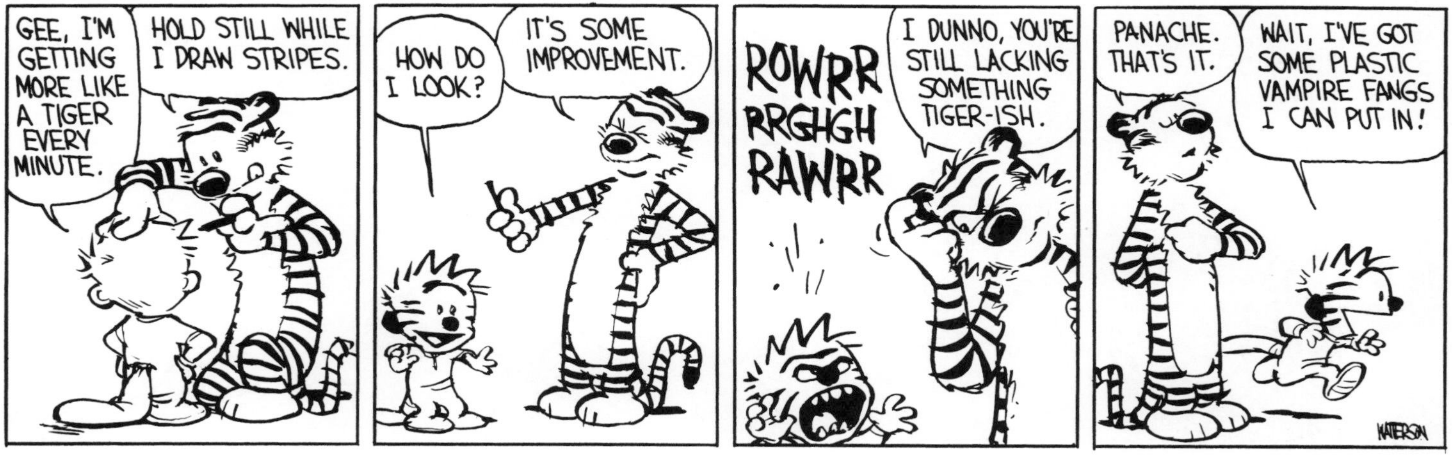
GEE, I'M GETTING MORE LIKE A TIGER EVERY MINUTE.
HOLD STILL WHILE I DRAW STRIPES.
HOW DO I LOOK?
IT'S SOME IMPROVEMENT.
ROWRR RRGHGH RAWRR
I DUNNO, YOU'RE STILL LACKING SOMETHING TIGER-ISH.
PANACHE. THAT'S IT.
WAIT, I'VE GOT SOME PLASTIC VAMPIRE FANGS I CAN PUT IN!

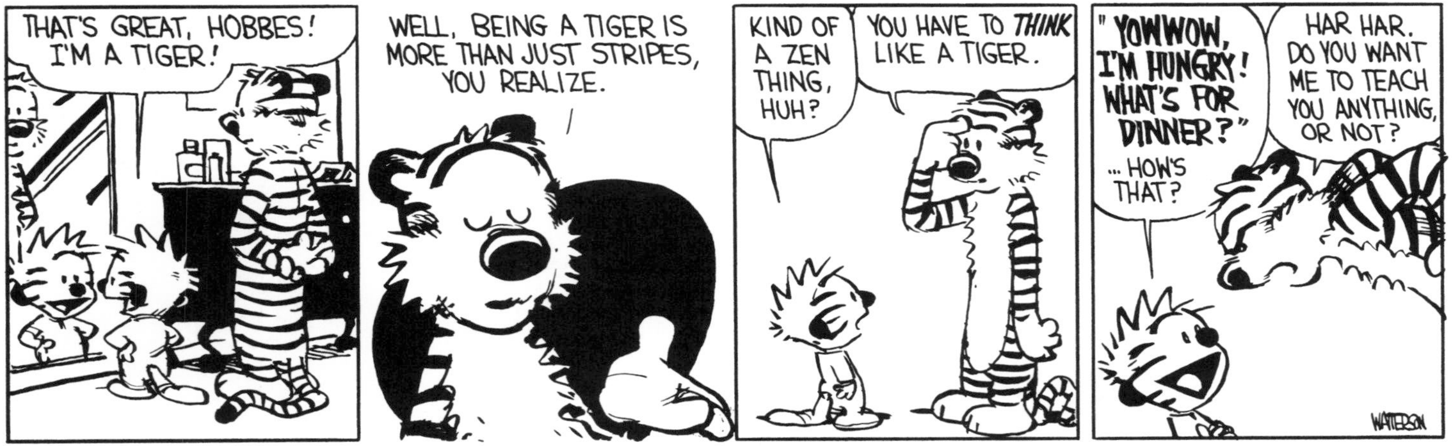
THAT'S GREAT, HOBBES! I'M A TIGER!
WELL, BEING A TIGER IS MORE THAN JUST STRIPES, YOU REALIZE.
KIND OF A ZEN THING, HUH?
YOU HAVE TO *THINK* LIKE A TIGER.
"YOWWOW, I'M HUNGRY! WHAT'S FOR DINNER?"
... HOW'S THAT?
HAR HAR. DO YOU WANT ME TO TEACH YOU ANYTHING, OR NOT?
WATTERSON

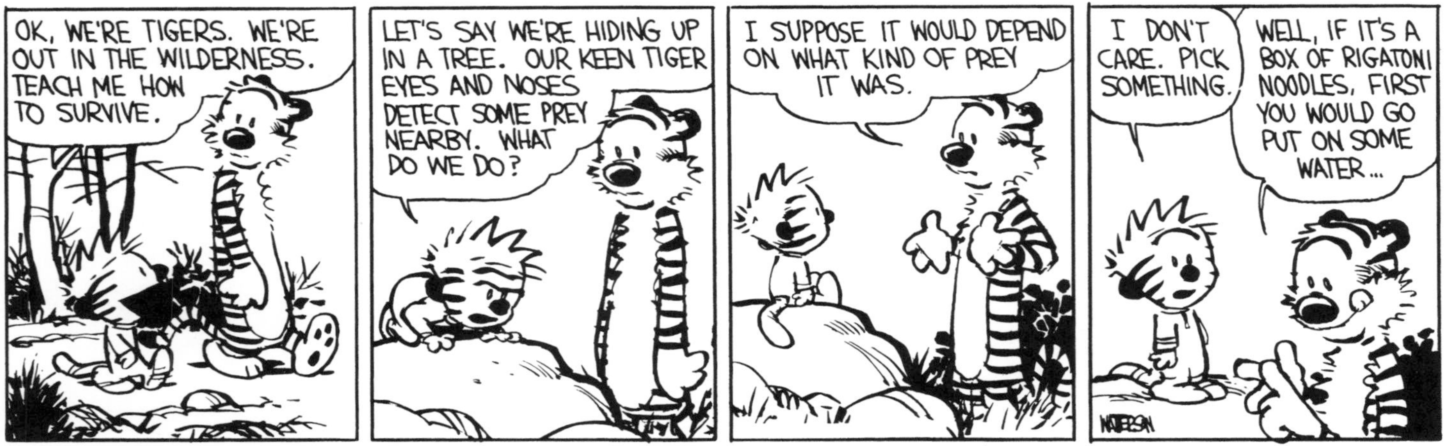
OK, WE'RE TIGERS. WE'RE OUT IN THE WILDERNESS. TEACH ME HOW TO SURVIVE.
LET'S SAY WE'RE HIDING UP IN A TREE. OUR KEEN TIGER EYES AND NOSES DETECT SOME PREY NEARBY. WHAT DO WE DO?
I SUPPOSE IT WOULD DEPEND ON WHAT KIND OF PREY IT WAS.
I DON'T CARE. PICK SOMETHING.
WELL, IF IT'S A BOX OF RIGATONI NOODLES, FIRST YOU WOULD GO PUT ON SOME WATER...
WATTERSON

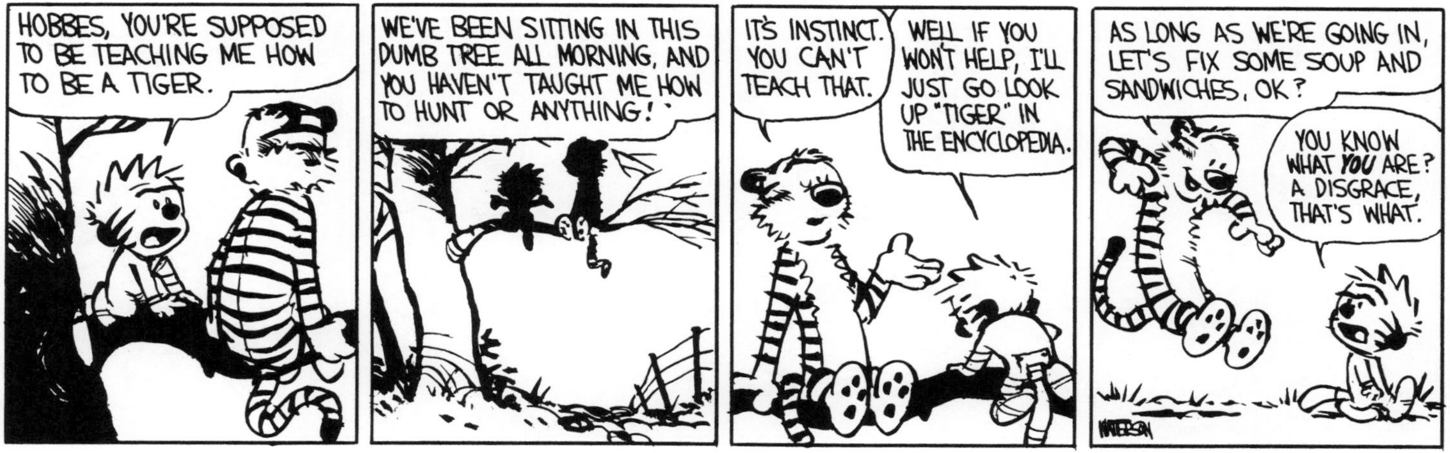
HOBBES, YOU'RE SUPPOSED TO BE TEACHING ME HOW TO BE A TIGER.
WE'VE BEEN SITTING IN THIS DUMB TREE ALL MORNING, AND YOU HAVEN'T TAUGHT ME HOW TO HUNT OR ANYTHING!
IT'S INSTINCT. YOU CAN'T TEACH THAT.
WELL IF YOU WON'T HELP, I'LL JUST GO LOOK UP "TIGER" IN THE ENCYCLOPEDIA.
AS LONG AS WE'RE GOING IN, LET'S FIX SOME SOUP AND SANDWICHES, OK?
YOU KNOW WHAT **YOU** ARE? A DISGRACE, THAT'S WHAT.

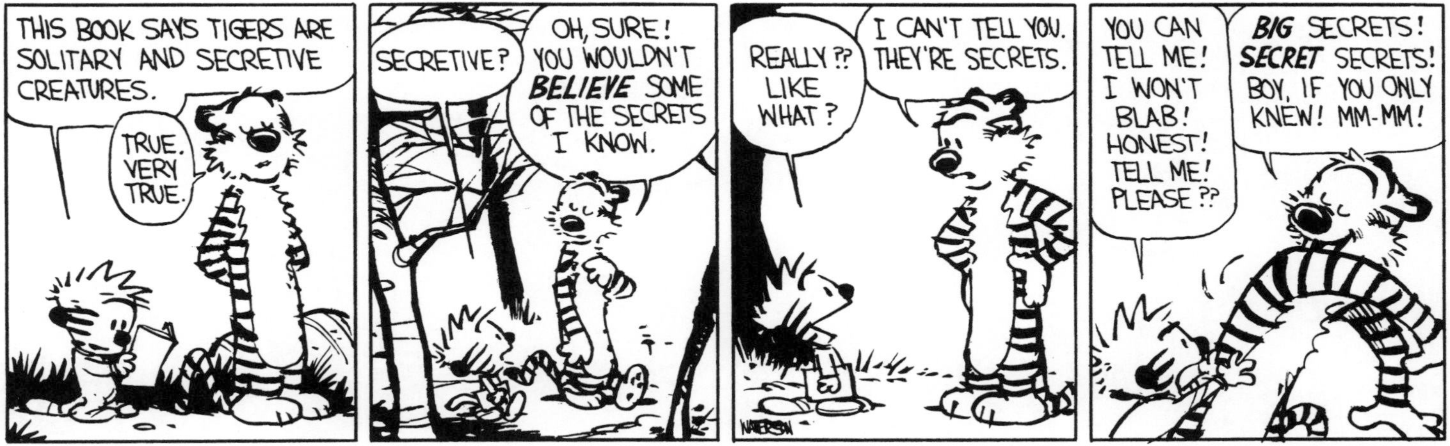
THIS BOOK SAYS TIGERS ARE SOLITARY AND SECRETIVE CREATURES.
TRUE. VERY TRUE.
SECRETIVE?
OH, SURE! YOU WOULDN'T **BELIEVE** SOME OF THE SECRETS I KNOW.
REALLY?? LIKE WHAT?
I CAN'T TELL YOU. THEY'RE SECRETS.
YOU CAN TELL ME! I WON'T BLAB! HONEST! TELL ME! PLEASE??
BIG SECRETS! **SECRET** SECRETS! BOY, IF YOU ONLY KNEW! MM-MM!

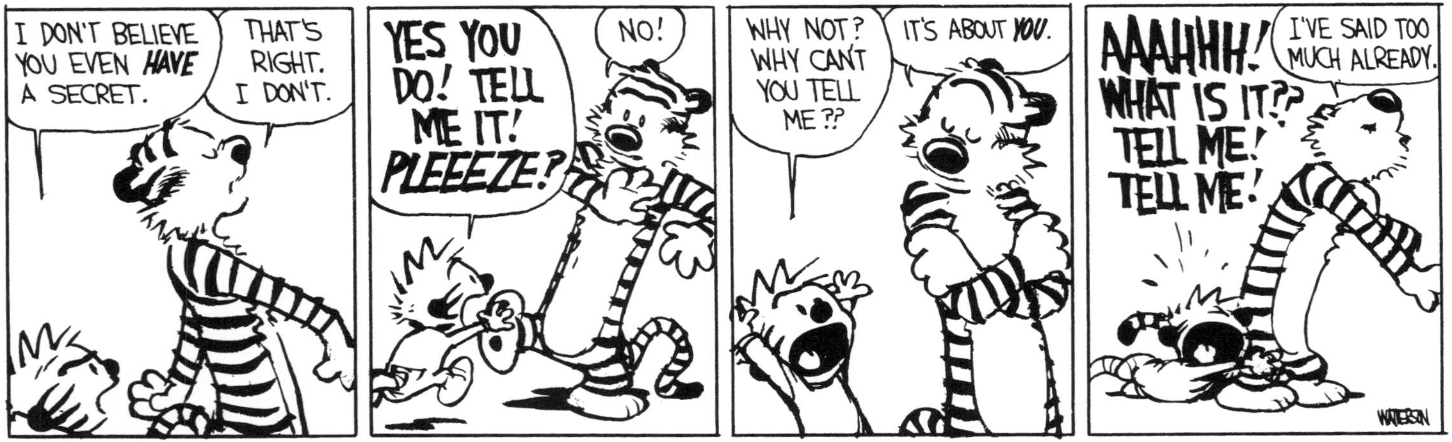
I DON'T BELIEVE YOU EVEN *HAVE* A SECRET.
THAT'S RIGHT. I DON'T.
YES YOU DO! TELL ME IT! *PLEEEZE?*
NO!
WHY NOT? WHY CAN'T YOU TELL ME??
IT'S ABOUT *YOU*.
AAAHHH! WHAT IS IT?? TELL ME! TELL ME!
I'VE SAID TOO MUCH ALREADY.

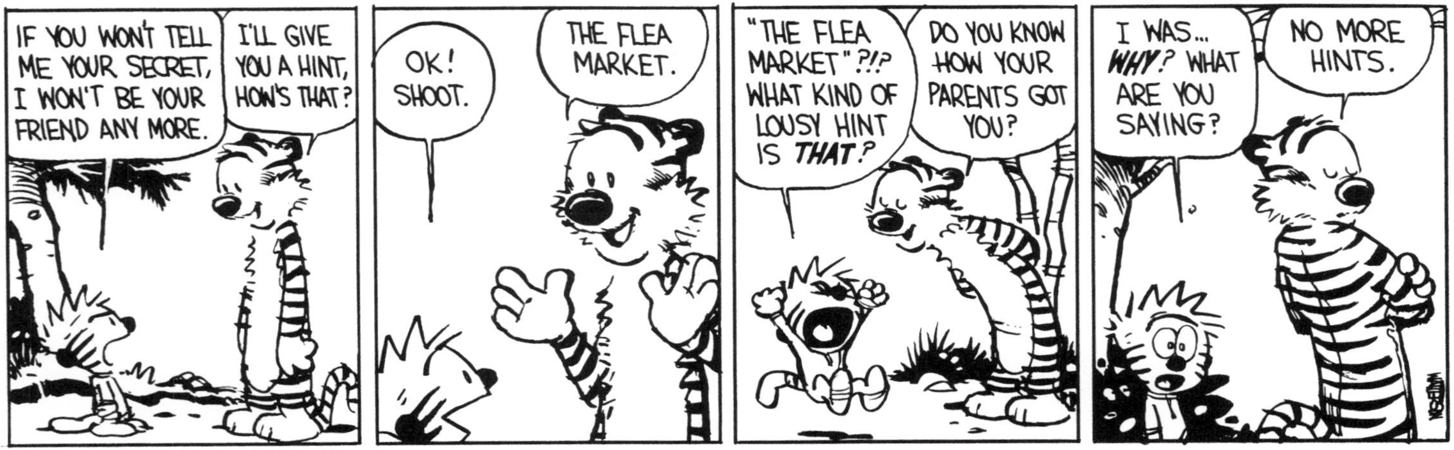
IF YOU WON'T TELL ME YOUR SECRET, I WON'T BE YOUR FRIEND ANY MORE.
I'LL GIVE YOU A HINT, HOW'S THAT?
OK! SHOOT.
THE FLEA MARKET.
"THE FLEA MARKET"?!? WHAT KIND OF LOUSY HINT IS *THAT*?
DO YOU KNOW HOW YOUR PARENTS GOT YOU?
I WAS... *WHY?* WHAT ARE YOU SAYING?
NO MORE HINTS.

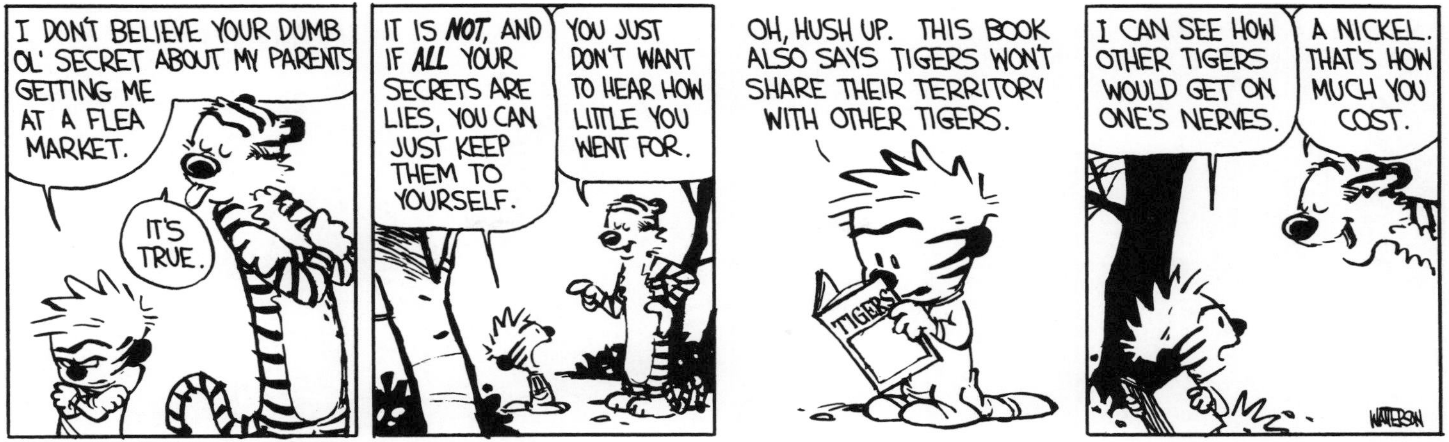
I DON'T BELIEVE YOUR DUMB OL' SECRET ABOUT MY PARENTS GETTING ME AT A FLEA MARKET.
IT'S TRUE.
IT IS NOT, AND IF ALL YOUR SECRETS ARE LIES, YOU CAN JUST KEEP THEM TO YOURSELF.
YOU JUST DON'T WANT TO HEAR HOW LITTLE YOU WENT FOR.
OH, HUSH UP. THIS BOOK ALSO SAYS TIGERS WON'T SHARE THEIR TERRITORY WITH OTHER TIGERS.
TIGERS
I CAN SEE HOW OTHER TIGERS WOULD GET ON ONE'S NERVES.
A NICKEL. THAT'S HOW MUCH YOU COST.
WATTERSON

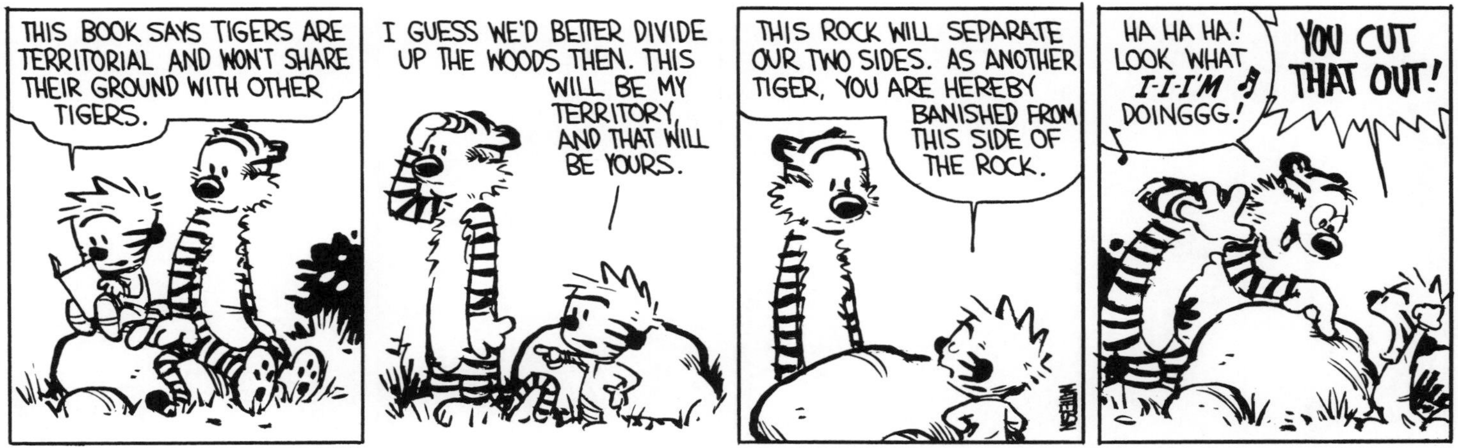
THIS BOOK SAYS TIGERS ARE TERRITORIAL AND WON'T SHARE THEIR GROUND WITH OTHER TIGERS.
I GUESS WE'D BETTER DIVIDE UP THE WOODS THEN. THIS WILL BE MY TERRITORY, AND THAT WILL BE YOURS.
THIS ROCK WILL SEPARATE OUR TWO SIDES. AS ANOTHER TIGER, YOU ARE HEREBY BANISHED FROM THIS SIDE OF THE ROCK.
HA HA HA! LOOK WHAT I-I-I'M DOINGGG!
YOU CUT THAT OUT!

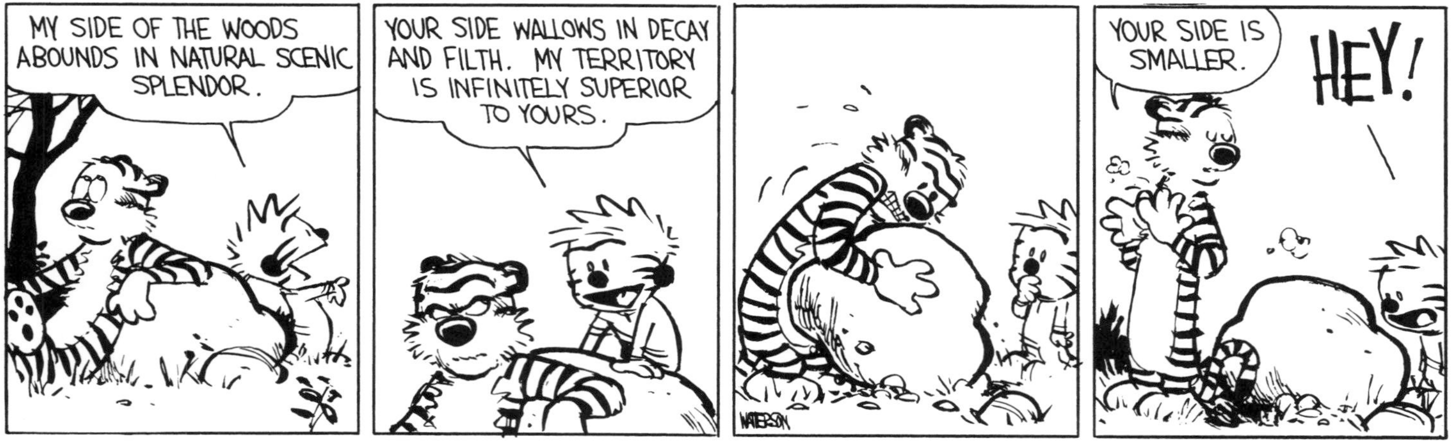
MY SIDE OF THE WOODS ABOUNDS IN NATURAL SCENIC SPLENDOR.
YOUR SIDE WALLOWS IN DECAY AND FILTH. MY TERRITORY IS INFINITELY SUPERIOR TO YOURS.
YOUR SIDE IS SMALLER.
HEY!

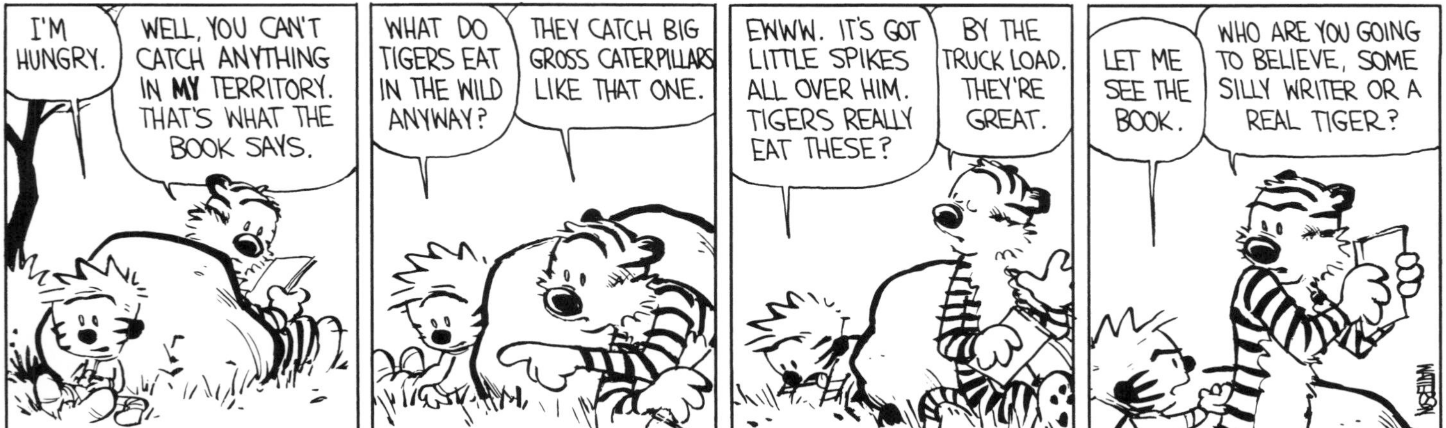
I'M HUNGRY.
WELL, YOU CAN'T CATCH ANYTHING IN **MY** TERRITORY. THAT'S WHAT THE BOOK SAYS.
WHAT DO TIGERS EAT IN THE WILD ANYWAY?
THEY CATCH BIG GROSS CATERPILLARS LIKE THAT ONE.
EWWW. IT'S GOT LITTLE SPIKES ALL OVER HIM. TIGERS REALLY EAT THESE?
BY THE TRUCK LOAD. THEY'RE GREAT.
LET ME SEE THE BOOK.
WHO ARE YOU GOING TO BELIEVE, SOME SILLY WRITER OR A REAL TIGER?

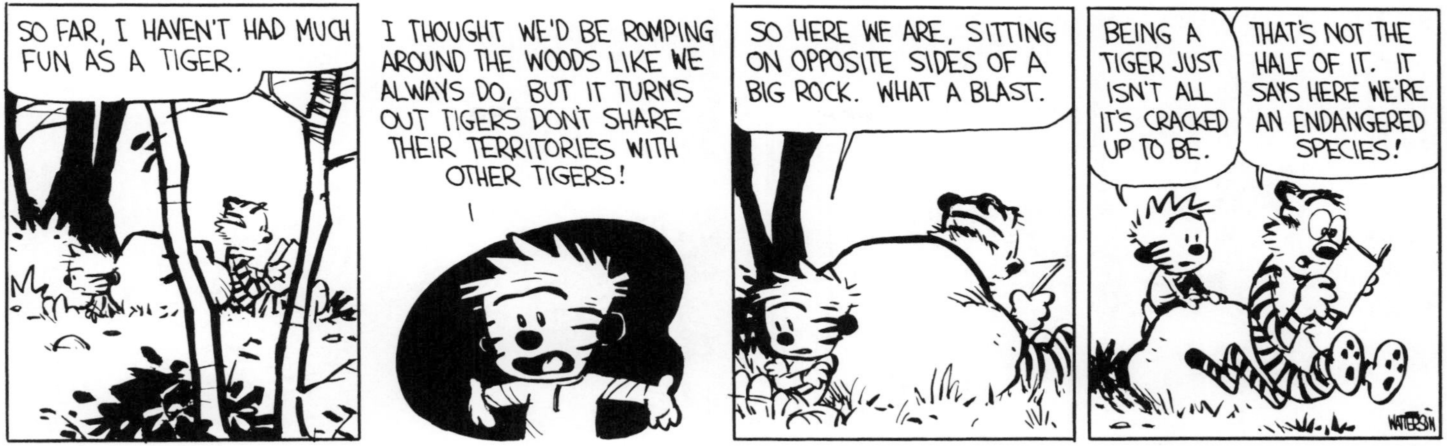
SO FAR, I HAVEN'T HAD MUCH FUN AS A TIGER.
I THOUGHT WE'D BE ROMPING AROUND THE WOODS LIKE WE ALWAYS DO, BUT IT TURNS OUT TIGERS DON'T SHARE THEIR TERRITORIES WITH OTHER TIGERS!
SO HERE WE ARE, SITTING ON OPPOSITE SIDES OF A BIG ROCK. WHAT A BLAST.
BEING A TIGER JUST ISN'T ALL IT'S CRACKED UP TO BE.
THAT'S NOT THE HALF OF IT. IT SAYS HERE WE'RE AN ENDANGERED SPECIES!
WATTERSON

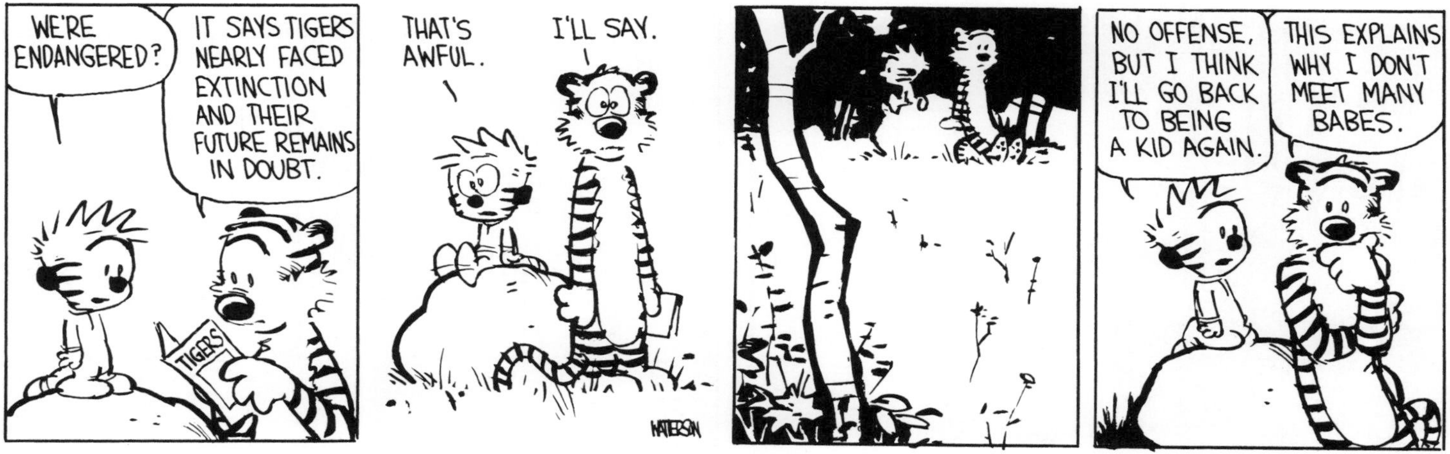
WE'RE ENDANGERED?
IT SAYS TIGERS NEARLY FACED EXTINCTION AND THEIR FUTURE REMAINS IN DOUBT.
TIGERS
THAT'S AWFUL.
I'LL SAY.
WATTERSON
NO OFFENSE, BUT I THINK I'LL GO BACK TO BEING A KID AGAIN.
THIS EXPLAINS WHY I DON'T MEET MANY BABES.

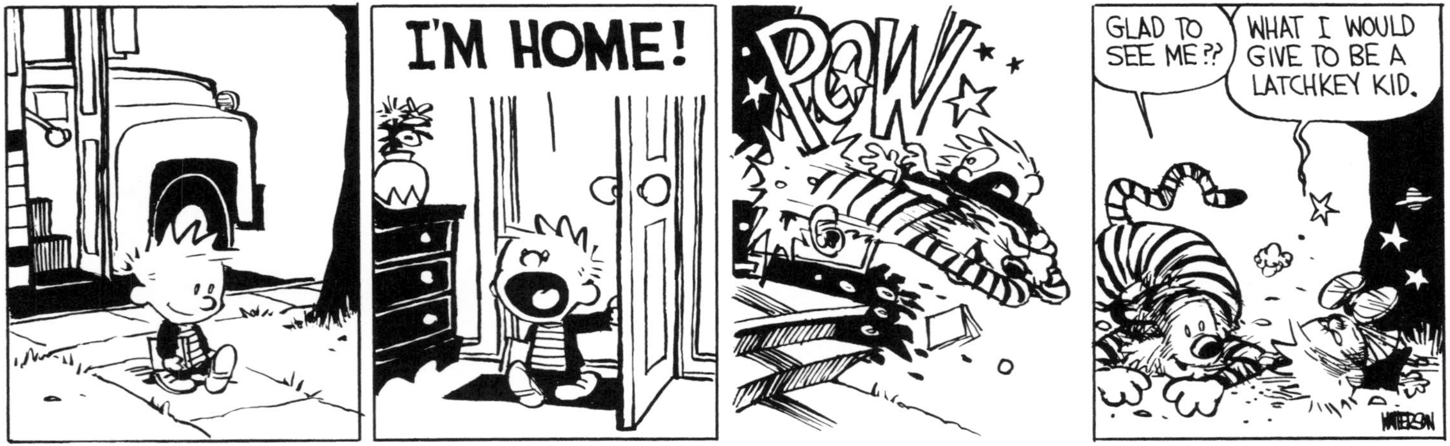
I'M HOME!
POW
GLAD TO SEE ME??
WHAT I WOULD GIVE TO BE A LATCHKEY KID.
WATTERSON

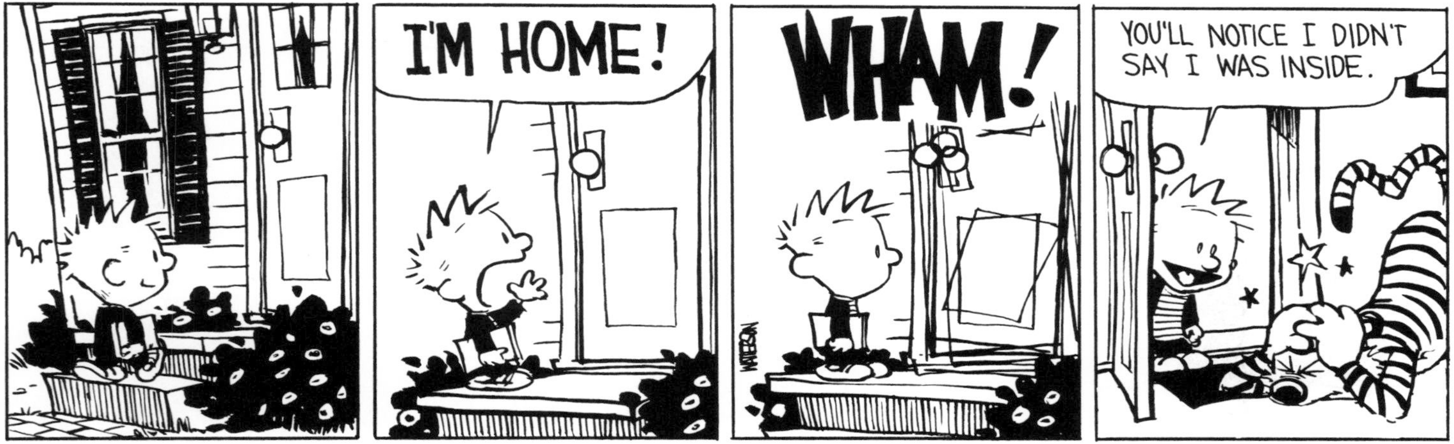
I'M HOME!
WATTERSON
WHAM!
YOU'LL NOTICE I DIDN'T SAY I WAS INSIDE.

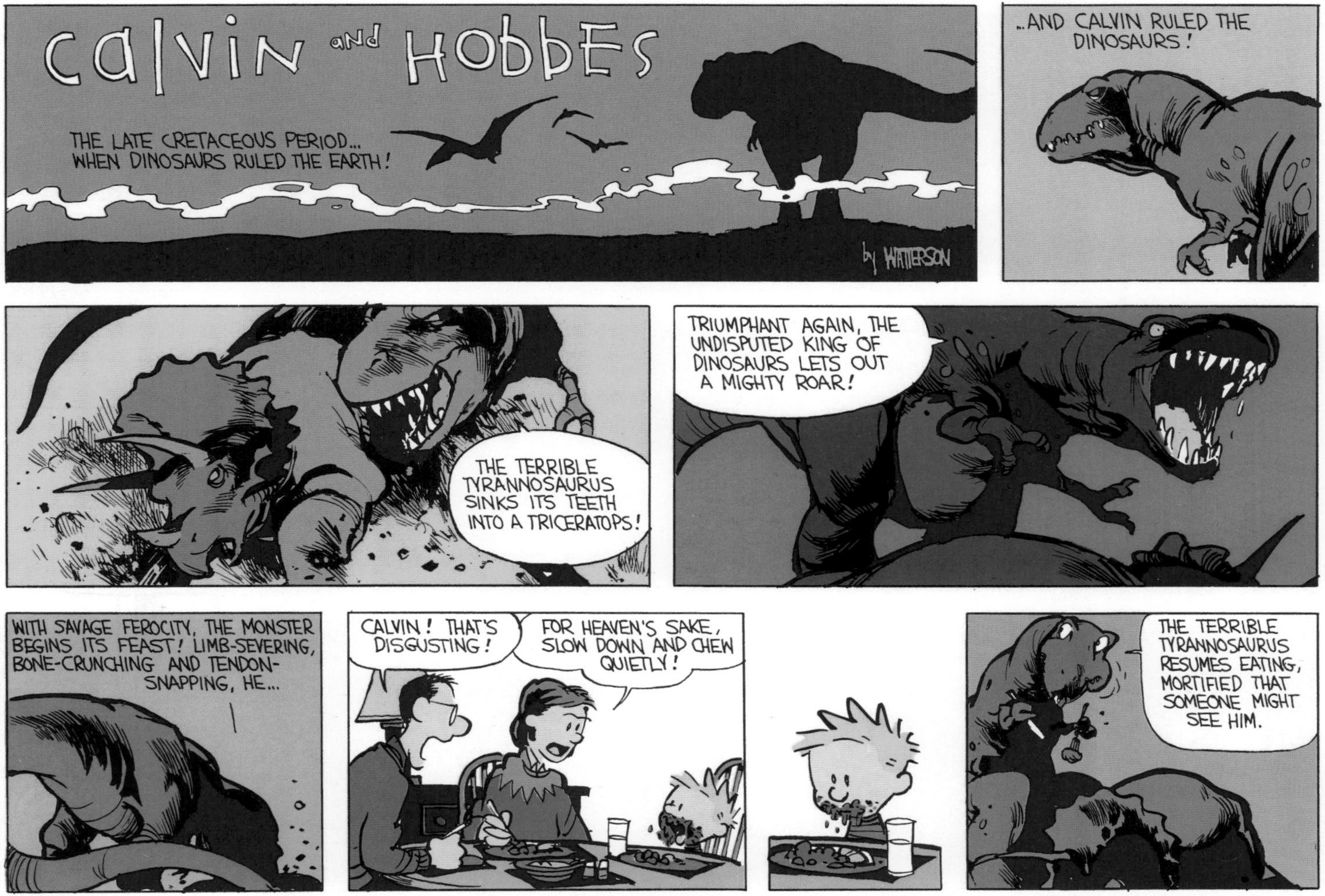
Calvin and HOBBES
THE LATE CRETACEOUS PERIOD... WHEN DINOSAURS RULED THE EARTH!
by WATTERSON
..AND CALVIN RULED THE DINOSAURS!
THE TERRIBLE TYRANNOSAURUS SINKS ITS TEETH INTO A TRICERATOPS!
TRIUMPHANT AGAIN, THE UNDISPUTED KING OF DINOSAURS LETS OUT A MIGHTY ROAR!
WITH SAVAGE FEROCITY, THE MONSTER BEGINS ITS FEAST! LIMB-SEVERING, BONE-CRUNCHING AND TENDON-SNAPPING, HE...
CALVIN! THAT'S DISGUSTING!
FOR HEAVEN'S SAKE, SLOW DOWN AND CHEW QUIETLY!
THE TERRIBLE TYRANNOSAURUS RESUMES EATING, MORTIFIED THAT SOMEONE MIGHT SEE HIM.

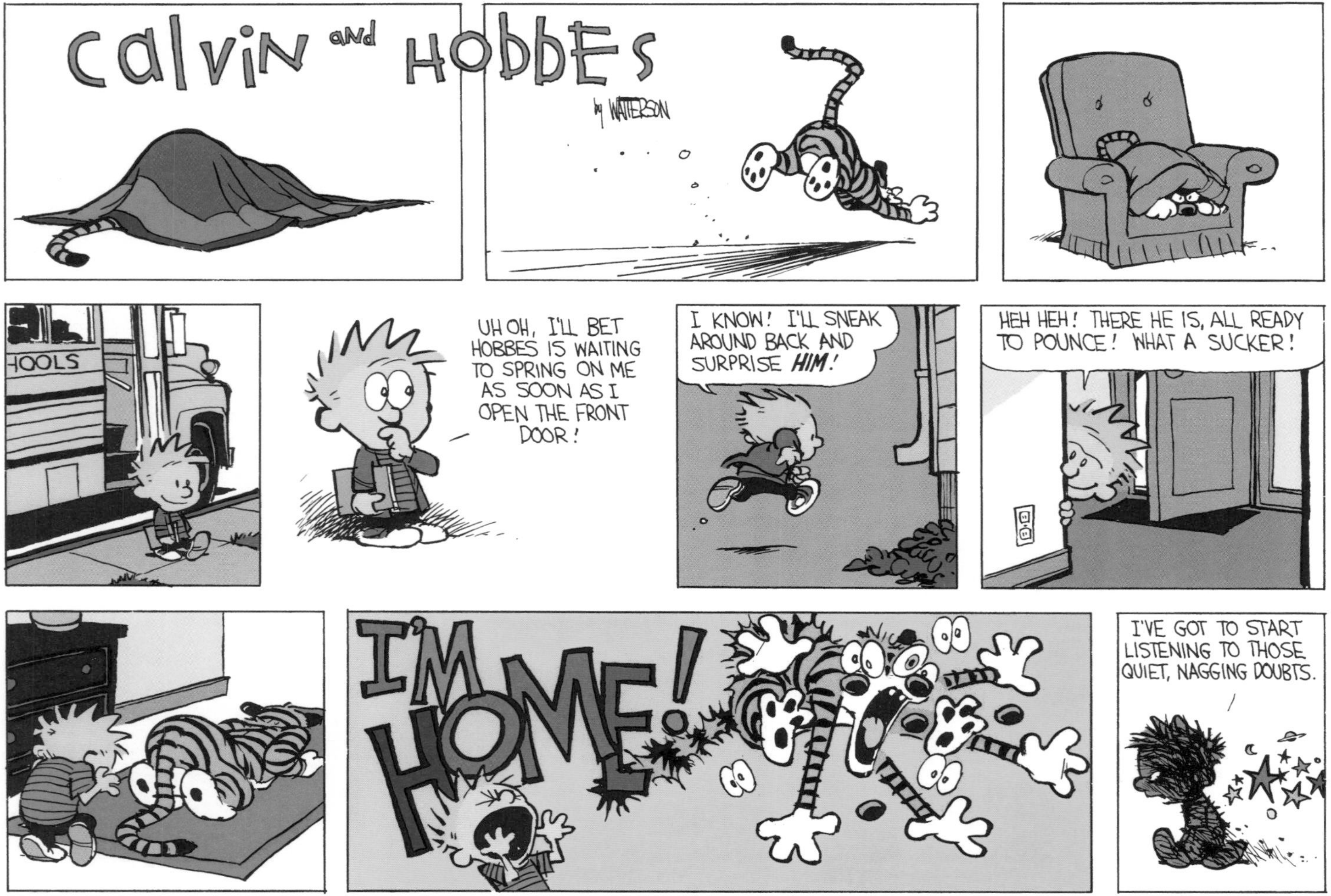
Calvin and HOBBES
by WATTERSON
HOOLS
UH OH, I'LL BET HOBBES IS WAITING TO SPRING ON ME AS SOON AS I OPEN THE FRONT DOOR!
I KNOW! I'LL SNEAK AROUND BACK AND SURPRISE HIM!
HEH HEH! THERE HE IS, ALL READY TO POUNCE! WHAT A SUCKER!
I'M HOME!
I'VE GOT TO START LISTENING TO THOSE QUIET, NAGGING DOUBTS.

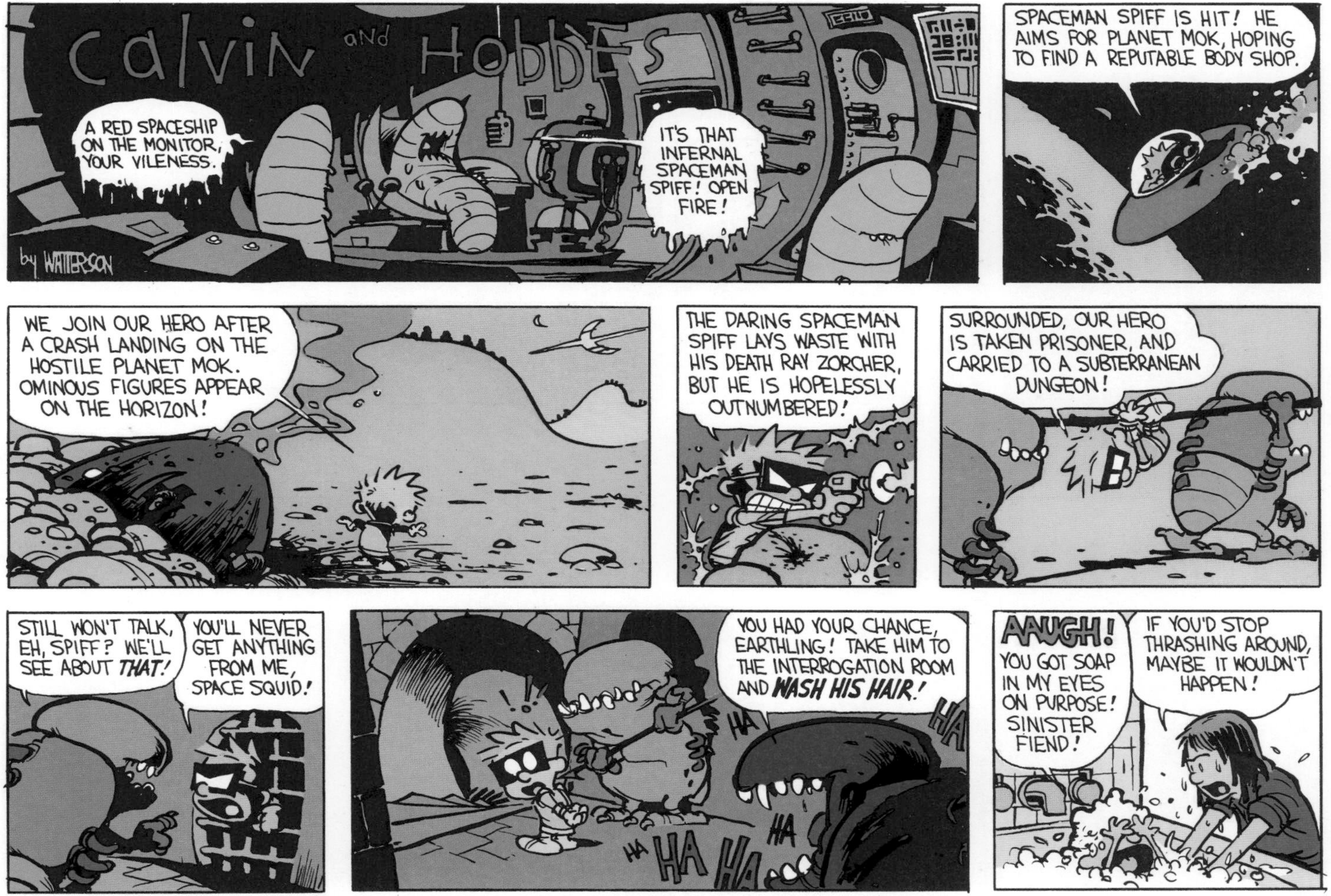
Calvin and Hobbes
by WATTERSON
A RED SPACESHIP ON THE MONITOR, YOUR VILENESS.
IT'S THAT INFERNAL SPACEMAN SPIFF! OPEN FIRE!
SPACEMAN SPIFF IS HIT! HE AIMS FOR PLANET MOK, HOPING TO FIND A REPUTABLE BODY SHOP.
WE JOIN OUR HERO AFTER A CRASH LANDING ON THE HOSTILE PLANET MOK. OMINOUS FIGURES APPEAR ON THE HORIZON!
THE DARING SPACEMAN SPIFF LAYS WASTE WITH HIS DEATH RAY ZORCHER, BUT HE IS HOPELESSLY OUTNUMBERED!
SURROUNDED, OUR HERO IS TAKEN PRISONER, AND CARRIED TO A SUBTERRANEAN DUNGEON!
STILL WON'T TALK, EH, SPIFF? WE'LL SEE ABOUT *THAT*!
YOU'LL NEVER GET ANYTHING FROM ME, SPACE SQUID!
YOU HAD YOUR CHANCE, EARTHLING! TAKE HIM TO THE INTERROGATION ROOM AND ***WASH HIS HAIR***!
HA HA HA HA HA HA HA
AAUGH!
YOU GOT SOAP IN MY EYES ON PURPOSE! SINISTER FIEND!
IF YOU'D STOP THRASHING AROUND, MAYBE IT WOULDN'T HAPPEN!

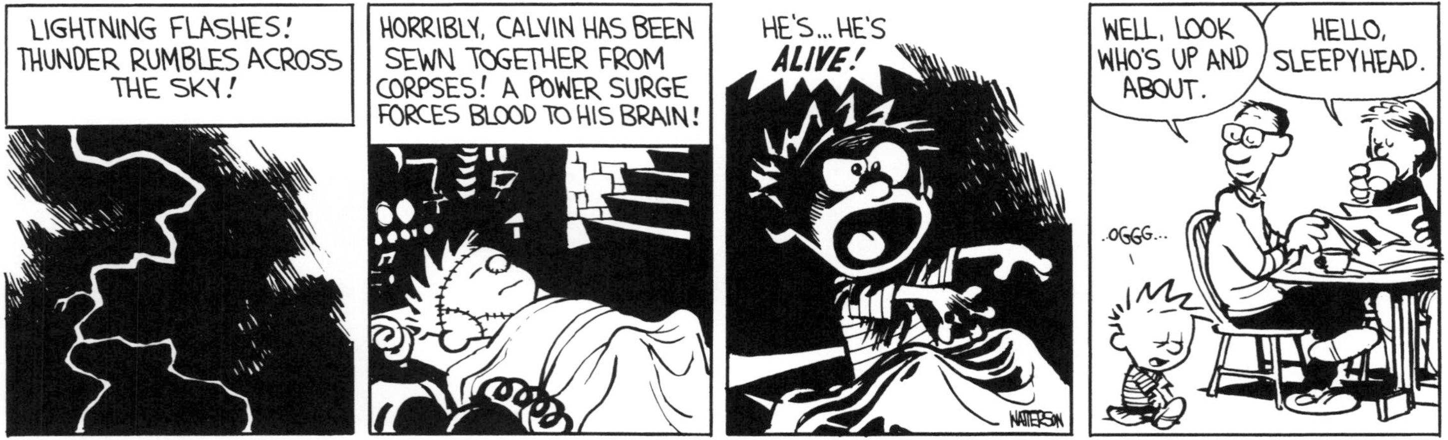
LIGHTNING FLASHES! THUNDER RUMBLES ACROSS THE SKY!
HORRIBLY, CALVIN HAS BEEN SEWN TOGETHER FROM CORPSES! A POWER SURGE FORCES BLOOD TO HIS BRAIN!
HE'S... HE'S ALIVE!
WATTERSON
WELL, LOOK WHO'S UP AND ABOUT.
HELLO, SLEEPYHEAD.
..OGGG..

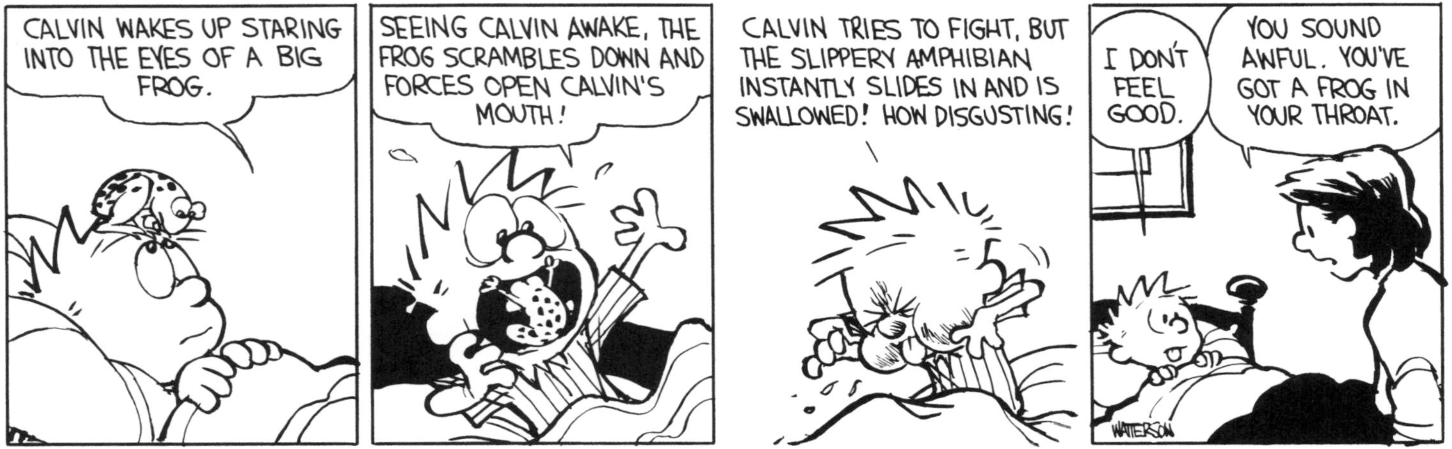
CALVIN WAKES UP STARING INTO THE EYES OF A BIG FROG.
SEEING CALVIN AWAKE, THE FROG SCRAMBLES DOWN AND FORCES OPEN CALVIN'S MOUTH!
CALVIN TRIES TO FIGHT, BUT THE SLIPPERY AMPHIBIAN INSTANTLY SLIDES IN AND IS SWALLOWED! HOW DISGUSTING!
I DON'T FEEL GOOD.
YOU SOUND AWFUL. YOU'VE GOT A FROG IN YOUR THROAT.
WATTERSON

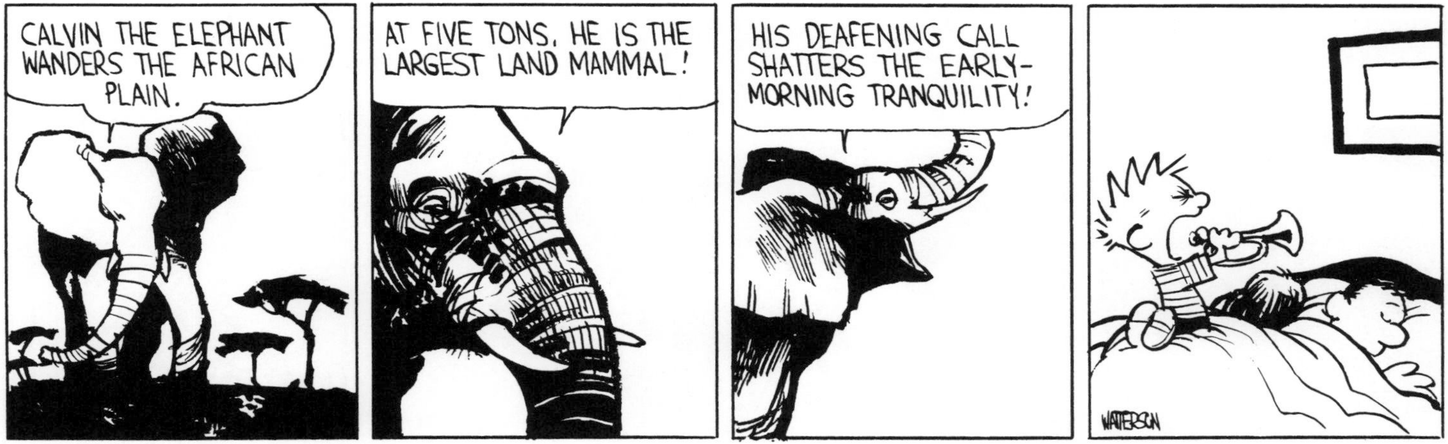
CALVIN THE ELEPHANT WANDERS THE AFRICAN PLAIN.
AT FIVE TONS, HE IS THE LARGEST LAND MAMMAL!
HIS DEAFENING CALL SHATTERS THE EARLY-MORNING TRANQUILITY!

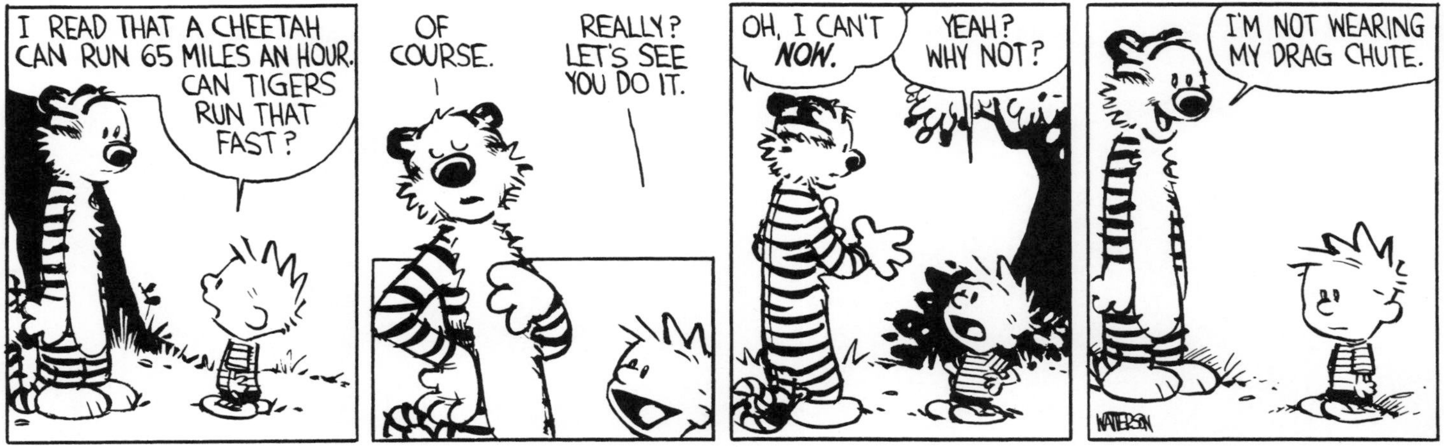
I READ THAT A CHEETAH CAN RUN 65 MILES AN HOUR.
CAN TIGERS RUN THAT FAST?
OF COURSE.
REALLY? LET'S SEE YOU DO IT.
OH, I CAN'T *NOW*.
YEAH? WHY NOT?
I'M NOT WEARING MY DRAG CHUTE.

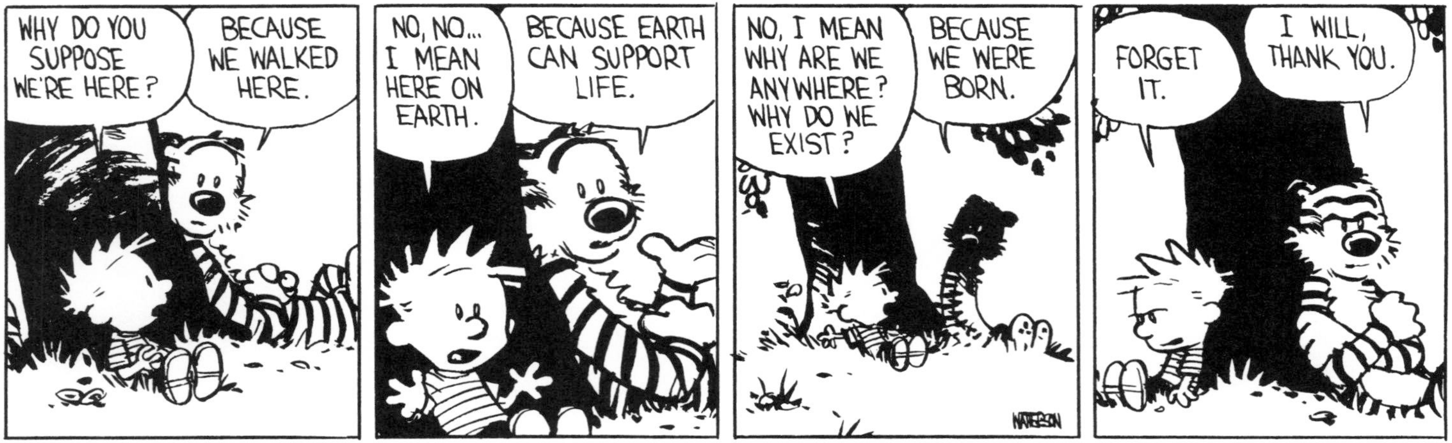
WHY DO YOU SUPPOSE WE'RE HERE?
BECAUSE WE WALKED HERE.
NO, NO... I MEAN HERE ON EARTH.
BECAUSE EARTH CAN SUPPORT LIFE.
NO, I MEAN WHY ARE WE ANYWHERE? WHY DO WE EXIST?
BECAUSE WE WERE BORN.
FORGET IT.
I WILL, THANK YOU.

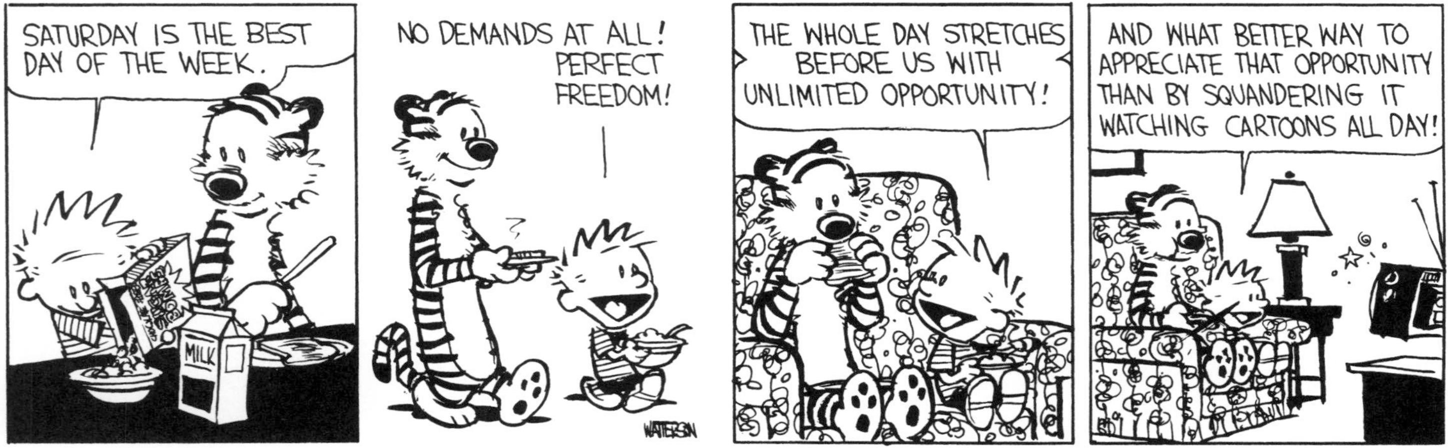
SATURDAY IS THE BEST DAY OF THE WEEK.
MILK
NO DEMANDS AT ALL! PERFECT FREEDOM!
THE WHOLE DAY STRETCHES BEFORE US WITH UNLIMITED OPPORTUNITY!
AND WHAT BETTER WAY TO APPRECIATE THAT OPPORTUNITY THAN BY SQUANDERING IT WATCHING CARTOONS ALL DAY!

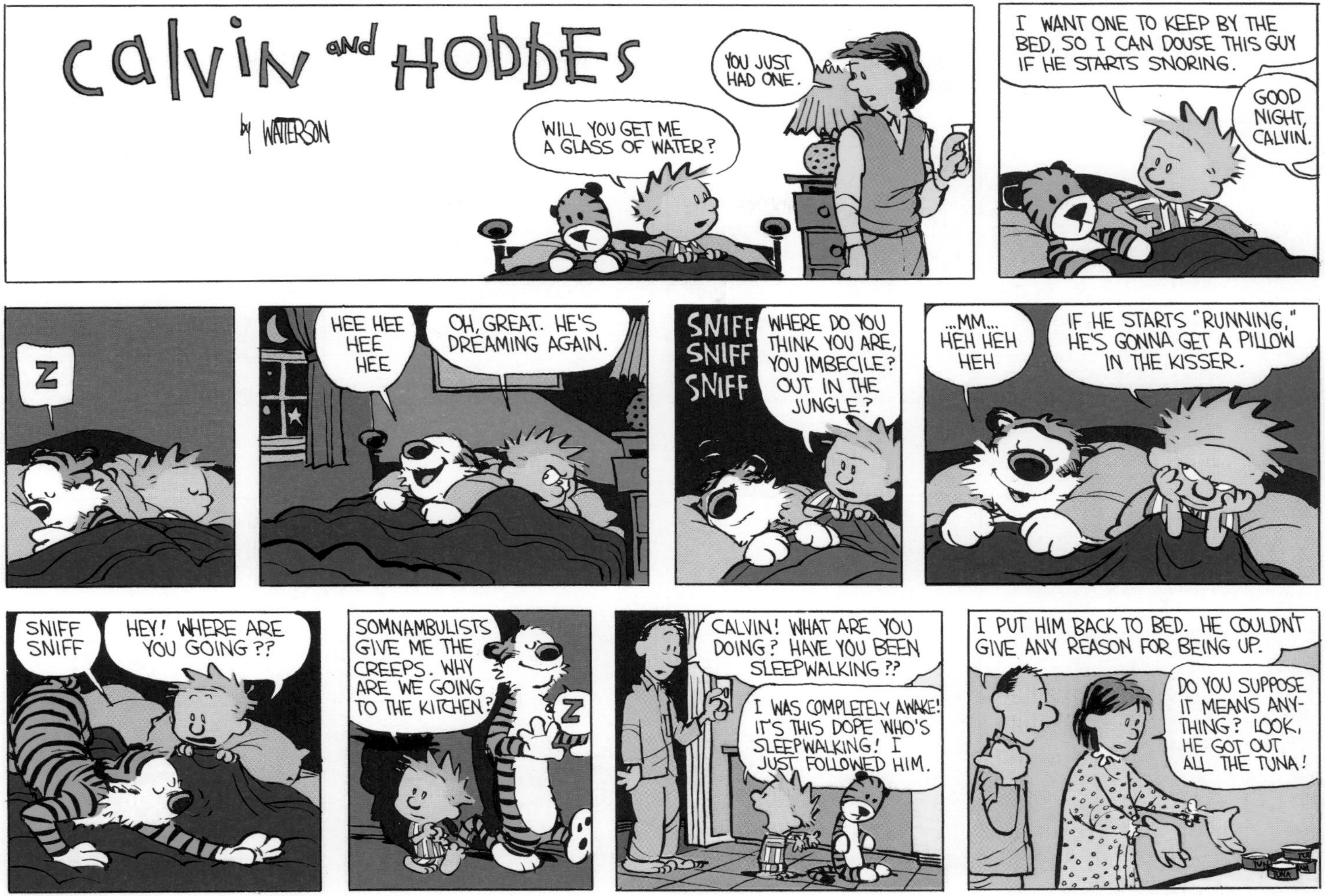

CALVIN AND HOBBES
by WATTERSON
WILL YOU GET ME A GLASS OF WATER?
YOU JUST HAD ONE.
I WANT ONE TO KEEP BY THE BED, SO I CAN DOUSE THIS GUY IF HE STARTS SNORING.
GOOD NIGHT, CALVIN.
Z
HEE HEE HEE HEE
OH, GREAT. HE'S DREAMING AGAIN.
SNIFF SNIFF SNIFF
WHERE DO YOU THINK YOU ARE, YOU IMBECILE? OUT IN THE JUNGLE?
...MM... HEH HEH HEH
IF HE STARTS "RUNNING," HE'S GONNA GET A PILLOW IN THE KISSER.
SNIFF SNIFF
HEY! WHERE ARE YOU GOING??
SOMNAMBULISTS GIVE ME THE CREEPS. WHY ARE WE GOING TO THE KITCHEN?
Z
CALVIN! WHAT ARE YOU DOING? HAVE YOU BEEN SLEEPWALKING??
I WAS COMPLETELY AWAKE! IT'S THIS DOPE WHO'S SLEEPWALKING! I JUST FOLLOWED HIM.
I PUT HIM BACK TO BED. HE COULDN'T GIVE ANY REASON FOR BEING UP.
DO YOU SUPPOSE IT MEANS ANYTHING? LOOK, HE GOT OUT ALL THE TUNA!

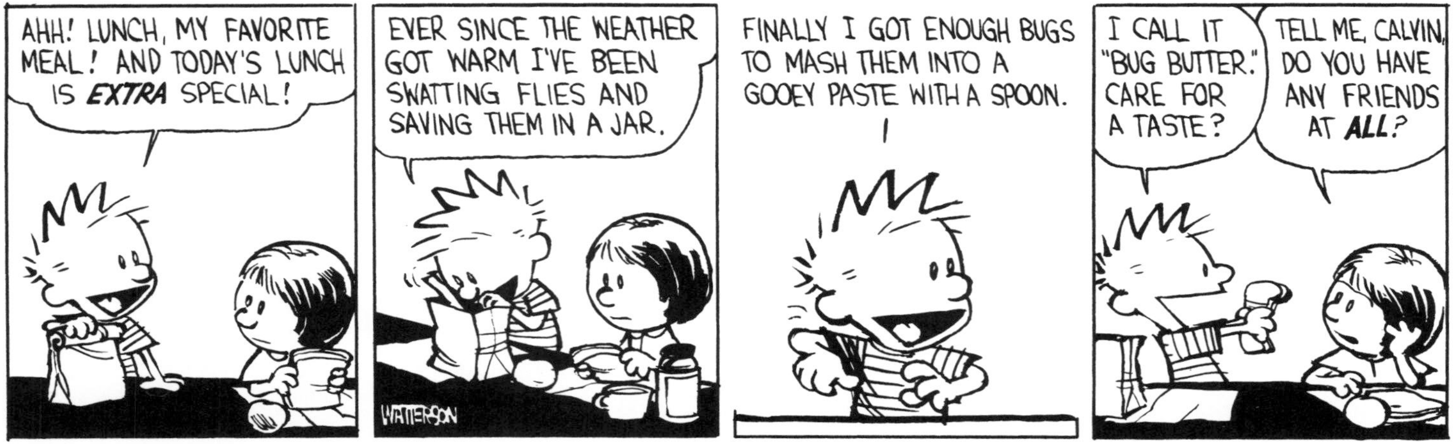
AHH! LUNCH, MY FAVORITE MEAL! AND TODAY'S LUNCH IS EXTRA SPECIAL!
EVER SINCE THE WEATHER GOT WARM I'VE BEEN SWATTING FLIES AND SAVING THEM IN A JAR.
WATTERSON
FINALLY I GOT ENOUGH BUGS TO MASH THEM INTO A GOOEY PASTE WITH A SPOON.
I CALL IT "BUG BUTTER." CARE FOR A TASTE?
TELL ME, CALVIN, DO YOU HAVE ANY FRIENDS AT ALL?

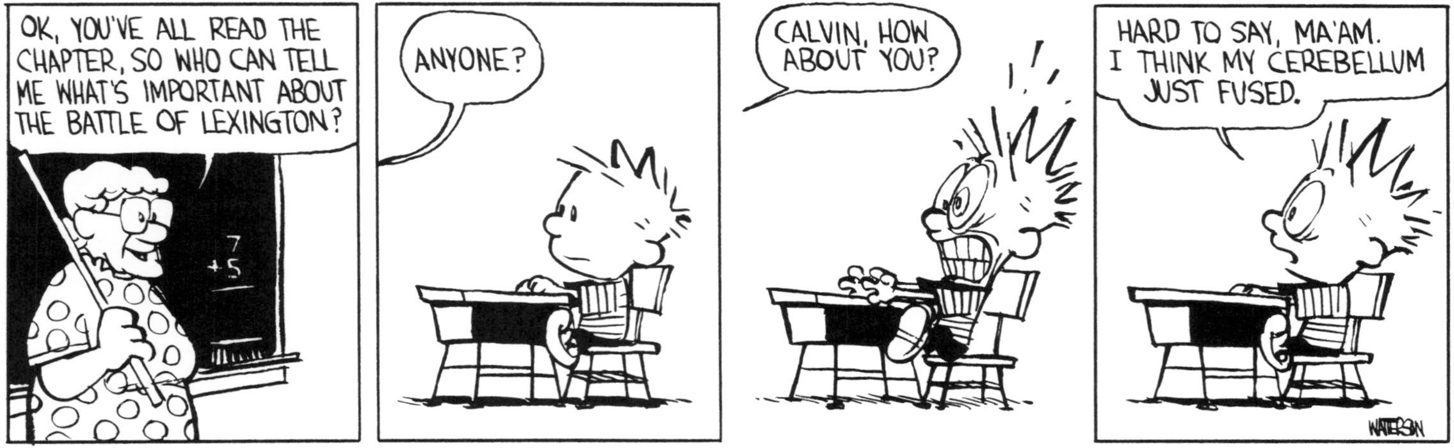
OK, YOU'VE ALL READ THE CHAPTER, SO WHO CAN TELL ME WHAT'S IMPORTANT ABOUT THE BATTLE OF LEXINGTON?
7
+5
ANYONE?
CALVIN, HOW ABOUT YOU?
HARD TO SAY, MA'AM. I THINK MY CEREBELLUM JUST FUSED.
WATTERSON

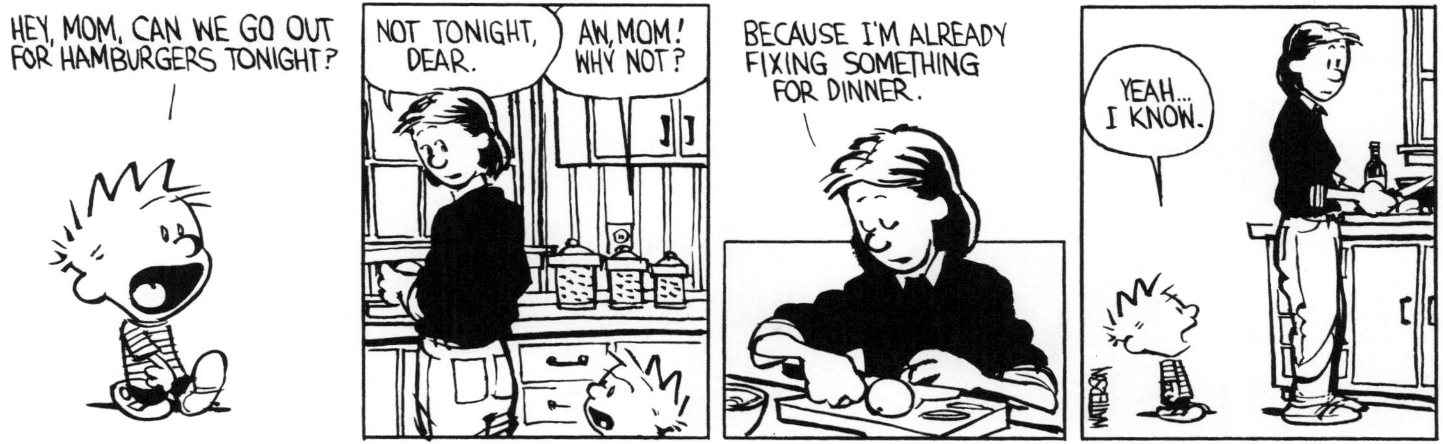
HEY, MOM, CAN WE GO OUT FOR HAMBURGERS TONIGHT?
NOT TONIGHT, DEAR.
AW, MOM! WHY NOT?
BECAUSE I'M ALREADY FIXING SOMETHING FOR DINNER.
YEAH... I KNOW.
WATTERSON

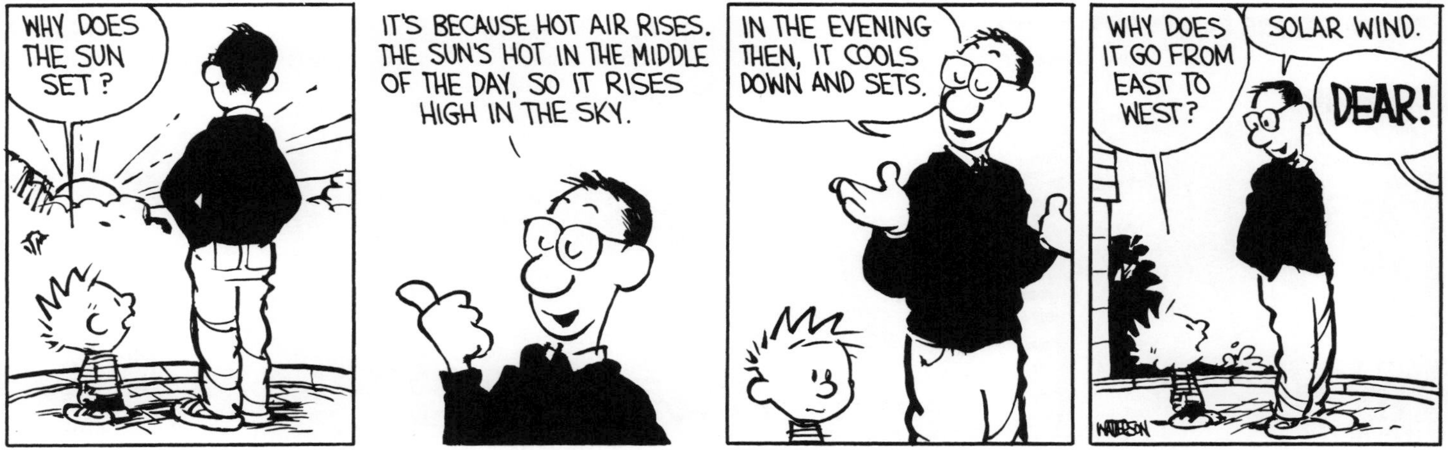
WHY DOES THE SUN SET?
IT'S BECAUSE HOT AIR RISES. THE SUN'S HOT IN THE MIDDLE OF THE DAY, SO IT RISES HIGH IN THE SKY.
IN THE EVENING THEN, IT COOLS DOWN AND SETS.
WHY DOES IT GO FROM EAST TO WEST?
SOLAR WIND.
DEAR!
WATTERSON

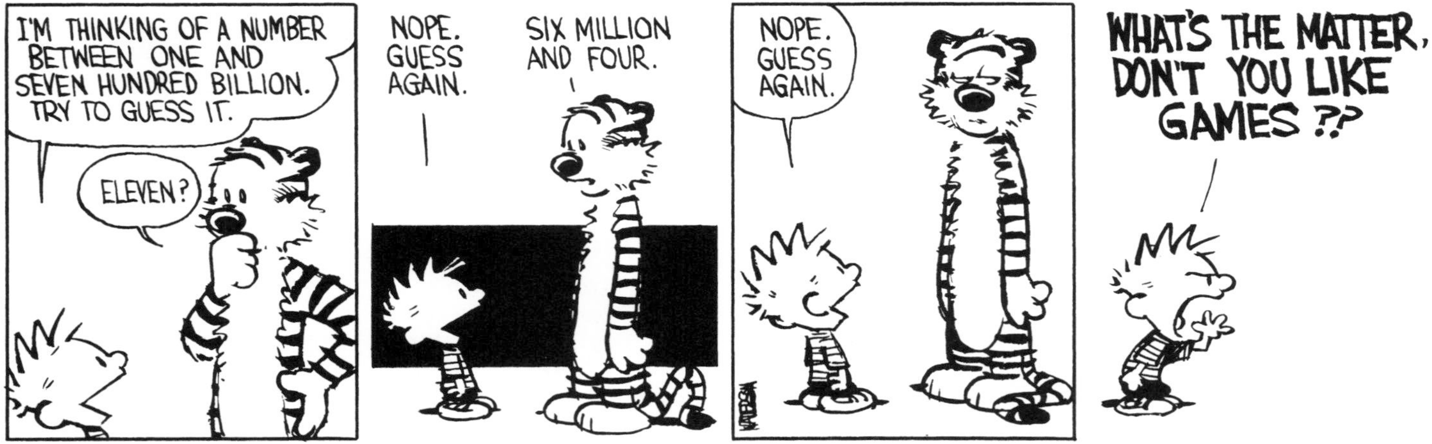
I'M THINKING OF A NUMBER BETWEEN ONE AND SEVEN HUNDRED BILLION. TRY TO GUESS IT.
ELEVEN?
NOPE. GUESS AGAIN.
SIX MILLION AND FOUR.
NOPE. GUESS AGAIN.
WHAT'S THE MATTER, DON'T YOU LIKE GAMES ??

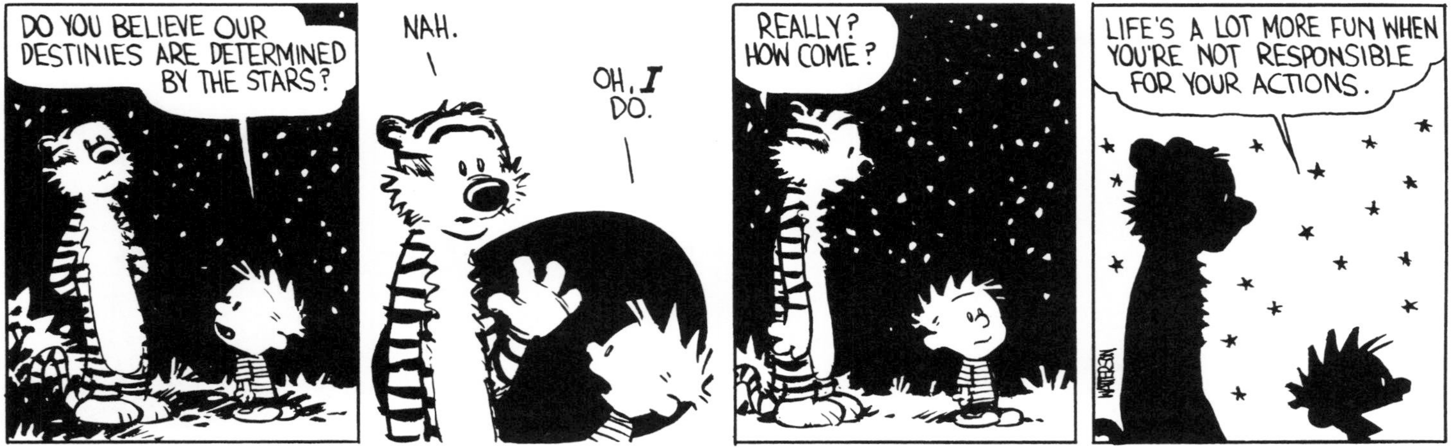
DO YOU BELIEVE OUR DESTINIES ARE DETERMINED BY THE STARS?
NAH.
OH, *I* DO.
REALLY? HOW COME?
LIFE'S A LOT MORE FUN WHEN YOU'RE NOT RESPONSIBLE FOR YOUR ACTIONS.

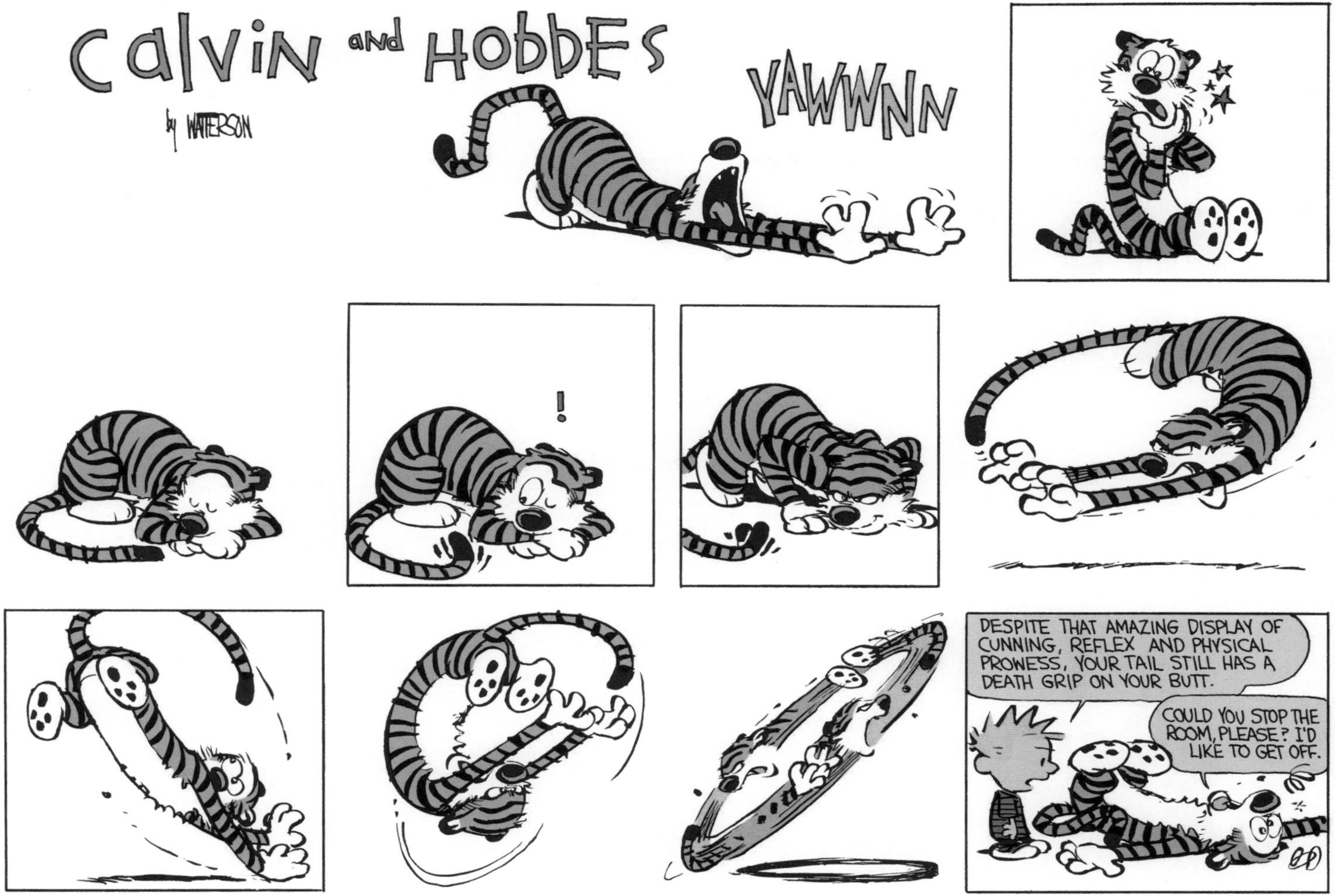
Calvin and HOBBES
by WATTERSON
YAWWNN
!
DESPITE THAT AMAZING DISPLAY OF CUNNING, REFLEX AND PHYSICAL PROWESS, YOUR TAIL STILL HAS A DEATH GRIP ON YOUR BUTT.
COULD YOU STOP THE ROOM, PLEASE? I'D LIKE TO GET OFF.

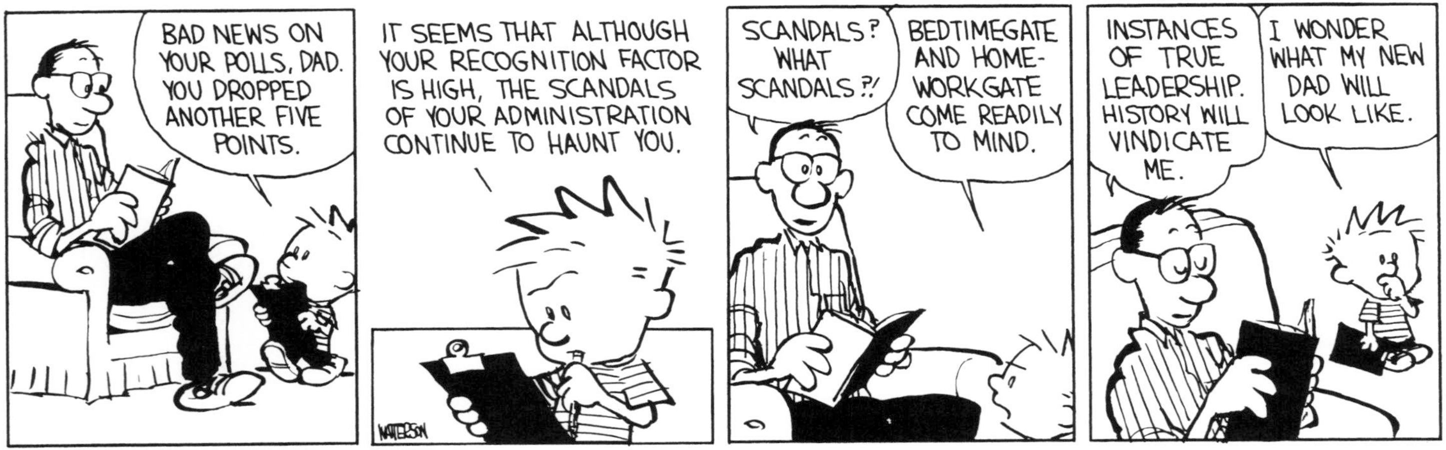
BAD NEWS ON YOUR POLLS, DAD. YOU DROPPED ANOTHER FIVE POINTS.
IT SEEMS THAT ALTHOUGH YOUR RECOGNITION FACTOR IS HIGH, THE SCANDALS OF YOUR ADMINISTRATION CONTINUE TO HAUNT YOU.
SCANDALS? WHAT SCANDALS?!
BEDTIMEGATE AND HOME-WORKGATE COME READILY TO MIND.
INSTANCES OF TRUE LEADERSHIP. HISTORY WILL VINDICATE ME.
I WONDER WHAT MY NEW DAD WILL LOOK LIKE.

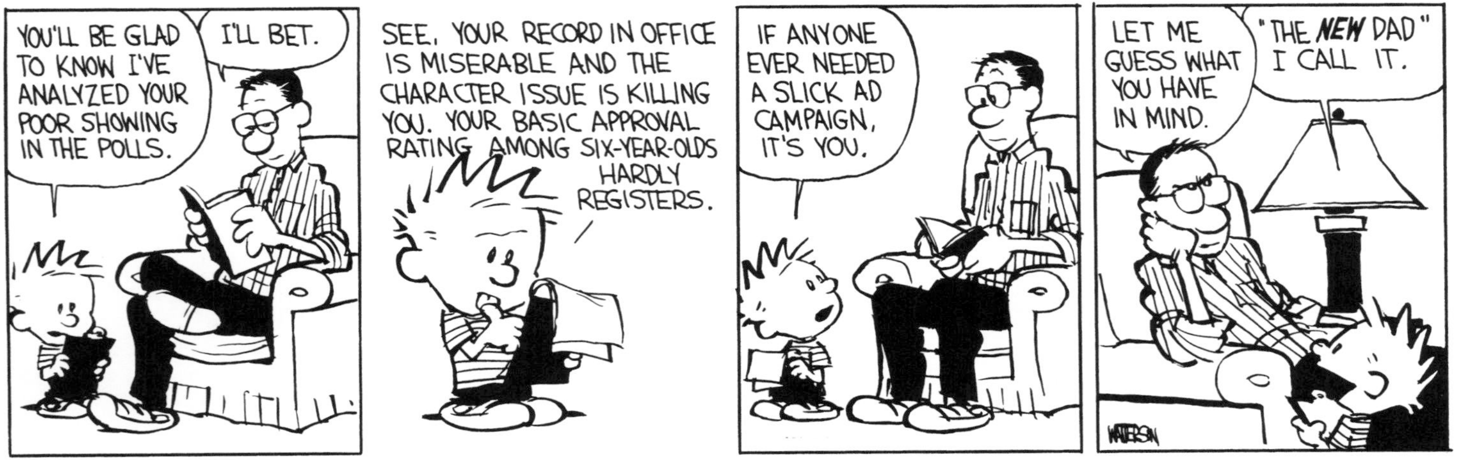
YOU'LL BE GLAD TO KNOW I'VE ANALYZED YOUR POOR SHOWING IN THE POLLS.
I'LL BET.
SEE. YOUR RECORD IN OFFICE IS MISERABLE AND THE CHARACTER ISSUE IS KILLING YOU. YOUR BASIC APPROVAL RATING AMONG SIX-YEAR-OLDS HARDLY REGISTERS.
IF ANYONE EVER NEEDED A SLICK AD CAMPAIGN, IT'S YOU.
LET ME GUESS WHAT YOU HAVE IN MIND.
"THE NEW DAD" I CALL IT.

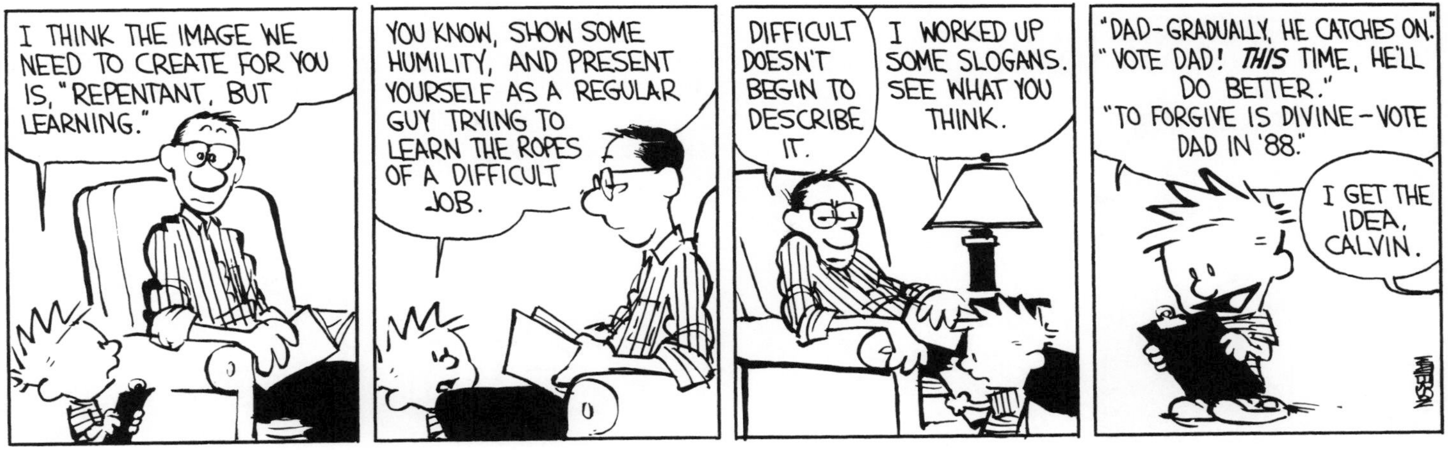
I THINK THE IMAGE WE NEED TO CREATE FOR YOU IS, "REPENTANT, BUT LEARNING."
YOU KNOW, SHOW SOME HUMILITY, AND PRESENT YOURSELF AS A REGULAR GUY TRYING TO LEARN THE ROPES OF A DIFFICULT JOB.
DIFFICULT DOESN'T BEGIN TO DESCRIBE IT.
I WORKED UP SOME SLOGANS. SEE WHAT YOU THINK.
"DAD-GRADUALLY, HE CATCHES ON." "VOTE DAD! *THIS* TIME, HE'LL DO BETTER." "TO FORGIVE IS DIVINE-VOTE DAD IN '88."
I GET THE IDEA, CALVIN.
WATTERSON

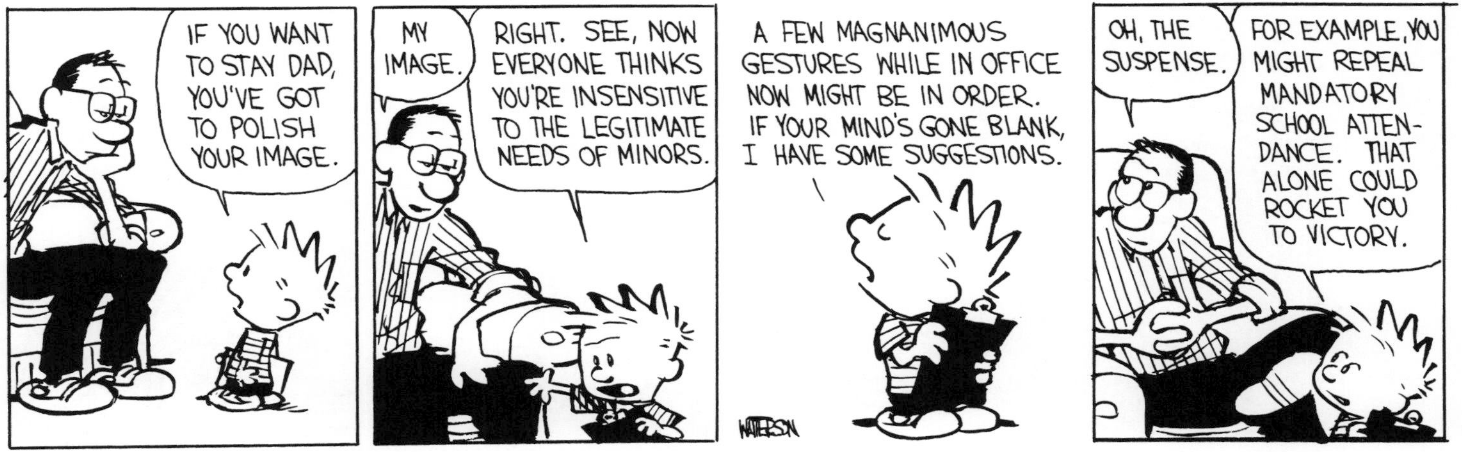
IF YOU WANT TO STAY DAD, YOU'VE GOT TO POLISH YOUR IMAGE.
MY IMAGE.
RIGHT. SEE, NOW EVERYONE THINKS YOU'RE INSENSITIVE TO THE LEGITIMATE NEEDS OF MINORS.
A FEW MAGNANIMOUS GESTURES WHILE IN OFFICE NOW MIGHT BE IN ORDER. IF YOUR MIND'S GONE BLANK, I HAVE SOME SUGGESTIONS.
WATTERSON
OH, THE SUSPENSE.
FOR EXAMPLE, YOU MIGHT REPEAL MANDATORY SCHOOL ATTENDANCE. THAT ALONE COULD ROCKET YOU TO VICTORY.

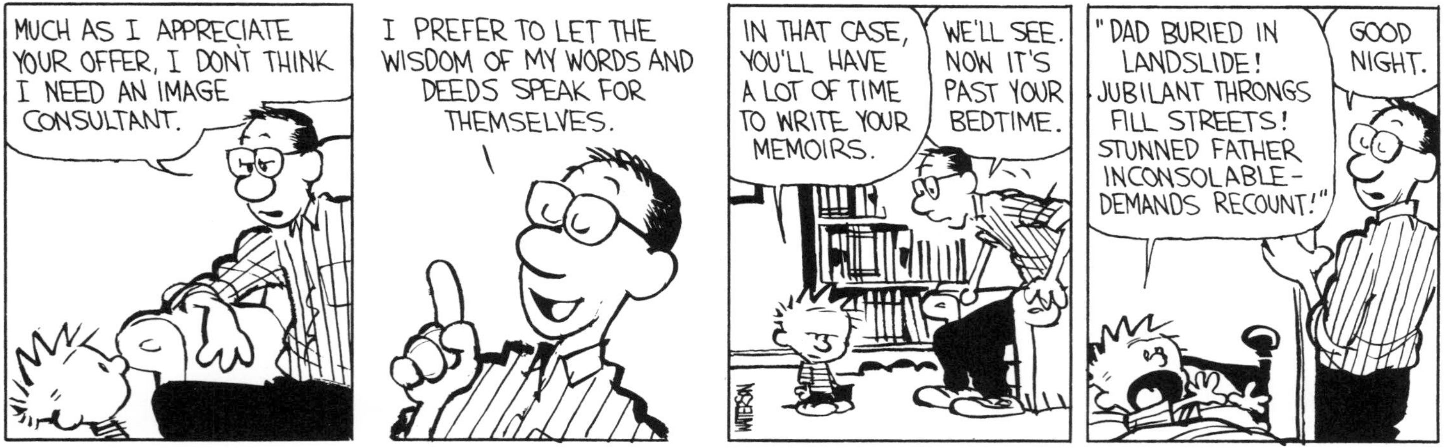
MUCH AS I APPRECIATE YOUR OFFER, I DON'T THINK I NEED AN IMAGE CONSULTANT.
I PREFER TO LET THE WISDOM OF MY WORDS AND DEEDS SPEAK FOR THEMSELVES.
IN THAT CASE, YOU'LL HAVE A LOT OF TIME TO WRITE YOUR MEMOIRS.
WE'LL SEE. NOW IT'S PAST YOUR BEDTIME.
"DAD BURIED IN LANDSLIDE! JUBILANT THRONGS FILL STREETS! STUNNED FATHER INCONSOLABLE- DEMANDS RECOUNT!"
GOOD NIGHT.

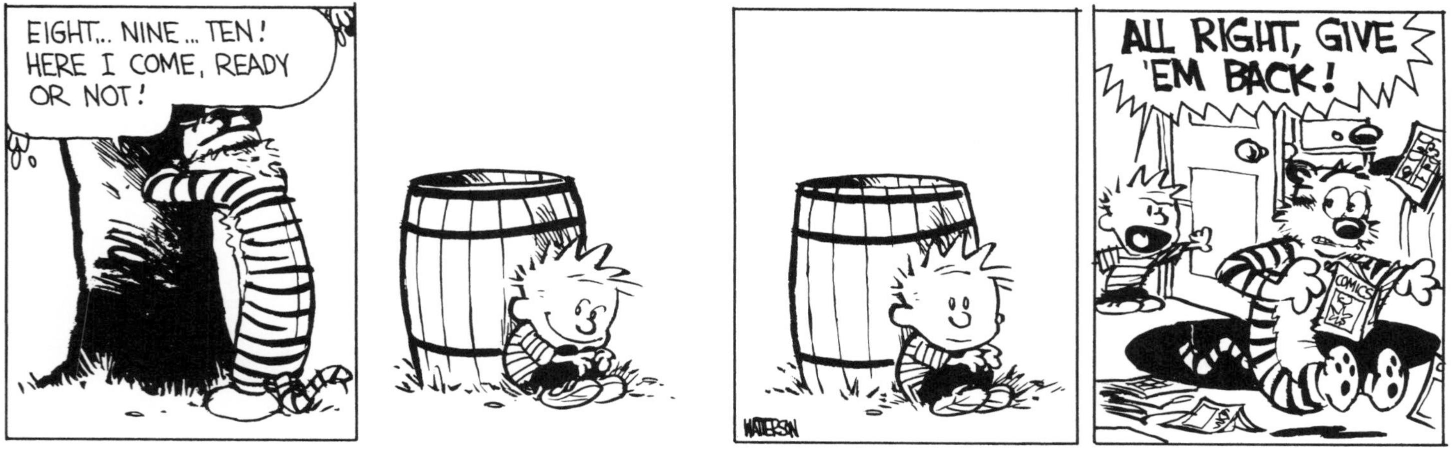
EIGHT... NINE... TEN! HERE I COME, READY OR NOT!
ALL RIGHT, GIVE 'EM BACK!
COMICS

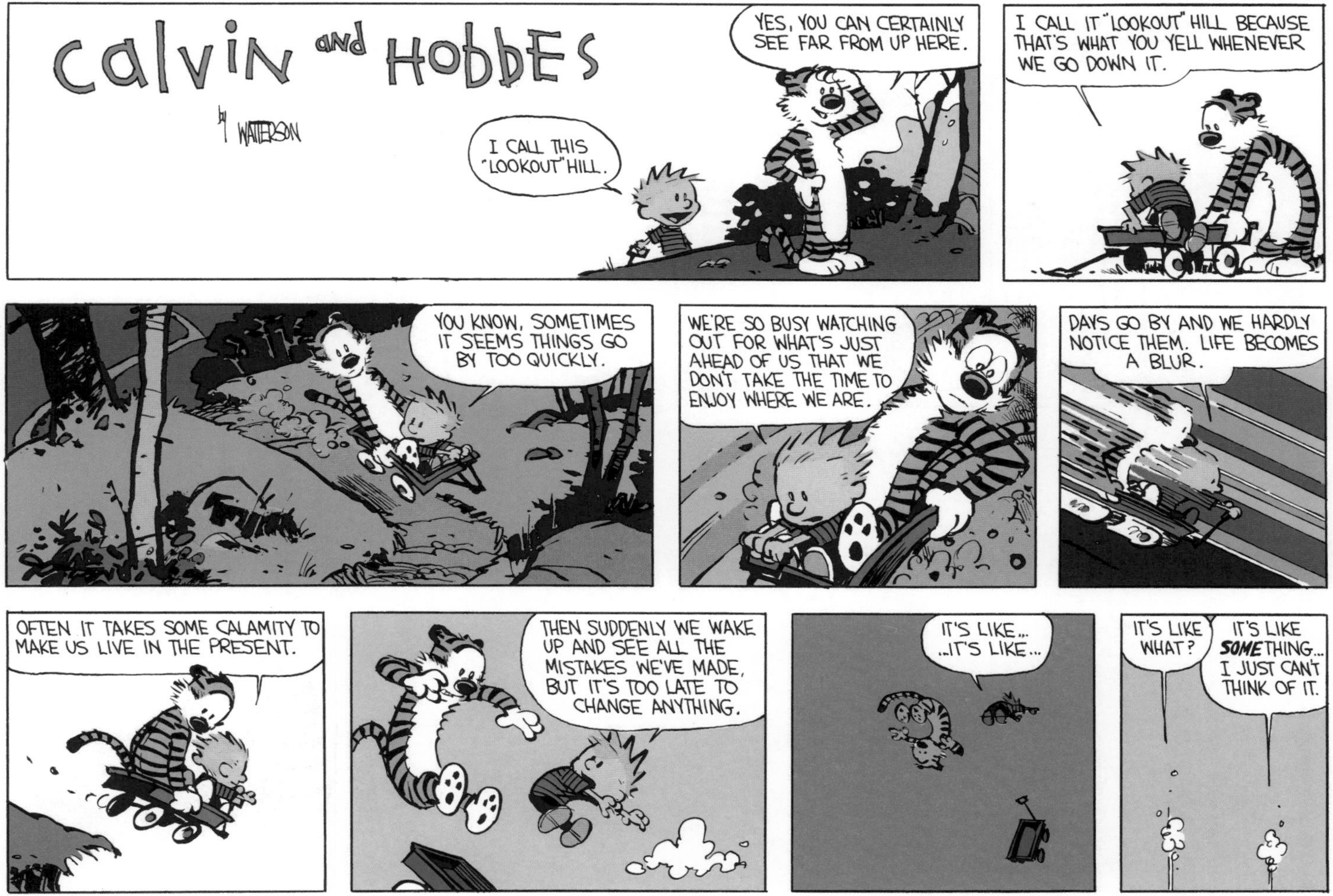
Calvin and HOBBES
by WATTERSON
I CALL THIS "LOOKOUT" HILL.
YES, YOU CAN CERTAINLY SEE FAR FROM UP HERE.
I CALL IT "LOOKOUT" HILL BECAUSE THAT'S WHAT YOU YELL WHENEVER WE GO DOWN IT.
YOU KNOW, SOMETIMES IT SEEMS THINGS GO BY TOO QUICKLY.
WE'RE SO BUSY WATCHING OUT FOR WHAT'S JUST AHEAD OF US THAT WE DON'T TAKE THE TIME TO ENJOY WHERE WE ARE.
DAYS GO BY AND WE HARDLY NOTICE THEM. LIFE BECOMES A BLUR.
OFTEN IT TAKES SOME CALAMITY TO MAKE US LIVE IN THE PRESENT.
THEN SUDDENLY WE WAKE UP AND SEE ALL THE MISTAKES WE'VE MADE, BUT IT'S TOO LATE TO CHANGE ANYTHING.
IT'S LIKE... ..IT'S LIKE...
IT'S LIKE WHAT?
IT'S LIKE SOMETHING... I JUST CAN'T THINK OF IT.

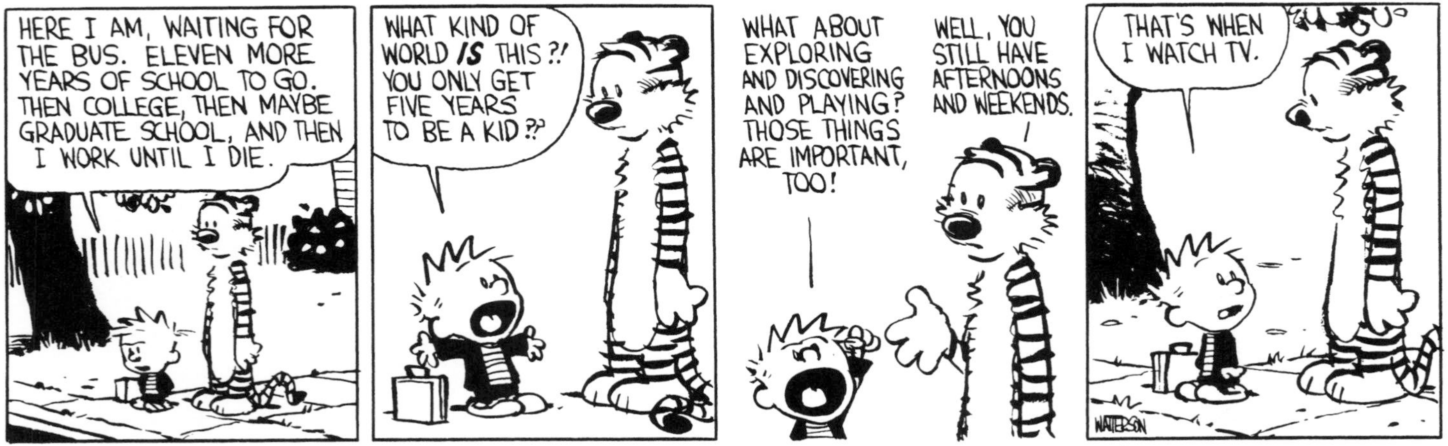
HERE I AM, WAITING FOR THE BUS. ELEVEN MORE YEARS OF SCHOOL TO GO. THEN COLLEGE, THEN MAYBE GRADUATE SCHOOL, AND THEN I WORK UNTIL I DIE.
WHAT KIND OF WORLD **IS** THIS?! YOU ONLY GET FIVE YEARS TO BE A KID??
WHAT ABOUT EXPLORING AND DISCOVERING AND PLAYING? THOSE THINGS ARE IMPORTANT, TOO!
WELL, YOU STILL HAVE AFTERNOONS AND WEEKENDS.
THAT'S WHEN I WATCH TV.
WATTERSON

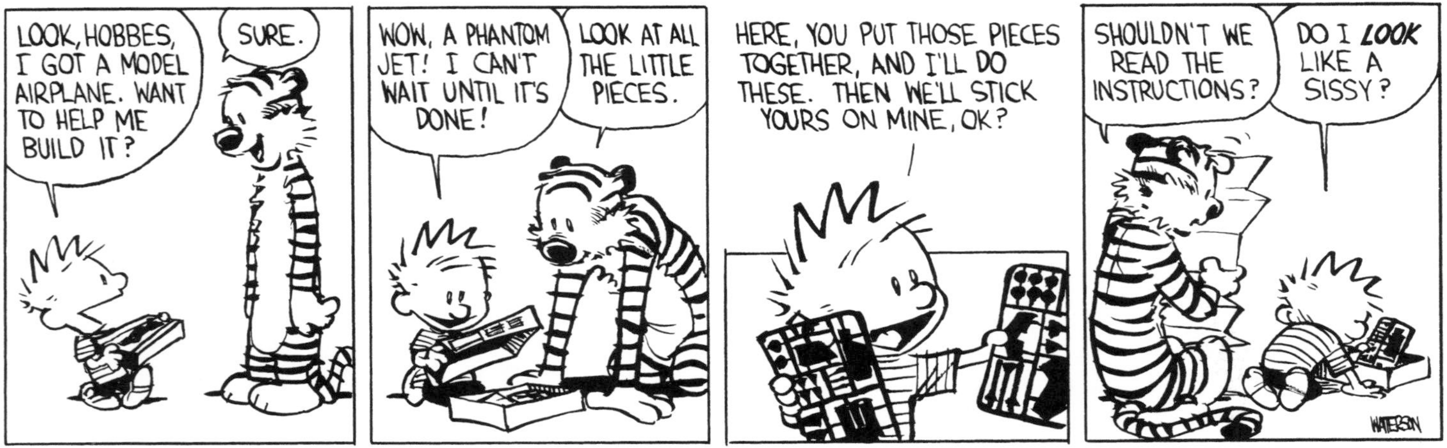
LOOK, HOBBES, I GOT A MODEL AIRPLANE. WANT TO HELP ME BUILD IT?
SURE.
WOW, A PHANTOM JET! I CAN'T WAIT UNTIL IT'S DONE!
LOOK AT ALL THE LITTLE PIECES.
HERE, YOU PUT THOSE PIECES TOGETHER, AND I'LL DO THESE. THEN WE'LL STICK YOURS ON MINE, OK?
SHOULDN'T WE READ THE INSTRUCTIONS?
DO I **LOOK** LIKE A SISSY?
WATTERSON

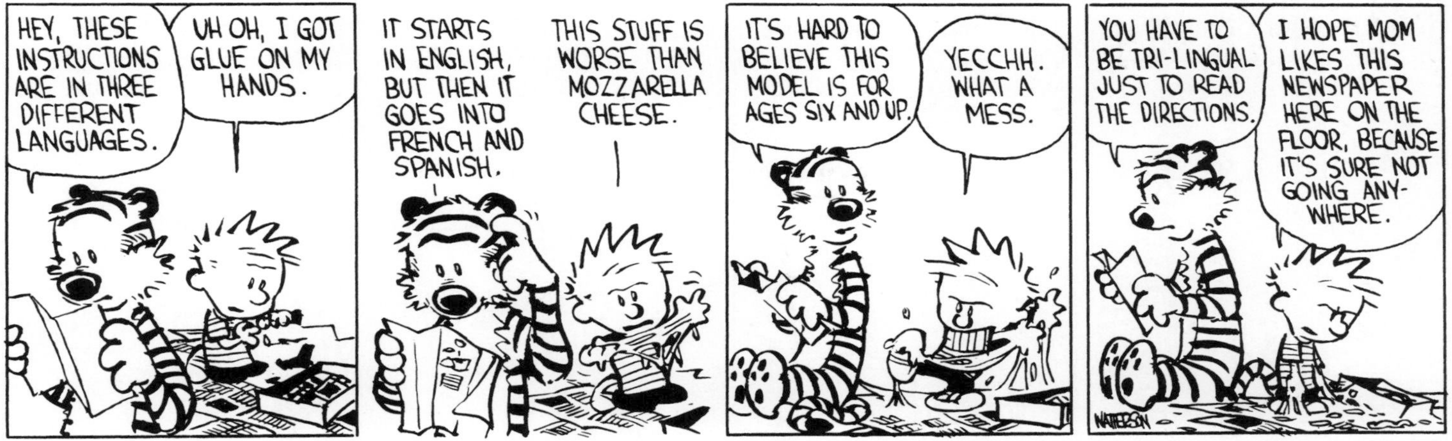
HEY, THESE INSTRUCTIONS ARE IN THREE DIFFERENT LANGUAGES.
UH OH, I GOT GLUE ON MY HANDS.
IT STARTS IN ENGLISH, BUT THEN IT GOES INTO FRENCH AND SPANISH.
THIS STUFF IS WORSE THAN MOZZARELLA CHEESE.
IT'S HARD TO BELIEVE THIS MODEL IS FOR AGES SIX AND UP.
YECCHH. WHAT A MESS.
YOU HAVE TO BE TRI-LINGUAL JUST TO READ THE DIRECTIONS.
I HOPE MOM LIKES THIS NEWSPAPER HERE ON THE FLOOR, BECAUSE IT'S SURE NOT GOING ANY-WHERE.

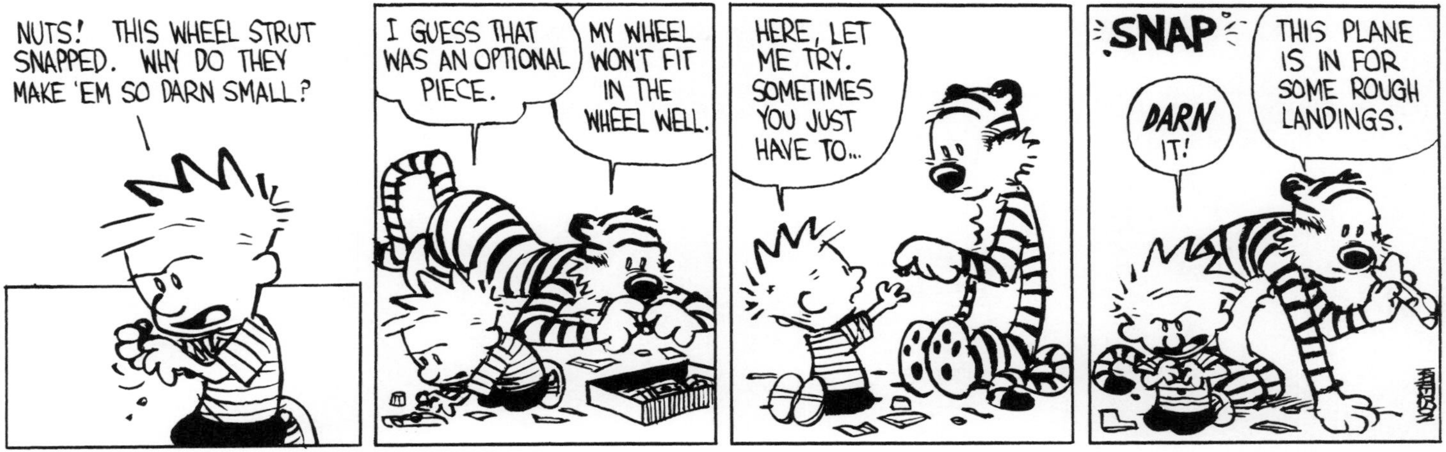
NUTS! THIS WHEEL STRUT SNAPPED. WHY DO THEY MAKE 'EM SO DARN SMALL?
I GUESS THAT WAS AN OPTIONAL PIECE.
MY WHEEL WON'T FIT IN THE WHEEL WELL.
HERE, LET ME TRY. SOMETIMES YOU JUST HAVE TO...
SNAP
DARN IT!
THIS PLANE IS IN FOR SOME ROUGH LANDINGS.

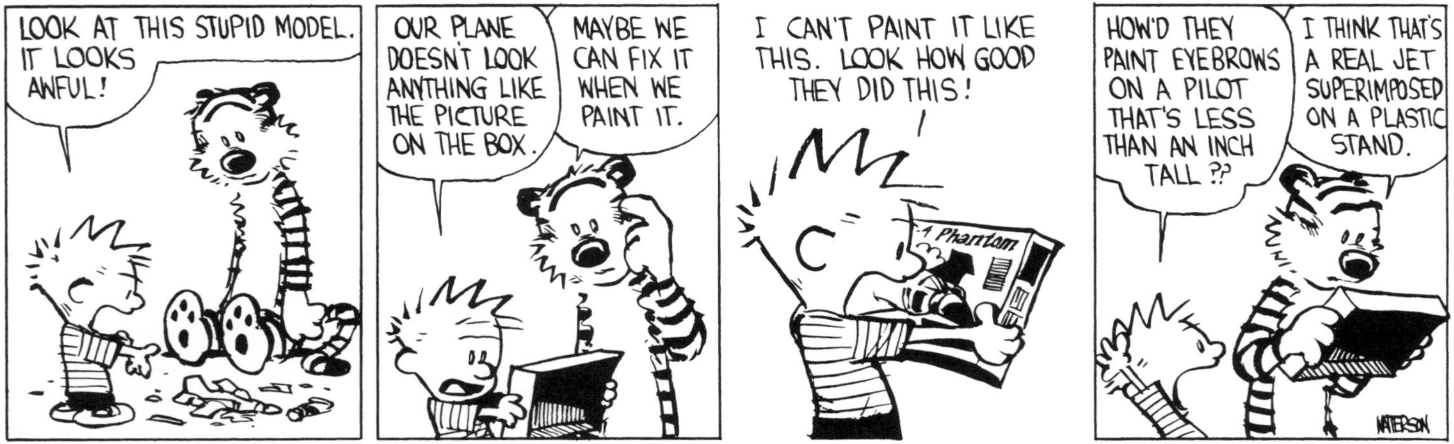
LOOK AT THIS STUPID MODEL. IT LOOKS AWFUL!
OUR PLANE DOESN'T LOOK ANYTHING LIKE THE PICTURE ON THE BOX.
MAYBE WE CAN FIX IT WHEN WE PAINT IT.
I CAN'T PAINT IT LIKE THIS. LOOK HOW GOOD THEY DID THIS!
Phantom
HOW'D THEY PAINT EYEBROWS ON A PILOT THAT'S LESS THAN AN INCH TALL ??
I THINK THAT'S A REAL JET SUPERIMPOSED ON A PLASTIC STAND.
WATTERSON

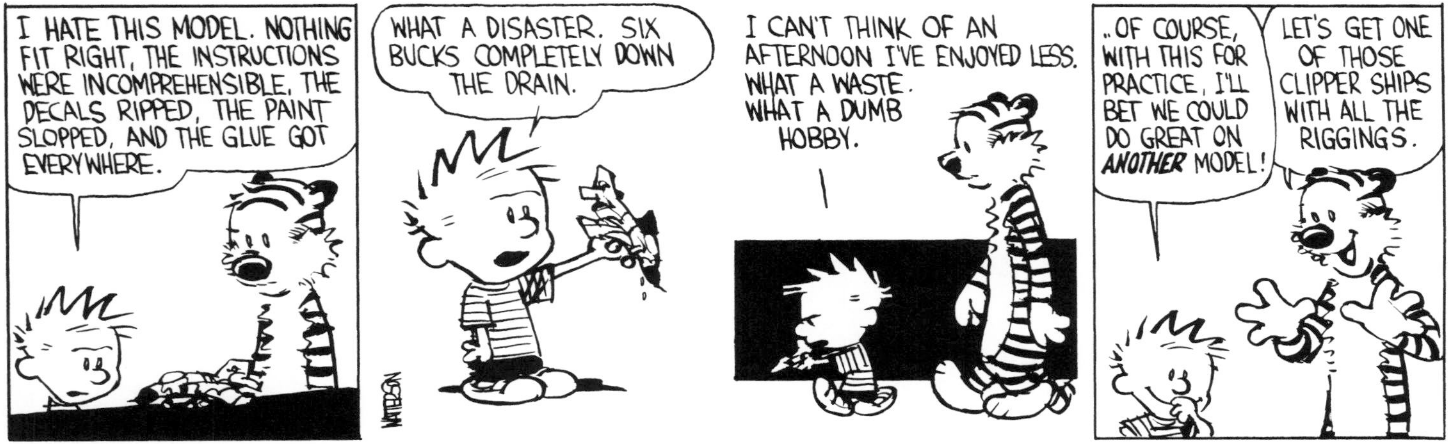
I HATE THIS MODEL. NOTHING FIT RIGHT, THE INSTRUCTIONS WERE INCOMPREHENSIBLE, THE DECALS RIPPED, THE PAINT SLOPPED, AND THE GLUE GOT EVERYWHERE.
WATTERSON
WHAT A DISASTER. SIX BUCKS COMPLETELY DOWN THE DRAIN.
I CAN'T THINK OF AN AFTERNOON I'VE ENJOYED LESS. WHAT A WASTE. WHAT A DUMB HOBBY.
..OF COURSE, WITH THIS FOR PRACTICE, I'LL BET WE COULD DO GREAT ON ANOTHER MODEL!
LET'S GET ONE OF THOSE CLIPPER SHIPS WITH ALL THE RIGGINGS.

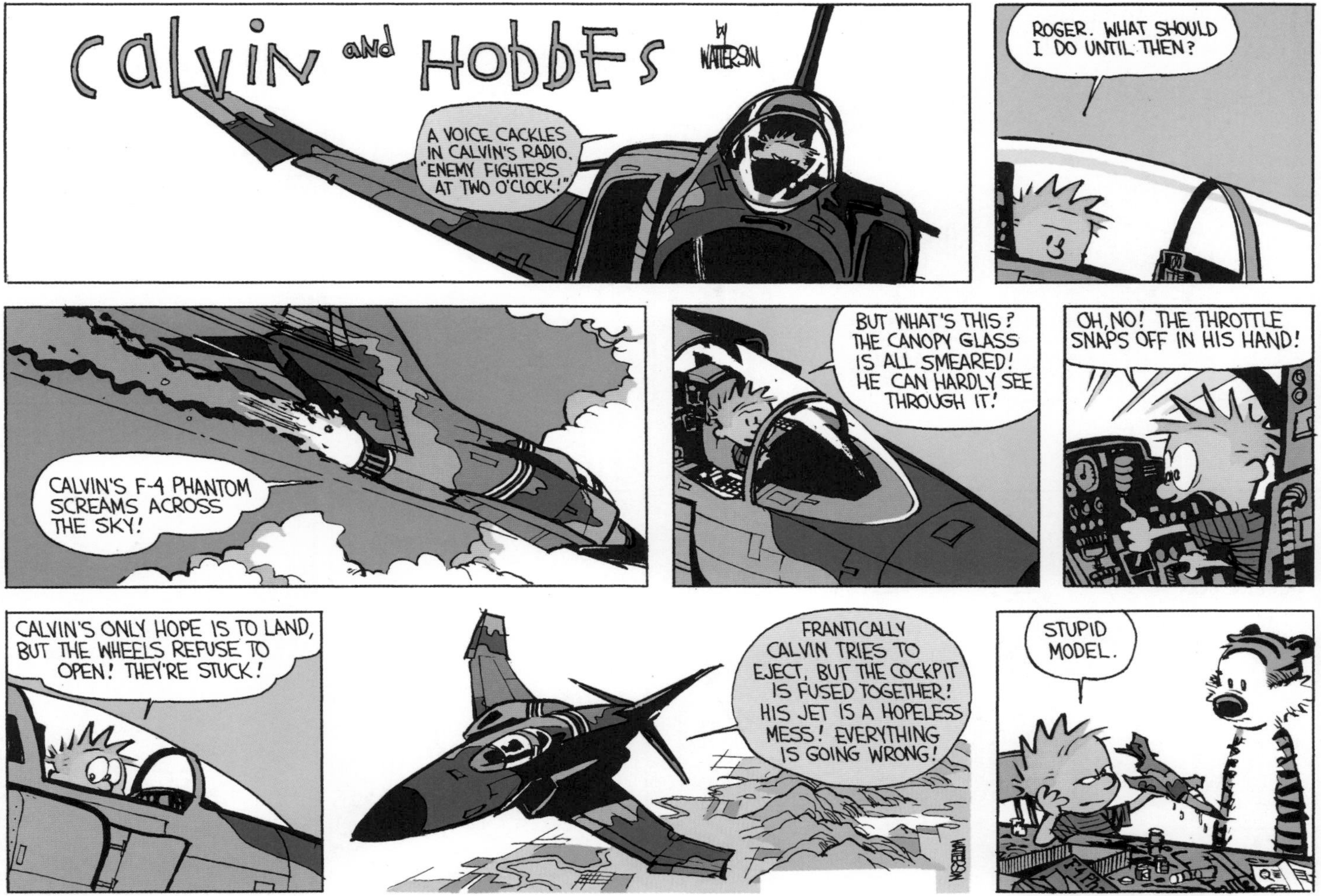
Calvin and HOBBES by WATTERSON
A VOICE CACKLES IN CALVIN'S RADIO. "ENEMY FIGHTERS AT TWO O'CLOCK!"
ROGER. WHAT SHOULD I DO UNTIL THEN?
CALVIN'S F-4 PHANTOM SCREAMS ACROSS THE SKY!
BUT WHAT'S THIS? THE CANOPY GLASS IS ALL SMEARED! HE CAN HARDLY SEE THROUGH IT!
OH, NO! THE THROTTLE SNAPS OFF IN HIS HAND!
CALVIN'S ONLY HOPE IS TO LAND, BUT THE WHEELS REFUSE TO OPEN! THEY'RE STUCK!
FRANTICALLY CALVIN TRIES TO EJECT, BUT THE COCKPIT IS FUSED TOGETHER! HIS JET IS A HOPELESS MESS! EVERYTHING IS GOING WRONG!
WATTERSON
STUPID MODEL.

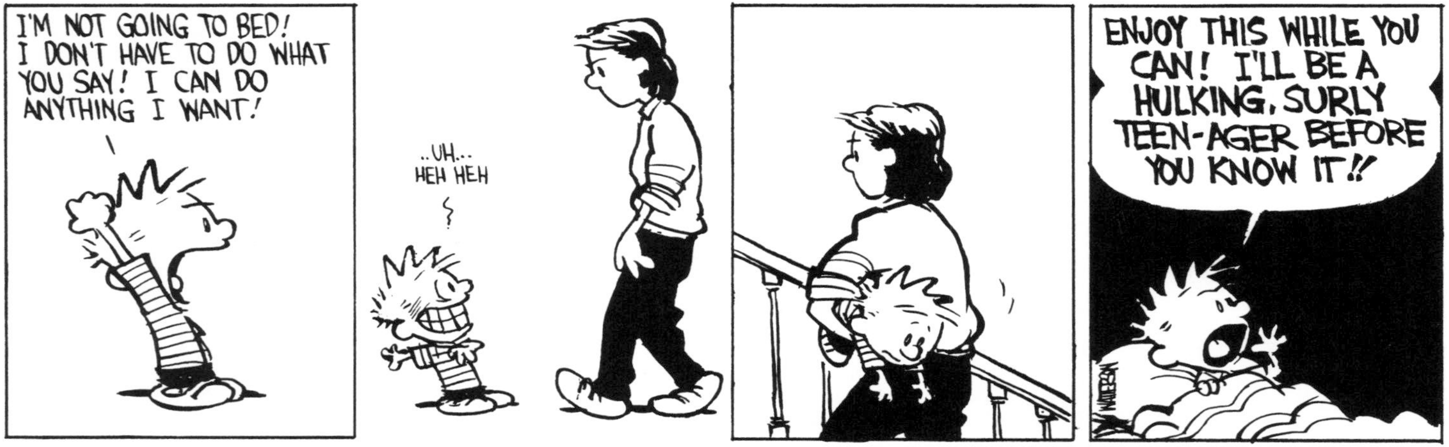
I'M NOT GOING TO BED! I DON'T HAVE TO DO WHAT YOU SAY! I CAN DO ANYTHING I WANT!
..UH... HEH HEH
ENJOY THIS WHILE YOU CAN! I'LL BE A HULKING, SURLY TEEN-AGER BEFORE YOU KNOW IT!!
WATTERSON

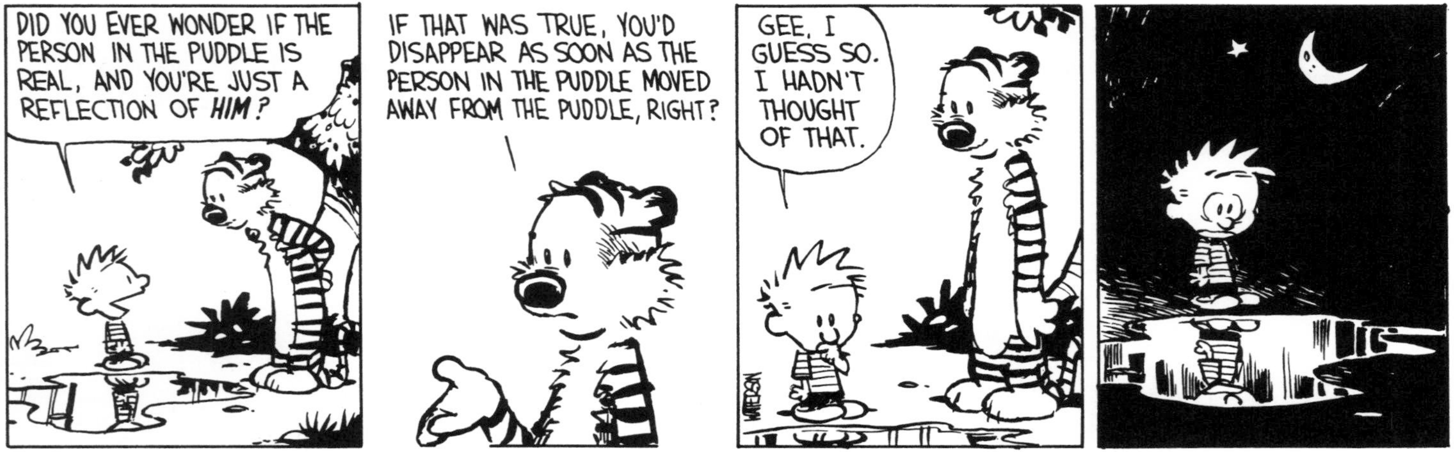
DID YOU EVER WONDER IF THE PERSON IN THE PUDDLE IS REAL, AND YOU'RE JUST A REFLECTION OF *HIM*?
IF THAT WAS TRUE, YOU'D DISAPPEAR AS SOON AS THE PERSON IN THE PUDDLE MOVED AWAY FROM THE PUDDLE, RIGHT?
GEE, I GUESS SO. I HADN'T THOUGHT OF THAT.
WATTERSON

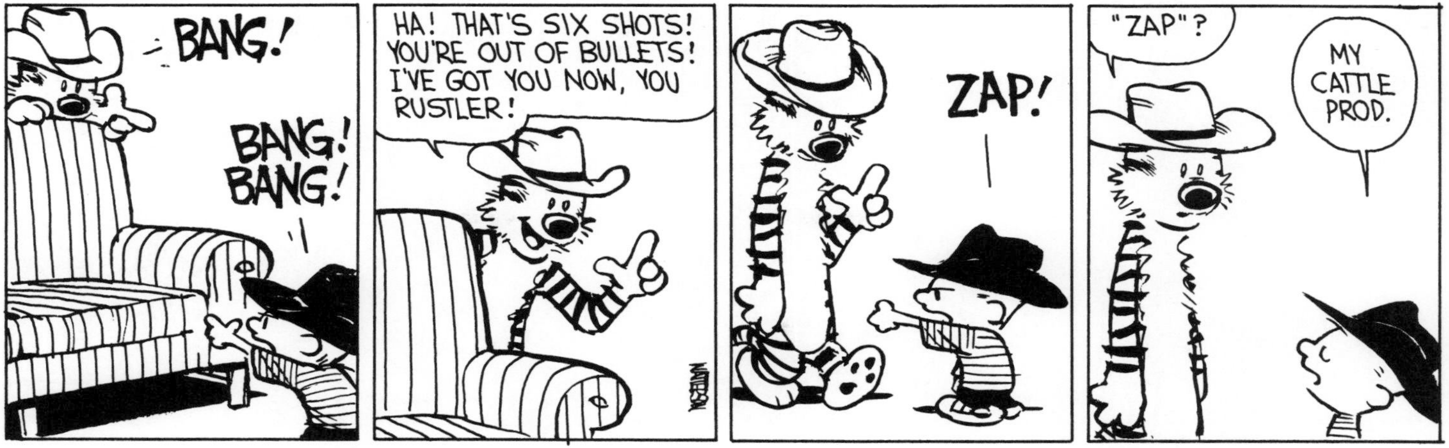
BANG!
BANG! BANG!
HA! THAT'S SIX SHOTS! YOU'RE OUT OF BULLETS! I'VE GOT YOU NOW, YOU RUSTLER!
WATTERSON
ZAP!
"ZAP"?
MY CATTLE PROD.

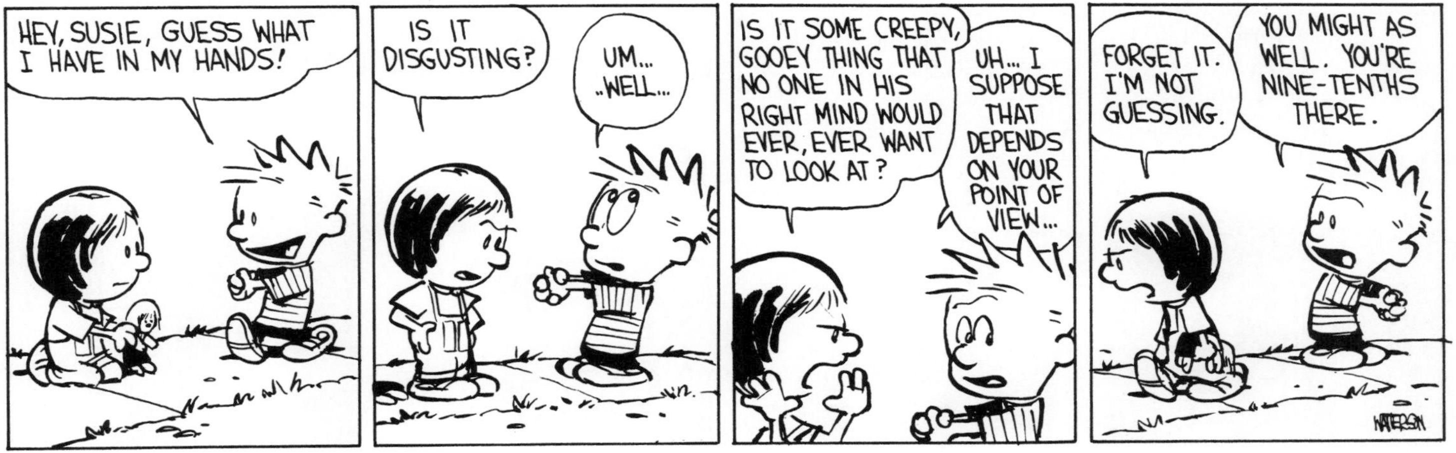
HEY, SUSIE, GUESS WHAT I HAVE IN MY HANDS!
IS IT DISGUSTING?
UM... ..WELL...
IS IT SOME CREEPY, GOOEY THING THAT NO ONE IN HIS RIGHT MIND WOULD EVER, EVER WANT TO LOOK AT?
UH... I SUPPOSE THAT DEPENDS ON YOUR POINT OF VIEW...
FORGET IT. I'M NOT GUESSING.
YOU MIGHT AS WELL. YOU'RE NINE-TENTHS THERE.
WATTERSON

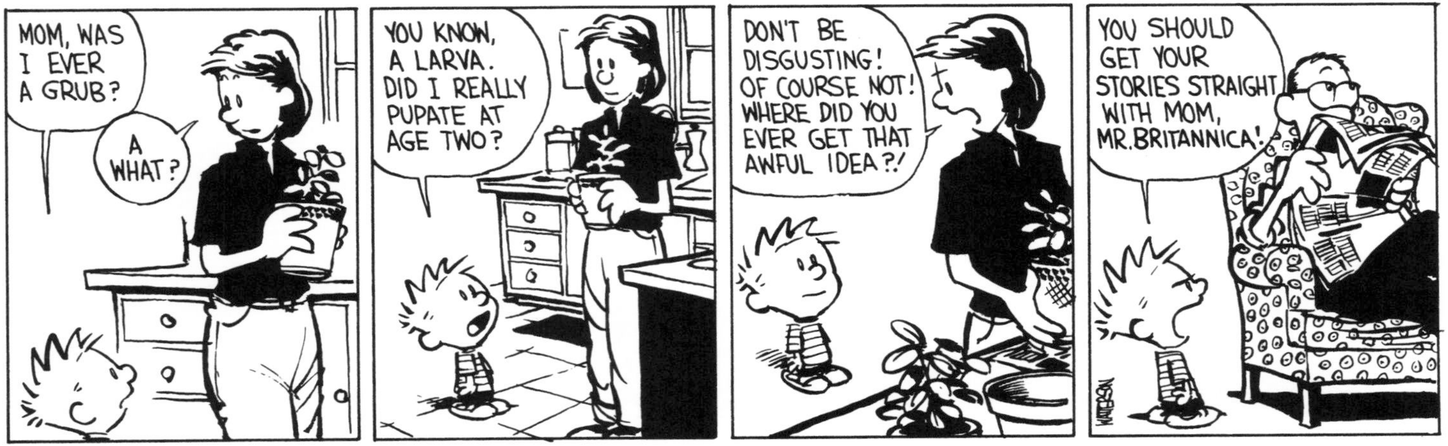
MOM, WAS I EVER A GRUB?
A WHAT?
YOU KNOW, A LARVA. DID I REALLY PUPATE AT AGE TWO?
DON'T BE DISGUSTING! OF COURSE NOT! WHERE DID YOU EVER GET THAT AWFUL IDEA?!
YOU SHOULD GET YOUR STORIES STRAIGHT WITH MOM, MR. BRITANNICA!
WATTERSON

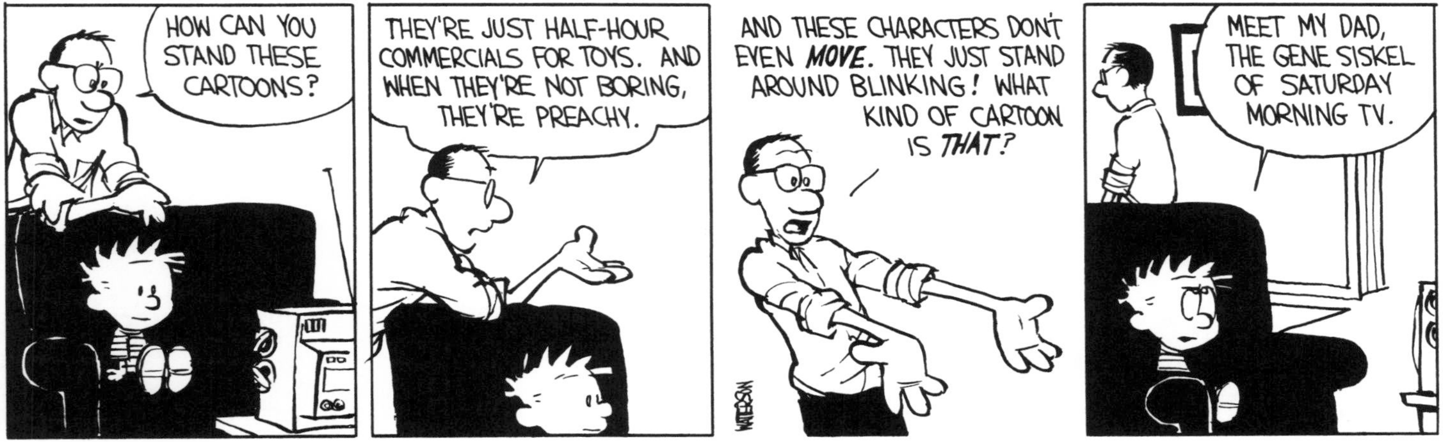
HOW CAN YOU STAND THESE CARTOONS?
THEY'RE JUST HALF-HOUR COMMERCIALS FOR TOYS. AND WHEN THEY'RE NOT BORING, THEY'RE PREACHY.
WATTERSON
AND THESE CHARACTERS DON'T EVEN ***MOVE***. THEY JUST STAND AROUND BLINKING! WHAT KIND OF CARTOON IS ***THAT***?
MEET MY DAD, THE GENE SISKEL OF SATURDAY MORNING TV.

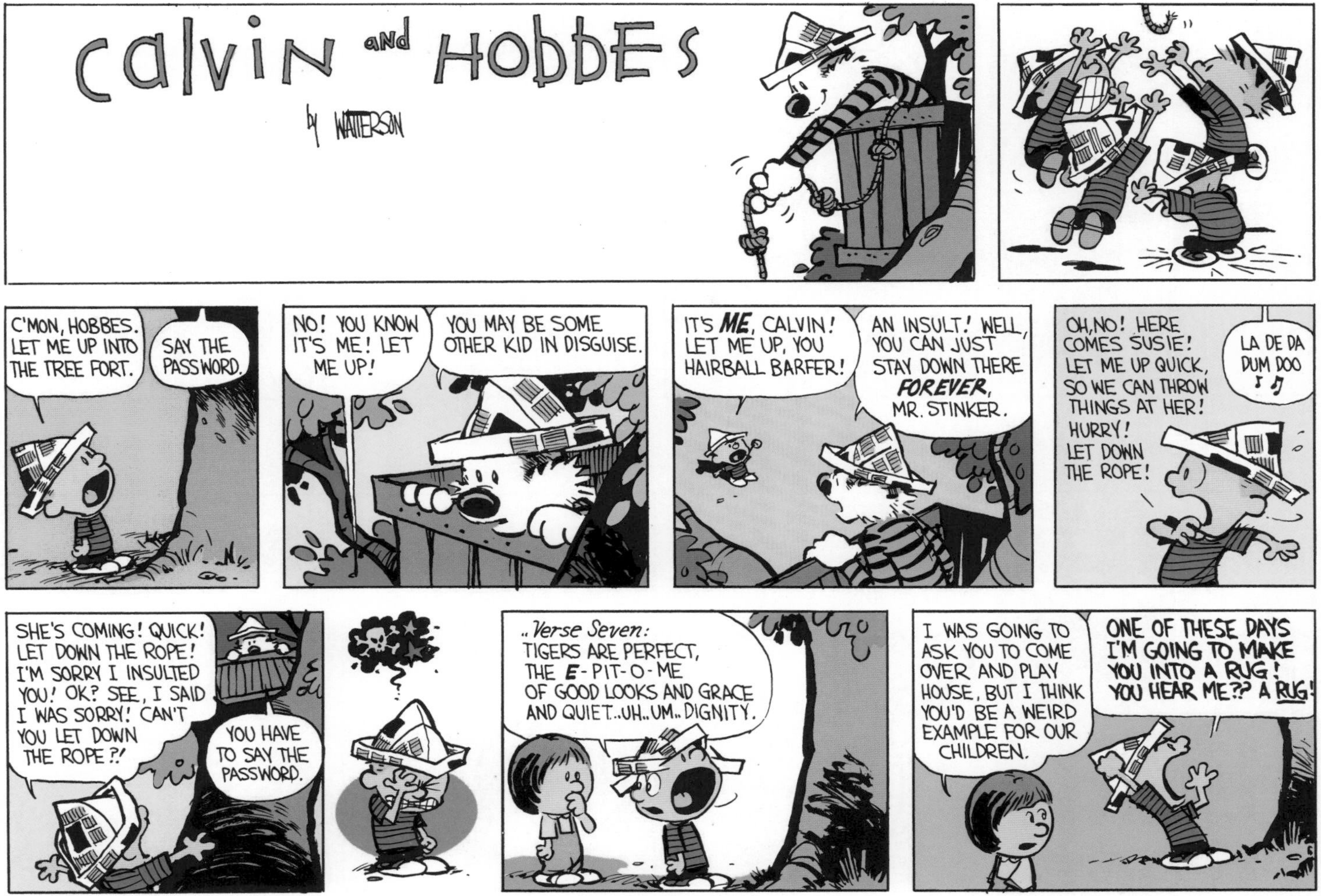
Calvin and HOBBES
by WATTERSON
C'MON, HOBBES. LET ME UP INTO THE TREE FORT.
SAY THE PASSWORD.
NO! YOU KNOW IT'S ME! LET ME UP!
YOU MAY BE SOME OTHER KID IN DISGUISE.
IT'S **ME**, CALVIN! LET ME UP, YOU HAIRBALL BARFER!
AN INSULT! WELL, YOU CAN JUST STAY DOWN THERE ***FOREVER***, MR. STINKER.
OH, NO! HERE COMES SUSIE! LET ME UP QUICK, SO WE CAN THROW THINGS AT HER! HURRY! LET DOWN THE ROPE!
LA DE DA DUM DOO
SHE'S COMING! QUICK! LET DOWN THE ROPE! I'M SORRY I INSULTED YOU! OK? SEE, I SAID I WAS SORRY! CAN'T YOU LET DOWN THE ROPE?!
YOU HAVE TO SAY THE PASSWORD.
..Verse Seven: TIGERS ARE PERFECT, THE **E**-PIT-O-ME OF GOOD LOOKS AND GRACE AND QUIET..UH..UM..DIGNITY.
I WAS GOING TO ASK YOU TO COME OVER AND PLAY HOUSE, BUT I THINK YOU'D BE A WEIRD EXAMPLE FOR OUR CHILDREN.
ONE OF THESE DAYS I'M GOING TO MAKE YOU INTO A RUG! YOU HEAR ME?? A RUG!

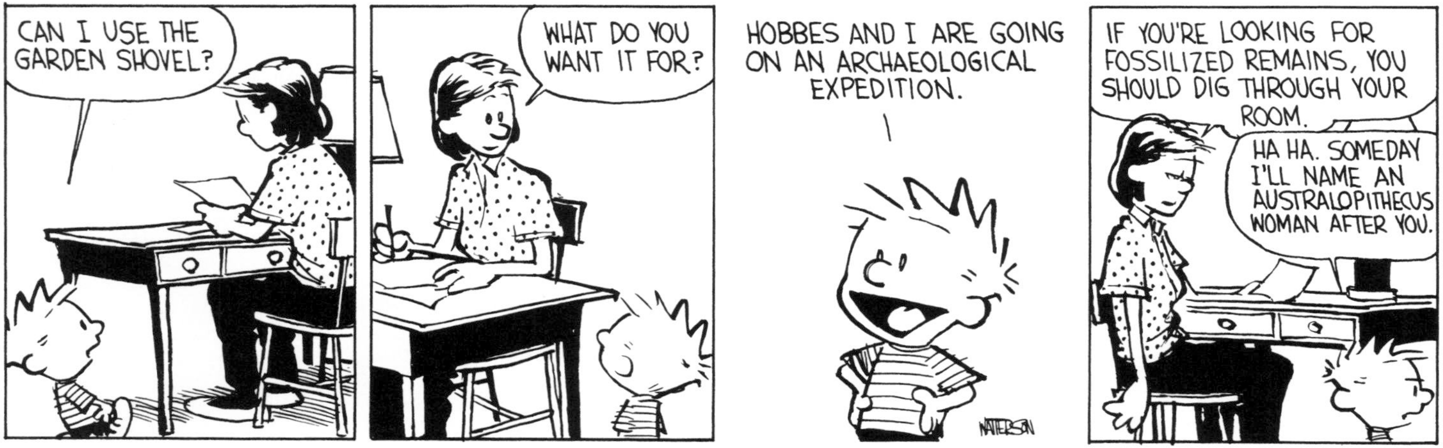
CAN I USE THE GARDEN SHOVEL?
WHAT DO YOU WANT IT FOR?
HOBBES AND I ARE GOING ON AN ARCHAEOLOGICAL EXPEDITION.
IF YOU'RE LOOKING FOR FOSSILIZED REMAINS, YOU SHOULD DIG THROUGH YOUR ROOM.
HA HA. SOMEDAY I'LL NAME AN AUSTRALOPITHECUS WOMAN AFTER YOU.
WATTERSON

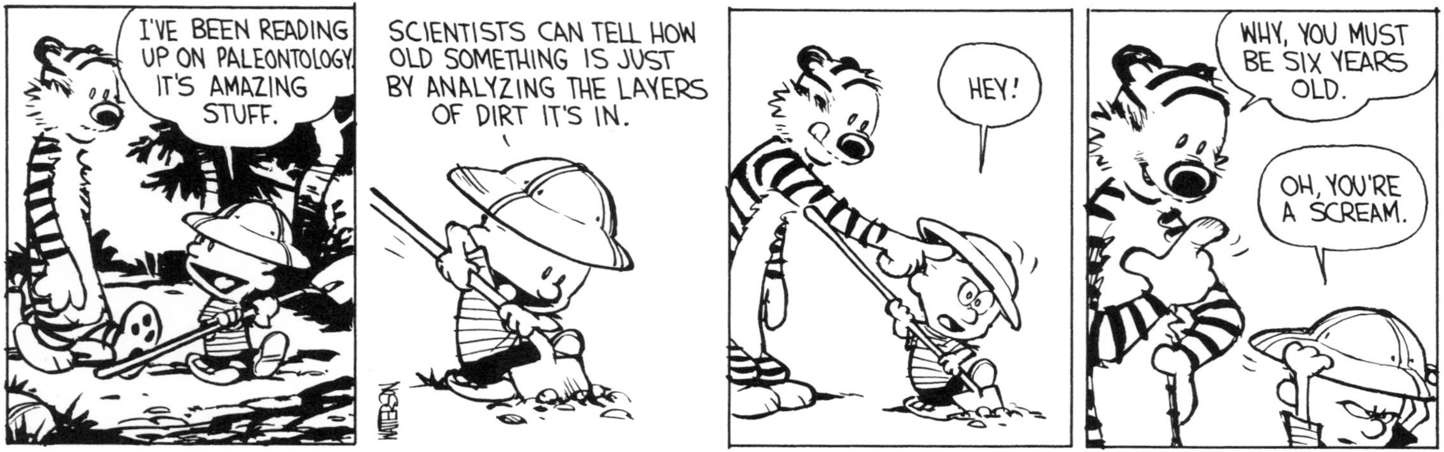
I'VE BEEN READING UP ON PALEONTOLOGY. IT'S AMAZING STUFF.
SCIENTISTS CAN TELL HOW OLD SOMETHING IS JUST BY ANALYZING THE LAYERS OF DIRT IT'S IN.
WATTERSON
HEY!
WHY, YOU MUST BE SIX YEARS OLD.
OH, YOU'RE A SCREAM.

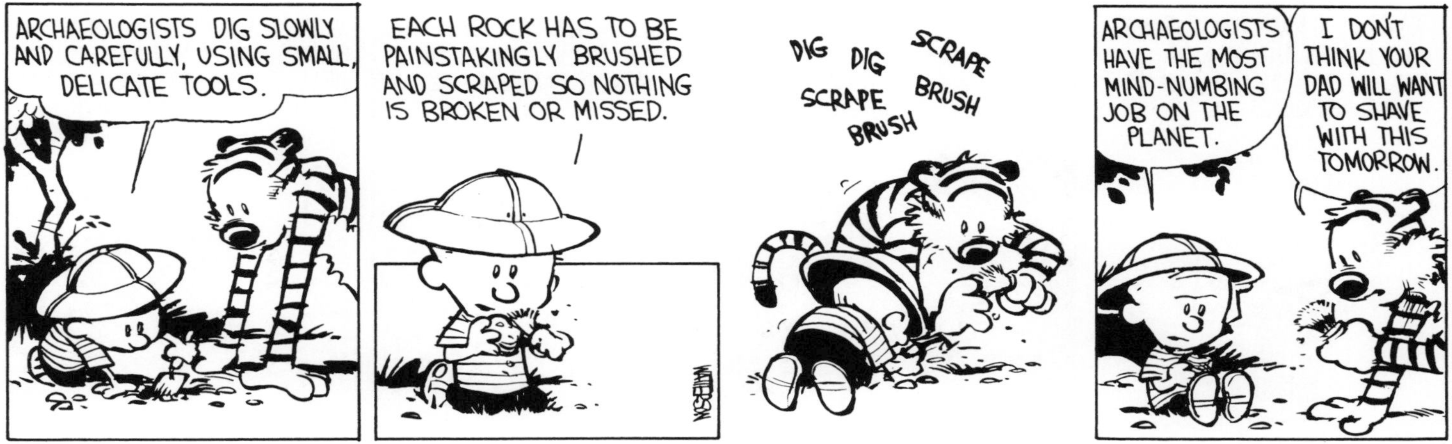
ARCHAEOLOGISTS DIG SLOWLY AND CAREFULLY, USING SMALL, DELICATE TOOLS.
EACH ROCK HAS TO BE PAINSTAKINGLY BRUSHED AND SCRAPED SO NOTHING IS BROKEN OR MISSED.
DIG DIG SCRAPE SCRAPE BRUSH BRUSH
ARCHAEOLOGISTS HAVE THE MOST MIND-NUMBING JOB ON THE PLANET.
I DON'T THINK YOUR DAD WILL WANT TO SHAVE WITH THIS TOMORROW.

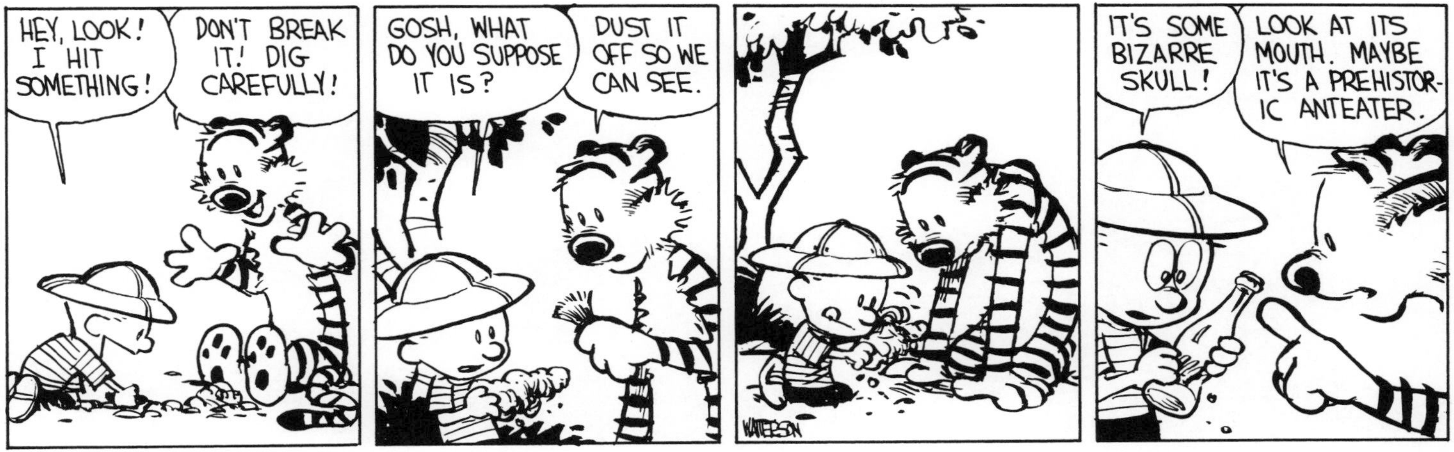
HEY, LOOK! I HIT SOMETHING!
DON'T BREAK IT! DIG CAREFULLY!
GOSH, WHAT DO YOU SUPPOSE IT IS?
DUST IT OFF SO WE CAN SEE.
IT'S SOME BIZARRE SKULL!
LOOK AT ITS MOUTH. MAYBE IT'S A PREHISTORIC ANTEATER.

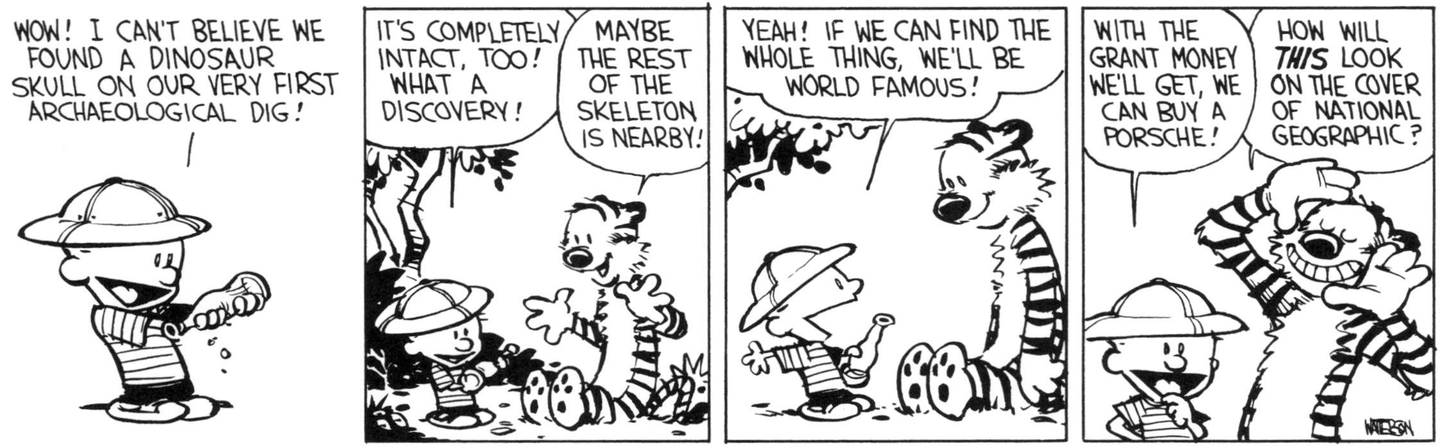
WOW! I CAN'T BELIEVE WE FOUND A DINOSAUR SKULL ON OUR VERY FIRST ARCHAEOLOGICAL DIG!
IT'S COMPLETELY INTACT, TOO! WHAT A DISCOVERY!
MAYBE THE REST OF THE SKELETON IS NEARBY!
YEAH! IF WE CAN FIND THE WHOLE THING, WE'LL BE WORLD FAMOUS!
WITH THE GRANT MONEY WE'LL GET, WE CAN BUY A PORSCHE!
HOW WILL **THIS** LOOK ON THE COVER OF NATIONAL GEOGRAPHIC?
WATTERSON

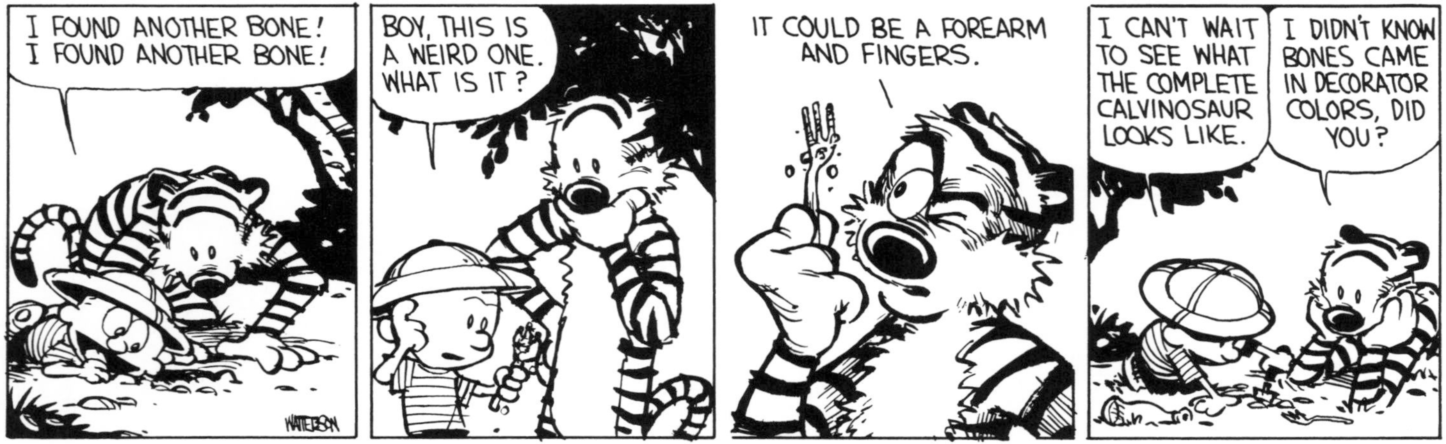
I FOUND ANOTHER BONE! I FOUND ANOTHER BONE!
BOY, THIS IS A WEIRD ONE. WHAT IS IT?
IT COULD BE A FOREARM AND FINGERS.
I CAN'T WAIT TO SEE WHAT THE COMPLETE CALVINOSAUR LOOKS LIKE.
I DIDN'T KNOW BONES CAME IN DECORATOR COLORS, DID YOU?
WATTERSON

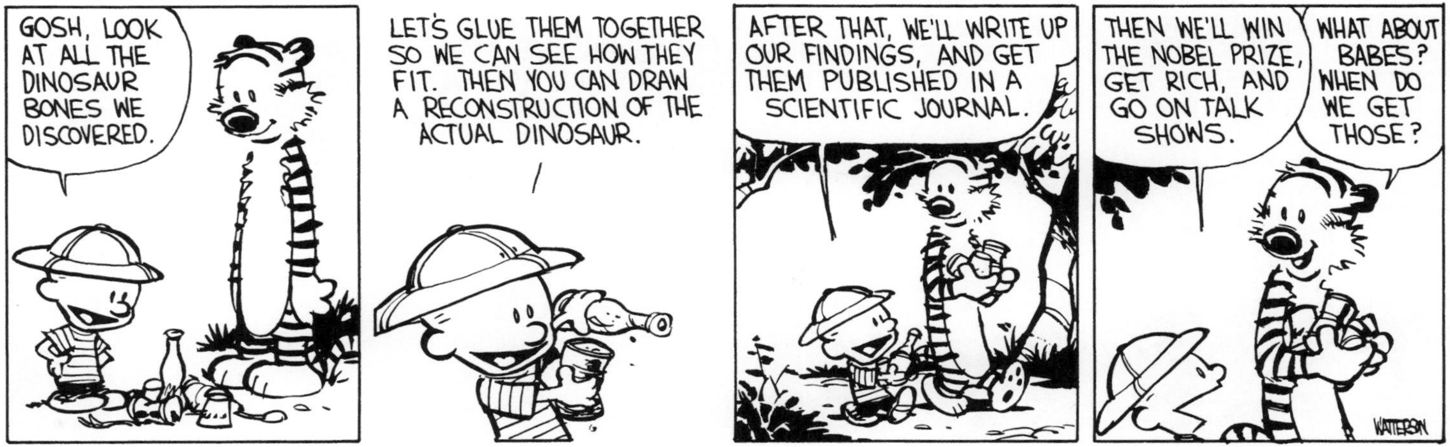
GOSH, LOOK AT ALL THE DINOSAUR BONES WE DISCOVERED.
LET'S GLUE THEM TOGETHER SO WE CAN SEE HOW THEY FIT. THEN YOU CAN DRAW A RECONSTRUCTION OF THE ACTUAL DINOSAUR.
AFTER THAT, WE'LL WRITE UP OUR FINDINGS, AND GET THEM PUBLISHED IN A SCIENTIFIC JOURNAL.
THEN WE'LL WIN THE NOBEL PRIZE, GET RICH, AND GO ON TALK SHOWS.
WHAT ABOUT BABES? WHEN DO WE GET THOSE?
WATTERSON

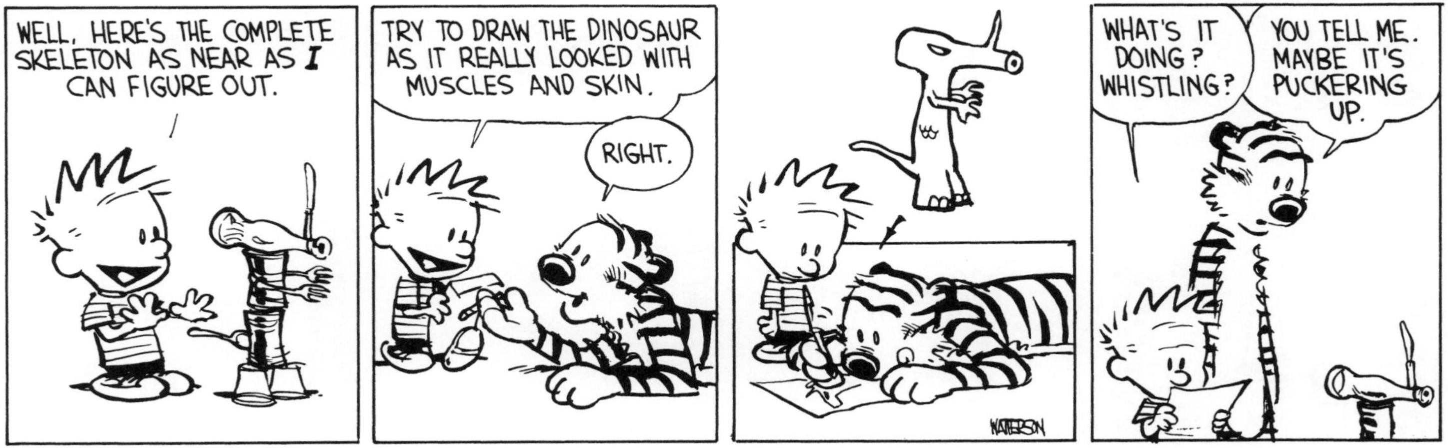
WELL, HERE'S THE COMPLETE SKELETON AS NEAR AS *I* CAN FIGURE OUT.
TRY TO DRAW THE DINOSAUR AS IT REALLY LOOKED WITH MUSCLES AND SKIN.
RIGHT.
WATTERSON
WHAT'S IT DOING? WHISTLING?
YOU TELL ME. MAYBE IT'S PUCKERING UP.

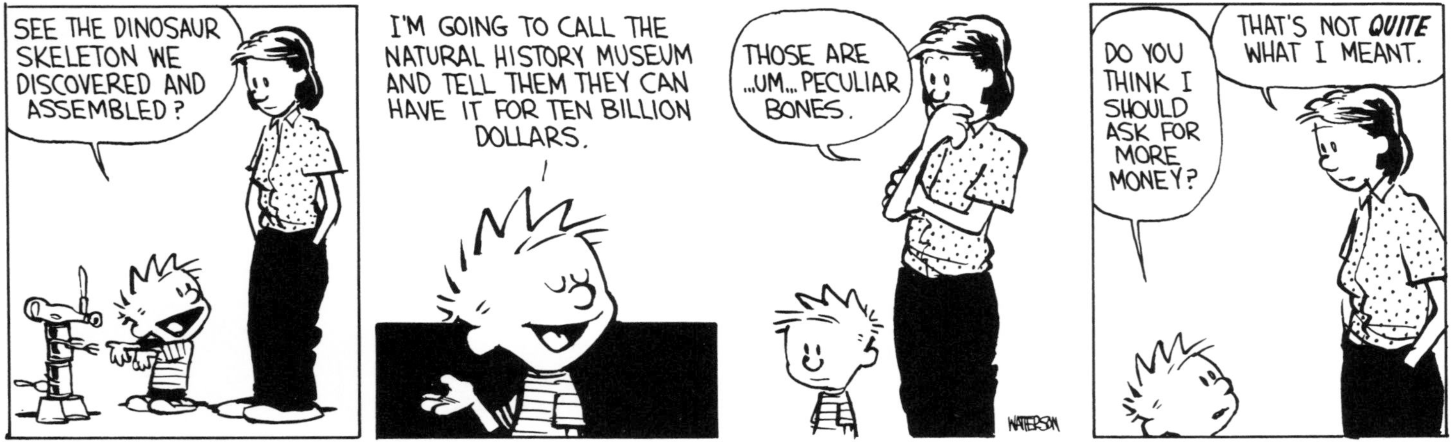
SEE THE DINOSAUR SKELETON WE DISCOVERED AND ASSEMBLED?
I'M GOING TO CALL THE NATURAL HISTORY MUSEUM AND TELL THEM THEY CAN HAVE IT FOR TEN BILLION DOLLARS.
THOSE ARE ...UM... PECULIAR BONES.
WATTERSON
DO YOU THINK I SHOULD ASK FOR MORE MONEY?
THAT'S NOT **QUITE** WHAT I MEANT.

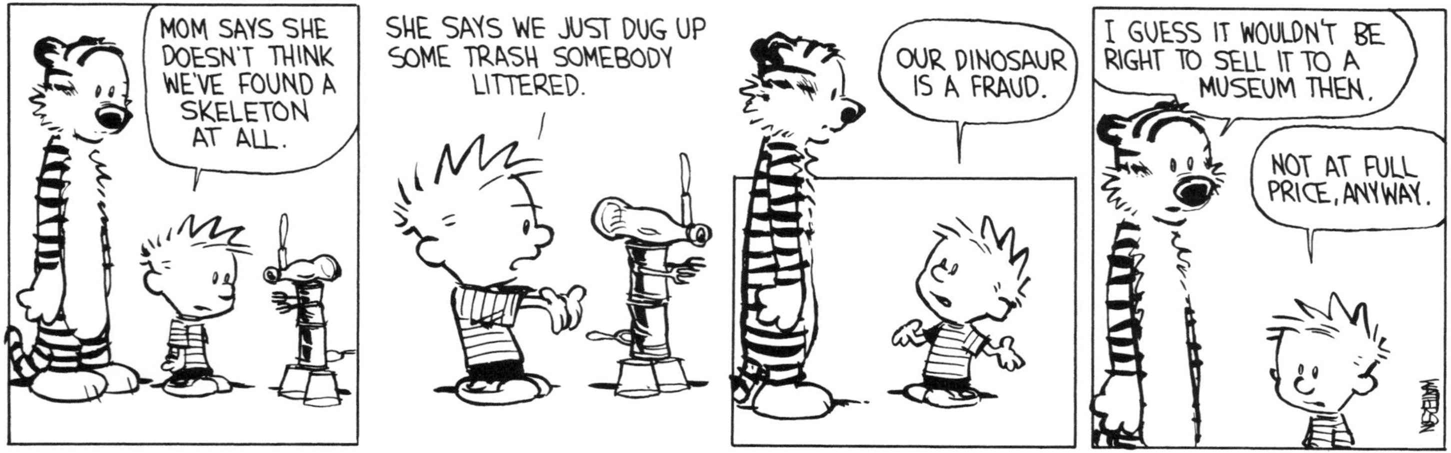
MOM SAYS SHE DOESN'T THINK WE'VE FOUND A SKELETON AT ALL.
SHE SAYS WE JUST DUG UP SOME TRASH SOMEBODY LITTERED.
OUR DINOSAUR IS A FRAUD.
I GUESS IT WOULDN'T BE RIGHT TO SELL IT TO A MUSEUM THEN.
NOT AT FULL PRICE, ANYWAY.

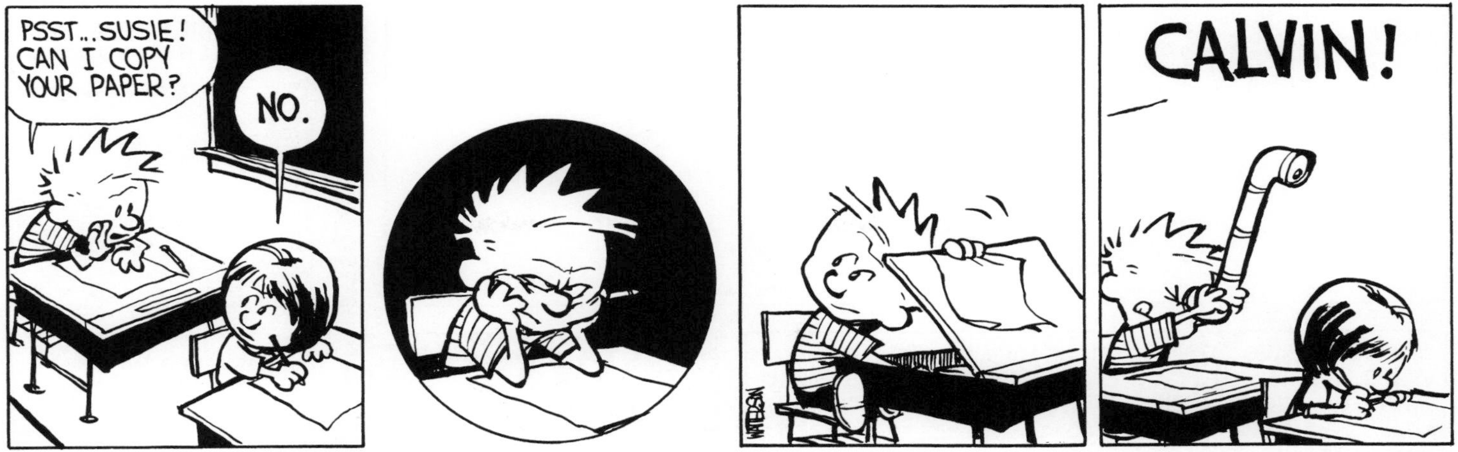
PSST... SUSIE! CAN I COPY YOUR PAPER?
NO.
CALVIN!

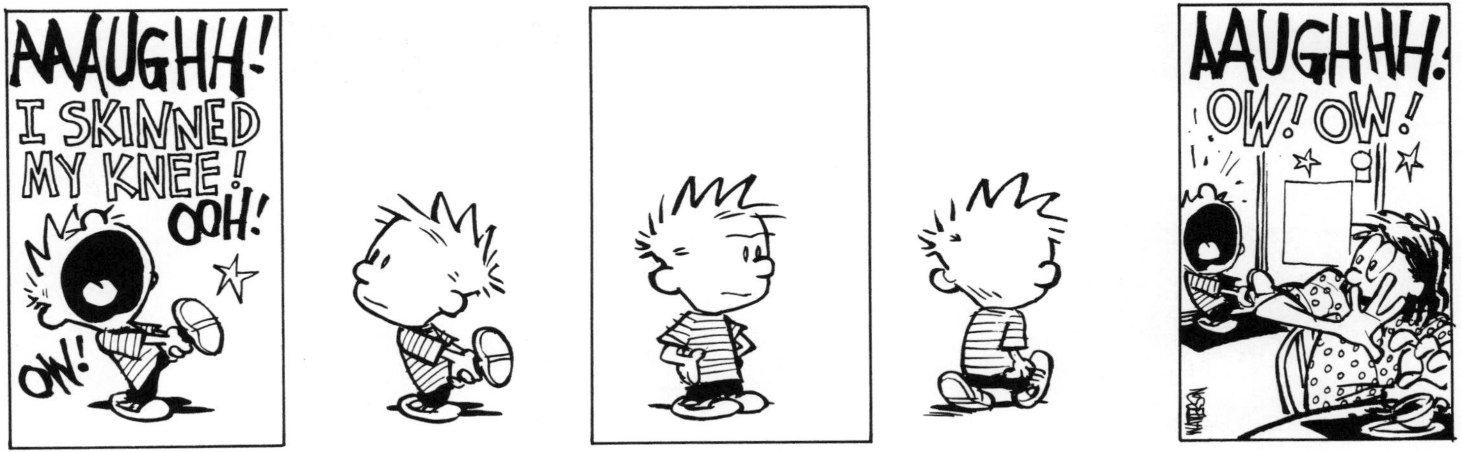
AAAUGHH!
I SKINNED MY KNEE!
OOH!
OW!
AAUGHHH!
OW! OW!

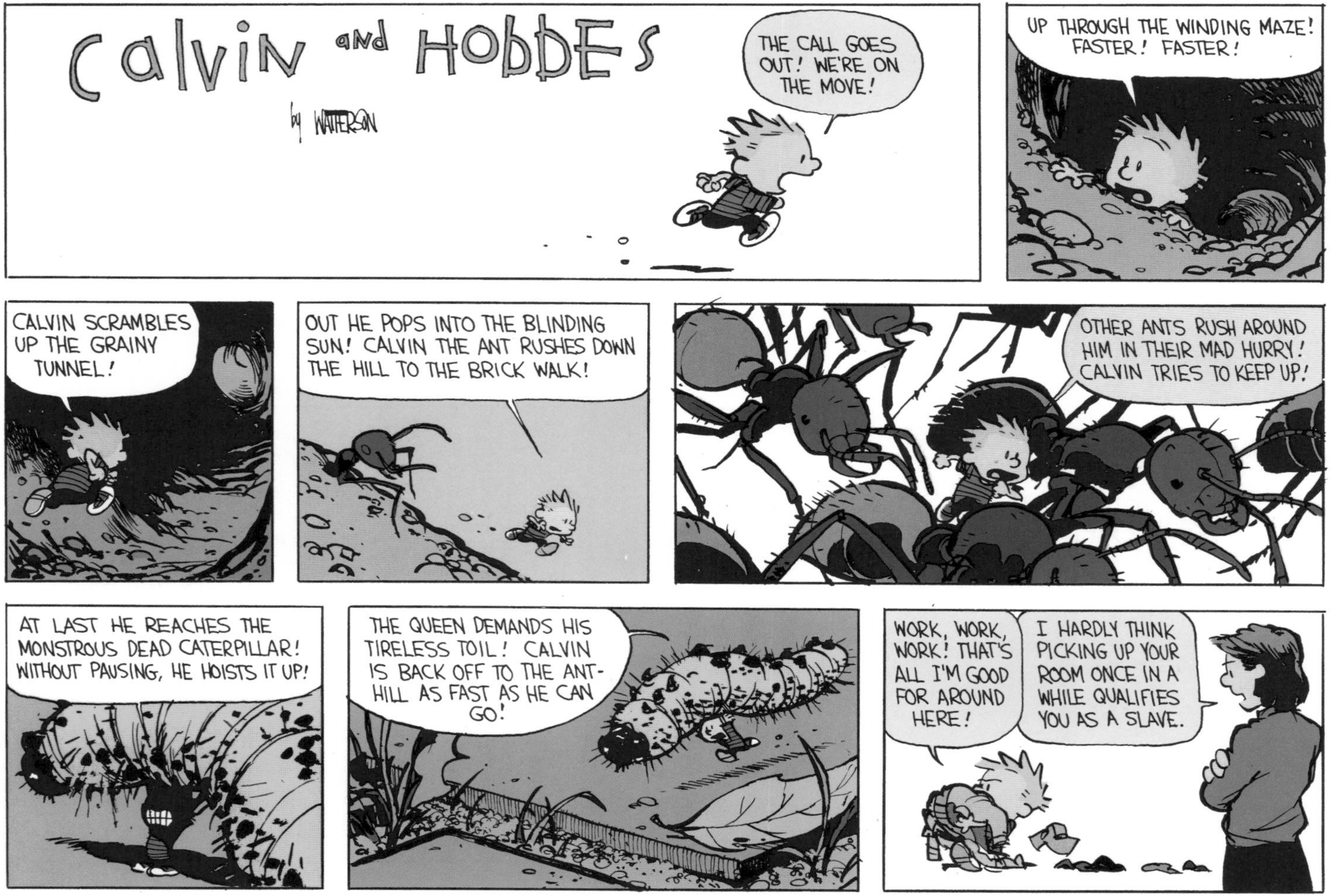
Calvin and HOBBES
by WATTERSON
THE CALL GOES OUT! WE'RE ON THE MOVE!
UP THROUGH THE WINDING MAZE! FASTER! FASTER!
CALVIN SCRAMBLES UP THE GRAINY TUNNEL!
OUT HE POPS INTO THE BLINDING SUN! CALVIN THE ANT RUSHES DOWN THE HILL TO THE BRICK WALK!
OTHER ANTS RUSH AROUND HIM IN THEIR MAD HURRY! CALVIN TRIES TO KEEP UP!
AT LAST HE REACHES THE MONSTROUS DEAD CATERPILLAR! WITHOUT PAUSING, HE HOISTS IT UP!
THE QUEEN DEMANDS HIS TIRELESS TOIL! CALVIN IS BACK OFF TO THE ANT-HILL AS FAST AS HE CAN GO!
WORK, WORK, WORK! THAT'S ALL I'M GOOD FOR AROUND HERE!
I HARDLY THINK PICKING UP YOUR ROOM ONCE IN A WHILE QUALIFIES YOU AS A SLAVE.

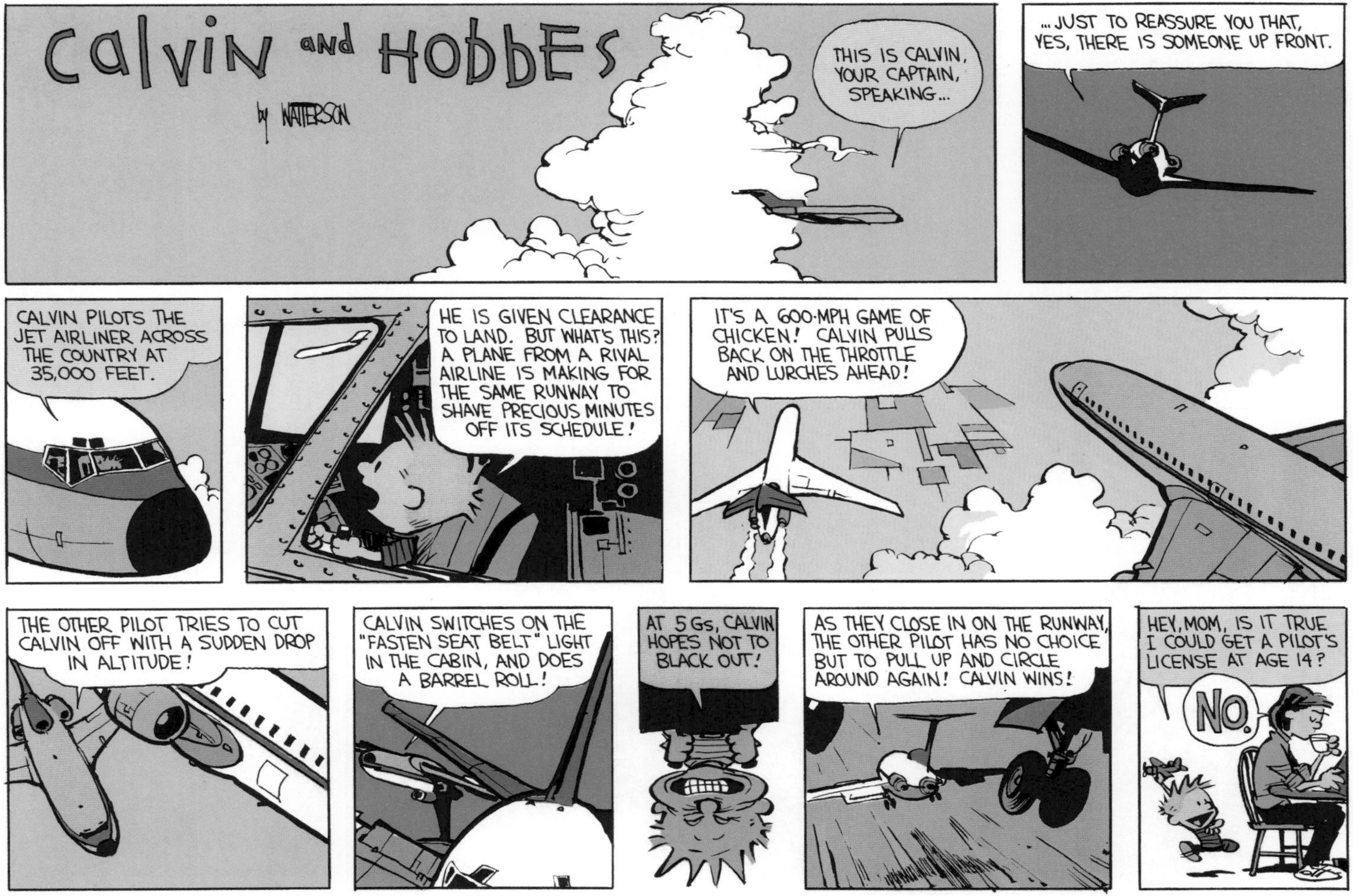
Calvin and HOBBES
by WATTERSON
THIS IS CALVIN, YOUR CAPTAIN, SPEAKING...
...JUST TO REASSURE YOU THAT, YES, THERE IS SOMEONE UP FRONT.
CALVIN PILOTS THE JET AIRLINER ACROSS THE COUNTRY AT 35,000 FEET.
HE IS GIVEN CLEARANCE TO LAND. BUT WHAT'S THIS? A PLANE FROM A RIVAL AIRLINE IS MAKING FOR THE SAME RUNWAY TO SHAVE PRECIOUS MINUTES OFF ITS SCHEDULE!
IT'S A 600-MPH GAME OF CHICKEN! CALVIN PULLS BACK ON THE THROTTLE AND LURCHES AHEAD!
THE OTHER PILOT TRIES TO CUT CALVIN OFF WITH A SUDDEN DROP IN ALTITUDE!
CALVIN SWITCHES ON THE "FASTEN SEAT BELT" LIGHT IN THE CABIN, AND DOES A BARREL ROLL!
AT 5 Gs, CALVIN HOPES NOT TO BLACK OUT!
AS THEY CLOSE IN ON THE RUNWAY, THE OTHER PILOT HAS NO CHOICE BUT TO PULL UP AND CIRCLE AROUND AGAIN! CALVIN WINS!
HEY, MOM, IS IT TRUE I COULD GET A PILOT'S LICENSE AT AGE 14?
NO.

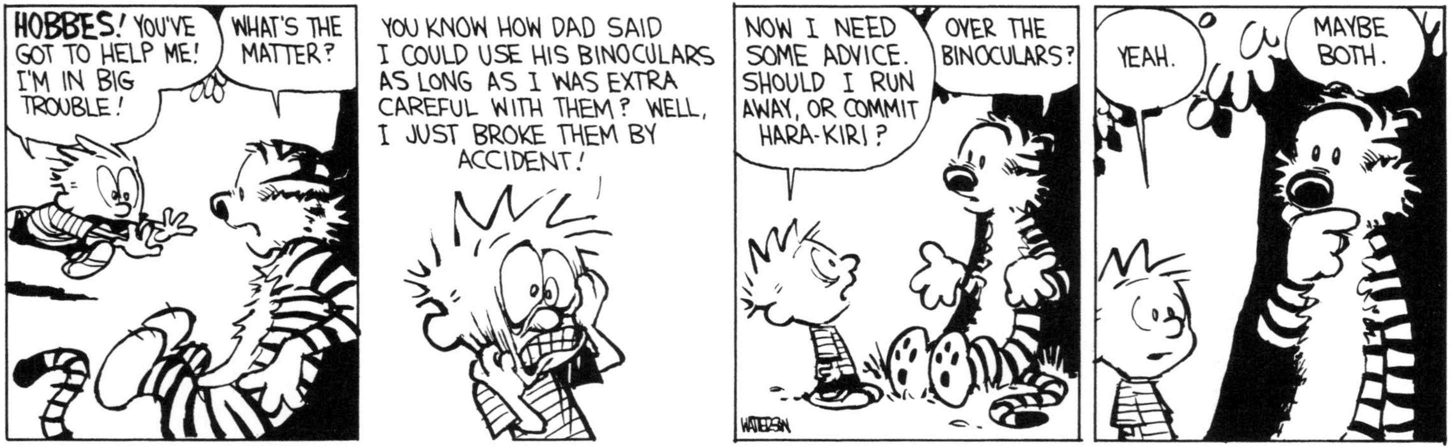
HOBBES! YOU'VE GOT TO HELP ME! I'M IN BIG TROUBLE!
WHAT'S THE MATTER?
YOU KNOW HOW DAD SAID I COULD USE HIS BINOCULARS AS LONG AS I WAS EXTRA CAREFUL WITH THEM? WELL, I JUST BROKE THEM BY ACCIDENT!
NOW I NEED SOME ADVICE. SHOULD I RUN AWAY, OR COMMIT HARA-KIRI?
OVER THE BINOCULARS?
YEAH.
MAYBE BOTH.
WATTERSON

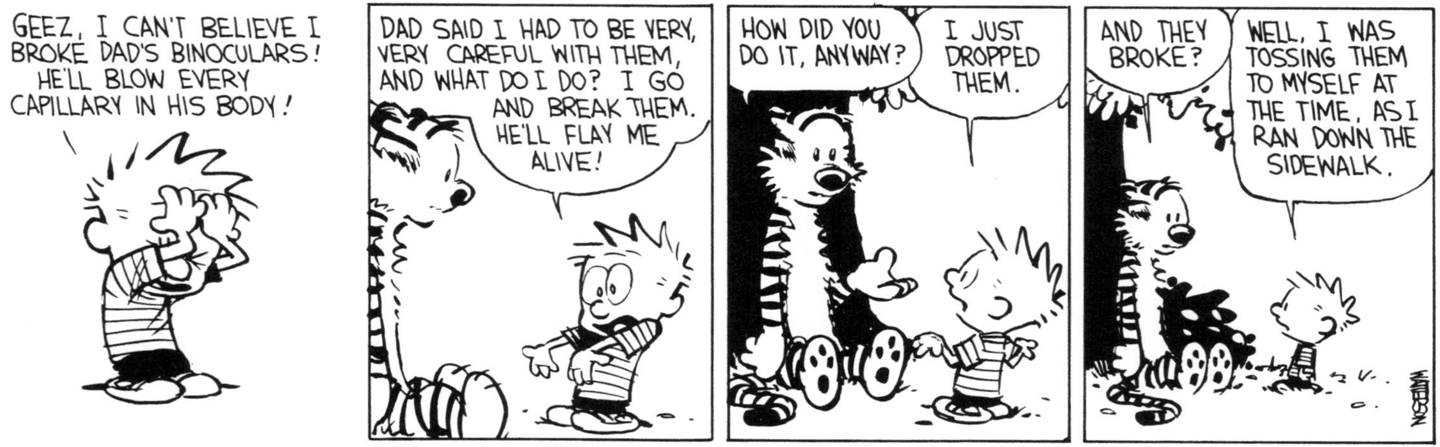
GEEZ, I CAN'T BELIEVE I BROKE DAD'S BINOCULARS! HE'LL BLOW EVERY CAPILLARY IN HIS BODY!
DAD SAID I HAD TO BE VERY, VERY CAREFUL WITH THEM, AND WHAT DO I DO? I GO AND BREAK THEM. HE'LL FLAY ME ALIVE!
HOW DID YOU DO IT, ANYWAY?
I JUST DROPPED THEM.
AND THEY BROKE?
WELL, I WAS TOSSING THEM TO MYSELF AT THE TIME, AS I RAN DOWN THE SIDEWALK.
WATTERSON

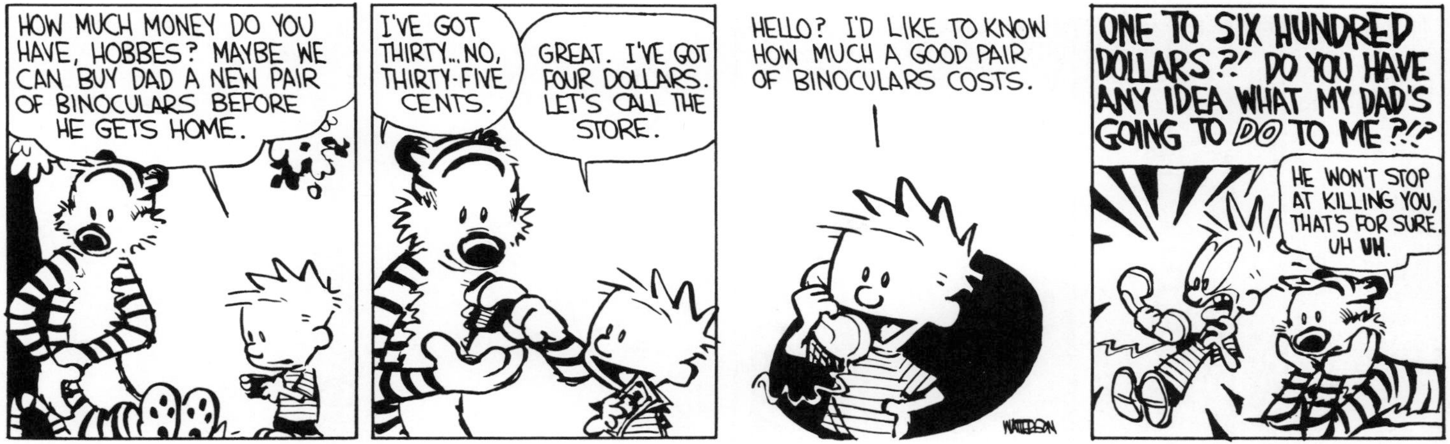
HOW MUCH MONEY DO YOU HAVE, HOBBES? MAYBE WE CAN BUY DAD A NEW PAIR OF BINOCULARS BEFORE HE GETS HOME.
I'VE GOT THIRTY...NO, THIRTY-FIVE CENTS.
GREAT. I'VE GOT FOUR DOLLARS. LET'S CALL THE STORE.
HELLO? I'D LIKE TO KNOW HOW MUCH A GOOD PAIR OF BINOCULARS COSTS.
WATTERSON
ONE TO SIX HUNDRED DOLLARS?! DO YOU HAVE ANY IDEA WHAT MY DAD'S GOING TO *DO* TO ME?!?
HE WON'T STOP AT KILLING YOU, THAT'S FOR SURE. UH **UH**.

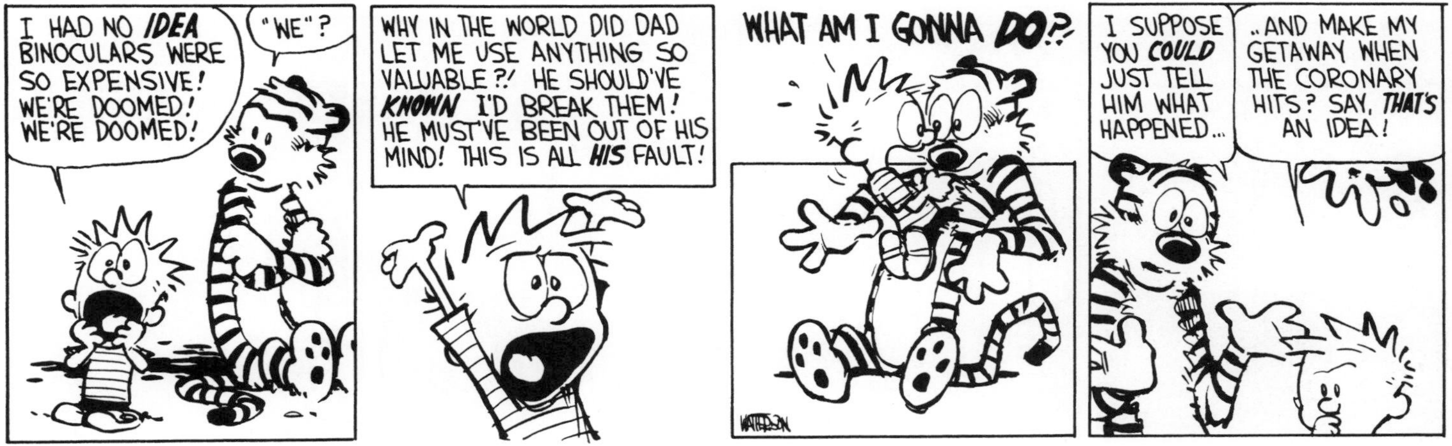
I HAD NO ***IDEA*** BINOCULARS WERE SO EXPENSIVE! WE'RE DOOMED! WE'RE DOOMED!
"WE"?
WHY IN THE WORLD DID DAD LET ME USE ANYTHING SO VALUABLE?! HE SHOULD'VE ***KNOWN*** I'D BREAK THEM! HE MUST'VE BEEN OUT OF HIS MIND! THIS IS ALL ***HIS*** FAULT!
WHAT AM I GONNA ***DO***?!
WATTERSON
I SUPPOSE YOU ***COULD*** JUST TELL HIM WHAT HAPPENED...
..AND MAKE MY GETAWAY WHEN THE CORONARY HITS? SAY, ***THAT'S*** AN IDEA!

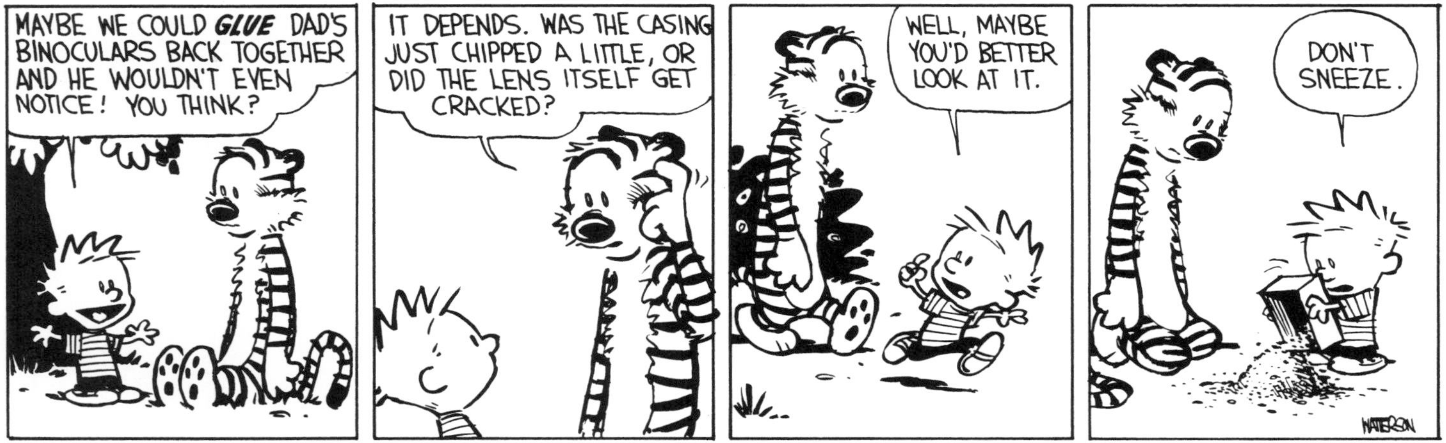
MAYBE WE COULD GLUE DAD'S BINOCULARS BACK TOGETHER AND HE WOULDN'T EVEN NOTICE! YOU THINK?
IT DEPENDS. WAS THE CASING JUST CHIPPED A LITTLE, OR DID THE LENS ITSELF GET CRACKED?
WELL, MAYBE YOU'D BETTER LOOK AT IT.
DON'T SNEEZE.
WATTERSON

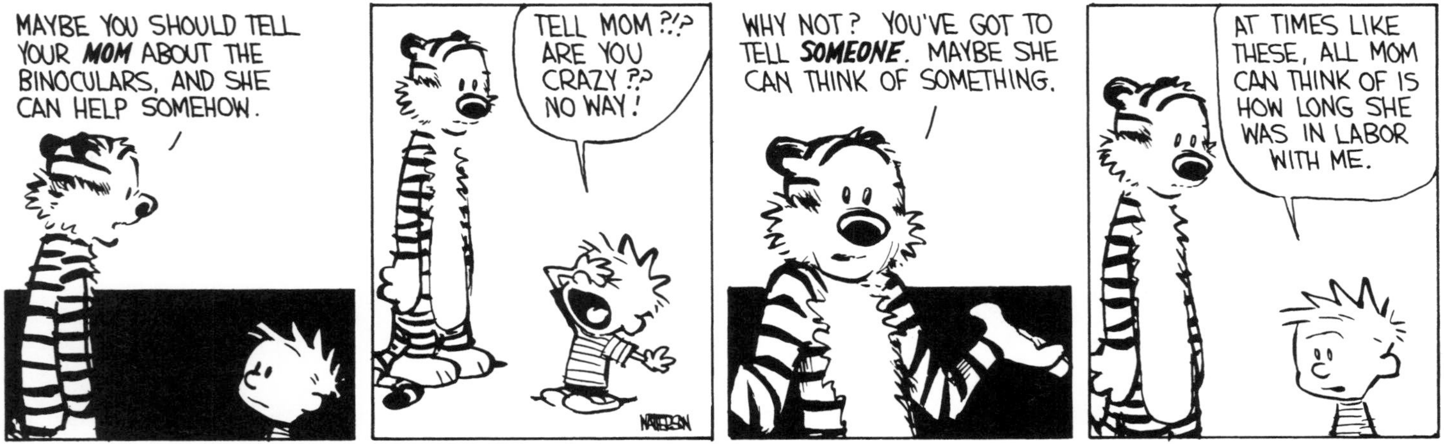
MAYBE YOU SHOULD TELL YOUR MOM ABOUT THE BINOCULARS, AND SHE CAN HELP SOMEHOW.
TELL MOM ?!? ARE YOU CRAZY ?!? NO WAY!
WATTERSON
WHY NOT? YOU'VE GOT TO TELL SOMEONE. MAYBE SHE CAN THINK OF SOMETHING.
AT TIMES LIKE THESE, ALL MOM CAN THINK OF IS HOW LONG SHE WAS IN LABOR WITH ME.

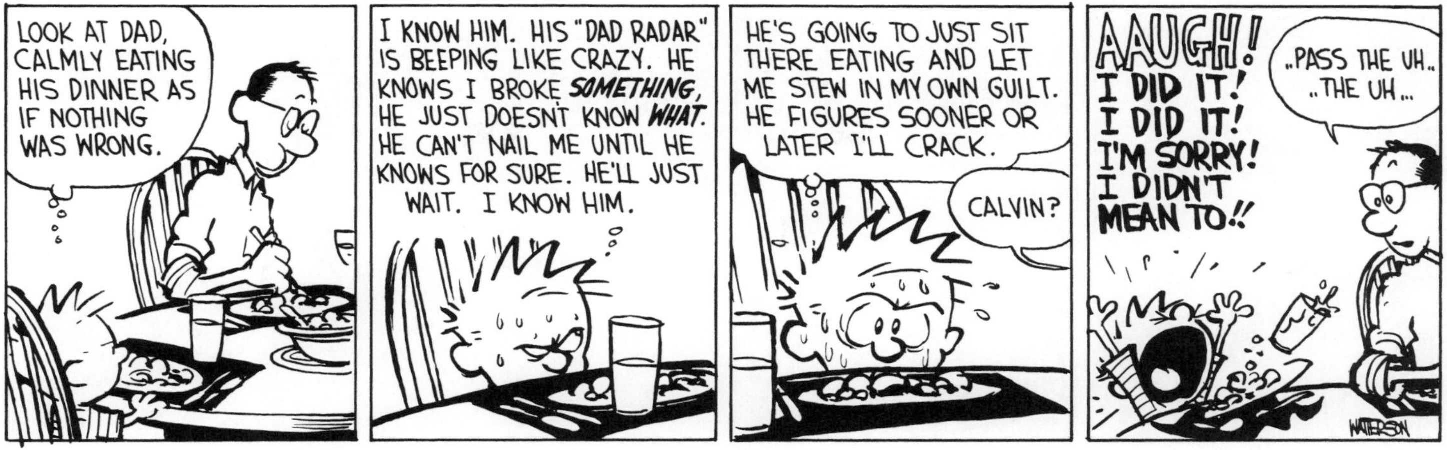
LOOK AT DAD, CALMLY EATING HIS DINNER AS IF NOTHING WAS WRONG.
I KNOW HIM. HIS "DAD RADAR" IS BEEPING LIKE CRAZY. HE KNOWS I BROKE *SOMETHING*, HE JUST DOESN'T KNOW *WHAT*. HE CAN'T NAIL ME UNTIL HE KNOWS FOR SURE. HE'LL JUST WAIT. I KNOW HIM.
HE'S GOING TO JUST SIT THERE EATING AND LET ME STEW IN MY OWN GUILT. HE FIGURES SOONER OR LATER I'LL CRACK.
CALVIN?
AAUGH! I DID IT! I DID IT! I'M SORRY! I DIDN'T MEAN TO!!
..PASS THE UH.. ..THE UH...
WATTERSON

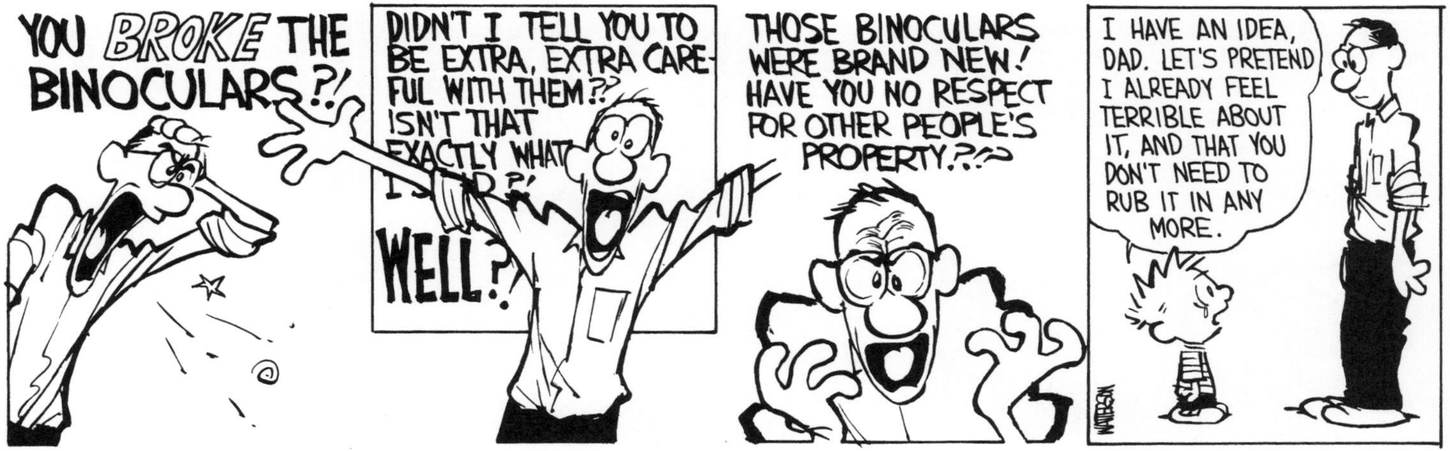
YOU *BROKE* THE BINOCULARS?!
DIDN'T I TELL YOU TO BE EXTRA, EXTRA CAREFUL WITH THEM?? ISN'T THAT EXACTLY WHAT
WELL?!
THOSE BINOCULARS WERE BRAND NEW! HAVE YOU NO RESPECT FOR OTHER PEOPLE'S PROPERTY?!?
I HAVE AN IDEA, DAD. LET'S PRETEND I ALREADY FEEL TERRIBLE ABOUT IT, AND THAT YOU DON'T NEED TO RUB IT IN ANY MORE.
WATTERSON

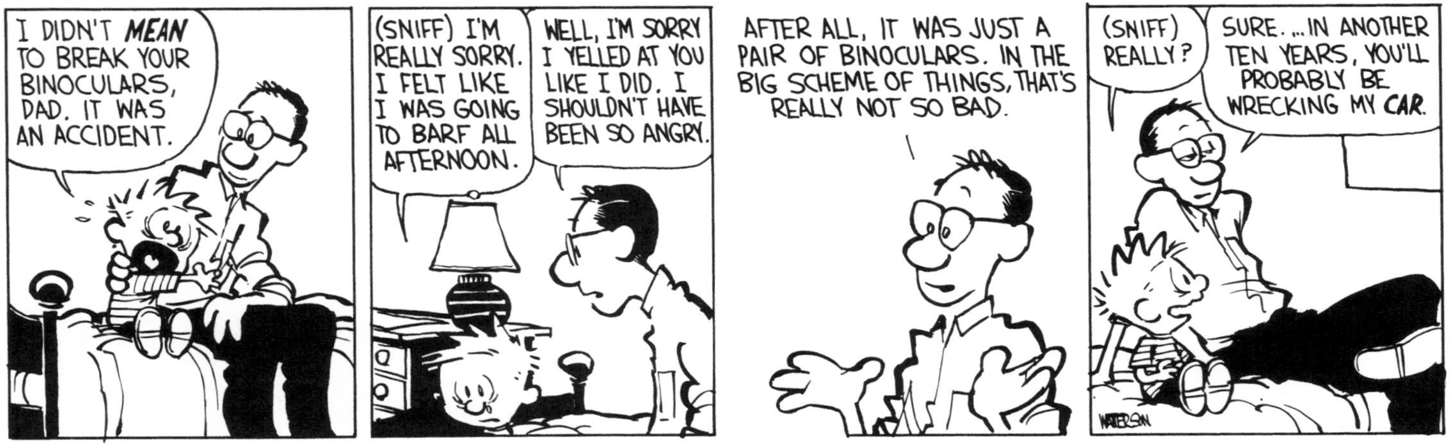
I DIDN'T MEAN TO BREAK YOUR BINOCULARS, DAD. IT WAS AN ACCIDENT.
(SNIFF) I'M REALLY SORRY. I FELT LIKE I WAS GOING TO BARF ALL AFTERNOON.
WELL, I'M SORRY I YELLED AT YOU LIKE I DID. I SHOULDN'T HAVE BEEN SO ANGRY.
AFTER ALL, IT WAS JUST A PAIR OF BINOCULARS. IN THE BIG SCHEME OF THINGS, THAT'S REALLY NOT SO BAD.
(SNIFF) REALLY?
SURE. ...IN ANOTHER TEN YEARS, YOU'LL PROBABLY BE WRECKING MY CAR.
WATTERSON

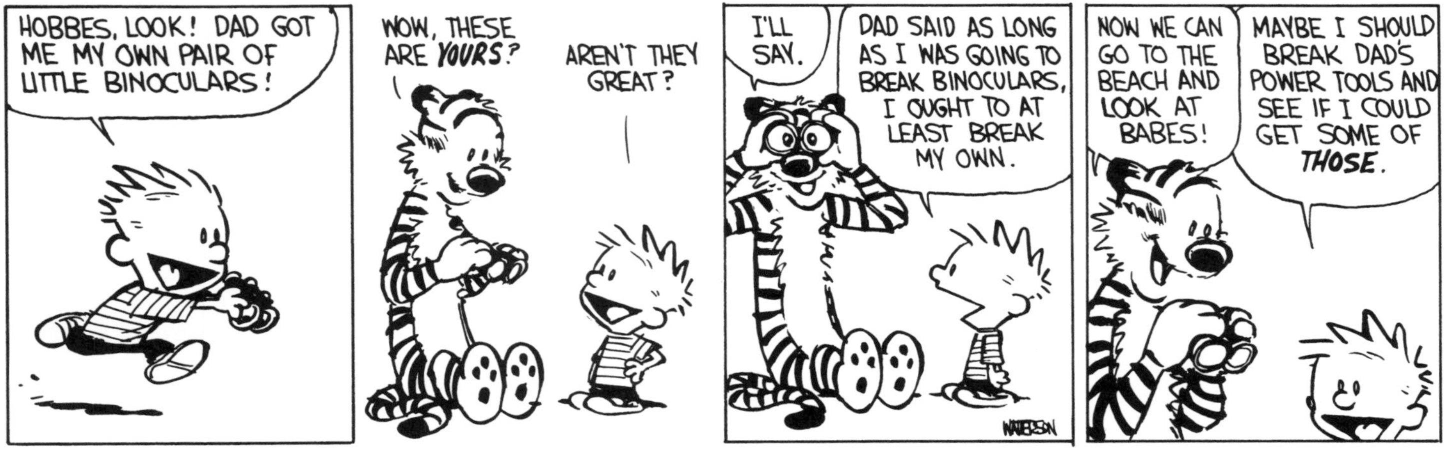
HOBBES, LOOK! DAD GOT ME MY OWN PAIR OF LITTLE BINOCULARS!
WOW, THESE ARE YOURS?
AREN'T THEY GREAT?
I'LL SAY.
DAD SAID AS LONG AS I WAS GOING TO BREAK BINOCULARS, I OUGHT TO AT LEAST BREAK MY OWN.
WATTERSON
NOW WE CAN GO TO THE BEACH AND LOOK AT BABES!
MAYBE I SHOULD BREAK DAD'S POWER TOOLS AND SEE IF I COULD GET SOME OF THOSE.

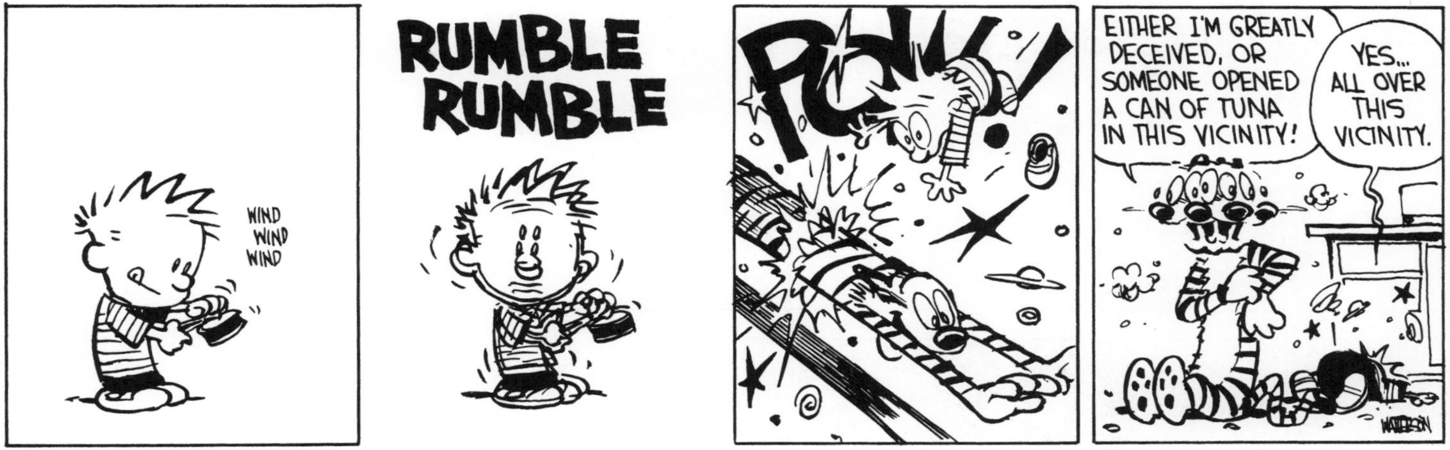
WIND
WIND
WIND
RUMBLE
RUMBLE
POW!
EITHER I'M GREATLY DECEIVED, OR SOMEONE OPENED A CAN OF TUNA IN THIS VICINITY!
YES... ALL OVER THIS VICINITY.
WATTERSON

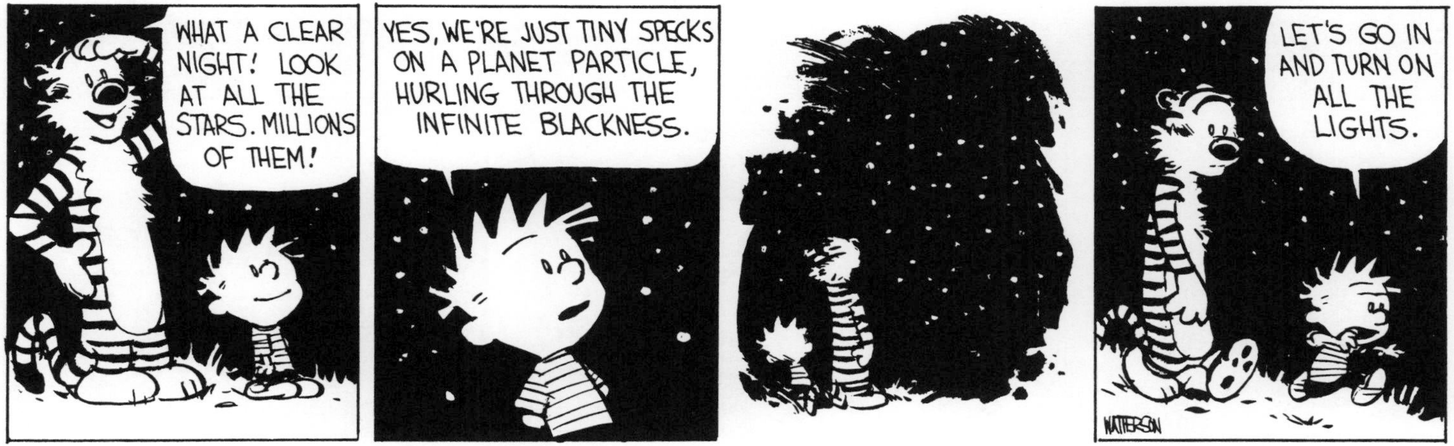
WHAT A CLEAR NIGHT! LOOK AT ALL THE STARS. MILLIONS OF THEM!
YES, WE'RE JUST TINY SPECKS ON A PLANET PARTICLE, HURLING THROUGH THE INFINITE BLACKNESS.
LET'S GO IN AND TURN ON ALL THE LIGHTS.
WATTERSON

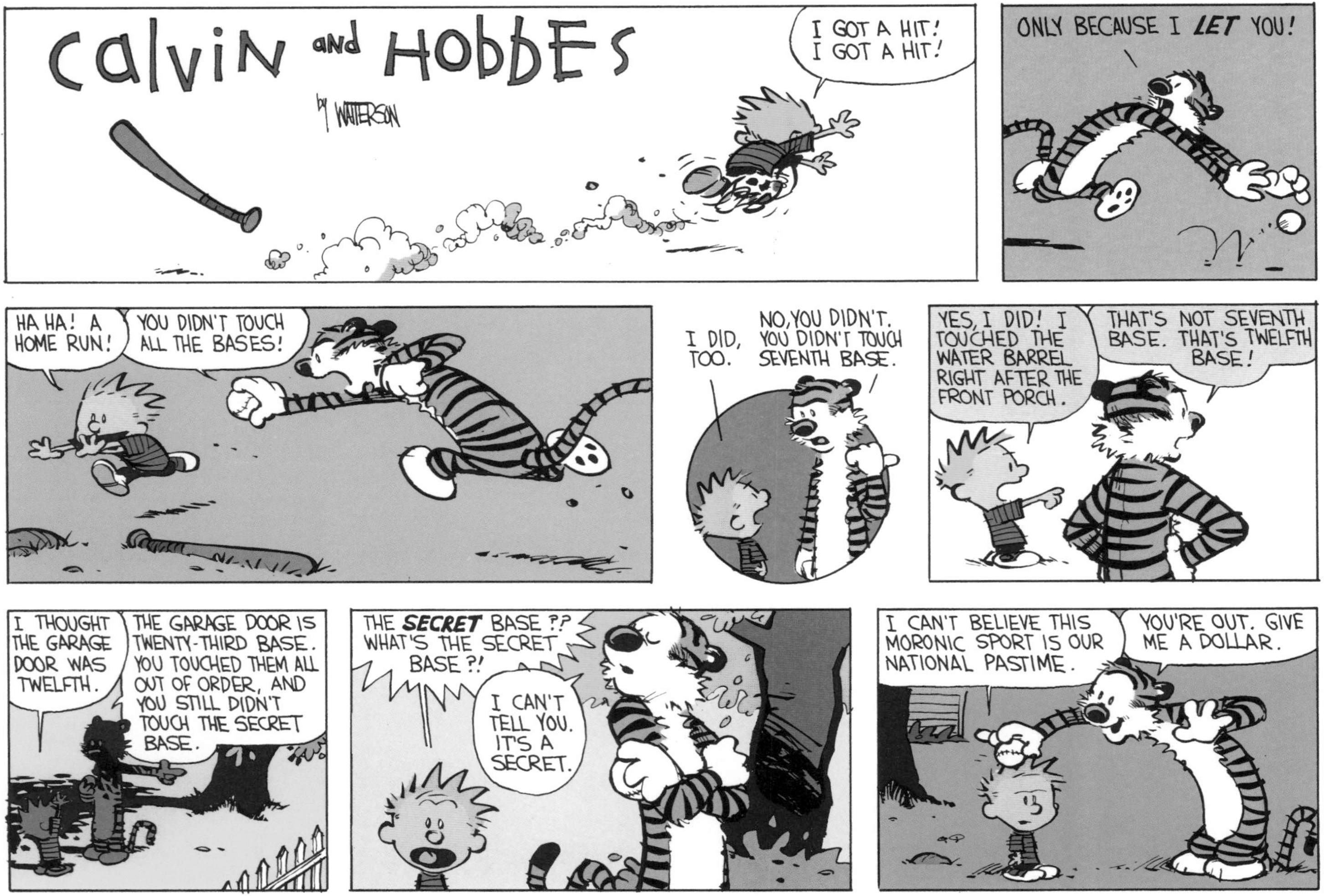
Calvin and HobbEs
by WATTERSON
I GOT A HIT! I GOT A HIT!
ONLY BECAUSE I LET YOU!
HA HA! A HOME RUN!
YOU DIDN'T TOUCH ALL THE BASES!
I DID, TOO.
NO, YOU DIDN'T. YOU DIDN'T TOUCH SEVENTH BASE.
YES, I DID! I TOUCHED THE WATER BARREL RIGHT AFTER THE FRONT PORCH.
THAT'S NOT SEVENTH BASE. THAT'S TWELFTH BASE!
I THOUGHT THE GARAGE DOOR WAS TWELFTH.
THE GARAGE DOOR IS TWENTY-THIRD BASE. YOU TOUCHED THEM ALL OUT OF ORDER, AND YOU STILL DIDN'T TOUCH THE SECRET BASE.
THE SECRET BASE ?? WHAT'S THE SECRET BASE ?!
I CAN'T TELL YOU. IT'S A SECRET.
I CAN'T BELIEVE THIS MORONIC SPORT IS OUR NATIONAL PASTIME.
YOU'RE OUT. GIVE ME A DOLLAR.

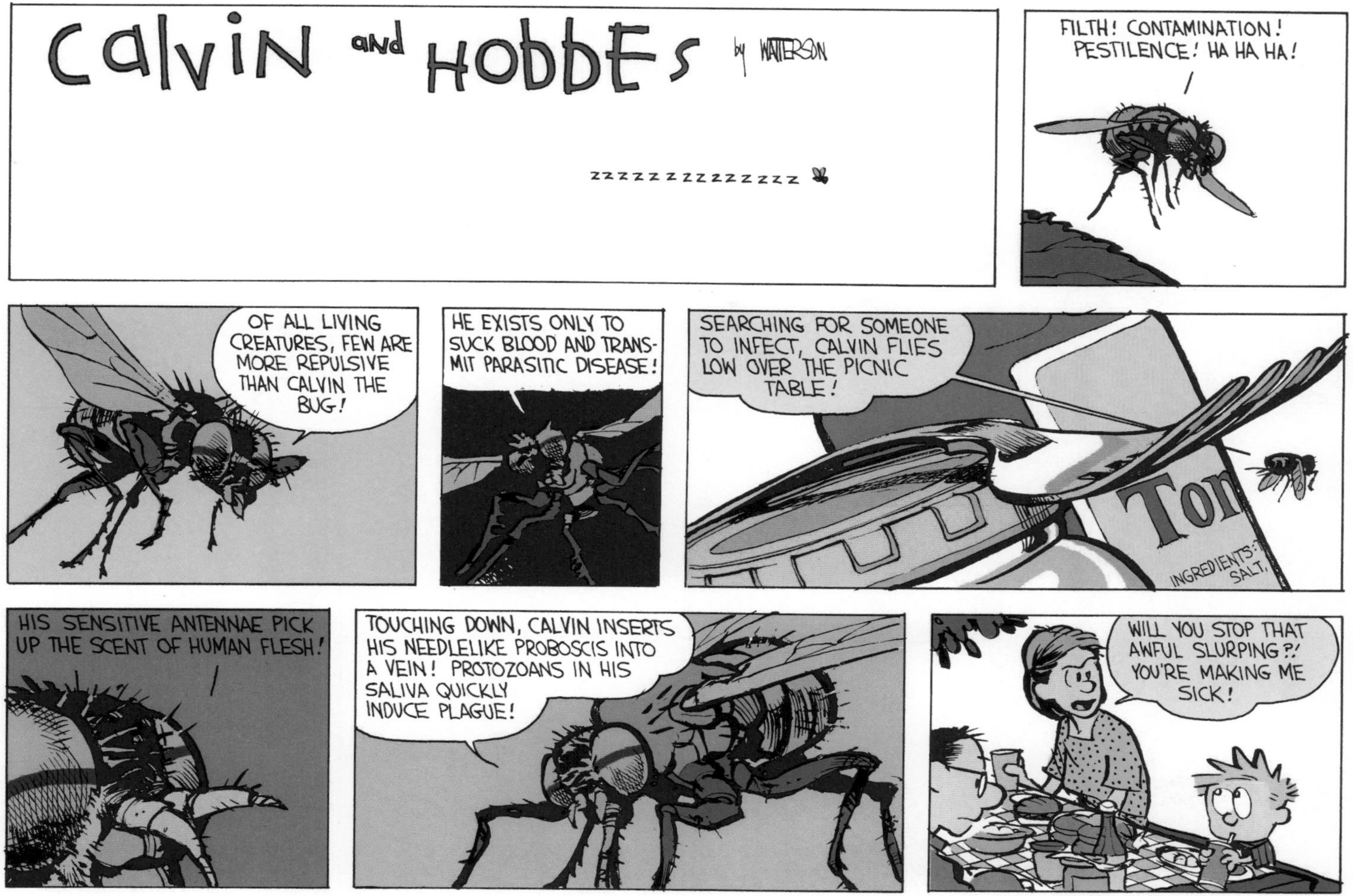
Calvin and HOBBES by WATTERSON
ZZZZZZZZZZZZZZZ
FILTH! CONTAMINATION! PESTILENCE! HA HA HA!
OF ALL LIVING CREATURES, FEW ARE MORE REPULSIVE THAN CALVIN THE BUG!
HE EXISTS ONLY TO SUCK BLOOD AND TRANSMIT PARASITIC DISEASE!
SEARCHING FOR SOMEONE TO INFECT, CALVIN FLIES LOW OVER THE PICNIC TABLE!
Tom
INGREDIENTS: SALT,
HIS SENSITIVE ANTENNAE PICK UP THE SCENT OF HUMAN FLESH!
TOUCHING DOWN, CALVIN INSERTS HIS NEEDLELIKE PROBOSCIS INTO A VEIN! PROTOZOANS IN HIS SALIVA QUICKLY INDUCE PLAGUE!
WILL YOU STOP THAT AWFUL SLURPING?! YOU'RE MAKING ME SICK!

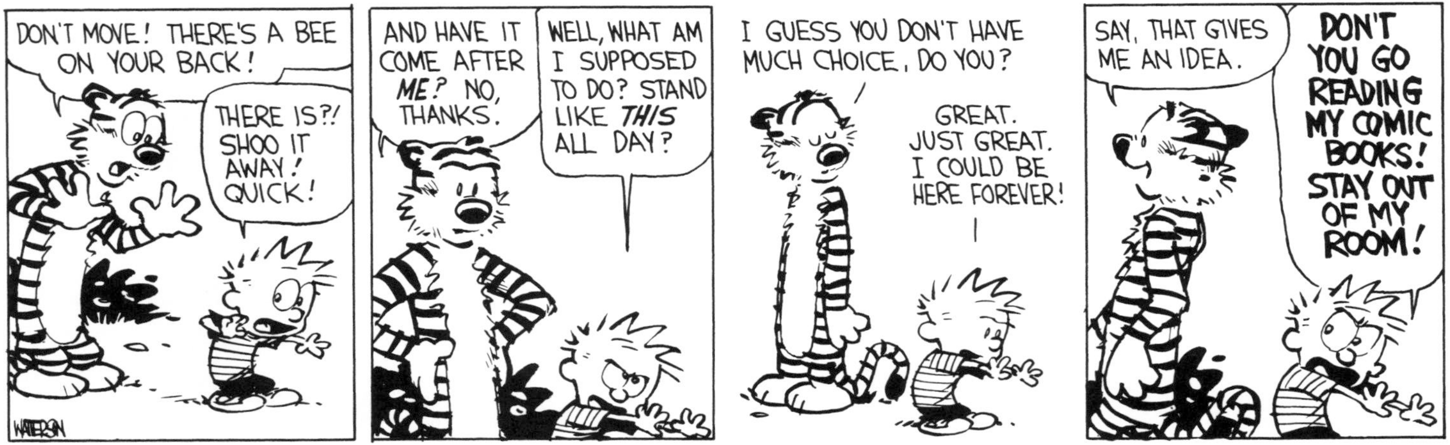
DON'T MOVE! THERE'S A BEE ON YOUR BACK!
THERE IS?! SHOO IT AWAY! QUICK!
AND HAVE IT COME AFTER *ME?* NO, THANKS.
WELL, WHAT AM I SUPPOSED TO DO? STAND LIKE *THIS* ALL DAY?
I GUESS YOU DON'T HAVE MUCH CHOICE, DO YOU?
GREAT. JUST GREAT. I COULD BE HERE FOREVER!
SAY, THAT GIVES ME AN IDEA.
DON'T YOU GO READING MY COMIC BOOKS! STAY OUT OF MY ROOM!

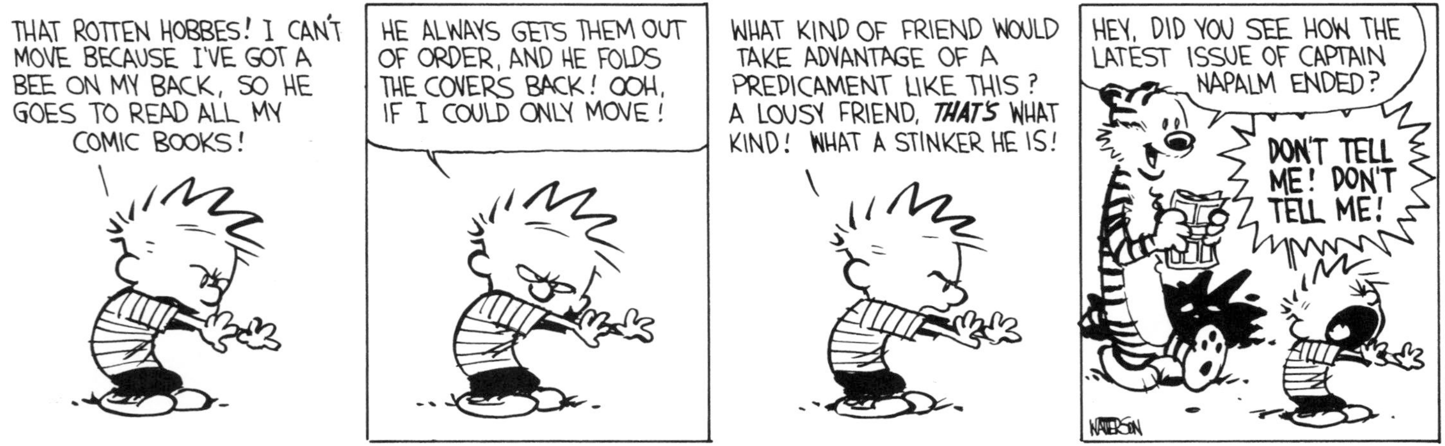
THAT ROTTEN HOBBES! I CAN'T MOVE BECAUSE I'VE GOT A BEE ON MY BACK, SO HE GOES TO READ ALL MY COMIC BOOKS!
HE ALWAYS GETS THEM OUT OF ORDER, AND HE FOLDS THE COVERS BACK! OOH, IF I COULD ONLY MOVE!
WHAT KIND OF FRIEND WOULD TAKE ADVANTAGE OF A PREDICAMENT LIKE THIS? A LOUSY FRIEND, *THAT'S* WHAT KIND! WHAT A STINKER HE IS!
HEY, DID YOU SEE HOW THE LATEST ISSUE OF CAPTAIN NAPALM ENDED?
DON'T TELL ME! DON'T TELL ME!

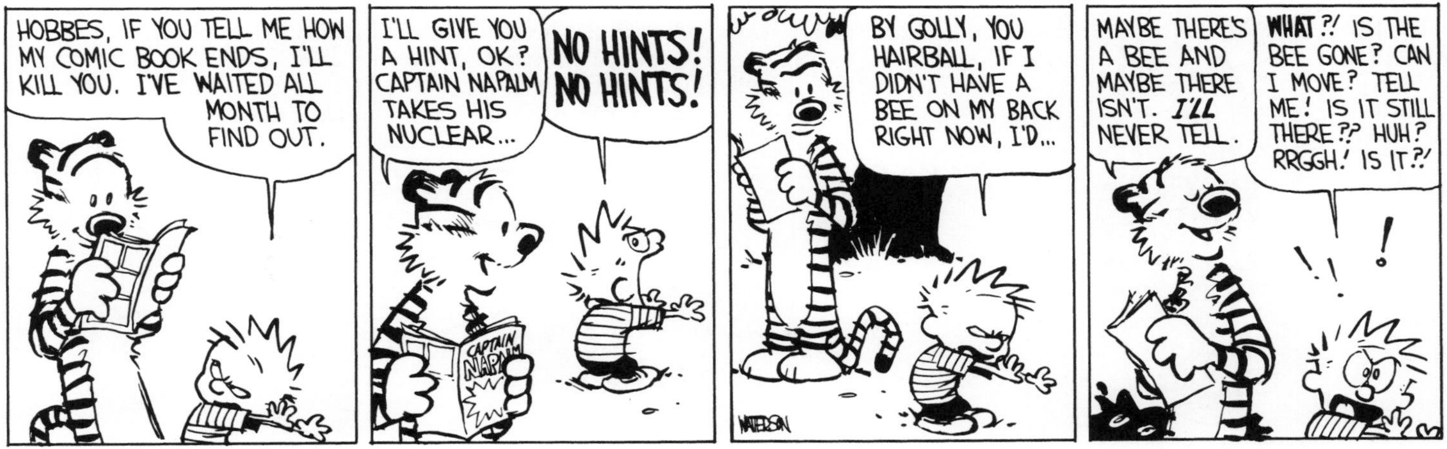
HOBBES, IF YOU TELL ME HOW MY COMIC BOOK ENDS, I'LL KILL YOU. I'VE WAITED ALL MONTH TO FIND OUT.
I'LL GIVE YOU A HINT, OK? CAPTAIN NAPALM TAKES HIS NUCLEAR...
NO HINTS! NO HINTS!
CAPTAIN NAPALM
BY GOLLY, YOU HAIRBALL, IF I DIDN'T HAVE A BEE ON MY BACK RIGHT NOW, I'D...
WATTERSON
MAYBE THERE'S A BEE AND MAYBE THERE ISN'T. I'LL NEVER TELL.
WHAT?! IS THE BEE GONE? CAN I MOVE? TELL ME! IS IT STILL THERE?? HUH? RRGGH! IS IT?!

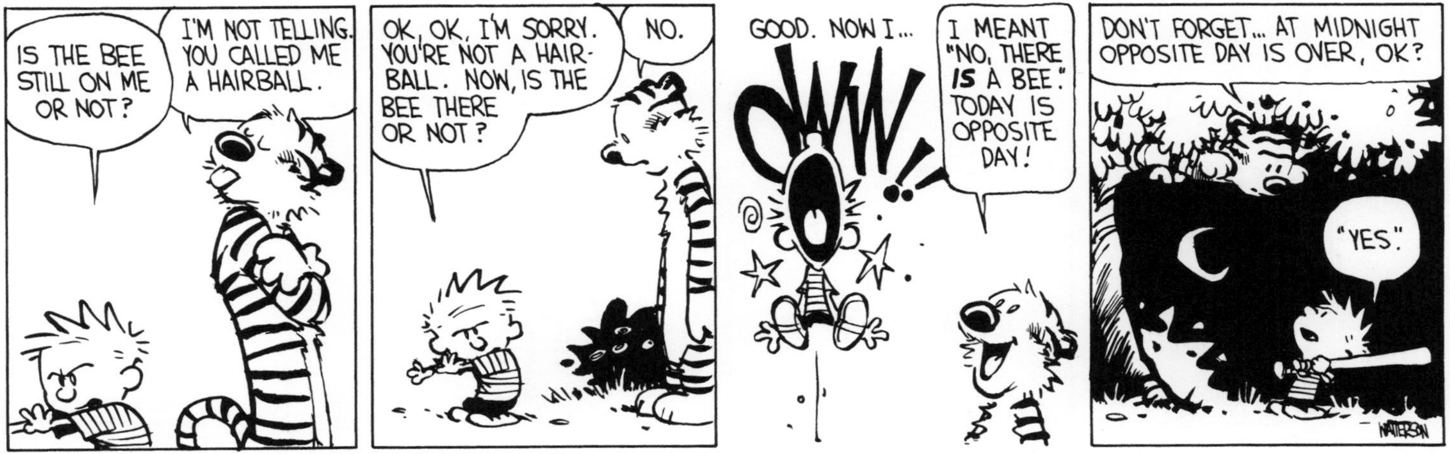
IS THE BEE STILL ON ME OR NOT?
I'M NOT TELLING. YOU CALLED ME A HAIRBALL.
OK, OK, I'M SORRY. YOU'RE NOT A HAIRBALL. NOW, IS THE BEE THERE OR NOT?
NO.
GOOD. NOW I...
OWW!!
I MEANT "NO, THERE IS A BEE." TODAY IS OPPOSITE DAY!
DON'T FORGET... AT MIDNIGHT OPPOSITE DAY IS OVER, OK?
"YES."
WATTERSON

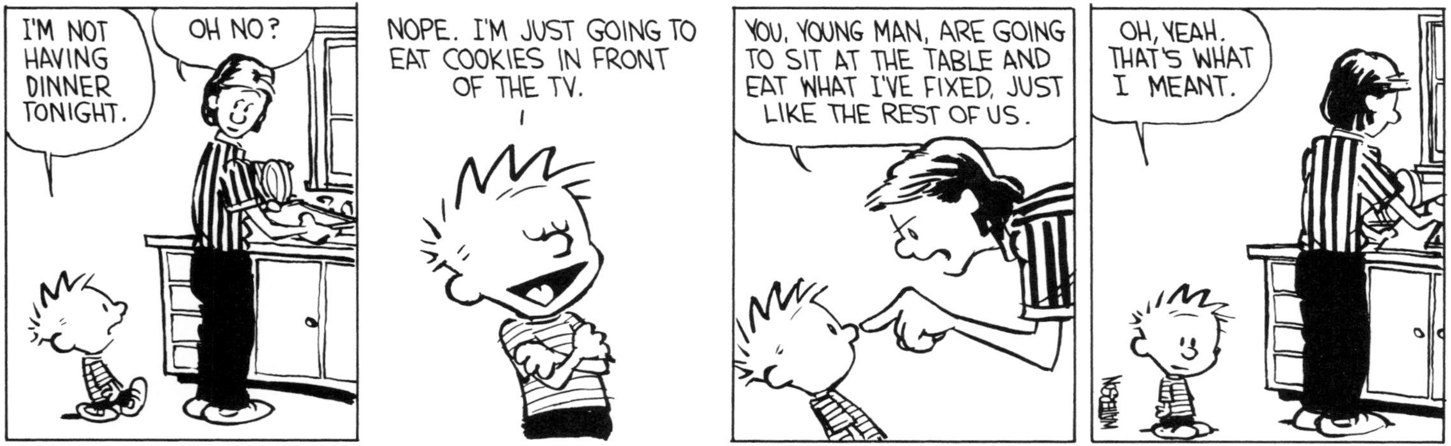
I'M NOT HAVING DINNER TONIGHT.
OH NO?
NOPE. I'M JUST GOING TO EAT COOKIES IN FRONT OF THE TV.
YOU, YOUNG MAN, ARE GOING TO SIT AT THE TABLE AND EAT WHAT I'VE FIXED, JUST LIKE THE REST OF US.
OH, YEAH. THAT'S WHAT I MEANT.
WATTERSON

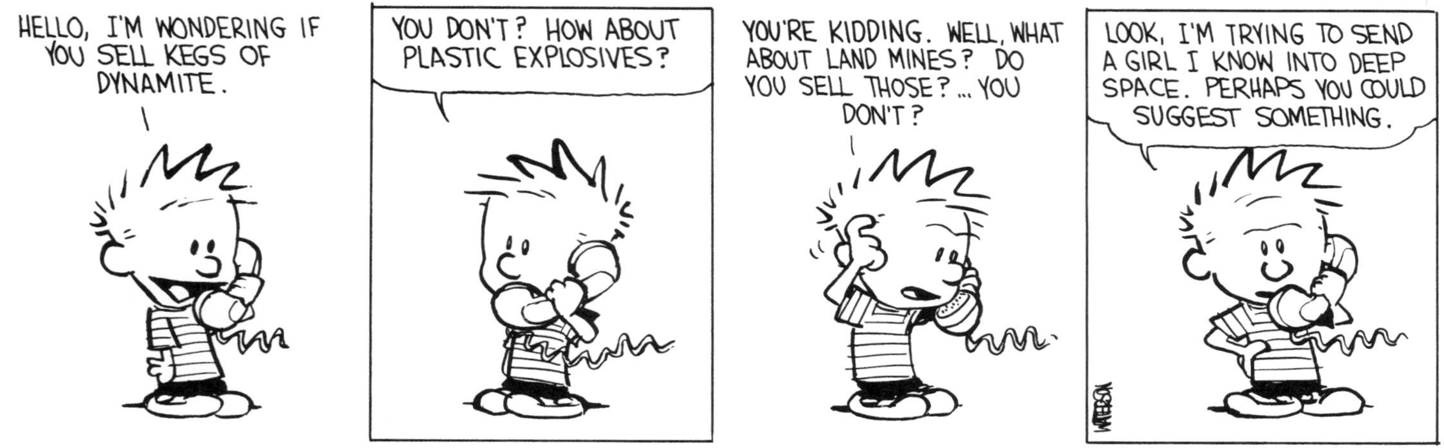
HELLO, I'M WONDERING IF YOU SELL KEGS OF DYNAMITE.
YOU DON'T? HOW ABOUT PLASTIC EXPLOSIVES?
YOU'RE KIDDING. WELL, WHAT ABOUT LAND MINES? DO YOU SELL THOSE? ... YOU DON'T?
LOOK, I'M TRYING TO SEND A GIRL I KNOW INTO DEEP SPACE. PERHAPS YOU COULD SUGGEST SOMETHING.
WATTERSON

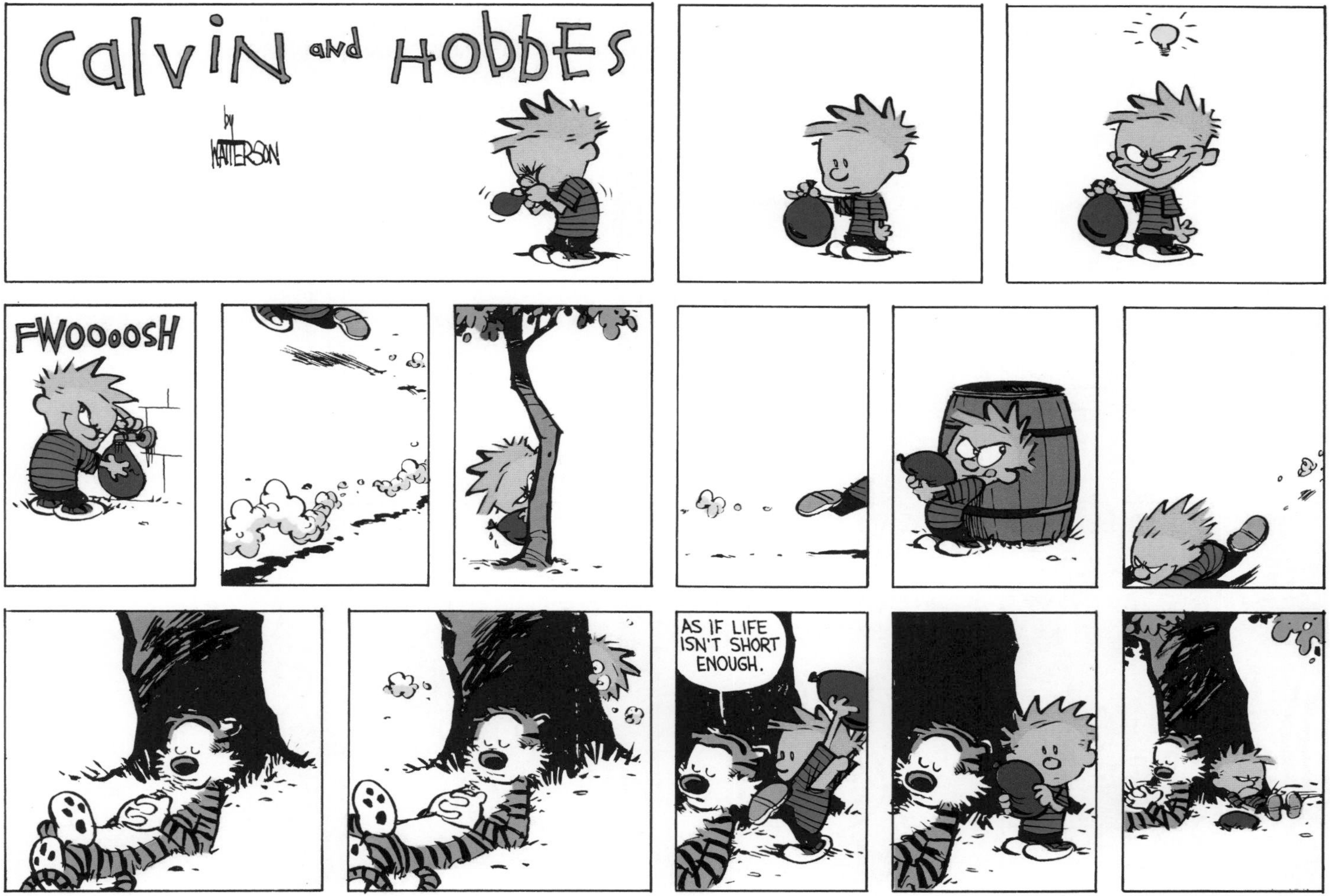
Calvin and HOBBES
by WATTERSON
FWOOooSH
AS IF LIFE ISN'T SHORT ENOUGH.

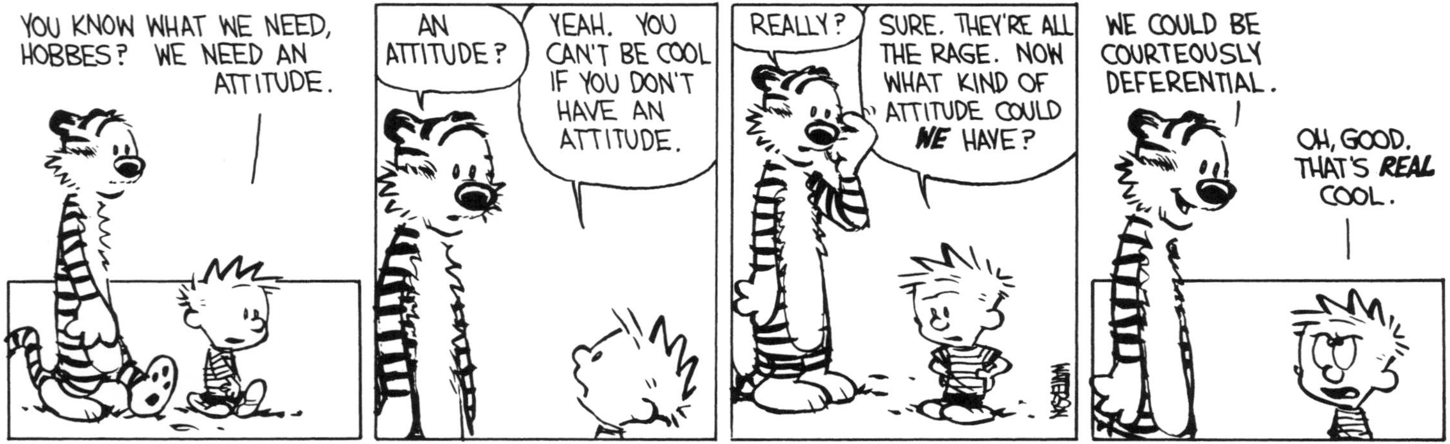
YOU KNOW WHAT WE NEED, HOBBES? WE NEED AN ATTITUDE.
AN ATTITUDE?
YEAH. YOU CAN'T BE COOL IF YOU DON'T HAVE AN ATTITUDE.
REALLY?
SURE. THEY'RE ALL THE RAGE. NOW WHAT KIND OF ATTITUDE COULD **WE** HAVE?
WE COULD BE COURTEOUSLY DEFERENTIAL.
OH, GOOD. THAT'S **REAL** COOL.

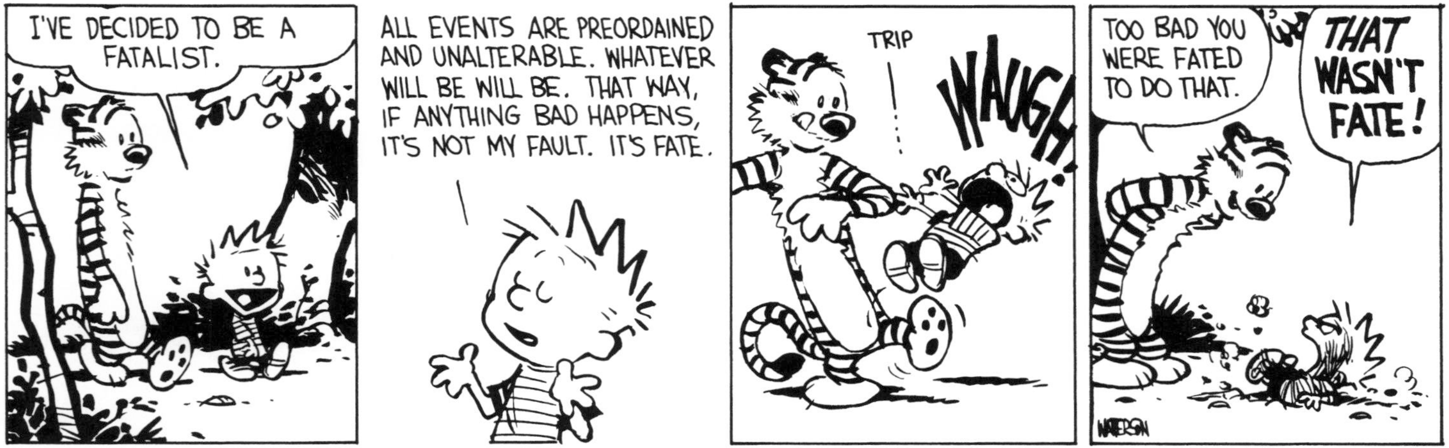
I'VE DECIDED TO BE A FATALIST.
ALL EVENTS ARE PREORDAINED AND UNALTERABLE. WHATEVER WILL BE WILL BE. THAT WAY, IF ANYTHING BAD HAPPENS, IT'S NOT MY FAULT. IT'S FATE.
TRIP
WAUGH!
TOO BAD YOU WERE FATED TO DO THAT.
THAT WASN'T FATE!

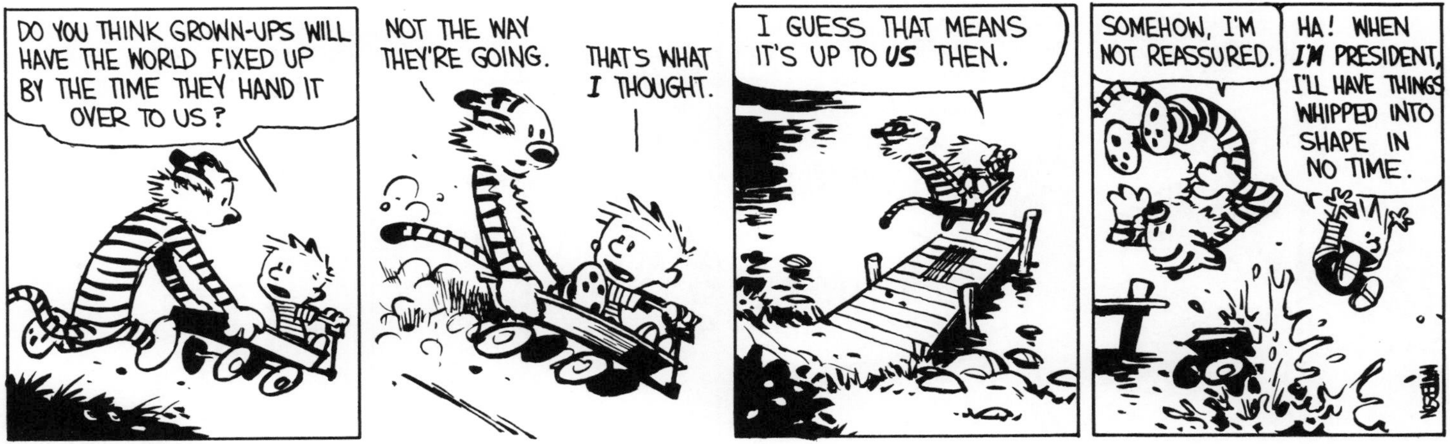
DO YOU THINK GROWN-UPS WILL HAVE THE WORLD FIXED UP BY THE TIME THEY HAND IT OVER TO US?
NOT THE WAY THEY'RE GOING.
THAT'S WHAT I THOUGHT.
I GUESS THAT MEANS IT'S UP TO US THEN.
SOMEHOW, I'M NOT REASSURED.
HA! WHEN I'M PRESIDENT, I'LL HAVE THINGS WHIPPED INTO SHAPE IN NO TIME.

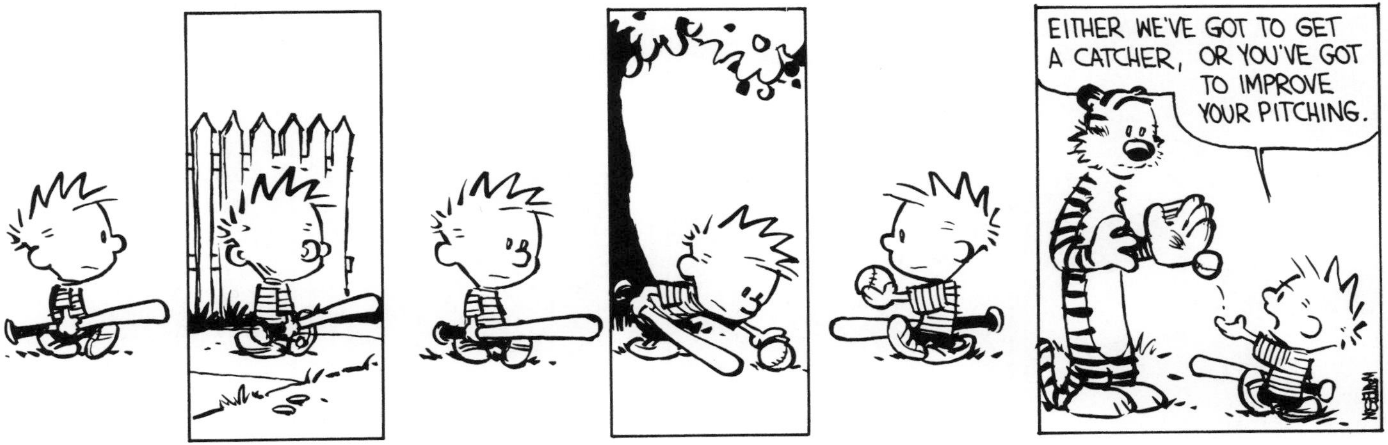
EITHER WE'VE GOT TO GET A CATCHER, OR YOU'VE GOT TO IMPROVE YOUR PITCHING.

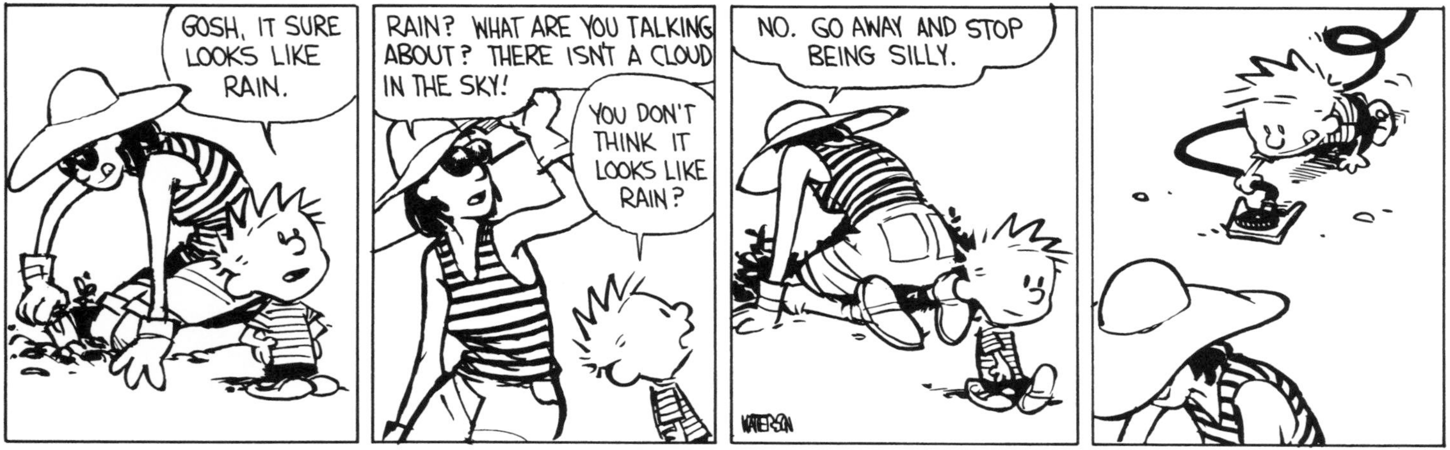
GOSH, IT SURE LOOKS LIKE RAIN.
RAIN? WHAT ARE YOU TALKING ABOUT? THERE ISN'T A CLOUD IN THE SKY!
YOU DON'T THINK IT LOOKS LIKE RAIN?
NO. GO AWAY AND STOP BEING SILLY.
WATTERSON

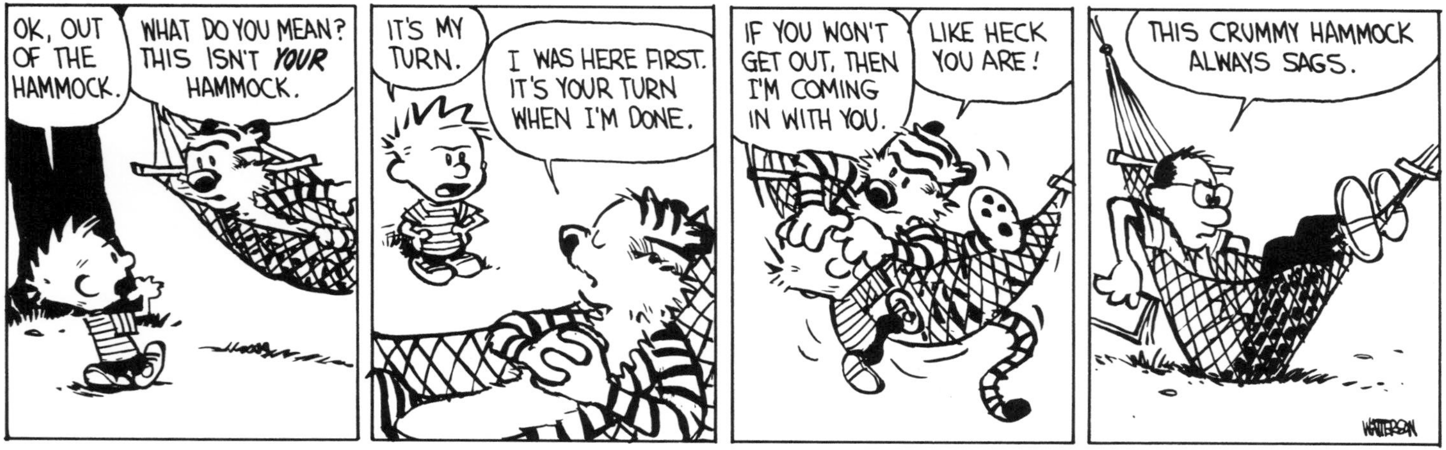
OK, OUT OF THE HAMMOCK.
WHAT DO YOU MEAN? THIS ISN'T *YOUR* HAMMOCK.
IT'S MY TURN.
I WAS HERE FIRST. IT'S YOUR TURN WHEN I'M DONE.
IF YOU WON'T GET OUT, THEN I'M COMING IN WITH YOU.
LIKE HECK YOU ARE!
THIS CRUMMY HAMMOCK ALWAYS SAGS.
WATTERSON

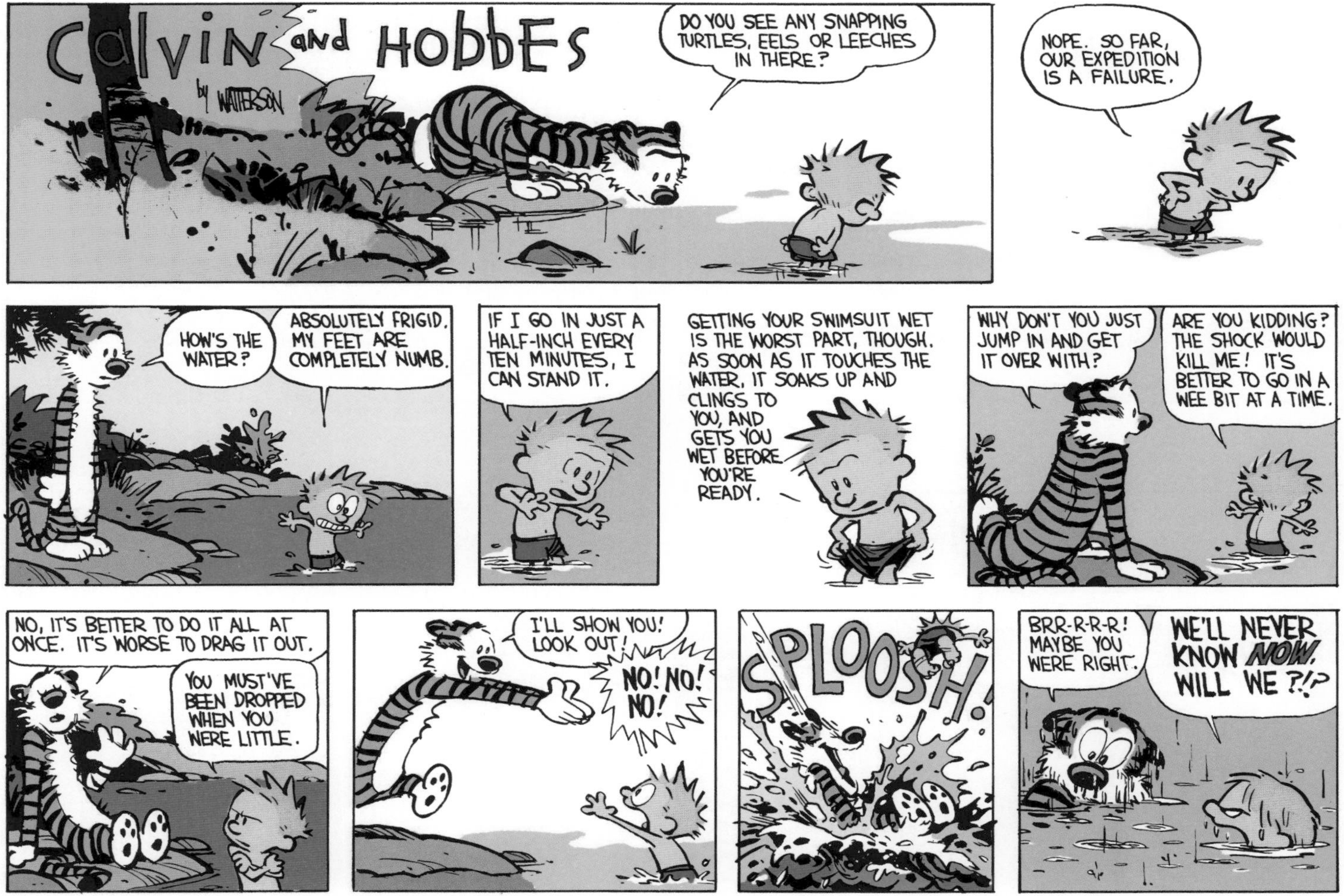
Calvin and HOBBES
by WATTERSON
DO YOU SEE ANY SNAPPING TURTLES, EELS OR LEECHES IN THERE?
NOPE. SO FAR, OUR EXPEDITION IS A FAILURE.
HOW'S THE WATER?
ABSOLUTELY FRIGID. MY FEET ARE COMPLETELY NUMB.
IF I GO IN JUST A HALF-INCH EVERY TEN MINUTES, I CAN STAND IT.
GETTING YOUR SWIMSUIT WET IS THE WORST PART, THOUGH. AS SOON AS IT TOUCHES THE WATER, IT SOAKS UP AND CLINGS TO YOU, AND GETS YOU WET BEFORE YOU'RE READY.
WHY DON'T YOU JUST JUMP IN AND GET IT OVER WITH?
ARE YOU KIDDING? THE SHOCK WOULD KILL ME! IT'S BETTER TO GO IN A WEE BIT AT A TIME.
NO, IT'S BETTER TO DO IT ALL AT ONCE. IT'S WORSE TO DRAG IT OUT.
YOU MUST'VE BEEN DROPPED WHEN YOU WERE LITTLE.
I'LL SHOW YOU! LOOK OUT!
NO! NO! NO!
SPLOOSH!
BRR-R-R-R! MAYBE YOU WERE RIGHT.
WE'LL NEVER KNOW NOW, WILL WE ?!?

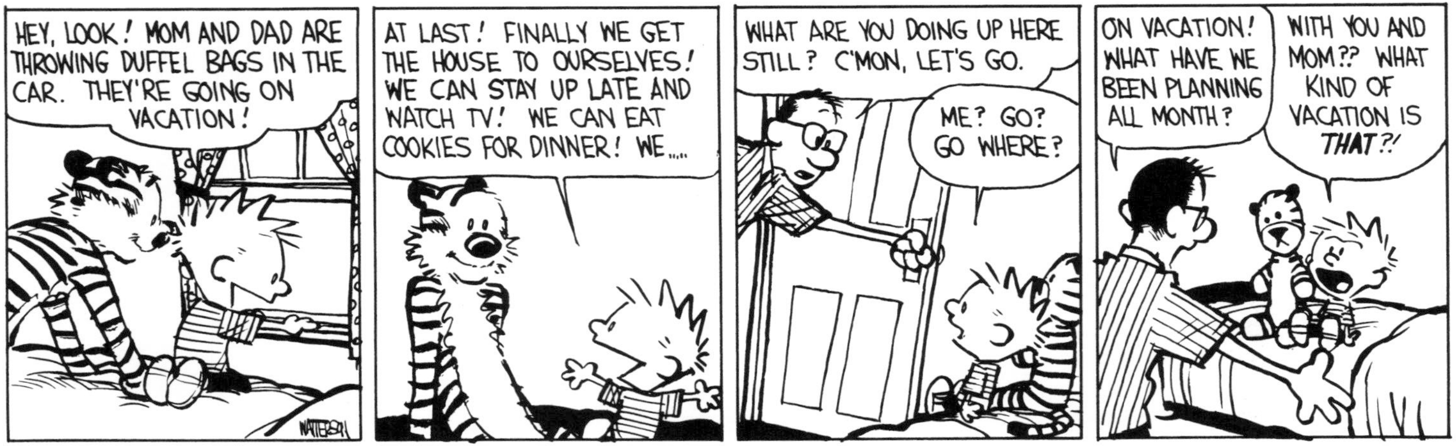
HEY, LOOK! MOM AND DAD ARE THROWING DUFFEL BAGS IN THE CAR. THEY'RE GOING ON VACATION!
AT LAST! FINALLY WE GET THE HOUSE TO OURSELVES! WE CAN STAY UP LATE AND WATCH TV! WE CAN EAT COOKIES FOR DINNER! WE.....
WHAT ARE YOU DOING UP HERE STILL? C'MON, LET'S GO.
ME? GO? GO WHERE?
ON VACATION! WHAT HAVE WE BEEN PLANNING ALL MONTH?
WITH YOU AND MOM?? WHAT KIND OF VACATION IS ***THAT***?!
WATTERSON

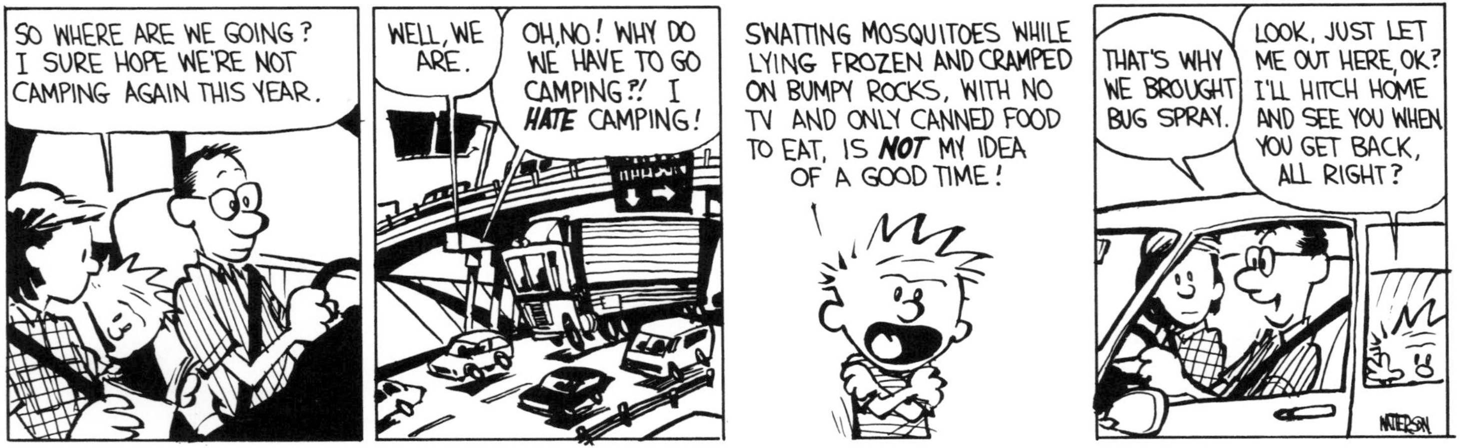
SO WHERE ARE WE GOING? I SURE HOPE WE'RE NOT CAMPING AGAIN THIS YEAR.
WELL, WE ARE.
OH, NO! WHY DO WE HAVE TO GO CAMPING?! I ***HATE*** CAMPING!
SWATTING MOSQUITOES WHILE LYING FROZEN AND CRAMPED ON BUMPY ROCKS, WITH NO TV AND ONLY CANNED FOOD TO EAT, IS ***NOT*** MY IDEA OF A GOOD TIME!
THAT'S WHY WE BROUGHT BUG SPRAY.
LOOK, JUST LET ME OUT HERE, OK? I'LL HITCH HOME AND SEE YOU WHEN YOU GET BACK, ALL RIGHT?
WATTERSON

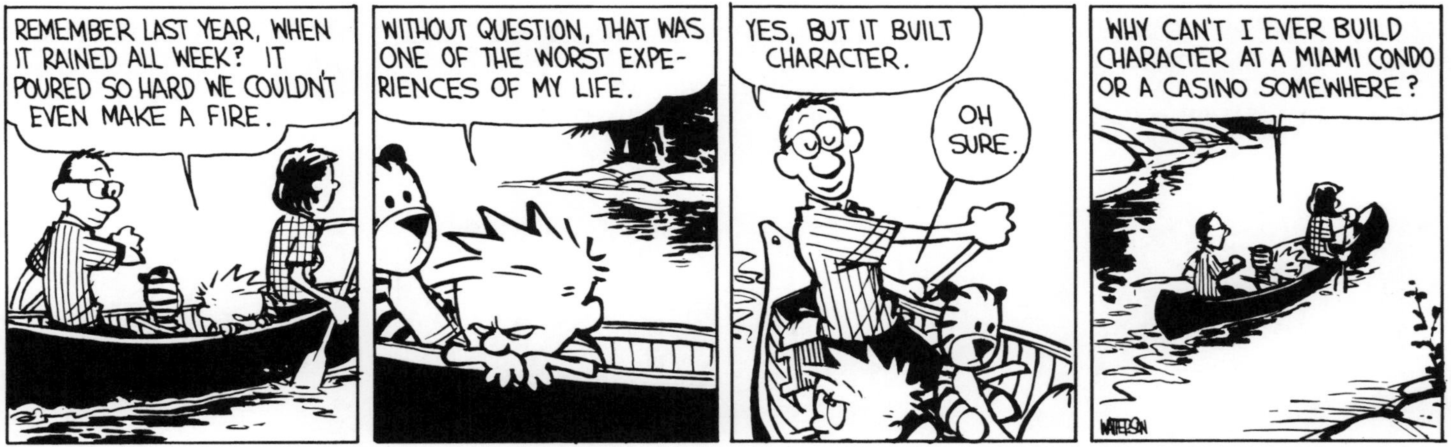
REMEMBER LAST YEAR, WHEN IT RAINED ALL WEEK? IT POURED SO HARD WE COULDN'T EVEN MAKE A FIRE.
WITHOUT QUESTION, THAT WAS ONE OF THE WORST EXPE-RIENCES OF MY LIFE.
YES, BUT IT BUILT CHARACTER.
OH SURE.
WHY CAN'T I EVER BUILD CHARACTER AT A MIAMI CONDO OR A CASINO SOMEWHERE?
WATTERSON

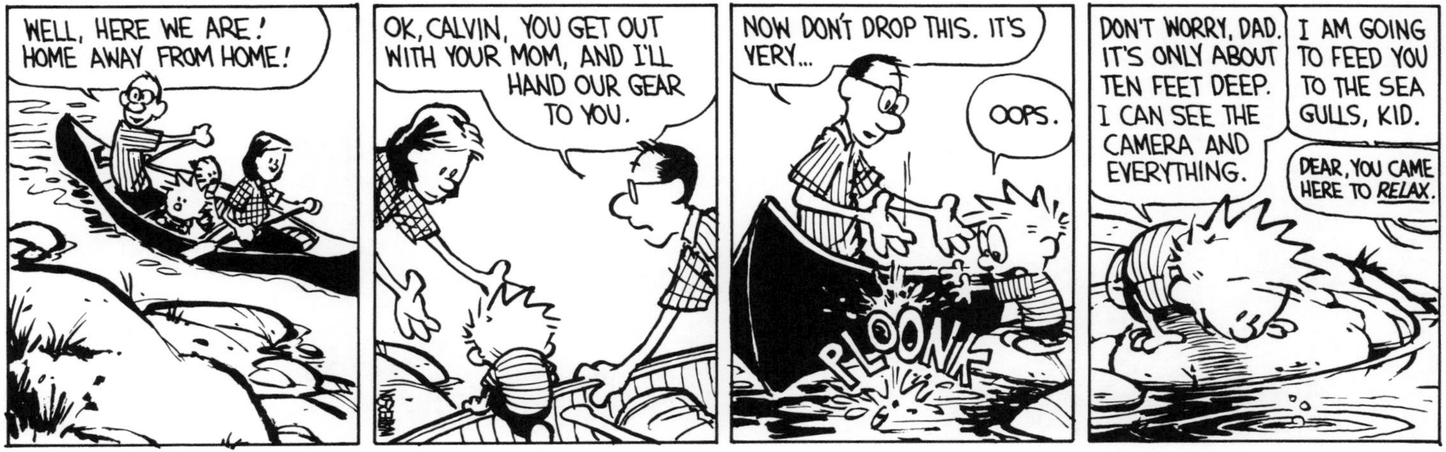
WELL, HERE WE ARE! HOME AWAY FROM HOME!
OK, CALVIN, YOU GET OUT WITH YOUR MOM, AND I'LL HAND OUR GEAR TO YOU.
WATTERSON
NOW DON'T DROP THIS. IT'S VERY...
OOPS.
PLOONK
DON'T WORRY, DAD. IT'S ONLY ABOUT TEN FEET DEEP. I CAN SEE THE CAMERA AND EVERYTHING.
I AM GOING TO FEED YOU TO THE SEA GULLS, KID.
DEAR, YOU CAME HERE TO *RELAX*.

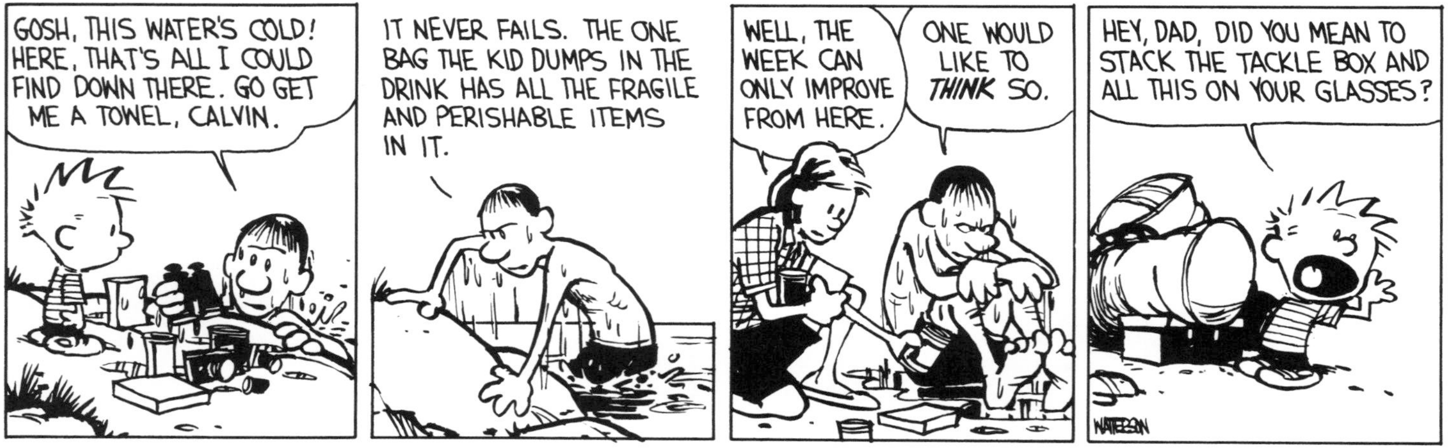
GOSH, THIS WATER'S COLD! HERE, THAT'S ALL I COULD FIND DOWN THERE. GO GET ME A TOWEL, CALVIN.
IT NEVER FAILS. THE ONE BAG THE KID DUMPS IN THE DRINK HAS ALL THE FRAGILE AND PERISHABLE ITEMS IN IT.
WELL, THE WEEK CAN ONLY IMPROVE FROM HERE.
ONE WOULD LIKE TO *THINK* SO.
HEY, DAD, DID YOU MEAN TO STACK THE TACKLE BOX AND ALL THIS ON YOUR GLASSES?
WATTERSON

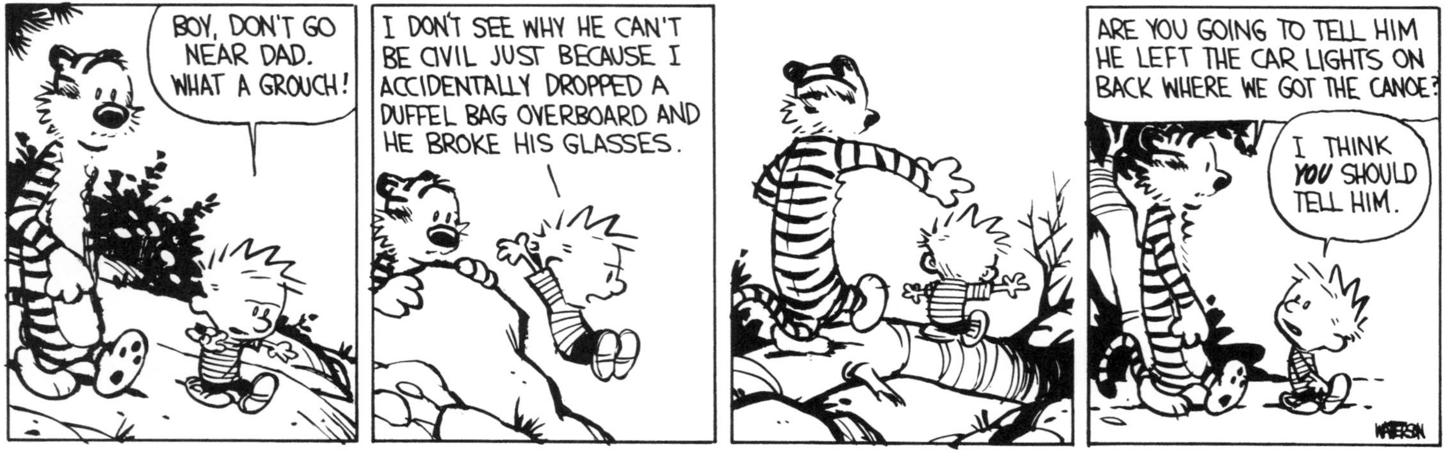
BOY, DON'T GO NEAR DAD. WHAT A GROUCH!
I DON'T SEE WHY HE CAN'T BE CIVIL JUST BECAUSE I ACCIDENTALLY DROPPED A DUFFEL BAG OVERBOARD AND HE BROKE HIS GLASSES.
ARE YOU GOING TO TELL HIM HE LEFT THE CAR LIGHTS ON BACK WHERE WE GOT THE CANOE?
I THINK *YOU* SHOULD TELL HIM.
WATTERSON

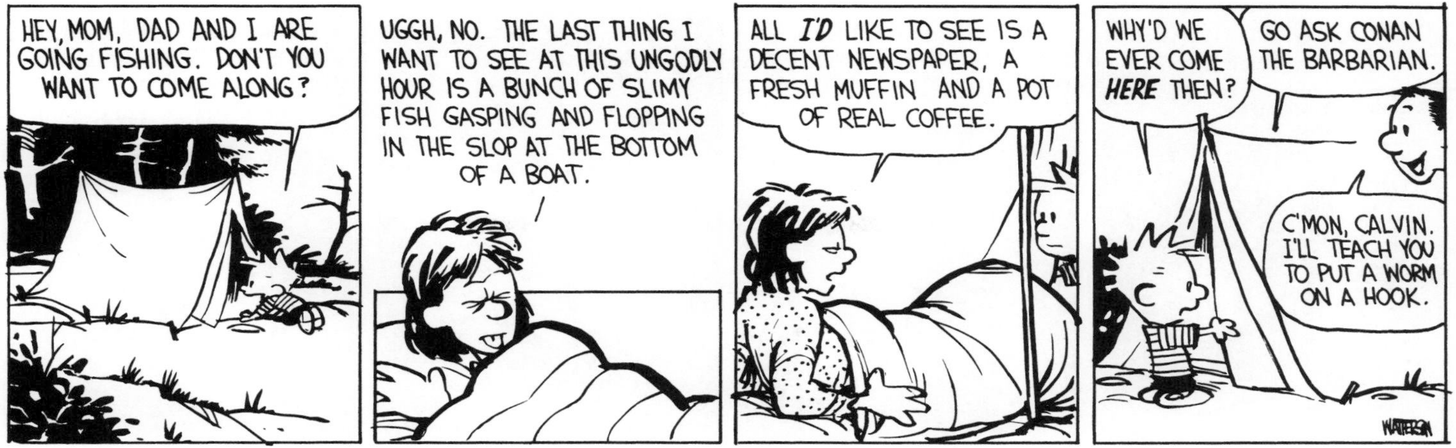
HEY, MOM, DAD AND I ARE GOING FISHING. DON'T YOU WANT TO COME ALONG?
UGGH, NO. THE LAST THING I WANT TO SEE AT THIS UNGODLY HOUR IS A BUNCH OF SLIMY FISH GASPING AND FLOPPING IN THE SLOP AT THE BOTTOM OF A BOAT.
ALL *I'D* LIKE TO SEE IS A DECENT NEWSPAPER, A FRESH MUFFIN AND A POT OF REAL COFFEE.
WHY'D WE EVER COME **HERE** THEN?
GO ASK CONAN THE BARBARIAN.
C'MON, CALVIN. I'LL TEACH YOU TO PUT A WORM ON A HOOK.
WATTERSON

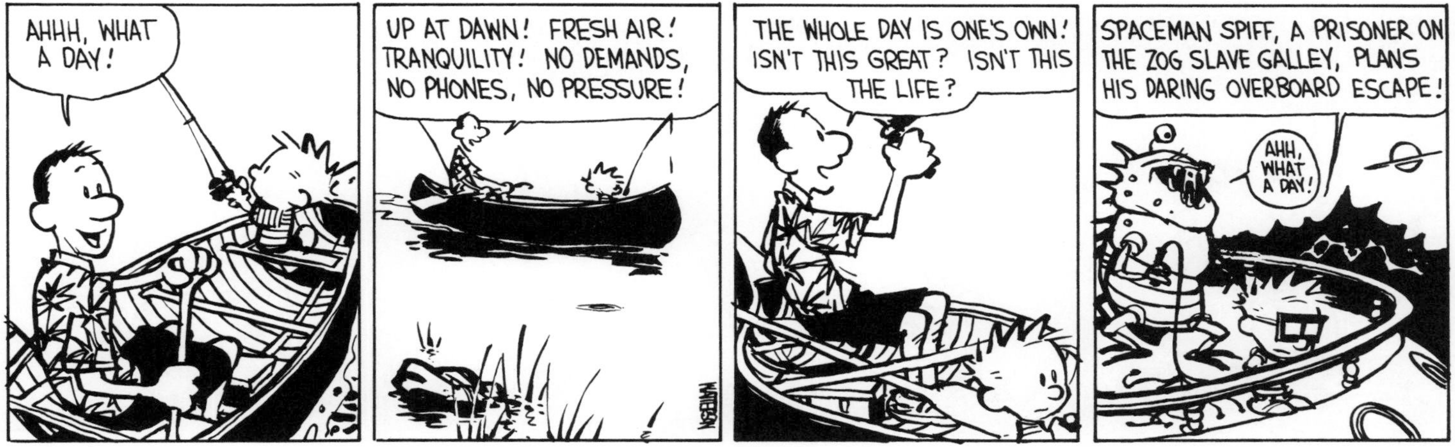
AHHH, WHAT A DAY!
UP AT DAWN! FRESH AIR! TRANQUILITY! NO DEMANDS, NO PHONES, NO PRESSURE!
WATTERSON
THE WHOLE DAY IS ONE'S OWN! ISN'T THIS GREAT? ISN'T THIS THE LIFE?
SPACEMAN SPIFF, A PRISONER ON THE ZOG SLAVE GALLEY, PLANS HIS DARING OVERBOARD ESCAPE!
AHH, WHAT A DAY!

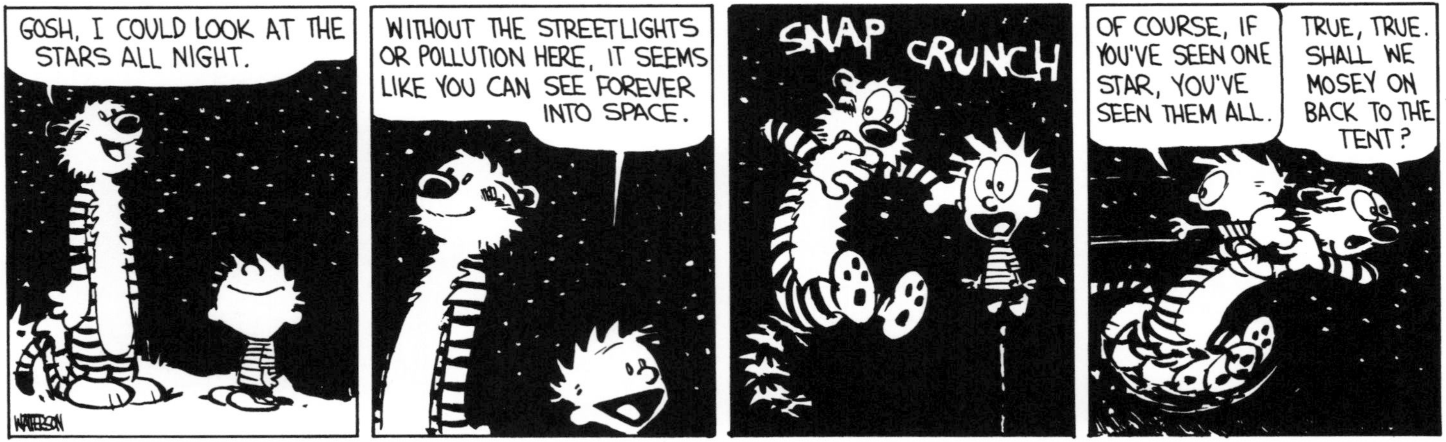
GOSH, I COULD LOOK AT THE STARS ALL NIGHT.
WITHOUT THE STREETLIGHTS OR POLLUTION HERE, IT SEEMS LIKE YOU CAN SEE FOREVER INTO SPACE.
SNAP
CRUNCH
OF COURSE, IF YOU'VE SEEN ONE STAR, YOU'VE SEEN THEM ALL.
TRUE, TRUE. SHALL WE MOSEY ON BACK TO THE TENT?

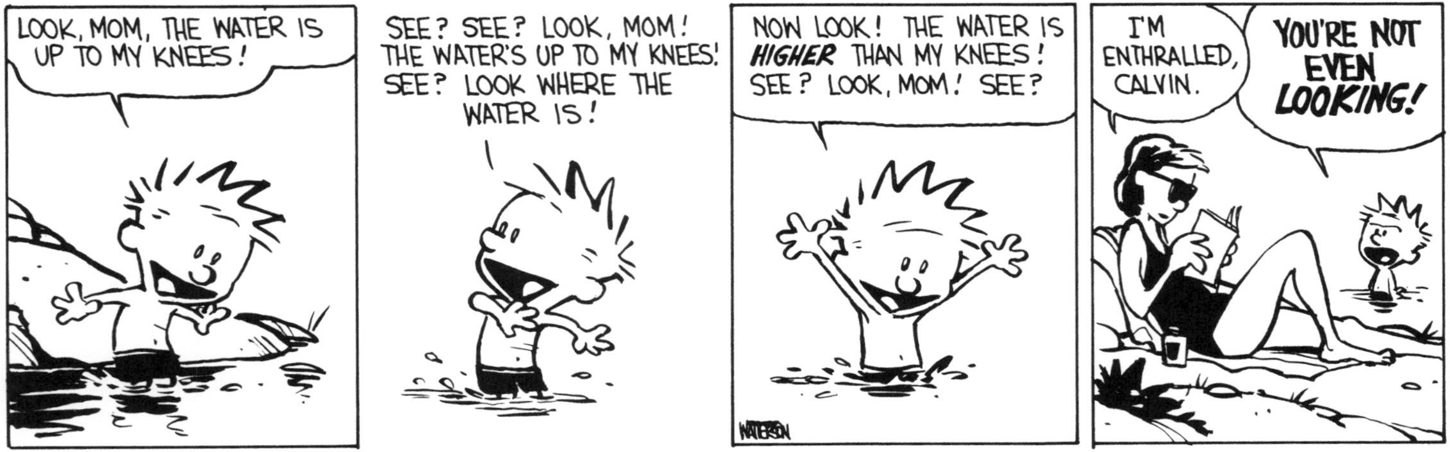
LOOK, MOM, THE WATER IS UP TO MY KNEES!
SEE? SEE? LOOK, MOM! THE WATER'S UP TO MY KNEES! SEE? LOOK WHERE THE WATER IS!
NOW LOOK! THE WATER IS HIGHER THAN MY KNEES! SEE? LOOK, MOM! SEE?
I'M ENTHRALLED, CALVIN.
YOU'RE NOT EVEN LOOKING!

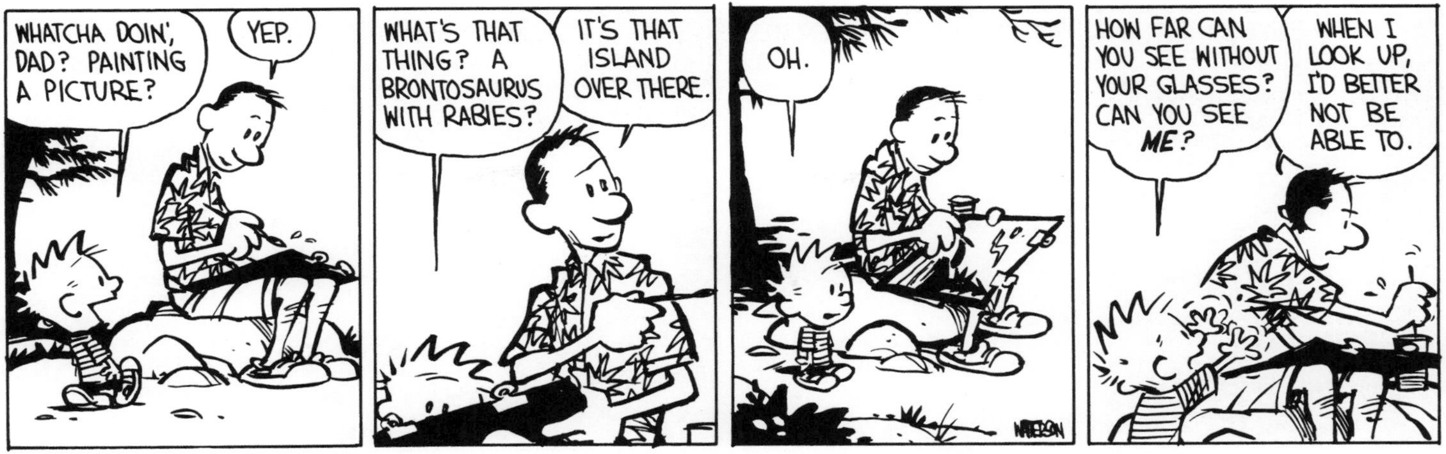
WHATCHA DOIN', DAD? PAINTING A PICTURE?
YEP.
WHAT'S THAT THING? A BRONTOSAURUS WITH RABIES?
IT'S THAT ISLAND OVER THERE.
OH.
HOW FAR CAN YOU SEE WITHOUT YOUR GLASSES? CAN YOU SEE *ME*?
WHEN I LOOK UP, I'D BETTER NOT BE ABLE TO.
WATTERSON

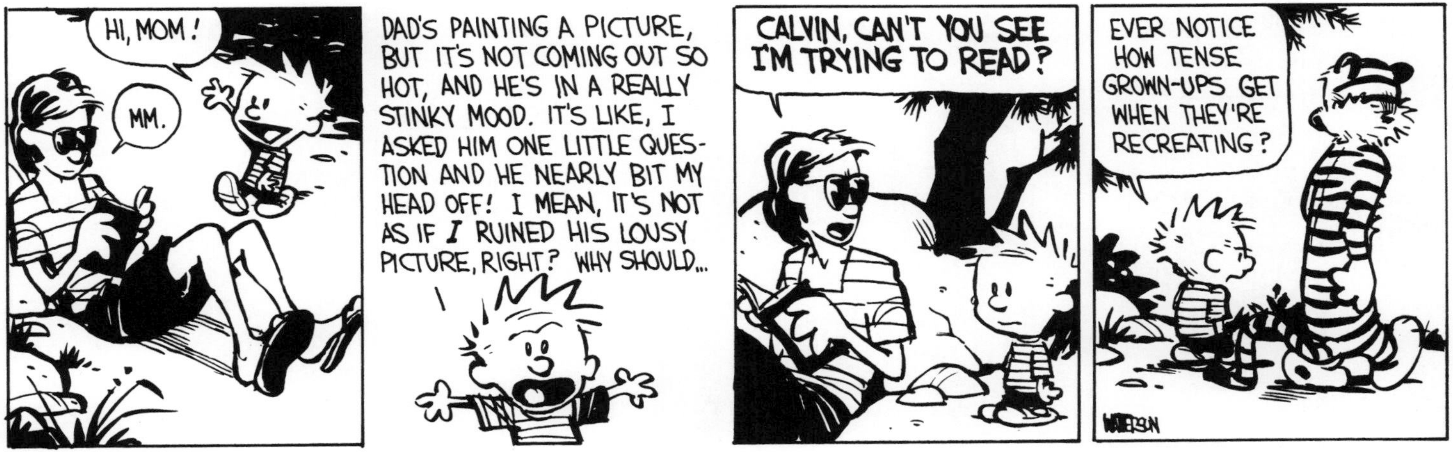
HI, MOM!
MM.
DAD'S PAINTING A PICTURE, BUT IT'S NOT COMING OUT SO HOT, AND HE'S IN A REALLY STINKY MOOD. IT'S LIKE, I ASKED HIM ONE LITTLE QUESTION AND HE NEARLY BIT MY HEAD OFF! I MEAN, IT'S NOT AS IF *I* RUINED HIS LOUSY PICTURE, RIGHT? WHY SHOULD...
CALVIN, CAN'T YOU SEE I'M TRYING TO READ?
EVER NOTICE HOW TENSE GROWN-UPS GET WHEN THEY'RE RECREATING?
WATTERSON

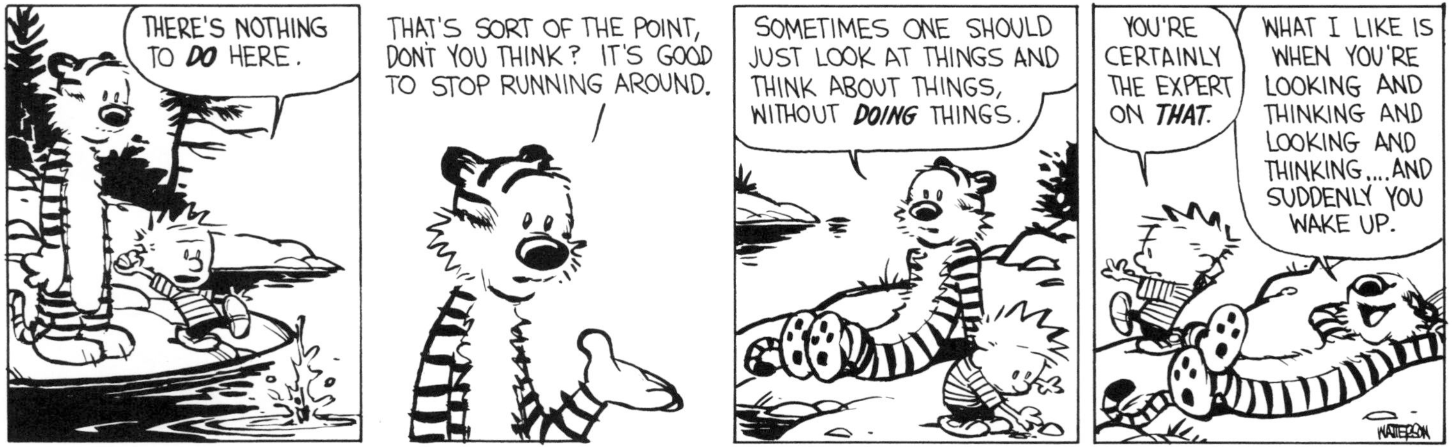
THERE'S NOTHING TO DO HERE.
THAT'S SORT OF THE POINT, DON'T YOU THINK? IT'S GOOD TO STOP RUNNING AROUND.
SOMETIMES ONE SHOULD JUST LOOK AT THINGS AND THINK ABOUT THINGS, WITHOUT DOING THINGS.
YOU'RE CERTAINLY THE EXPERT ON THAT.
WHAT I LIKE IS WHEN YOU'RE LOOKING AND THINKING AND LOOKING AND THINKING.... AND SUDDENLY YOU WAKE UP.
WATTERSON

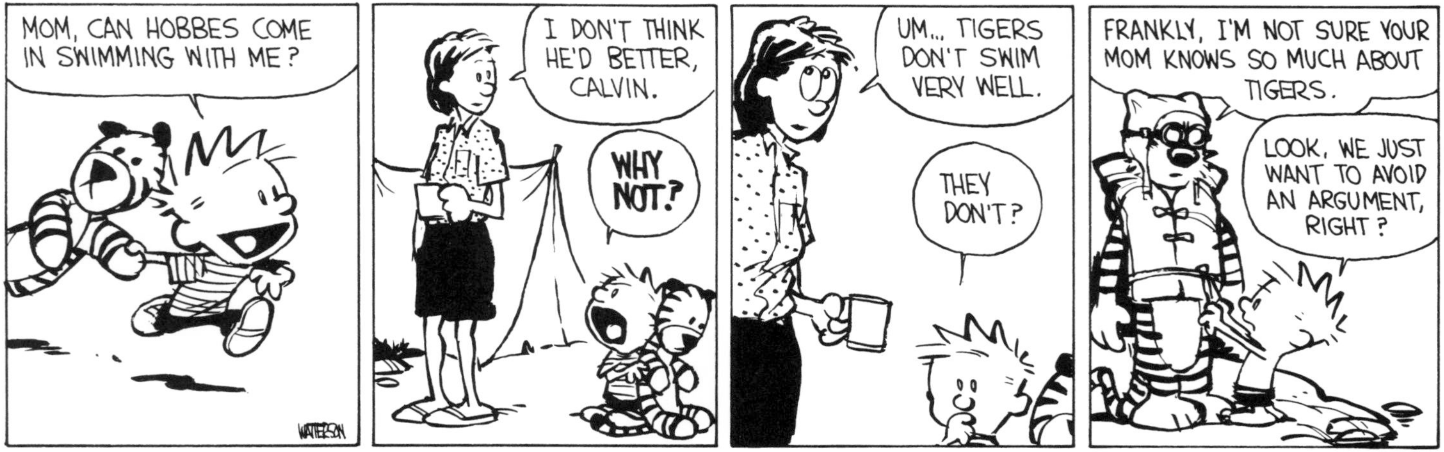
MOM, CAN HOBBES COME IN SWIMMING WITH ME?
WATTERSON
I DON'T THINK HE'D BETTER, CALVIN.
WHY NOT?
UM... TIGERS DON'T SWIM VERY WELL.
THEY DON'T?
FRANKLY, I'M NOT SURE YOUR MOM KNOWS SO MUCH ABOUT TIGERS.
LOOK, WE JUST WANT TO AVOID AN ARGUMENT, RIGHT?

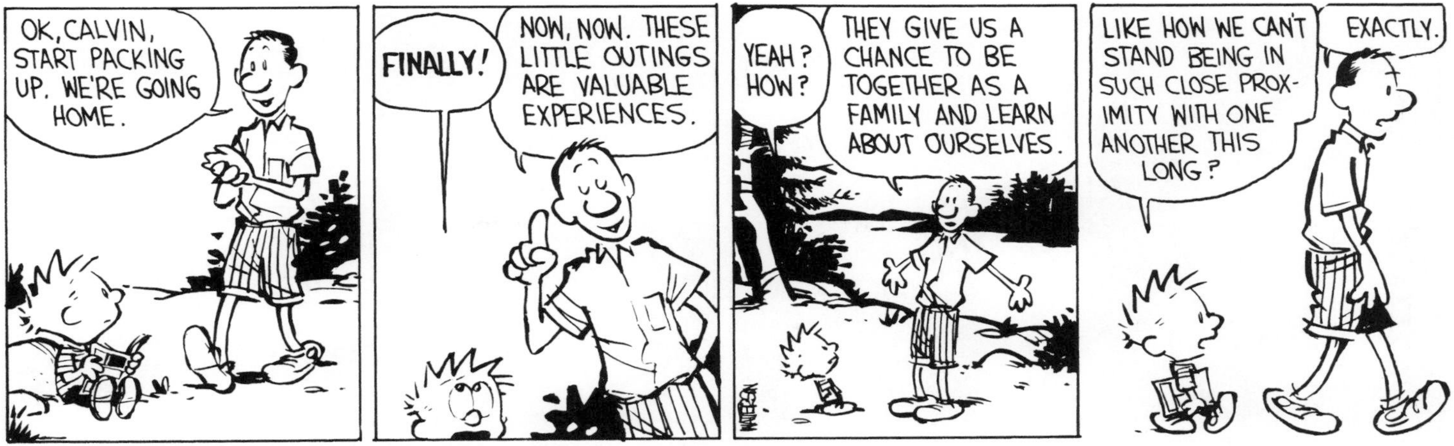
OK, CALVIN, START PACKING UP. WE'RE GOING HOME.
FINALLY!
NOW, NOW. THESE LITTLE OUTINGS ARE VALUABLE EXPERIENCES.
YEAH? HOW?
THEY GIVE US A CHANCE TO BE TOGETHER AS A FAMILY AND LEARN ABOUT OURSELVES.
LIKE HOW WE CAN'T STAND BEING IN SUCH CLOSE PROXIMITY WITH ONE ANOTHER THIS LONG?
EXACTLY.

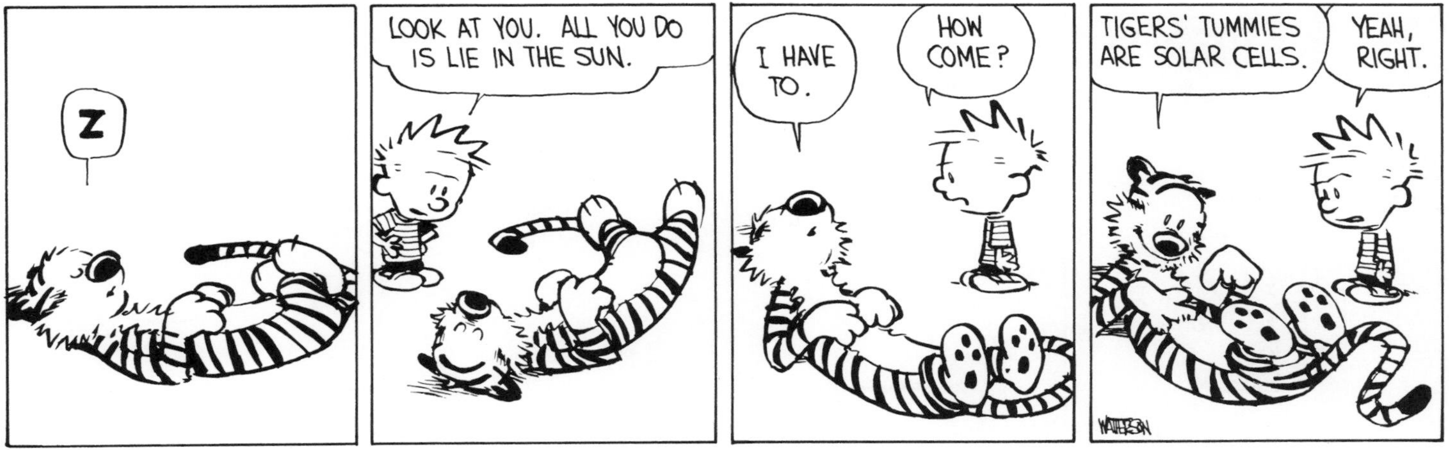
Z
LOOK AT YOU. ALL YOU DO IS LIE IN THE SUN.
I HAVE TO.
HOW COME?
TIGERS' TUMMIES ARE SOLAR CELLS.
YEAH, RIGHT.
WATTERSON

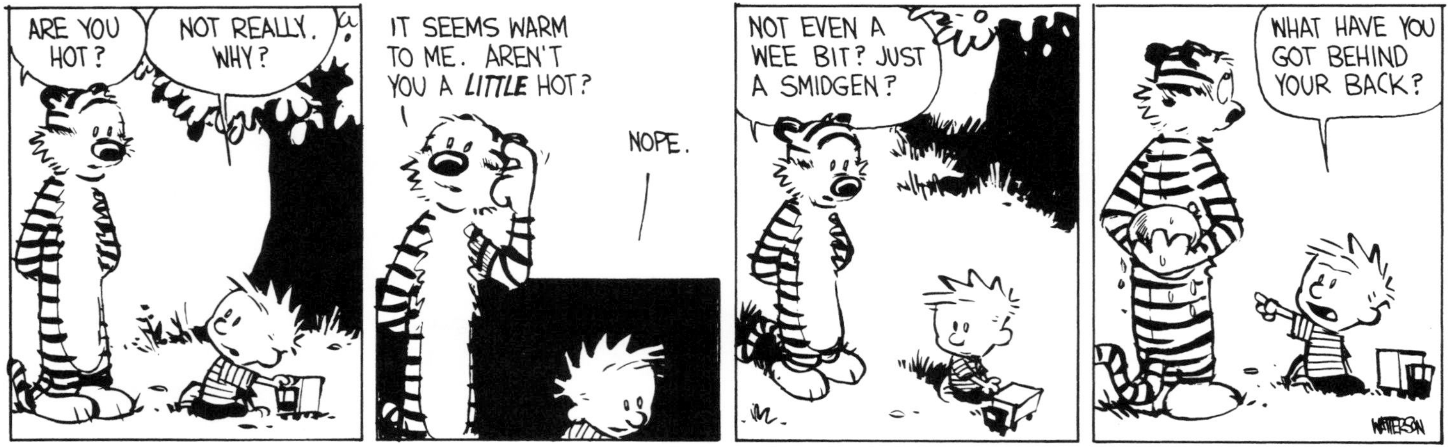
ARE YOU HOT?
NOT REALLY. WHY?
IT SEEMS WARM TO ME. AREN'T YOU A *LITTLE* HOT?
NOPE.
NOT EVEN A WEE BIT? JUST A SMIDGEN?
WHAT HAVE YOU GOT BEHIND YOUR BACK?

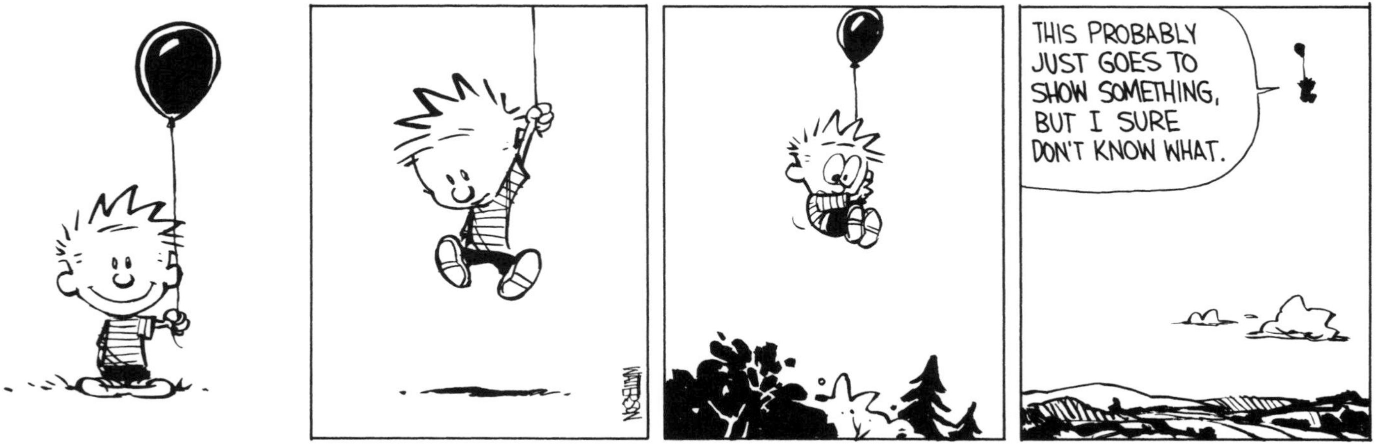
THIS PROBABLY JUST GOES TO SHOW SOMETHING, BUT I SURE DON'T KNOW WHAT.

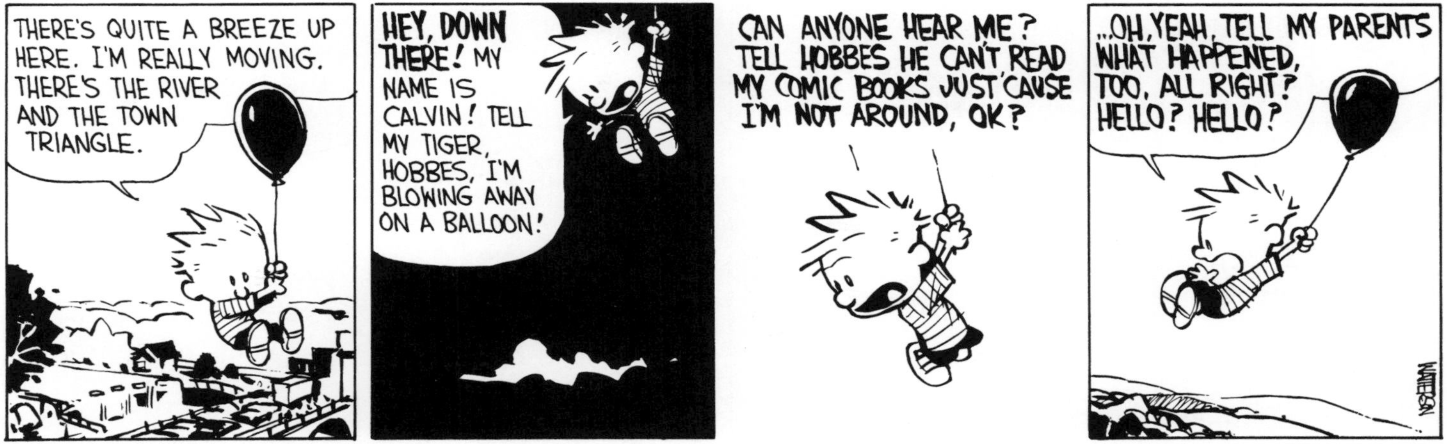
THERE'S QUITE A BREEZE UP HERE. I'M REALLY MOVING. THERE'S THE RIVER AND THE TOWN TRIANGLE.
HEY, DOWN THERE! MY NAME IS CALVIN! TELL MY TIGER, HOBBES, I'M BLOWING AWAY ON A BALLOON!
CAN ANYONE HEAR ME? TELL HOBBES HE CAN'T READ MY COMIC BOOKS JUST 'CAUSE I'M NOT AROUND, OK?
...OH, YEAH, TELL MY PARENTS WHAT HAPPENED, TOO, ALL RIGHT? HELLO? HELLO?

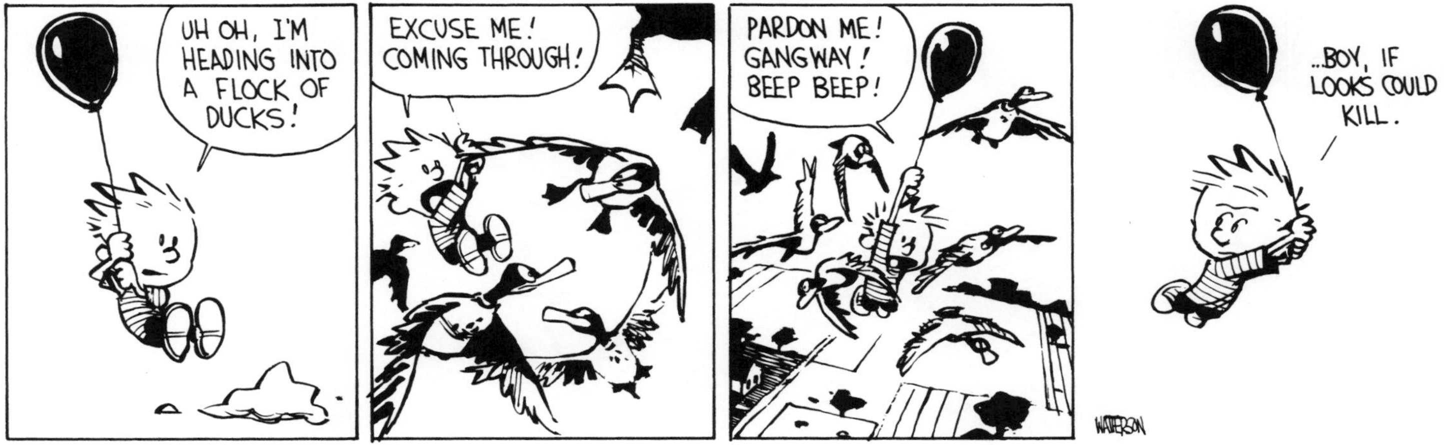
UH OH, I'M HEADING INTO A FLOCK OF DUCKS!
EXCUSE ME! COMING THROUGH!
PARDON ME! GANGWAY! BEEP BEEP!
...BOY, IF LOOKS COULD KILL.

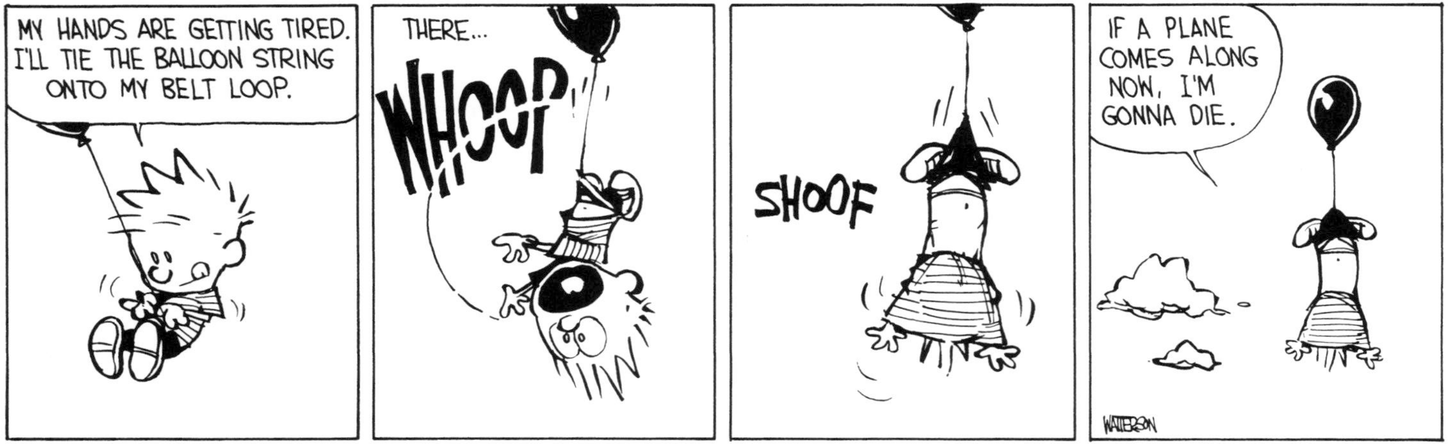
MY HANDS ARE GETTING TIRED. I'LL TIE THE BALLOON STRING ONTO MY BELT LOOP.
THERE...
WHOOP
SHOOF
IF A PLANE COMES ALONG NOW, I'M GONNA DIE.
WATTERSON

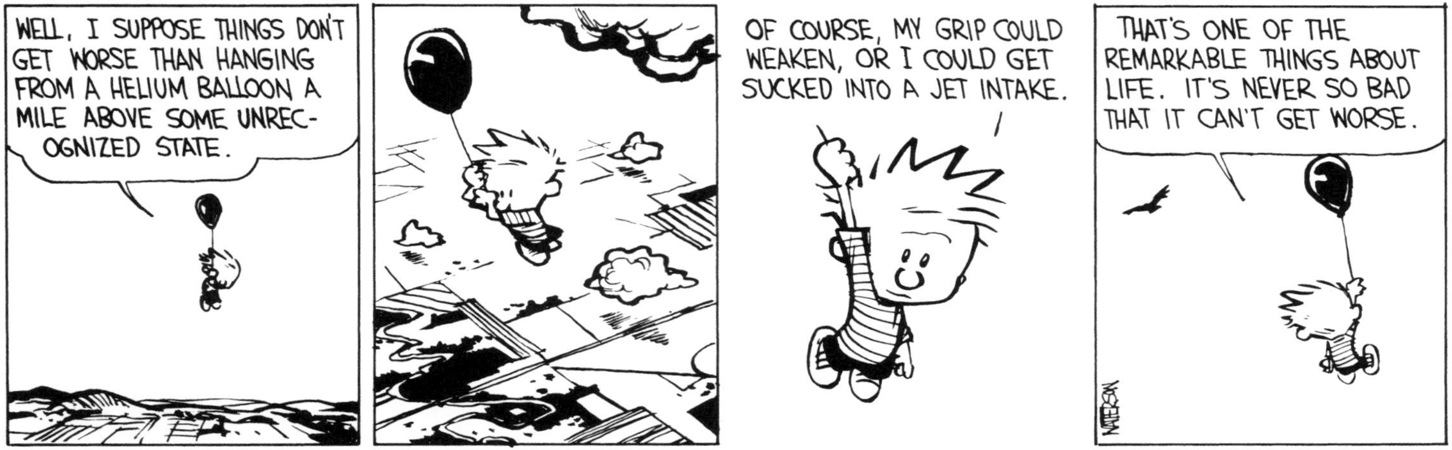
WELL, I SUPPOSE THINGS DON'T GET WORSE THAN HANGING FROM A HELIUM BALLOON A MILE ABOVE SOME UNRECOGNIZED STATE.
OF COURSE, MY GRIP COULD WEAKEN, OR I COULD GET SUCKED INTO A JET INTAKE.
THAT'S ONE OF THE REMARKABLE THINGS ABOUT LIFE. IT'S NEVER SO BAD THAT IT CAN'T GET WORSE.
WATTERSON

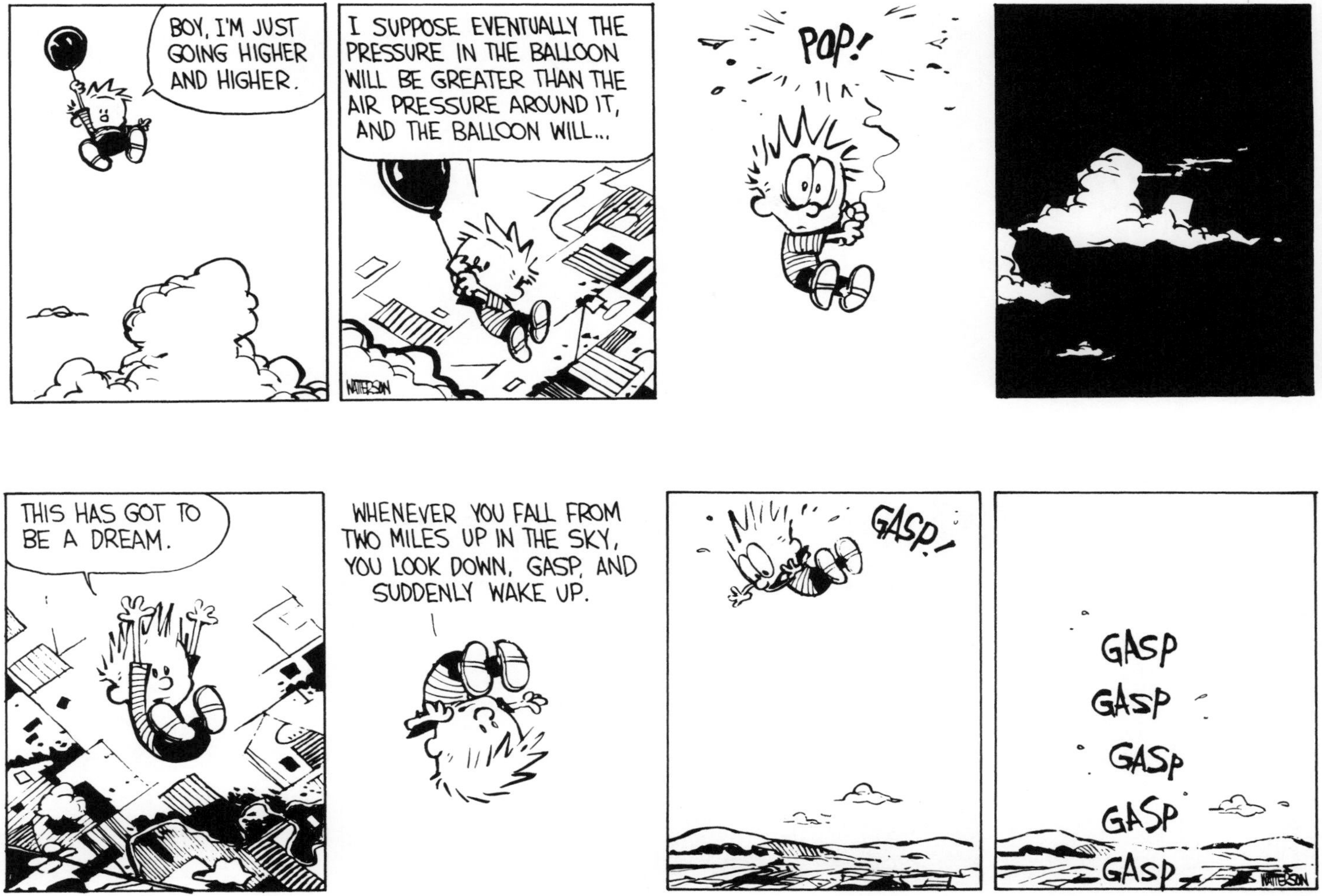
BOY, I'M JUST GOING HIGHER AND HIGHER.
I SUPPOSE EVENTUALLY THE PRESSURE IN THE BALLOON WILL BE GREATER THAN THE AIR PRESSURE AROUND IT, AND THE BALLOON WILL...
WATTERSON
POP!
THIS HAS GOT TO BE A DREAM.
WHENEVER YOU FALL FROM TWO MILES UP IN THE SKY, YOU LOOK DOWN, GASP, AND SUDDENLY WAKE UP.
GASP!
GASP
GASP
GASP
GASP
GASP
WATTERSON

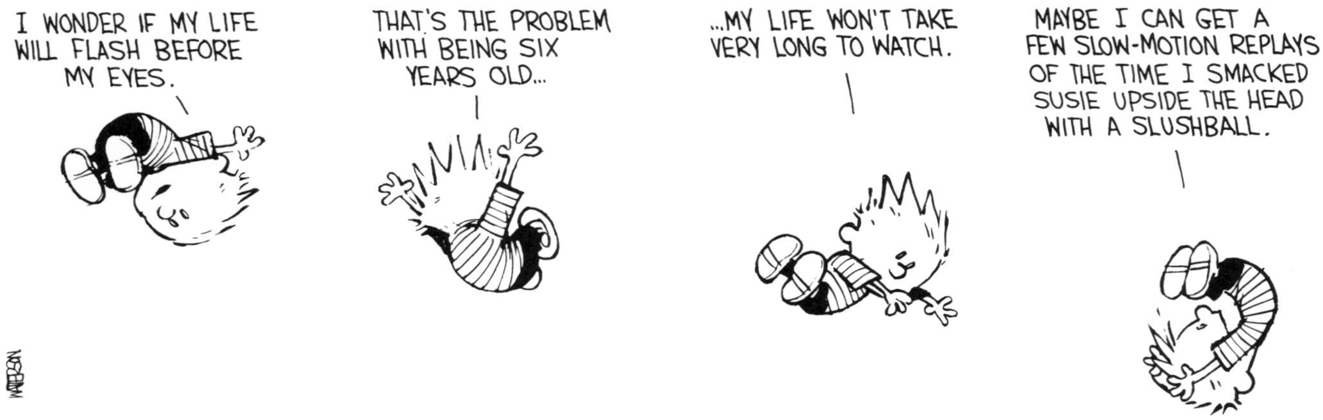
I WONDER IF MY LIFE WILL FLASH BEFORE MY EYES.
THAT'S THE PROBLEM WITH BEING SIX YEARS OLD...
...MY LIFE WON'T TAKE VERY LONG TO WATCH.
MAYBE I CAN GET A FEW SLOW-MOTION REPLAYS OF THE TIME I SMACKED SUSIE UPSIDE THE HEAD WITH A SLUSHBALL.

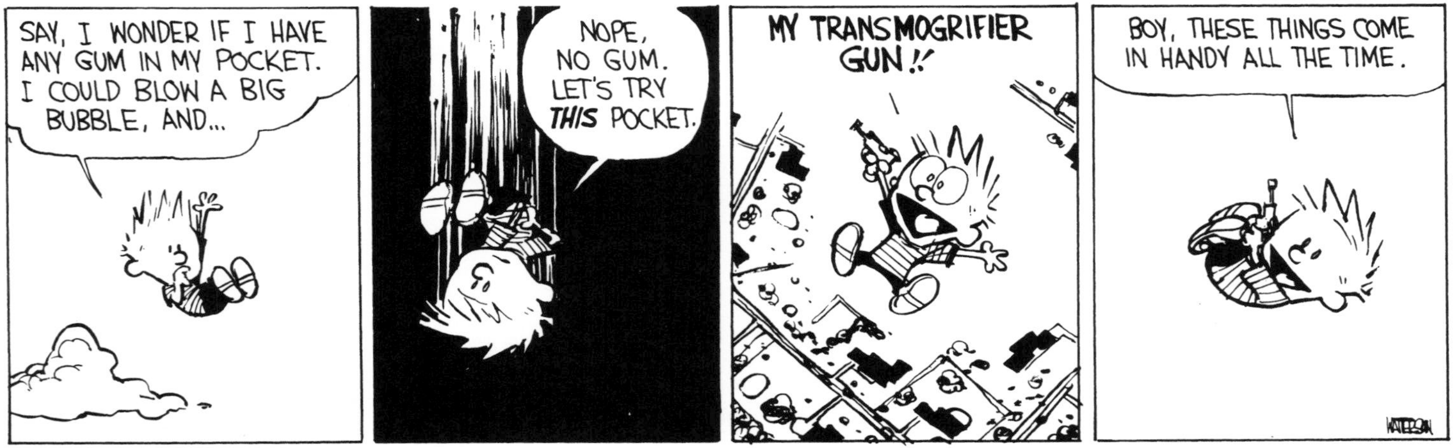
SAY, I WONDER IF I HAVE ANY GUM IN MY POCKET. I COULD BLOW A BIG BUBBLE, AND...
NOPE, NO GUM. LET'S TRY *THIS* POCKET.
MY TRANSMOGRIFIER GUN!!
BOY, THESE THINGS COME IN HANDY ALL THE TIME.

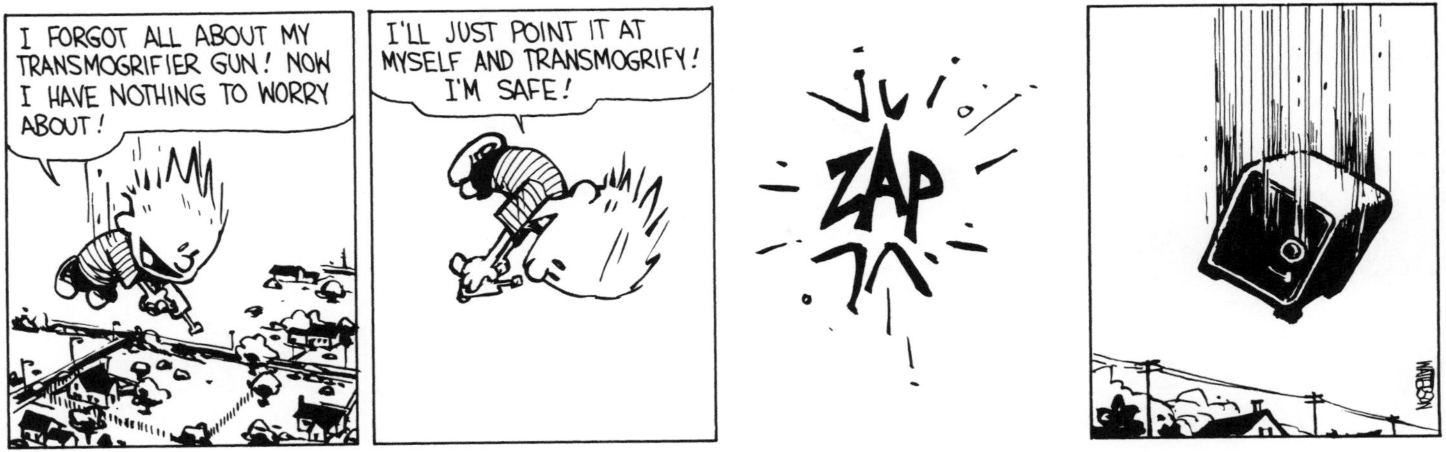
I FORGOT ALL ABOUT MY TRANSMOGRIFIER GUN! NOW I HAVE NOTHING TO WORRY ABOUT!
I'LL JUST POINT IT AT MYSELF AND TRANSMOGRIFY! I'M SAFE!
ZAP
WATTERSON

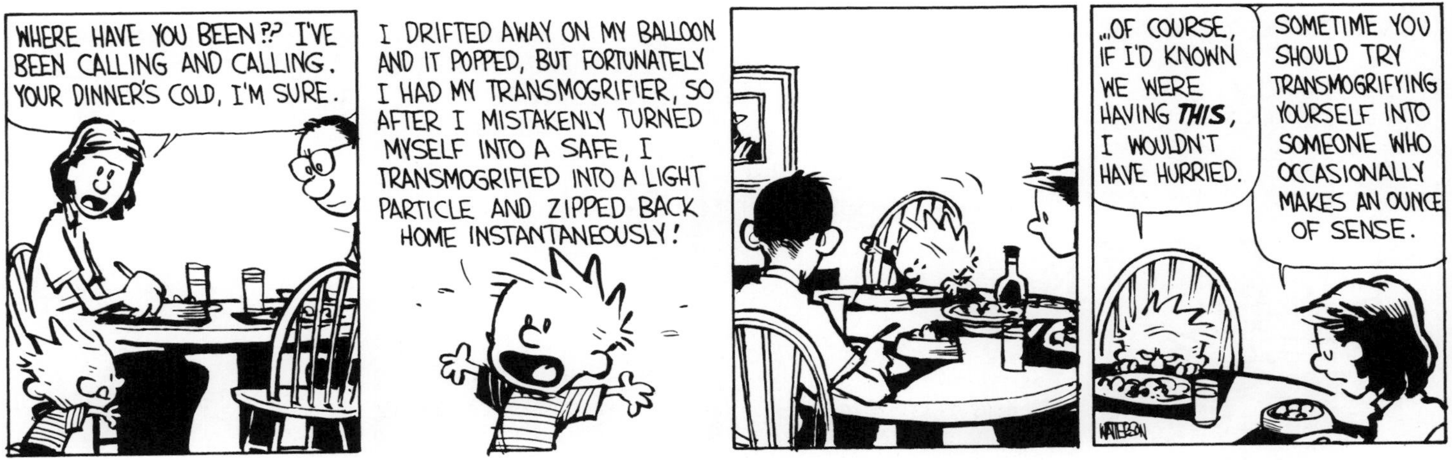
WHERE HAVE YOU BEEN?? I'VE BEEN CALLING AND CALLING. YOUR DINNER'S COLD, I'M SURE.
I DRIFTED AWAY ON MY BALLOON AND IT POPPED, BUT FORTUNATELY I HAD MY TRANSMOGRIFIER, SO AFTER I MISTAKENLY TURNED MYSELF INTO A SAFE, I TRANSMOGRIFIED INTO A LIGHT PARTICLE AND ZIPPED BACK HOME INSTANTANEOUSLY!
...OF COURSE, IF I'D KNOWN WE WERE HAVING ***THIS***, I WOULDN'T HAVE HURRIED.
SOMETIME YOU SHOULD TRY TRANSMOGRIFYING YOURSELF INTO SOMEONE WHO OCCASIONALLY MAKES AN OUNCE OF SENSE.
WATTERSON

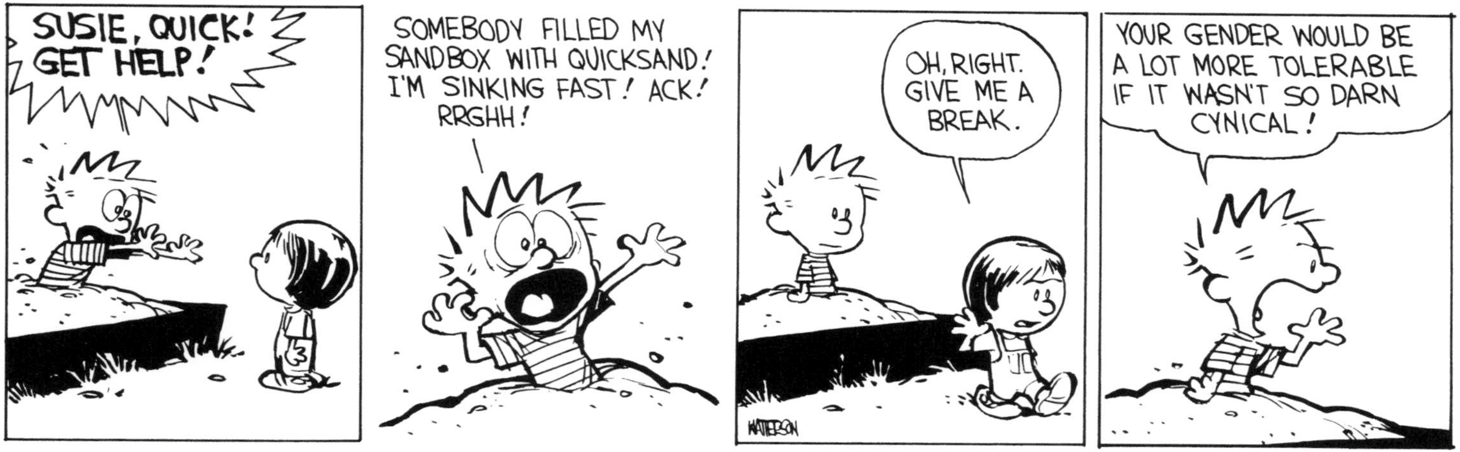
SUSIE, QUICK! GET HELP!
SOMEBODY FILLED MY SANDBOX WITH QUICKSAND! I'M SINKING FAST! ACK! RRGHH!
OH, RIGHT. GIVE ME A BREAK.
YOUR GENDER WOULD BE A LOT MORE TOLERABLE IF IT WASN'T SO DARN CYNICAL!
WATTERSON

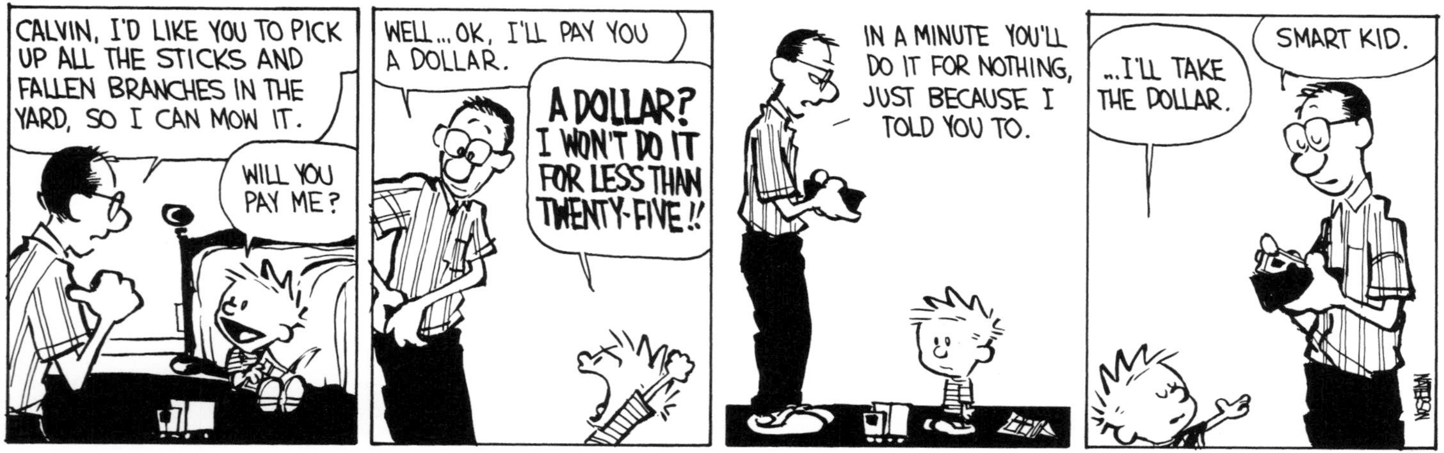
CALVIN, I'D LIKE YOU TO PICK UP ALL THE STICKS AND FALLEN BRANCHES IN THE YARD, SO I CAN MOW IT.
WILL YOU PAY ME?
WELL... OK, I'LL PAY YOU A DOLLAR.
A DOLLAR? I WON'T DO IT FOR LESS THAN TWENTY-FIVE!!
IN A MINUTE YOU'LL DO IT FOR NOTHING, JUST BECAUSE I TOLD YOU TO.
...I'LL TAKE THE DOLLAR.
SMART KID.
WATTERSON

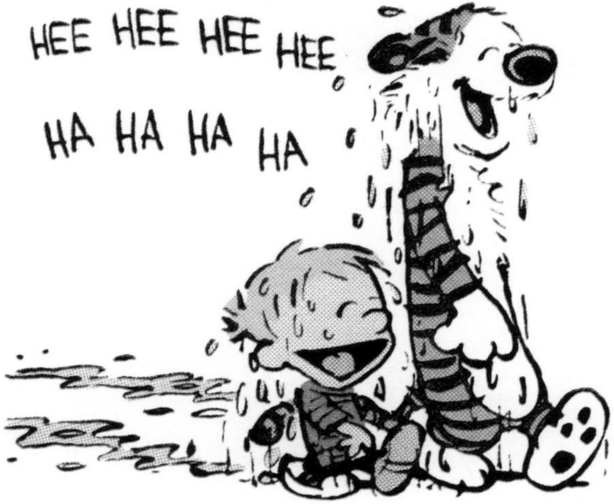
HEE HEE HEE HEE
HA HA HA HA

Andrews McMeel Publishing
a division of Andrews McMeel Universal
1130 Walnut Street, Kansas City, Missouri 64106

www.andrewsmcmeel.com

24 25 26 27 28 SDB 10 9 8 7 6 5 4 3 2

ISBN: 978-1-5248-8804-6

Library of Congress Control Number: 2023944888

ATTENTION: SCHOOLS AND BUSINESSES

Andrews McMeel books are available at quantity discounts with bulk purchase for educational, business, or sales promotional use. For information, please e-mail the Andrews McMeel Publishing Special Sales Department: sales@amuniversal.com.